Literature, Religion, and Postsecular Studies
Lori Branch, Series Editor

Joanna Southcott (1812). Engraving by William Sharp
© Trustees of the British Museum

Lake Methodism

Polite Literature and Popular Religion in England, 1780–1830

JASPER CRAGWALL

THE OHIO STATE UNIVERSITY PRESS · COLUMBUS

Copyright © 2013 by The Ohio State University.
All rights reserved.
Library of Congress Cataloging-in-Publication Data
Cragwall, Jasper Albert, 1977–
Lake Methodism : polite literature and popular religion in England, 1780–1830 / Jasper Cragwall.
p. cm.
(Literature, religion, and postsecular studies)
Includes bibliographical references and index.
ISBN-13: 978-0-8142-1227-1 (cloth : alk. paper)
ISBN-10: 0-8142-1227-1 (cloth : alk. paper)
ISBN-13: 978-0-8142-9329-4 (cd)
1. English literature—19th century—History and criticism. 2. Religion and literature—Great Britain—History—19th century. 3. English literature—18th century—History and criticism. 4. Religion and literature—Great Britain—History—18th century. 5. Romanticism—Great Britain. 6. Methodism in literature. 7. Methodism—History. 8. Methodism—Influence. 9. Great Britain—Intellectual life—19th century. 10. Great Britain—Intellectual life—18th century. I. Title. II. Series: Literature, religion, and postsecular studies.
PR468.R44C73 2013
820.9'382—dc23
                    2013004710

Cover design by Juliet Williams
Text design by Juliet Williams
Type set in Sabon

∞ The paper used in this publication meets the minimum requirements of the American National Standard for Information Sciences—Permanence of Paper for Printed Library Materials. ANSI Z39.48-1992.

9 8 7 6 5 4 3 2 1

To Nadya, with all my love

Contents

Acknowledgments ix

Chapter 1 Introduction:
"Lake Methodism" and the Lows of High Argument 1

Chapter 2 "Elocution to the Mute":
Anglican Authority and the Cultural Revolt of Methodism 33

Chapter 3 Wordsworth and the Ragged Legion:
Poets, Priests, and Preachers 77

Chapter 4 Sage or Sibyl? A Lay Sermon 112

Chapter 5 Joanna Southcott's Body, and the Posthumous Life of
Romantic Prophecy 150

Chapter 6 Resurrection, the New Birth, and Vital Christianity:
The Methodism to Frankenstein's Madness 184

Postscript 225

Works Cited 229

Index 247

Acknowledgments

Writing a book, I've found, is a good counter to the romance of the solitary author. I won't ever be able to express adequate gratitude for the generosities I've received, though it's my great pleasure to make an attempt here.

Over many years, this book developed with support from the Mrs. Giles Whiting Foundation, as well as with timely grant and leave support from Loyola University Chicago. Loyola has given me a community of scholars and students without whom this book would never have been possible. Steve Jones has been my mentor, inspiration, and friend—the best senior colleague, I'm convinced, in all academia. Joyce Wexler has given me countless hours of sage advice, and I owe almost as much to every other member of the department.

My readers, Adam Potkay and Dan White, brought heroic sharpness of thought and welcome critique to the manuscript. They saw clearly what I only glimpsed, saving this book from many blunders, and revealing many new paths. The book and I would have been immeasurably poorer without the suggestions and conversation of Lori Branch, John Bugg,

Fred Burwick, Mark Canuel, Billy Galperin, Marilyn Gaull, Susan Green, Colin Jager, Scott Krawczyk, Ron Levao, Larry Lipking, Fred Lock, Peter Manning, Jon Mee, Jeanne Moskal, Dahlia Porter, Bob Ryan, Starry Schor, Stuart Sherman, Jerry Singerman, Gene Stelzig, Helen Thompson, Tim Whelan, Caroline Winschel, and Sarah Zimmerman. Most of all, I'd like to thank Sandy Crooms, Eugene O'Connor, Kristen Ebert-Wagner, and the entire editorial staff at The Ohio State University Press, who have expertly shepherded this book.

For invitations to take my arguments on the road, I'm grateful to Tom Kaminski and the Johnsonian Society, Tavia Nyong'o and the Center for the Study of Sexuality and Gender, New York University, and Richard Gibson and the Department of English, Wheaton College, as well as colleagues at the North American Society for the Study of Romanticism and the Association of Literary Scholars and Critics. Earlier versions of Chapters Three and Six appeared in the *Huntington Library Quarterly* 68.4 (2005) and *Romantic Autobiography in England,* ed. Eugene Stelzig (Ashgate, 2009). I'm grateful to the publishers for permission to rethink some of this material here.

Years ago, Henry Abelove gave me his "Methodism," before I knew it was possible to know any other. I've only since learned it's not possible to know any better. For this, and for years of kind guidance and good friendship, I thank him.

My greatest debts, and my deepest thanks, are to Susan Wolfson. She has given me so much, and for so long, that no indexing could possibly be sufficient. She has read, at every stage of its development, every inch of this book, with indefatigable genius and astonishing generosity. This has been more than I deserve: and yet more than this, Susan has taught me to read, write, teach, and think. I owe to her my professional self.

To my wife, I dedicate this book—small recompense for years of boundless love.

Chapter 1

Introduction

"Lake Methodism" and the Lows of High Argument

> I feel that I am all unfit
> For such high argument.
>
> —Wordsworth, *Peter Bell* (1798 version, lines 929–30)

he title of this book, *Lake Methodism,* is doubled, bearing an argument for the doublings of Romanticism. *Methodism* figures the first claim: although religion has been an underutilized concept in Romantic studies, recently it has been emerging as one of the most powerful lenses for focusing late eighteenth- and early nineteenth-century British literature. We are beginning to appreciate how, against intellectually privileged and socially restricted experiments in secularization, "the religious" retained, if not an absolute political and cultural hegemony, then something close to it throughout the period. The ironic consequence of the Historicist intervention was the dismissal of a major agent for historical meaning, as "religion" came to be understood as one of the most extreme "spiritual" resolutions that displaced or denied ideological contradictions re-emphasized by critical practice. *Lake Methodism* adopts historicist technique in order to unsettle this historicism, joining new scholarship that has explored the ways religious discourse—vitally embedded in mate-

rial life as well as the afterlife—affected and constituted a variety of romanticisms.[1]

Yet even within this invigorated conversation, there remain moments of striking isolation. D. Bruce Hindmarsh, for example, begins *The Evangelical Conversion Narrative* (2005) with surprise at his solitary interest in the most salable autobiographical genre of the Romantic period.[2] Moreover, if the classroom—or its metaphor, the anthology—is the final arbiter of which arguments have persuaded (or at least interested) the academy, "religion" still has achieved only a tenuous connection with "Romanticism." The canonical landscape has shifted tectonically over the last decades, as many new anthologies have emerged with aggressively revisionist programs, yet the sermons, spiritual lessons, hymns, theological disquisitions, and at times sanctimoniously moralizing prose and verse that were some of the best-read texts of the Romantic period remain largely unrepresented.[3]

---

1. Especially Lori Branch, *Rituals of Spontaneity: Sentiment and Secularism from Free Prayer to Wordsworth* (Waco, TX: Baylor University Press, 2006); Richard E. Brantley, *Locke, Wesley, and the Method of English Romanticism* (Gainesville: University of Florida Press, 1984) and *Wordsworth's "Natural Methodism"* (New Haven, CT, and London: Yale University Press, 1975); Mark Canuel, *Religion, Toleration, and British Writing, 1790–1830* (Cambridge: Cambridge University Press, 2002); Brian Goldberg, *The Lake Poets and Professional Identity* (Cambridge: Cambridge University Press, 2007); Diane Long Hoeveler, *Gothic Riffs: Secularizing the Uncanny in the European Imaginary, 1780–1820* (Columbus: The Ohio State University Press, 2010); Colin Jager, *The Book of God: Secularization and Design in the Romantic Era* (Philadelphia: University of Pennsylvania Press, 2007); Jon Mee, *Romanticism, Enthusiasm, and Regulation: Poetics and the Policing of Culture in the Romantic Period* (Oxford: Oxford University Press, 2003); Robert Ryan, *The Romantic Reformation: Religious Politics in English Literature, 1789–1824* (Cambridge: Cambridge University Press, 1997); and Daniel E. White, *Early Romanticism and Religious Dissent* (Cambridge: Cambridge University Press, 2007).

2. Hindmarsh observes, "Although I could find dozens of studies of the Puritan conversion narrative in the seventeenth century, I could not point to a single book-length study of the genre as it reappeared and proliferated in England during the Evangelical Revival." *The Evangelical Conversion Narrative: Spiritual Autobiography in Early Modern England* (Oxford: Oxford University Press, 2005), vi. For a recent engagement with other versions of the genre, see *Romantic Autobiography in England*, ed. Eugene Stelzig (Aldershot; Burlington, VT: Ashgate, 2009).

3. So, for example, Anne Mellor and Richard Matlak's admirable *British Literature 1780–1830*, though "motivated by a desire to give a comprehensive sense of the range of writing produced in England between 1780 and 1830, including works by women as well as men, by lower-class as well as middle-class and aristocratic writers, by men and women of differing races and ethnicities, and spanning in genre productions in poetry, drama, fiction, nonfictional prose essays, journals, and letters," does not include a category of "religion" within its generous scope (*British Literature 1780–1830*, ed. Anne K. Mellor and Richard E. Matlak [Harcourt Brace, 1996], 2). The stimulating *Broadview Anthology of Literature of the Revolutionary Period*, ed. D. L. Macdonald and Anne McWhir (2010) constructs its

But even as *Lake Methodism* will argue for the critical ways in which religion structured many aspects of Romantic-era Britain—nearly everyone was some sort of Christian, and even after violent wrangling in the 1790s, the "constitution" was still usually taken to signify not a codification of rights, but the union of the state with the Church of England—ubiquity wasn't unanimity. Religion was universal, but it was also universally fractured, a discourse in which disagreements began rather than ended. Religion was a primary mechanism for registering difference in the early nineteenth century. Though the nation was probably no longer a "confessional state," in which every person was born an Anglican, "civil rights" in the Romantic period were consistently understood as religious in nature, as some of the largest Parliamentary contests were fought over the legal status of Catholics, Dissenters, and the Church of England itself, while many arguments for abolition, the Rights of Man and Woman, prison reform and animal rights appealed to the tenets of "Reasonable Christianity," rather than the conclusions of secularized reason. Denomination was as significant a vehicle for identity as race, class, gender, or sexuality—and it was frequently the way these other categories were themselves signified.

This broad historical disposition sets the stage for my more local, and explicitly literary, turn to *Lake Methodism:* what I will call "the lows of high argument." My claim is that Romanticism's rhetorics of privilege trafficked in some of the most socially toxic religious forms of the eighteenth and nineteenth centuries. It was John Gibson Lockhart who, in the *Blackwood's* of 1824, gleefully (and tellingly) pilloried the "Lake Methodists" for their war with the "Established Church of Poetry."[4] The Lake sect was proffering an arrestingly unstable compound of literary prestige and embarrassing enthusiasm—an awkward, anxious, and deeply productive suspension of cultural authority and risible disreputability. If Lockhart's gibe has lost some of its precision for us today, restoring its edge reveals

---

welcome argument for an Anglophone culture through an "inclusive editorial practice" which "reclaims a broad canon that might have been more familiar to writers of the Revolutionary Period" (xxxiv), with, nevertheless, almost no representation from the religious texts that very often formed the most important cultural bonds within the English-speaking world. *The Norton Anthology of English Literature: The Romantic Period,* ed. Jack Stillinger and Deidre Shauna Lynch (8th ed., 2006) is perhaps even more traditional in its choices; *The Longman Edition of British Literature: The Romantics and Their Contemporaries,* ed. Susan J. Wolfson, Peter J. Manning, and Amelia Klein (5th ed., 2012), provides an excellent collection of "Perspectives" on a variety of important cultural and political contexts, but no coverage of the denominational convulsions of Repeal, Relief, and Toleration which occupied Parliament and the public sphere for the whole of the Romantic period.

4. "Southey's *Life of Wesley,*" *Blackwood's Edinburgh Magazine* 15 (February 1824): 208–19 (208).

its target, namely some of Romanticism's most enduring tropes. The Lake Poets—Robert Southey and William Wordsworth, Poets-Laureate regnant and future, along with the Sage of Highgate Samuel Taylor Coleridge—might have seemed to offer an exhilaratingly rarefied poetics of spontaneous inspiration and prophetic imagination, couched within lexicons of experimental simplicity and lyrical concision. But all these—as Lockhart and many diverse, even antagonistic referees of taste including Francis Jeffrey, William Hazlitt, and Leigh Hunt would agree time and again—were the familiar vulgarities of popular Methodism, warmed over as an egregiously self-canonizing art.

In gauging the demographic and doctrinal specificity of the culture that provoked Lockhart's charge, *Lake Methodism* shows how an understanding of the contests between the Church of England and an increasingly organized and influential body of Methodists can transform the way we read key Romantic texts. Wesleyans and Anglicans debated the terms of "Romanticism" more ferociously than any poet, struggling over the character and even existence of inspiration, prophecy, the moral and Providential significance of the natural world, and the value of autobiographical and lyrical forms. *Lake Methodism* treats these spiritualizing figures not as obvious vehicles for an unproblematic cultural capital or a reactionary "Romantic Ideology," but as urgent political signifiers in a country still largely organized along religious lines: lines which the languages of high romanticism blurred, erased, and reinscribed in unpredictable plays upon the social ironies lurking within ostensibly elevated aesthetics. Ragged men and women earnestly claiming divine visitations and the Pentecostal overflow of powerful feelings posed a profound challenge to the Church and constitution of England in the early nineteenth century, and long after what is usually taken as the final resting point of an irreversible slide from youthful radicalisms into disenchantment, default, or apostasy, the Lakers remained acutely aware of (if not entirely comfortable with) the way their cherished rhetorical ecstasies identified with, and were sometimes wholly owned by, the threadbare subversions of the Methodists and a broader culture of religious enthusiasm.

My keywords play into my revisionary agenda. "Romantic" is no longer a stable or reliable category, and the "romanticisms" that have supplanted the unitary vision constellated by late nineteenth-century receptions, while indicting it as an ideologically motivated mirage, may ultimately operate only as self-conscious shorthand for a collection of decades.[5] "High Argument" has undergone even more explicit critique—

---

5. David Simpson, for example, introduced readers to *The Cambridge Companion*

the postures of oracular transcendence which for M. H. Abrams had cast the poet as a heroic "philosopher-seer and poet-prophet, an elected spokesman for the Western tradition," have been re-read as the specific and limited investments of a masculine, bourgeois or gentry power, mystified into specious universalism: in Jerome McGann's influential revision, as "extreme forms of displacement and poetic conceptualization whereby the actual human issues with which the poetry is concerned are resituated in a variety of idealized localities."[6] But both New Critical and New Historical representations of high argument, while diverging in their ethical evaluation of Romantic privilege, agree that it has been privileged as a deep, almost unique reserve of cultural capital: what had seemed a genuinely admirable form of rhetorical authority might also sound like rhetoric comfortably in service to political authoritarianism. In rehearsing these arguments, I don't mean to revisit a dispute that has already shifted our field of study, but rather to gather this cluster of discussion under the banner of "Lake Methodism." To do so isn't to accede to the satires of periodical reviewers, nor to limit the gathering to texts so targeted. It's instead to resituate a Romanticism that has been cleansed of its low-cultural company, back into revealing proximity. Wordsworth and Coleridge receive sustained attention in my story, and few paragraphs go by without Southey, but further chapters discuss the Shelleys, the writings of Methodist preachers and Anglican clerics, and the cultural panic swirling around Romanticism's most famous poet-prophet, Joanna Southcott.

"Lake," then, has a considerable range beyond the Lake District. But "Methodism" too is an unsteady signifier, and historically and geographically plural "Methodisms" have taken up residence in work over the past several decades.[7] This is a modern reclamation of an old formation, since

---

to *British Romanticism* (1993) with a strategic skepticism of the title's nominal coherence: "By *Romanticism* I mean, very roughly, the writings of the late eighteenth and early nineteenth centuries, sharing a general historical situation but not necessarily held together by any essential or prescriptive characteristics." "Romanticism, Criticism and Theory," in *The Cambridge Companion to British Romanticism*, ed. Stuart Curran (Cambridge: Cambridge University Press, 1993), 1.

6. M. H. Abrams, *Natural Supernaturalism: Tradition and Revolution in Romantic Literature* (New York: Norton, 1971), 12. Jerome J. McGann, *The Romantic Ideology: A Critical Investigation* (Chicago and London: University of Chicago Press, 1983), 1. Anne Mellor argues that prophecy and apocalyptic millenarianism were gender-bound discourses, "antithetical to . . . the 'feminine mode of thought' in the Romantic period"; see "Blake, the Apocalypse, and Romantic Women Writers," in *Romanticism and Millenarianism*, ed. Tim Fulford (New York: Palgrave, 2002), 139–52 (140). I will address Mellor's arguments more fully in the fifth chapter.

7. See, for example (and in spite of the apparent unity of the title), David Hempton, *Methodism and Politics in British Society, 1750–1850* (Stanford, CA: Stanford University Press, 1984), 11.

"Methodism" operated with little social or theological clarity in the eighteenth and nineteenth centuries. Sometimes joining Arminian Wesleyans with Calvinist Evangelicals inside and outside the Church of England, self-identified members of the "Society" with unrelated and unregulated enthusiasts, priggish moralizers of no particular sect with drunkards and scoundrels, "Methodist" was very often only a strategically indistinct slur. As the lay preacher John Pawson granted in 1806, the most predictable meaning of "Methodist" was someone held "in supreme contempt, as that name implied everything that was low, mean, and despicable in the opinion of the world."[8] The semantic vagrancy of "Methodism" is an important social fact, reflected throughout this book in rhetorical, bodily, and generic practices, rather than through confessions of faith or habits of worship. Language and performance were often how Methodism and its expressive "enthusiasm" were identified, smearing together the irregularities of tramping ministers and perambulating poets.[9]

Unlike a traditional historian of religion, I'm most interested in the firm persuasions—rather than firm facts—that characterized polite treatments of Methodism. To dismiss, for example, Southey's lifetime of writing on the Wesleyans because it's often falsified by evidence recovered from parish records two centuries later seems to me to miss the atmospherics of Romantic culture, what went without saying, and what was always being said: those ideological pressures shaping lived experience as surely as empirical truths often recognized only after all concerned were long dead. If fictive history shapes a different base from positive scholarship, it also captures the heated tempers and temperatures of Methodism and its critics. "Methodism" often suggested an affective and spiritual mode that might vertiginously leap across social divides, while defying any historical specificity—it was at times the only abbreviation for the "denial

---

8. *Wesley's Veterans: Lives of Early Methodist Preachers Told by Themselves,* [ed. Thomas Jackson], with additions and annotations by Rev. John Telford (London: Robert Culley, 1909–14), 4:4. Cited hereafter as *WV*.

9. While "Methodism" was never entirely equivalent with "enthusiasm," both discourses, especially when handled critically, superimposed a cognitive and political order upon experiences and practices connected distantly, if at all. Jon Mee suggests that "enthusiasm" especially was recast across the eighteenth century as a descriptor for "any kind of socially disruptive mania" (*Romanticism, Enthusiasm, and Regulation,* 30). John Downes argued in 1759 that "a Suspicion" of Methodism was frequently charged upon the "weak and slender Ground" of affect and appearance, rather than doctrine or discipline: "Sometimes a preacher unhappily incurs it by his Voice, Manner, Gestures, Pronunciation, nay, even by his very Countenance." John Downes, *Methodism Examined and Exposed: or, the Clergy's Duty of Guarding their Flocks against False Teachers* (London: J. Rivington, 1759), 94.

of history" available to Romantic culture. The "Methodism" of *Lake Methodism* is as much a fiction of the Romantic imaginary as a collection of archival evidences, configuring the sort of eternal formation that Hazlitt suggested in the defamiliarizing gambit opening his savage essay "On the Causes of Methodism": "The first Methodist on record was David."[10] Infecting ancient Israel as well as modern England, Hazlitt's "Methodism" was a timeless capability for material and discursive disability, a mode of politicking, feeling, and writing independent of theology, shared by "the maudling sentimentalist, the religious prostitute, the disinterested poet-laureate": "the same reason makes a man a religious enthusiast that makes a man an enthusiast in any other way, an uncomfortable mind in an uncomfortable body."[11] Leigh Hunt, whose bitter disgust at the Methodists surpassed even Hazlitt's, was only slightly more precise in his terms: "by the followers of this sect," he understood "not only the immediate followers of WHITFIELD and WESLEY, but all that enthusiast multitude who in the spirit of Christian modesty call themselves the *Godly.*"[12]

The incoherence of "Methodism" is a signal ambiguity of Romantic religion, unfolding in convenient misrepresentations and weird intimacies, often more striking than clear doctrines. Reliable desynonymizations—between "enthusiasm," "fanaticism," and "superstition"; "Methodism" and "enthusiasm"; or even, at times, "Methodism" and "Anglicanism"—privilege the Coleridgean epistemological hygiene found more readily in academic writings on Romantic culture, than in that culture. "Methodist," like "Papist" before it, was a category readily unmoored and sometimes adrift; fixing it in place lets go of some of its weight. But it's still important not to lose sight of Methodism's specific histories, as it emerged in Oxford in the 1730s, grew into a defining formation for the Anglophone world, and resonated across Britain and America even as other connections unraveled.[13] In England, it had magnetized the poorest members of

---

10. William Hazlitt, "On the Causes of Methodism," *The Round Table* [1817], in *The Complete Works of William Hazlitt*, ed. P. P. Howe, 21 vols. (London and Toronto: J. M. Dent and Sons, 1930–34), 4:57.

11. Hazlitt, "On the Causes of Methodism," 4:60, 58.

12. [Leigh Hunt], *An Attempt to Shew the Folly and Danger of Methodism in a Series of Essays*, Essay I: "On the Ignorance and Vulgarity of the Methodists," in *Examiner* 19 (May 8, 1808): 301.

13. For trans-Atlantic Methodisms, see David Hempton, *Methodism: Empire of the Spirit* (New Haven, CT: Yale University Press, 2005); W. R. Ward, *The Protestant Evangelical Awakening* (Cambridge: Cambridge University Press, 1992); and David S. Lovejoy, *Religious Enthusiasm in the New World: Heresy to Revolution* (Cambridge, MA: Harvard University Press, 1985). *Black Atlantic Writers of the Eighteenth Century: Living the New Exodus in England and the Americas*, ed. Adam Potkay and Sandra Burr (New York: St.

the country into unnerving articulation and organization: its unexpected marriage of rapturous excess to steely-eyed discipline was a serious corrosive to existing political and literary orthodoxy, but the complicated ideological commitments of Methodism have proven enduringly difficult to parse. Providing much of the political muscle for the dissolution of the constitution across the nineteenth century, mainstream Methodists represented themselves as sedulously loyalist. Coleridge deplored the Methodists' "equivocal state, as Dissenters & pretended non-Dissenters,"[14] an equivocation inherited by many influential twentieth-century critics, as Bernard Semmel celebrated "The Methodist Revolution," while E. P. Thompson assaulted the "chiliasm of despair" utterly complicit with Old Corruption and New Capital.[15]

Yet if its politics are susceptible to divergent narratives, Methodism's cultural presence was unarguably pervasive. Methodist sermons, songs, autobiographies, and periodicals spectacularly outsold the productions of many "respectable" authors during the Romantic period, and they solidified an emergent popular readership in advance of the better known, and ostensibly secular and politically radical, reorganizations of the public sphere in the 1790s. To orthodox monitors, these literary innovations were the dark corollary of Methodism's political project, irritating *Blackwood's* into a huffed declaration in 1819 (shortly after its very positive review of Wordsworth's pseudo-Methodist conversion poem, *Peter Bell*) for "the aversion of men of cultivated taste to evangelical religion," "hateful" to "all men of right feeling." Methodism, warned *Blackwood's*, was a shocking aesthetic insurgency:

> the most dread ideas are associated with those of the most familiar sort—a rude eagerness takes the place of a lofty enthusiasm—and words, that the soul fears to hear unless in hours of high and solemn preparation, are impiously vollied out by ignorant and uneducated men, among all the hideousness or meanness of their own sectarian jargon.[16]

Martin's, 1995), provides valuably annotated texts, as well as an important argument for the "appearance" of George Whitefield as an organizing "motif of black autobiography" (9).

14. *The Notebooks of Samuel Taylor Coleridge*, ed. Kathleen Coburn, 5 vols. (Princeton, NJ: Princeton University Press, 1957–2002), 3:3901.

15. Bernard Semmel, *The Methodist Revolution* (New York: Basic Books, 1973); E. P. Thompson, *The Making of the English Working Class* (New York: Vintage, 1966), 350–400.

16. "Chalmers's Sermons," *Blackwood's Edinburgh Magazine* 5.28 (July 1819): 462–68 (464). Adam Potkay reads *Peter Bell* against its adjacent Methodisms, in *Wordsworth's Ethics* (Baltimore: Johns Hopkins University Press, 2012).

Lake Methodism locates the sociolect of high romanticism in this "rude eagerness" mixed with "lofty enthusiasm," the collision of sublime "dread" with the homely "familiar," the decorum of a highly managed "solemn preparation" with the raucous vulgarity of the "ignorant and uneducated."

The Lows of High Argument

The volatility of this meeting appears in the give-and-take in *Blackwood's* own pages. The year 1819 witnessed the ferocity with which the gentry could respond to popular speech and politics, but *Blackwood's* dogged commitment to a habituated recoil in "men of cultivated taste" from evangelical excesses would be complicated by Lockhart's (well-hedged) appreciation for "Lake Methodism" merely five years later. This unresolved tension, of a high culture volubly contemptuous of and surreptitiously attracted to disreputable Christianities, is an animating spirit of Romanticism. Many of the most establishmentarian, even authoritarian gestures of early nineteenth-century English culture were built knowingly on a fault line of equivocation between the vatic prestige of pristinely classical or Miltonic traditions, and the coarse enthusiasms of an underclass that produced highly visible, widely read, and problematically normative constructions of prophecy and inspiration. But contaminating pollinations between popular and polite enthusiasms, properly and improperly regulated spiritualisms—and most typically, obsessive discriminations between different social groups engaged in similarly transcendentalizing practices—had been a recurring anxiety in England at least since the Reformation. Recently, Jon Mee has taught us to read the "striking and important continuities in the attitudes expressed towards enthusiasm" across the centuries; Leigh Hunt's 1808 smear campaign, *An Attempt to Shew the Folly and Danger of Methodism,* isn't unlike the hysterical outrages of earlier centuries.[17]

---

17. Mee, *Romanticism, Enthusiasm, and Regulation,* 4. Some accounts of enthusiasm in literature outside the Romantic period that I've found particularly helpful, especially in their explorations of the complex class positions of religious excitement, are Clement Hawes, *Mania and Literary Style: The Rhetoric of Enthusiasm from the Ranters to Christopher Smart* (Cambridge: Cambridge University Press, 1996); Christopher Hill, *Milton and the English Revolution* (New York: Viking, 1978) and *The World Turned Upside Down: Radical Ideas during the English Revolution* (London: Penguin, 1991 [1972]); Nigel Smith, *Perfection Proclaimed: Language and Literature in English Radical Religion,1640–1660* (Oxford: Clarendon, 1989); and John Stachniewski, *The Persecutory Imagination: English Puritanism and the Literature of Religious Despair* (Oxford: Clarendon, 1991).

Yet Romanticism was a peculiar moment when experiments in self-consciously high culture resynonymized within themselves the rhetorical and social formations from which they had been scrupulously distinguished. If the authority of the respectable imagination had long relied on a distinction from the "enthusiasm" which J. G. A. Pocock defines as "the delusion or imposture of those who falsely believe or profess that they are or have been possessed by the Spirit,"[18] Lockhart's "Lake Methodism" signaled the unsettling relay of polite privilege back into these vanities. The Oxbridge poet could be heard harping the same tune as the ranting prophet—with the unexpected addendum that the poet was promising, rather than compromising, the truth of the imagination. "High romantic argument," I'll demonstrate, was a risky innovation in cultural capital, never entirely able to disavow—and never entirely interested in disavowing—the social lives its tropes led beyond the respectable text, in the surrounding world of devoted sectarians who claimed the disruptive credentials of flashing eyes and floating hair against the rigid hierarchies of the Established Church. "Inspiration" may have been uniquely prized in the Romantic period, but it was also frantically pathologized by a squirearchy and clergy besieged by the Inspired. In the hazy confusion of distinction and disgust that resulted, the precise elevation of high argument could be very hard to measure.

My argument pushes against the critical genealogy running from Matthew Arnold, through Raymond Williams, and into recent scholarship that ties Romanticism, especially in its masculine and politically conservative forms, to a larger (and largely problematic) pattern of the sacralization of "Culture" against the atomizing pressures of "History" or "Society." I'll be measuring the complications to this masculine tradition, and especially those arguments that Romanticism fabricated an enduring (and enduringly mystified) "prestige of literature" founded upon "extravagant claims for the imagination."[19] Extravagance within the sacred imaginary might vulgarize as well as dignify, depending on its specific doctrinal and demographic resonances: the "sacred" wasn't a homogenous discourse of transcendental value, but a space for profound ideological conflicts, and spiritual exuberance was hardly an automatic guarantee of social privilege. While Shaun Irlam investigates the "legitimate . . . varieties of suprarational or Enthusiastic experiences," in which the poet, "however

---

18. J. G. A. Pocock, "Enthusiasm: The Antiself of Enlightenment," *Huntington Library Quarterly* 60 (1998): 7–28 (10).

19. David G. Riede, *Oracles and Hierophants: Constructions of Romantic Authority* (Ithaca, NY, and London: Cornell University Press, 1991), 2, ix.

dithyrambic or corybantic his demeanor becomes, is always conceived as a figure of knowledge, virtue, truth, and moral authority," the Hellenic nuance of his lexicon of "demeanor" is also an argument.[20] It was only insofar as enthusiasm was performed within safely classical grammars and histories, and the politics of the ruling class they encoded, that it might, as John Lawson granted in 1758, be admitted as "the Essence of Poetry."[21] This ethereal essence, which attached modern poets to an illustriously ancient pedigree, could be appreciated only by complacently overlooking the contemporary enthusiasts who stalked the country's parishes and filled its printing presses, and many Englishmen viewed an insistence on the universal "moral authority" of the spiritually aroused subject as a transparent, even disingenuous ploy. Isaac Taylor, an eminent Patristic scholar writing in the 1830s, a time when Dissenting "enthusiasm" and Catholic "superstition" were dealing savage wounds to the National Church, was furious at the "preposterous ... pedantry of [any] writer, who in discoursing, for example, of Superstition, or Enthusiasm, should confine himself to such a definition of those terms as might comport with the senses they bore, centuries ago, in the minds of Lucan, Plutarch, Epictetus, or Aristotle."[22]

Taylor's agitation wasn't entirely outside the mainstream. Across the eighteenth and early nineteenth centuries, the Anglican pulpit relentlessly preached against an "enthusiasm" uniformly diagnosed as poisonous. Even in 1767, the notion that "enthusiasm" signified merely a particularly intense form of poetic insight already looked like a willful blindness to the reality of English religious politics. William Duff, carefully distinguishing between classically moribund and vitally Methodistical meanings of the

---

20. Shaun Irlam, *Elations: The Poetics of Enthusiasm in Eighteenth-Century Britain* (Stanford, CA: Stanford University Press, 1999), 6–7. Likewise, Lori Branch argues for the orthodox religiosity of Wordsworth's most authoritative imaginative positions, tracing his "engagement with the long moral tradition that sought to ground morality in spontaneous emotional responses" (*Rituals of Spontaneity*, 182). For an account of secularized, and intensely nationalized, forms of spontaneous enthusiasm in the Romantic period, see Angela Esterhammer, *Romanticism and Improvisation, 1750–1850* (Cambridge: Cambridge University Press, 2008).

21. John Lawson, *Lectures Concerning Oratory* (Dublin: G. Faulkner, 1758), 77. For a survey of this use of "enthusiasm," see Susie I. Tucker, *Enthusiasm: A Study in Semantic Change* (Cambridge: Cambridge University Press, 1972), 77–92.

22. [Isaac Taylor], *Fanaticism, By the Author of Natural History of Enthusiasm*, [London, 1833]; (New York: J. Leavitt, 1834), 19. Wordsworth seems to have owned this book, as well as the *Natural History of Enthusiasm*; see Brantley, *Wordsworth's "Natural Methodism,"* 67n1. Coleridge published his marginalia on *Natural History of Enthusiasm* as the awkward conclusion to *On the Constitution of Church and State*, which Taylor repaid by giving Coleridge's work one of its only notices, in the *Eclectic Review* 6 (July 1831): 1–28.

term, argued that in this "modern sense, [it] is in no respect a qualification of a Poet," only "an overheated and distempered imagination" that had incubated a damaging social instinct.[23] Watching the Establishment crumble in 1829, Taylor was less circumspect, casting enthusiasm as an expansive species of Prometheanism that was mad, bad, and dangerous to know: "Opportunity may be wanting, and habit may be wanting, but intrinsic qualification for the perpetration of the worst crimes is not wanting to those whose bosom heaves with enthusiasm"; enthusiastic "ambition" was "to rival the achievements, not of heroes, but of fiends."[24]

If not everyone shared Taylor's lurid nightmare of "enthusiasm" as a gateway drug to homicide, a broad consensus nonetheless identified it as an acute aesthetic and moral deficiency, which denigrated holy impulses into scabrous parodies.[25] Archbishops and arch-radicals coupled in opposition. Even the champion of avant-garde poetics and liberal politics, Leigh Hunt, was exercised into mounting an extensive campaign in *The Examiner* of 1808 against Methodism, and for years to come his paper ran articles attacking enthusiastic oratory, reviling the "indecencies and Profane Raptures of Methodists."[26] Rapture, rather than revolution, was Hunt's worry. His critique of "Methodism" was keyed to its deformation of sensibility: "the vulgar admire Methodism just as they do violent colours, violent noise, and violent swearing."[27] Likewise, when Hazlitt chewed over "The Causes of Methodism" at *The Round Table,* he choked on "the history of Methodism," which was "religion with its slabbering-bib and go-cart," "a bastard kind of Popery, stripped of its painted-

---

23. William Duff, *Essay on Original Genius, and its Various Modes of Exertion in Philosophy and the Fine Arts* [1767], ed. John L. Mahoney (Gainesville, FL: Scholars' Facsimiles and Reproductions, 1964), 170.

24. Isaac Taylor, *Natural History of Enthusiasm* [London, 1829]; 4th ed. (New York: J. Leavitt, 1834), 17.

25. Clement Hawes argues that the "manic rhetorical style" of enthusiasm in the seventeenth and eighteenth centuries was inherently political, "constituted, above all, by its rebellious stance toward traditional hierarchies of socio-economic privilege and their related hierarchies of discourse" (*Mania and Literary Style,* 2). Irlam critiques this argument as "a romantic fantasy," since "[t]here is no reason to suppose that the proletariat or (since this term is an anachronism in the eighteenth century) any underclass (serf, peasant, plebeian) possesses a monopoly on rebellion. . . . This seems to me to map a rather commonplace as well as dubious romance of the *pensée sauvage* onto the social body, as if one could tabulate a demography of sentiment according to class, race, or gender" (*Elations,* 237). While it's certainly true that the radical vulgarity of "enthusiasm" is an essentializing construct, it was one roundly authorized in the long eighteenth century. The "dubious romance" isn't a fiction of recent critics, but an important social fact of post-Restoration English culture.

26. [Hunt], "An Attempt VI," *Examiner* 33 (August 14, 1808): 524.

27. [Hunt], "An Attempt II, concluded," *Examiner* 21 (May 22, 1808): 335.

pomp and outward ornaments, and reduced to a state of pauperism."[28] The hostility to enthusiasm—and to Methodist tastes, even more than to Methodist doctrines—blended many otherwise dissonant ideological positions: such unexpected continuities suggest its importance in Romantic-period distinctions of high and low culture, bourgeois and plebeian. John Guillory identifies in the "distinction between a credentialed and a noncredentialed speech" the function of polite letters,[29] and many others have suggested that Romanticism, despite its incoherences, united in what William Keach calls a "resistance to the vulgar,"[30] an entire "sociology of culture" (in Jon Klancher's terms) that brooded on the vast "abyss between serious and mass culture."[31] But against this deep current of division tugged a sense that "enthusiasm," and Methodism especially, also charted a drifting course on which privileged and popular forms collided, and with alarming frequency at the most distinguished aesthetic coordinates—precisely the spaces that might have mapped the widest cultural separations.

For all of Hazlitt's insistence on Methodism's bastardy, and a "[place] of worship that combines the noise and turbulence of a drunken brawl at an ale-house, with the indecencies of a bagnio," he traced the lineage of its agitations back to poetic inspiration. Both Methodists and poets, he snorted, "strive to gain a vertigo by abandoning their reason, and give themselves up to the intoxications of a distempered zeal, that

'Dissolves them into ecstasies,
And brings all heaven before their eyes.'"[32]

Quoting *Il Penseroso,* Hazlitt deflated Milton's space of ecstasy ("the studious Cloysters pale" and "the high embowed Roof" echoing with the "full voic'd Quire below, / In Service High") into a parodic whorehouse,

---

28. Hazlitt, "On the Causes of Methodism," 4:60–61.
29. John Guillory, *Cultural Capital: The Problem of Literary Canon Formation* (Chicago and London: University of Chicago Press, 1993), 62.
30. William Keach, *Arbitrary Power: Romanticism, Language, and Politics* (Princeton, NJ: Princeton University Press, 2004), 72.
31. Jon Klancher, *The Making of English Reading Audiences, 1790–1832* (Madison: University of Wisconsin Press, 1987), 135. Philip Connell and Nigel Leask introduce their recent volume, *Romanticism and Popular Culture in Britain and Ireland,* arguing that "the emergence of the English literary canon is historically dependent upon an objectifying distinction between high and low, 'the people' and 'the public' (a distinction which Romantic theory itself did much to entrench)" ("What Is the People?" in Connell and Leask, *Romanticism and Popular Culture in Britain and Ireland* [Cambridge: Cambridge University Press, 2009], 3–48 [7]).
32. Hazlitt, "On the Causes of Methodism," 60–61.

where "Service High" descended to others less sacerdotal, cheered on by "the noise and turbulence of a drunken brawl." But though the ironies were waged at Methodism's expense, they cut into canonical poetics. As Hazlitt mordantly underscored, it was Milton himself who joined poetical to religious enthusiasm in order to claim a language of visionary transfiguration and political subversion, an "ecstasy" that "dissolves" any distinction of discourse, since the Methodists followed their own Heavn'ly Muse, and "plunge without remorse into hell-flames, soar on the wings of divine love, are carried away with the motions of the spirit, are lost in the abyss of unfathomable mysteries,—election, reprobation, predestination,—and revel in a sea of boundless nonsense."[33] Nor was Hazlitt alone. Romantic-era culture was nervously alive to the way poets and preachers, enthusiasts and gentlemen, could complicate each other's roles in an aesthetic stratosphere compounded out of abjection and exaltation.[34] "The sublime," Martin Shee complained in 1809, marked no separation between polite and plebeian cultures, but absorbed "credentialed" speech and enthusiastic rant equally. The "vague, irregular, and undefined" nature of sublimity, Shee argued, was an "intoxicating spirit" for everyone, not just the "disreputable examples" of "Methodists." The "sublime," he concluded, was "the insane point of the critical compass; for those who talk rationally on other subjects, no sooner touch on this, than they go off in a literary delirium; fancy themselves, like Longinus, 'the great sublime they draw,' and rave like Methodists, of inward lights, and enthusiastic emotions, which, if you cannot comprehend, you are set down as un-illumined by the grace of criticism, and excluded from the elect of Taste."[35]

This uneven ground, upon which high art and bourgeois respectability clashed with popular enthusiasm and plebeian culture, is the terrain of *Lake Methodism,* and its first and most formidable surveyor, Francis Jeffrey. Some of the vitriol in Jeffrey's campaign against the Lakers may be qualified as the bad-faith histrionics of a witty reviewer building his own reputation by sabotaging others; the heat of the inaugural salvo of 1802 against Southey's *Thalaba* and Wordsworth's "Preface" was in part meant to launch the *Edinburgh Review* with hot copy. But Jeffrey caught the spirit of the age, a Romantic climate evaporated not only from the consolatory narratives of Arnold and J. S. Mill, but also from New Histori-

---

33. Hazlitt, "On the Causes of Methodism," 61.
34. In Jon Mee's pithy formulation, "enthusiasm" straddled a social divide, signifying "both the fleshly seeing of the crowd and the highest flights of poetic inspiration" (*Romanticism, Enthusiasm, and Regulation,* 2).
35. Martin Archer Shee, *Elements of Art, A Poem* (London: W. Bulmer, 1809), 193.

cist arguments about spiritual displacement. For Jeffrey, this poetry wasn't apolitical literature, blissfully removed from the anxieties of the material world, but a poetics dangerously (even if ridiculously) flirting with energies that subverted the regime of polite taste governing staid churchmen and rational Dissenters alike.

The "splenetic and idle discontent" of the Lakers was a tripled perversion of theology, politics, and language. Jeffrey girded himself for an inquisition to preserve "the catholic poetical church" against "a *sect* of poets, . . . *dissenters* from the established systems": "Poetry has this much, at least, in common with religion, that its standards were fixed long ago, by certain inspired writers, whose authority it is no longer lawful to call into question." This was no casual metaphor system—the rhetorical and political disobediences of the Lakers were second-order defects, organized by primal devotional errors. Though the Lakers claimed "a creed and a revelation of their own," Jeffrey had little doubt that "their doctrines are of German *origin* . . . derived from some of the great modern reformers of that country," while "their leading principles . . . seem to have been borrowed from the great apostle of Geneva." The result was a nasty palimpsest of sedition and heresy, in which programs of secular and aesthetic revolution were haunted by the ghosts of spiritual Reformation, and poets eagerly prostituted themselves to any and every form of resentment in a strained reach at rhetorical novelty. "The great apostle of Geneva" invoked "the antisocial principles, and distempered sensibility of Rousseau" along with those of John Calvin, whose predestinarian determinism made his disciples bywords for brooding insularity after the Restoration, while "doctrines of German *origin*" signaled not only "the simplicity and energy (*horresco referens*) of Kotzebue and Schiller," but the aggressively styled "plain truth for plain people" of Luther, the infamous Moravian pursuit of a childlike mentality in adults, and the Wesleyan heirs of both.[36] The result was an incoherent miasma of bad English and foreign dogma, in which, as Daniel White argues, Jeffrey found "the doctrine of a zealous reforming sect" confounded with "Jacobin infidelity."[37]

What Bishop Lavington had deplored in 1749 as the iconic paradoxes of Methodism, "*sanctify'd singularities, low fooleries, and high pretensions,*" still signified in the Regency.[38] The more grandly mystical

---

36. [Francis Jeffrey], "Southey's Thalaba," *Edinburgh Review* 1 (October 1802): 63–83 (71; 63–65).

37. White, *Early Romanticism and Religious Dissent*, 156. See also Robert Ryan, *Romantic Reformation*, 31–32.

38. [George Lavington], *The Enthusiasm of Methodists and Papists, Compar'd* (London: J. and P. Knapton, 1749), "Preface," unpaged.

language became, the more thoroughly disreputable it might seem, indicative of a politically inflected lunacy that was recognizably current. Jeffrey's initial contempt was for the "absolute meanness and insipidity" of the *Lyrical Ballad*'s system for poetical diction rooted in a studied "neglect of the establishments of language," which, with double intent, indicted Wordsworth's joint revolts against grammatical and ecclesiastical Establishments. Yet Jeffrey reserved his heaviest fire, not for theories of verse built on a nostalgically pastoral "real language of men," but for Wordsworth's clearest attempt at self-styled "high argument" in *The Excursion*, and the accompanying "Prospectus" to *The Recluse*. The grand quarto of 1814 seemed to deflect many of the *Edinburgh Review*'s characteristic complaints: demotic experimentation was given over for Miltonic blank verse, and the potential radicalism of *Lyrical Ballad*'s catalogue of men and women freshly shattered by foreign war, sexual betrayal, and economic collapse was largely, if not entirely, replaced by establishmentarian fantasies of reconciliation within the Church of England.

But for Jeffrey, the prospect of a man promising to "breathe in worlds, / To which the Heaven of heavens is but a veil," while calling upon "thou Prophetic Spirit, Soul of Man" to "vouchsafe thy guidance" along the way, showed not that Wordsworth was finally singing of higher things, but that he had given way to his slumming instincts ("Prospectus," 29–30; 83). The high argument of the "Prospectus," Jeffrey insisted, was a climax of vulgarized poetics, confusing the cardinal directions of cultural capital, and crashing to earth when it thought it soared. Wordsworth seemed inexplicably determined to erode himself by tarting up an almost comically worthless "tissue of moral and devotional ravings" into specious profundity: "all sorts of commonplace notions and expressions are sanctified in his eyes, by the sublime ends for which they are employed; and the mystical verbiage of the Methodist pulpit is repeated, till the speaker entertains no doubt that he is the elected organ of divine truth and persuasion."[39] Jeffrey's assault evidences what will be one of my major arguments in *Lake Methodism*: had anyone in the early nineteenth century cared to enact the denial of history, or to partition polite from popular cultures, a grandiosely transcendent subjectivity preaching imaginative displacement would have been a fatally compromised vehicle. If such discourses signified material abstraction and intellectualized serenity, they also encoded emphatically disreputable doctrines and demographics, and high "romanticism"

---

39. [Jeffrey], "Wordsworth's *Excursion*," *Edinburgh Review* 47 (November 1814): 1–30 (4).

emerged out of a sometimes agonizing, and sometimes thrilling, conflation of what had seemed durable opposites.

Jeffrey's double-vision of high argument—at once imaginatively provocative and socially unsound—wasn't just a misprision sparked by a critic grinding his axe. The Lakers themselves played up and upon their equivocal sympathies with Methodism, vexing the transferences between reputable rhetoric and visceral literalism into an energetic sociopolitical uncertainty: in effect, the historical propulsion for the formal and metaphysical "Irony" we've come to identify as uniquely "Romantic." Such connections could be telegraphed with cheerfully resigned wit; Wordsworth jovially shrugged that, like it or not, the rollicking enthusiasm of his best-selling poem would always keep him "as much Peter Bell as ever" for the reading public.[40] Other times, the lines could be darkly tangled, as in Robert Southey's lifelong obsession with spiritual derangement, which challenged and reconstructed its scholars as well as its zealots. But the abiding alertness of Romantic-era culture to the twinned authority and vulgarity of the enthusiastic imagination had to do with the difficulty of policing the boundaries between polite literature and popular religion. My attention to this difficulty tells a different story from Jon Mee's, that Romanticism disciplined and regulated enthusiasm in a Foucauldian play—different, too, from Robert Miles's elaboration of a "marginalize[d] and finally discard[ed]" enthusiasm.[41]

In Chapter Two, "'Elocution to the Mute': Anglican Authority and the Cultural Revolt of Methodism," I show how enthusiasm, particularly in its Methodistical forms, posed an intractable puzzle to the eighteenth- and nineteenth-century Anglican disciplinary order. Stories of the secularization of politics and culture, I argue, make poor sense of Romantic England, which was still governed by the Church of England. The civil service hadn't yet been invented, and the Anglican hierarchy reserved for itself the legal and bureaucratic functions that would be dispersed among various institutions later in the nineteenth century. But while hegemonic, Anglican authority was surprisingly diffuse in self-conception, identified by habits of thought, speech, and affect, rather than clear confessions of faith. Methodism reversed this status quo, figuring a revolution in language and feeling more dangerous than any explicitly theological or political program. Unlike Paineite radicalism or intellectualized Dissent, answered by

---

40. *The Letters of William and Dorothy Wordsworth: The Later Years*, ed. Ernest de Selincourt, 2nd ed., rev. Alan G. Hill (Oxford: Clarendon, 1978–79), 2:439.
41. Robert Miles, *Romantic Misfits* (New York: Palgrave Macmillan, 2008), 173.

the State, Law, and Church, Methodism disrupted the nebulous cloud of the Anglican constitution, while professing a loyalism that insulated it from prosecution, and even successful opposition. The ensuing cultural panic, I argue, turns the story of Romanticism upside down, as Parliament debated the threat of Methodistical "Inspiration" one year after the *Lyrical Ballads* were published, bishops anathematized spiritual excitement, and Methodist songs, periodicals, and autobiographies reshaped the public sphere.

The rest of the book reads a set of situations—iconic and unsuspected—that cast the shadow of "Lake Methodism" across Romanticism. Chapter Three, "Wordsworth and the Ragged Legion: Poets, Priests, and Preachers," considers the effect of the tensions between Methodist preachers and Anglican priests on *The Prelude,* and especially its revisions and long-delayed publication. I historicize the mystically transcendental accreditations informing Wordsworth's spiritual autobiography in ways not evident in received "high Romanticism": the poet as "chosen son," the telling of "prophecy" to "the open fields," the attentions of a providential power shaping the subject through "ministry more palpable." Such figures, I argue, were more legible as the rhetoric of Wesleyan itinerants, whose "holy" powers defied the professional forms of Anglican priests, and their ground of social respectability and political orthodoxy. Sensitive to this resonance, Wordsworth revised, across several decades, Methodistical extravagance into normative Anglicanism. This revisionary process wasn't, as we usually hear, a youthfully vigorous pantheism tempered into the piety of old age: it was a shift between the sociopolitical significances of two determinate Christianities. Wordsworth never abandoned his enthusiasm entirely, and the trouble it entailed was much of its attraction. *The Prelude* often harnessed "high argument"—rhetorically sublime, spiritually potent, socially ridiculous, and politically subversive—into some of its deepest thinking on the work of the poet, and the ironies of cultural production.

What Wordsworth kept quiet, Coleridge noisily announced. Chapter Four, "Sage or Sibyl? A Lay Sermon," takes the titles of Coleridge's middle-aged philosophizing as its subject. The *Lay Sermons* were some of his densest, most reactionary work, turning in disgust from the emerging "READING PUBLIC," while struggling to give sinecures, place-men, and passive obedience the aura of categorical imperatives. Yet the generic history of "lay sermons" was at odds with Coleridge's politics. Expressly forbidden within the Anglican communion and marginalized by most respectable Dissenters, "lay preaching" was the proprietary business of the

Methodist upstarts I treat in chapter three. No wonder that form trumped content in the reception of the *Lay Sermons,* and Coleridge's budding reputation as a gentleman-Sage was blasted by a diagnosis of religious enthusiasm and demotic argument. Coleridge's malady found its only parallel in the pathetic writings and false pregnancy of Joanna Southcott, the "Woman to Deliver Her People" and "Second Eve" raised in Coleridge's home parish, who had alarmed the nation with her prophecies until her death two years earlier. Worse, the Sage was seen courting the acquaintance of the Southcottian Sibyl with his perversely named *Sibylline Leaves.* Most contemporaries washed their hands of this public self-mortification—but Hazlitt, in some of his most sustained and intense reviewing, suggested that this unlikely amalgamation was a covert petition for rhetorical authority, Coleridge's willful vulgarity the cover for his most extreme authoritarian tendencies.

Chapter Five, "Joanna Southcott's Body, and the Posthumous Life of Romantic Prophecy," turns to the real focus of the jokes considered in the preceding chapter, the servant-*cum*-prophetess who was one of the best read, and most gossiped about, figures of the Romantic period. Southcott's fame died with her, and she has largely disappeared from recent critical accounts, her brief notices usually confined to footnotes or dismissive concessionary clauses. I don't mean to contest this absence, but rather to write its history: the vanishing of Joanna Southcott was one of the great mystifications of the Regency, the endurance of this evaporation one of the fullest examples of the "Romantic Ideology," criticism's reproduction of the period's own self-representations. Much contemporary coverage painted Southcott as anachronistic, a clown of female mysticism from before the Reformation, who proclaimed enthusiastic prophecies impossible since the birth of Christ or the foundation of his Church. But it was Southcott's *modernity* that worried polite England: her meteorically successful books and celebrity were carried by print culture and mass marketing no less than Byron's or Scott's, suggesting that literacy, print, and publicity might be the organs of Enthusiasm rather than Enlightenment. The fascination with her suggested that the norms of politeness and popularity were being rewritten without the consultation of culturally privileged tastemakers, and that marginal Methodisms were now strong enough to crowd out reputable competitors. The mistaken "pregnancy" that closed her life also solved the conundrum she posed, transforming an ideological offense into a physical one, recasting a crisis in Englishness as the personal excrescence of the body of a solitary old woman—a body in which it could be buried forever.

But as Chapter Six, "Resurrection, the New Birth, and Vital Christianity: The Methodism to Frankenstein's Madness," argues, enthusiasm had a way of reanimating its corpses. My *Frankenstein* isn't a grim parable of technology gone awry at the hands of a secular Prometheanism, but an account of spiritual warfare, with a cast of saints, sinners, martyrs, and prophets—all enacted by the star, Victor Frankenstein. My study produces Victor as the climax of "Lake Methodism," marrying his privileges of class, gender, and education to the doctrinal heart of Methodism, the raw enthusiasms of life-in-death, "new creatures," and the figural, and often literal, promise of Resurrection. A university-trained prophet, Victor is the ironic mirror of Percy Shelley's attempts to uncouple the energies of poetic inspiration from plebeian agitation, distinctions that refuse difference. The discourses of creation in *Frankenstein* have a specific history in the popular Christianities of the late eighteenth and early nineteenth centuries, even as the Creature himself plangently voices an Enlightenment rationalism which had supposedly triumphed over such spiritualisms by 1818. In the novel's critique, Reason has its own delusions, and the Creature is haplessly rewritten as the "Devil," a broken antagonist without the rhetorical sublimity, social distinction, or skeptical credentials of Milton's Satan: the abject confirmation of the power of enthusiasm to re-determine the figures which would contain it.

Against Secularization

If "Lake Methodism" is a diffuse collection, its unifying argument is the homology of the foundational rhetorics of high romanticism: inspiration, visionary election, prophetic transcendence were themselves diffuse, though not defused. The most patently imaginary and magical conceits, such as giving new birth to dead flesh, were live wires rather than dead metaphors for many people in the early nineteenth century. The age of Saints, Apostles, and Prophets hadn't ended in the 1640s, and the vibrant spiritualisms of Britain during the French Wars weren't confined to peripheral cranks and subalterns, but flourished in commercially sophisticated editions that were major agents in the public sphere. If anything, a common (and respectable) concern was that the large (and surprisingly profitable) demand for religious enthusiasm revealed that print culture was powered by irrational and uncontainable desire, rather than politely scripted sociability. "Enthusiasm," and especially "Methodism," bundled together old practices with modern insecurities. In a marketplace overrun, high argument was overdetermined: former figures of cultural authority could turn into powerful tokens of the socially unacceptable, while nominally exclusive, exclusionary gestures of oracular retreat and clouded mystification could become the currency of clamoring materialisms.

A renewed sensitivity to religion—in all its enthusiasms, but also in the quieter forms that were broadly normative—can challenge our understanding of the "public sphere" in the Romantic period, often read in the perspective of secularizing practices and localities that emerged over the long eighteenth century. Jürgen Habermas, to take an exemplary instance, contends that "people's public use of their reason" marked the emergence of a transformative political technology in Europe well before the French Revolution, as a gradually cohering "citizenry" (or a bourgeois fraction mystified as a universal citizenry) leveraged rational discourse into an unofficial court of appeals against older forms of power.[42] This influential argument has focused much attention on how the authority of the *ancien regime,* built on spectacles of pomp and punishment at Court, military assemblies, and executions, was contested by what Paul Goring calls "the proliferation of new meeting places—clubs, salons, coffee-houses, assemblies, gardens—in which individuals could congregate and discuss the important issues of the day, and by a massive expansion in the production of printed matter."[43] In Habermas's story, this bourgeois public sphere is secular, in both situation and goal. As public "Reason" confronted the monarchical state and its client Church (especially in its Protestant forms), Enlightenment practices developed in various urbanities (such as the coffee-house) emancipated from religious management; print culture followed

---

42. Jürgen Habermas, *The Structural Transformation of the Public Sphere: An Inquiry into a Category of Bourgeois Society,* trans. Thomas Burger with Frederick Lawrence (Cambridge, MA: MIT Press, 1989), 26. For Habermas, the politicization of the "public use of Reason" is legible in a semantic doubling lost in English, as *"Räsonnement* unmistakably preserves the polemical nuances of both sides: simultaneously the invocation of reason and its disdainful disparagement as merely malcontent griping" (26).

43. Paul Goring, *The Rhetoric of Sensibility in Eighteenth-Century Culture* (Cambridge: Cambridge University Press, 2005), 21. See also Lee Erickson, *The Economy of Literary Form: English Literature and the Industrialization of Publishing, 1800–1850* (Baltimore: Johns Hopkins University Press, 1996); Paul Keen, *The Crisis of Literature in the 1790s: Print Culture and the Public Sphere* (Cambridge: Cambridge University Press, 1999); Jon Klancher, *The Making of English Reading Audiences, 1790–1832*; Anne Mellor, *Mothers of the Nation: Women's Political Writing in England, 1780–1830,* 2nd ed. (Bloomington: Indiana University Press, 2002); Robert Miles, *Romantic Misfits*; Lucy Newlyn, *Reading, Writing, and Romanticism: The Anxiety of Reception* (Oxford: Oxford University Press, 2000); Mark Schoenfield, *British Periodicals and Romantic Identity: The "Literary Lower Empire"* (New York: Palgrave, 2009); and William St. Clair, *The Reading Nation in the Romantic Period* (Cambridge: Cambridge University Press, 2004; paperback, 2007).

suit, producing a "public sphere of rational-critical debate in the world of letters" for a national market of readers.[44] As for "other institutions of the public reflecting critically on political issues," Habermas contends that these "counter-spheres" and "counter-publics" are still "oriented towards the intentions of the bourgeois public sphere" and its secularizing project.[45] Habermas's chief examples—Wilksite "public meetings" and "political associations," the fleeting "*plebeian* public sphere" of Revolutionary atheism under Robespierre, or its "continued but submerged existence manifested . . . in the Chartist Movement and especially in the anarchist traditions of the workers' movement on the continent"—are all read as forms of class association and political agency without religious dimension.[46]

This model has been complicated, with increased attention to its limits: the prospect of men coming together for a rational political discussion may tilt toward utopian fantasy, and its binding to locations that gate-keep class and gender reproduces the exclusions otherwise contested.[47] These limits and exclusions may be as useful as assuming a "pure" form of the rational public sphere, since the Romantic period's discursive and material shifts—changes in the publishing industry and transformations in copyright, the institutionalization of periodicals and novels as objects of cultural consumption, and the influence of new demographics on the market and the political arena—may mark the collapse (or, in Habermas's forecast, the structural transformation) of eighteenth-century consensus, and inaugurate the recognizable gaps of "modern" culture. By the 1790s, Paul Keen argues, the "ideal of literature as a public sphere had run aground on political anxieties about the sector of the populace which could reliably be included within the reading public, and on a deep suspicion that theoretical abstractions were politically dangerous rather than liberating";[48] a totalizing public sphere dissolved into paranoid segmentation of powerfully differentiated subjects and objects. The result, in

---

44. Habermas, *Structural Transformation*, 51.

45. Habermas, *Structural Transformation*, 65.

46. Habermas, *Structural Transformation*, xviii. Robert Hole argues that most parts of the political spectrum abandoned self-consciously "religious" arguments between 1790 and 1830: "[i]t could easily be made to appear, both to radical and conservative, that the removal of religious faith was a prerequisite of social change." *Pulpits, Politics, and Public Order in England, 1760–1832* (Cambridge: Cambridge University Press, 1989), 98.

47. Robert Miles surveys challenges to the "public sphere," and Habermas's responses, in *Romantic Misfits*, 13–18. Anne Mellor, shifting the model's attention to gender, critiques that "Habermas's conceptual limitation of the public sphere in England between 1780 and 1830 to men of property is historically incorrect" (*Mothers of the Nation*, 2).

48. Keen, *Crisis of Literature in the 1790s*, 75.

Jon Klancher's measure, was essentially hierarchical: "battle lines" erupted between "high culture and mass culture, bourgeoisie and working class."[49] For other critics, such as Mark Schoenfield, it was a guerilla campaign without uniforms, "a cultural war" of "clashing and allied voices across different discourses," with literary (and especially periodical) culture parrying and thrusting through perpetually shifting arrangements of cultural and economic capital.[50]

Yet these incisive critiques tend to take secularization for granted, and reinforce the grant by privileging non- and antireligious writing. At most, Romanticism often seems, as in M. H. Abrams's account, "the secularization of inherited theological ideas." Abrams presents this as "a historical commonplace," but the deepest power of his argument isn't its emphasis on "secularization," or its twin, the "naturalization of the supernatural," but the innocently adjectival "inherited."[51] The effect is to cast all religious discourse as the historical other of Romanticism—sources of inspiration alien to "The Spirit of the Age," which seems to be recognized in shrugging off this bequest. This critical formation is distinctly retrospective: the last breath of a Christian world-body, wheezing into poetical metaphor and cerebral Deism, or even the skepticism of a secularly minded academy, which sometimes internalizes the project of "Enlightenment" as its own.[52] The neglect of "religion" has been forcefully challenged by Robert Ryan's *The Romantic Reformation* (1997), which recovers "the national religious consciousness" as a structuring presence, and much later work owes a debt to Ryan's correction.[53] One may dispute the definite article in Ryan's title, but still welcome his argument that religion, like any other social form or classification, was a charged signifier ranging from the doctrinally grounded radicalism of Unitarians to the conservative tendencies of

---

49. Klancher, *Making of English Reading Audiences*, 13.
50. Schoenfield, *British Periodicals and Romantic Identity*, 1–2.
51. Abrams, *Natural Supernaturalism*, 12–13.
52. Colin Jager mounts a spectacular critique of some forms of contemporary "secularism," while arguing for a Romanticism already thinking beyond the axis of secular/spiritual, in "Shelley after Atheism," *Studies in Romanticism* 49 (Winter 2010): 611–31.
53. Ryan, *Romantic Reformation*, 1. Daniel E. White provides an excellent account of the ways in which rational Dissent comprised a "dissident middle-class language that suggests an influential and distinct fragment of the bourgeois public sphere" (*Early Romanticism and Religious Dissent*, 11). The Dissenting Gathered Churches, in which congregations not uncommonly had control over their own pulpits, may suggest a comfortable extension of the Habermasian public sphere out of a secularizing space, as the chapel could be home to much greater intellectual and political equality and philosophical freedom than the Established Church. See also Colin Jager for a challenge to the inevitability of secularization narratives, in *The Book of God*, especially 26–36.

the Established Church, and Ryan has inspired other scholars to parse the dense web of religious culture that mattered intensely for the discourses of Dissent, toleration, and enthusiasm.[54]

Joining these new approaches, *Lake Methodism* is skeptical of Romantic skepticism, and of the impact of a "secularization" more familiar to the period's modern students than its inhabitants. It's worth remembering not only that church and chapel were much more common communities than the coffee-house or the circulating library, but also that the "public sphere of ideas" was never obviously secular. A glance at the table of contents of any issue of *Blackwood's* or the *Edinburgh* or the *Quarterly* (let alone the widely circulating denominational periodicals) shows essays on religious books and issues alongside political, philosophical, or literary writing, and usually in ways that don't recognize any distinction between the various categories.[55] J. C. D. Clark warns against a nominalism which makes John Locke's work evidence of a "contractarian consensus," David Hume's (sometimes repressed and unpublished) philosophy for a widespread "secular pragmatism," or Adam Smith's writing for the emergence of the "acquisitive individual." This methodology is prone to finding "the inevitable political enfranchisement of the autonomous, and secular, individual" in an Enlightened public sphere: a serious misrepresentation of an English society that was, at least until the 1830s, a "confessional state dominated by providential status rather than contract, and structured vertically rather than horizontally."[56] While Habermas argues the Reformation transformed "the status of the church," making "religion . . . a private matter" and so securing "the first sphere of private autonomy," this elides the organizational force of denominational allegiances, formally and informally, across other groupings of identity.[57]

---

54. Especially White, *Early Romanticism and Religious Dissent*; Canuel, *Religion, Toleration, and British Writing*; and Mee, *Romanticism, Enthusiasm, and Regulation*.

55. Cf. Stephen Prickett's suggestion that Coleridge "belongs essentially to an undifferentiated world where literary criticism is *neither* a secular *nor* a religious activity, but one that unquestioningly partakes of both worlds." "The Ache in the Missing Limb: Coleridge and the Amputation of Meaning," in *Coleridge's Visionary Language*, ed. Tim Fulford and Morton D. Paley (Cambridge: D. S. Brewer, 1993), 123–35 (132).

56. J. C. D. Clark, *English Society 1660–1832: Religion, Ideology and Politics during the Ancien Regime*, 2nd ed. (Cambridge: Cambridge University Press, 2000), 125. Clark argues that the influence of Locke, especially, has been overstated—his political and economic thought was "briefly relevant" during the American Revolution, but "throughout the century, he was largely irrelevant to English political disputes," ignored by the enfranchised authorities of Parliament and the judiciary, and familiar mostly to Dissenters, who used him to critique genuinely hegemonic political thought (139–42).

57. Habermas, *Structural Transformation*, 11.

The dissolution of the confessional state was a slow process. For hundreds of years after the "Reformation," autonomously private religious identities could be extracted only through the renunciation of public identities; even after the back-and-forth ejections and reinstatements of priests within the Church of England in the seventeenth century, nonconforming Christians were officially barred from public office, and non-Trinitarians suffered more onerous disabilities. As we'll see in the next chapter, "politics" inevitably meant an engagement to some degree with the Church of England. "Establishment" signified not just a network of entrenched interests, but their concentration in the Anglican Church as a system for the maintenance of order and the redistribution of wealth through gentry patronage. Nor did the collapse of the confessional structure across the nineteenth century necessarily signal the rise, let alone triumph, of an emergent secular politics. The decades up to 1830, Clark argues, "saw no objective, quantifiable phenomenon which can be called 'the rise of the middle class' or 'the making of the working class.'" Rather, "the quantifiable phenomenon was the rise of Dissent and the spread of religious disengagement" from the Church of England. This was a transformation in religious organization and experience, not a transition from the primacy of religious ideologies into a differentiated secularism.[58] The dismantling of the Anglican constitution was brought about not by freethinking skeptics or secular radicals, but by denominational antagonists such as Catholics and Dissenters who understood their agenda as the necessary extension of their spiritual commitments.

Cultural as well as political preferences still evinced a broadly religious consensus. Certainly, the reading public was largely unaware of a secularizing "public" sphere, as William St. Clair's report of sales and circulation demonstrates. Even after copyright lapsed, William Godwin, Hume, and Smith were absent from the period's anthologies (an otherwise enormously popular textual form), and Edward Gibbon appeared only with the entirety of his thoughts on Christianity cut. Publishers "not only ignored the discoveries of the Enlightenment, but offered a Counter-Enlightenment to readers who knew nothing of the Enlightenment."[59] Now-canonical texts often had small print runs and very limited influence: Beilby Porteus, Bishop of London, Privy Councilor, and official organizer of the intellectual program for counterrevolution, had no idea who Godwin was and had never heard of *Political Justice* a year after its publication.[60]

---

58. Clark, *English Society 1660–1832*, 192.
59. St. Clair, *Reading Nation*, 134.
60. Hole, *Pulpits, Politics, and Public Order*, 102n12. See also St. Clair's account of

More typically, secularizing and spiritualizing practices cohabited in the "public sphere," and sometimes inhabited the same people. If the theater was a powerful site for the dissemination of standardized English, and the politics of region, race, and nation encoded in grammar,[61] the Anglican pulpit remained the only mouthpiece for polite elocution with which most people, particularly the rural and poor, would have had much experience. Notwithstanding salon or pub conversations, the rituals of worship punctuated the weekly rhythms of most people; the hierarchy of speaking clergyman and silent congregation, and the distinction between free chairs and gentry-owned pews in the church itself, wasn't necessarily challenged by Sunday afternoons with the hybridities of print culture. Organizing Romantic culture into dramatic binaries also imagines tensions not experienced in the eagerness of nearly every Christian to characterize his or her religion as "reasonable." Even the most conspicuous "enthusiasts" were called "Methodists" for the disciplinary rigor and "Experimental" empiricism they brought to their writings and subjectivities.

Christianity hadn't withered into a historical archive or a mythological registry by the turn of the nineteenth century. It only seems so in the histories that are attracted to disruptive intellectual practices, tracing vectors of secularization, such as skeptical freethought, scientific materialism, or the innovations in Biblical scholarship that Jerome Christensen suggests "vitiated scriptural authority and boded the metamorphosis of the Bible into just another popular text circulating in the promiscuous relations of writers, publishers, and readers."[62] Vitiated for whom? This "boding" is at odds with the late eighteenth century, where it was anticipated by very few people. True, Southey thought a "club of Atheists" were gathering in a Keswick tavern for weekly meetings in 1815, but local paranoia doesn't confirm a revolution.[63] "In the period up to 1870 there was little effec-

---

Mary Wollstonecraft's *Vindications*, in *Reading Nation*, 277–80.

61. See Andrew Elfenbein, *Romanticism and the Rise of English* (Stanford, CA: Stanford University Press, 2009), 75–77.

62. Jerome Christensen, *Coleridge's Blessed Machine of Language* (Ithaca, NY, and London: Cornell University Press, 1981), 24. Later chapters will more fully address Elinor Shaffer's seminal account of the Higher Criticism, *"'Kubla Khan'" and "The Fall of Jerusalem": The Mythological School in Biblical Criticism and Secular Literature, 1770–1880* (Cambridge: Cambridge University Press, 1975).

63. See Geoffrey Carnall, *Robert Southey and His Age: The Development of a Conservative Mind* (Oxford: Clarendon, 1960), 152–53. Philip Connell and Nigel Leask cite Hannah More's panic at what she called "speculative infidelity, brought down to the pockets and capacities of the poor, [which] forms a new aera in our history" as evidence for their own argument on "the rapid spread of radicalism and irreligion through the lower orders." This seems to me better evidence for the rapid spread of More's inexhaustible panic ("What Is the People?" 24).

tive challenge to a popular world-view that was recognizably Christian," argues historian Frances Knight:

> Most people continued to believe that their prayers, if uttered with sufficient conviction, could change the way in which the world worked, that all their deeds were being recorded in a great book that would be opened on the last day, and that their dead children were sleeping in the arms of Jesus. When it came to making choices between belief systems, the decision was between Anglicanism or Nonconformity or Roman Catholicism, rather than between Christianity and unbelief.[64]

Even scholarship that has studied a bookshelf of allusions to the Bible, Augustine, the church fathers, and doctrinally neutralized versions of Dante, Spenser, and Milton misses the pervasive culture of "Christianity" in Romantic England—as well as the bookshelf of James Lackington. A revolutionary bookseller unprecedentedly successful at marketing books to underserved readers, in 1791 Lackington provided a catalogue to his first library, astonishing (and exhausting) in its difference from our own sense of what "literature" looked like at the end of the eighteenth century:

> We all worked very hard, particularly Mr. John Jones and me, in order to get money to purchase books; and for some months every shilling we could spare was laid out at old book-shops, stalls, &c. insomuch that in a short time we had what *we* called a very good library. This choice collection consisted of Polhil on precious Faith; Polhil on the Decrees; Shepherd's sound believer; Bunyan's Pilgrim's Progress; Bunyan's Good News for the vilest of Sinners; Bunyan's Heavenly Footman; his Grace abounding to the chief of Sinners; his Life and Death of Mr. *Badman;* his Holy War in the town of *Mansoul;* Hervey's Meditations; Hervey's Dialogues; Roger's Seven Helps to Heaven; Hall's Jacob's Ladder; Divine Breathings of a Devout Soul; Adams on the second epistle of Peter; Adams's Sermon on the *black* Devil, the *white* Devil, &c. &c. Colling's Divine Cordial for the Soul; Pearse's Soul's Espousal to Christ; Erskine's Gospel Sonnets; The Death of Abel; The Faith of God's Elect; Manton on the epistle of St.

---

64. Frances Knight, *The Nineteenth-Century Church and English Society* (Cambridge: Cambridge University Press, 1995), 24. Knight also suggests that the pressures of Paley, Malthus, Darwin, and the doctrinal disputes between dons and bishops didn't much affect everyday Anglican clerics, let alone their congregations: "The party conflicts that undoubtedly raged at a higher level in the Church generally passed them by . . . with the exception of a relatively few urban areas, the Tractarian parish priest was rare indeed" before 1860 (19).

> James; Pamble's Works; Baxter's Shove for a *heavy-arsed* Christian; his Call to the Unconverted; Mary Magdalen's Funeral Tears; Mrs. Moore's Evidences for Heaven; Mead's Almost a Christian; The Three Steps to Heaven; Brooks on Assurance; God's Revenge against Murder; Heaven upon Earth; The Pathway to Heaven; Wilcox's Guide to eternal Glory; Derham's Unsearchable Riches of Christ; his Exposition of Revelations; Alleine's Sure guide to Heaven; The Sincere Convert; Watson's Heaven taken by Storm; Heaven's Vengeance; Wall's None but Christ; Aristotle's Masterpiece; Coles on God's Sovereignty; Charnock on Providence; Young's Short and sure Guide to Salvation; Wesley's Sermons, Journals, Tracts, &c. and others of the same description. . . . We had indeed a few of a better sort, as Gay's Fables; Pomfret's Poems; Milton's Paradise Lost; besides Hobbes's Homer, and Walker's Epictetus, mentioned in my former letter.[65]

Perhaps because so many current romanticisms are so heavily occupied, or preoccupied with varieties of exceptionalism—sexual, bodily, national, racial, scientific, political, philosophical, imaginative—the common ground of religion can slip from notice. But to cede this terrain is also to retreat from the battleground Romanticism, the rough-and-tumble of sectarian strife and passionate religiosity that characterized the national culture, in which doctrinal differences were fighting words, waged by men and women with few vocabularies for identity not inflected by denomination.

The "Reading Nation" wasn't yet the nation; neither would recognize themselves easily in some modern representations. There were probably still more readers of Bunyan than of Byron.[66] Linda Colley argues that the glue of an "intolerant," even "thuggish" Protestantism—taught by the antediluvian *Book of Martyrs*, ubiquitous in households of few books—bound together the diversities of the three kingdoms.[67] We've been so charmed by the "Romantic Revolution" in literature, and the Rise of the Novel, that we haven't recognized that the period's other great genre was the sermon. Hugh Blair's *Sermons* sold a quarter of a million copies

---

65. James Lackington, *Memoirs of the First Forty-Five Years of the Life of James Lackington* (London: Lackington, 1791), 91–93.

66. For the almost unique place of Bunyan in British publishing history, see St. Clair, *Reading Nation*, 73n28 and 131.

67. Linda Colley, *Britons: Forging the Nation, 1707–1837* (New Haven, CT: Yale University Press, 1992), 23–27. Colley also argues that "religious works formed easily the bulk of what every British printing press was producing in this period" (41).

between 1774 and 1815, and Thomas Chalmers's *Astronomical Discourses* (a set of sermons) rivaled Byron's *Corsair*, selling 6,000 copies in their first two months, and 20,000 in their first year.[68] Religious texts, moreover, enjoyed a privilege unmatched in universities without departments of modern literature. William Paley's *Moral Philosophy*, with fifteen editions during his lifetime, had a long influence over many intellectual (or at least well-bred) men; his works were required examination texts for all Cambridge students until the end of the nineteenth century.[69] Only by gauging the "religious" in Romantic culture can we appreciate Southey's report, none too happy, in the *Quarterly* of 1810: "No works in this country are so widely circulated, and studied by so many thousand readers, as the Evangelical and Methodist Magazines."[70]

Southey screeched, "Of these publications we have no hesitation in saying that they produce evil—great evil, nothing but evil."[71] But if there's hyperbole here, it's not off the charts. The *Journal* of John Wesley, published serially from 1738 to 1789, and collected thereafter, was one of the most visible of English autobiographies, eventually reaching more than a million words, with a total number of copies somewhere between 80,000 and 180,000.[72] In the 1790s, Wesley's *Arminian Magazine* had twice the circulation of the *Gentleman's Magazine*, and, under many names, would become the longest-running religious periodical in the world.[73] These works emerged from and sustained a strictly managed autocracy, governed first by Wesley (an ordained clergyman, and onetime fellow of Lincoln College), then by his hand-picked successors, all of whom controlled what, where, and how texts were printed, edited or anthologized, priced, and marketed within and beyond the Methodist Connexion. As the next chapter argues, Methodism was a particularly savvy brand in a country already

---

68. St. Clair, *Reading Nation*, 581, 591

69. Isabel Rivers, *Reason, Grace and Sentiment: A Study of the Language of Religion and Ethics in England, 1660–1780*, 2 vols. (Cambridge: Cambridge University Press, 1991–2000), 2:336. See also Jager, *Book of God*, 102–23. Aileen Fyfe reminds us that while Paley's *Evidences of Christianity* and *Moral Philosophy* were required texts, the *Natural Theology* wasn't, contrary to long-standing misconception; Fyfe, "The Reception of William Paley's *Natural Theology* in the University of Cambridge," *The British Journal for the History of Science* 30.3 (October 1997): 321–35.

70. Robert Southey, "On the Evangelical Sects," *Quarterly Review* 4 (November 1810): 480–514 (507–8). Southey's report is also his lament that "the bigotry, fanaticism, and uncharitableness of these publications are melancholy proofs of human weakness."

71. Southey, "On the Evangelical Sects," 508.

72. For estimates on publication figures, see Wesley, *Journal and Diaries* I (1735–38), ed. W. Reginald Ward and Richard P. Heitzenrater (Nashville: Abingdon, 1988), 41.

73. Brantley, *Locke, Wesley, and the Method of English Romanticism*, 118.

heavily invested in religious culture. Methodism offered novel intensities—the ecstatic spontaneity of its sermons against the rote recitations of the Establishment, the soaring melodies of its new hymns against an Anglican service almost entirely devoid of music, along with an entire library of cleverly segmented and accessibly edited texts—to previously neglected, even invisible publics. Methodist success surprised everyone, even its manager: in spite of a business model of marketing cheaply in order to maximize circulation, John Wesley realized a lifetime profit of £30,000, all of which he gave away.[74]

This print enterprise, coupled with an army of itinerant preachers crisscrossing the country and colonies, brought Methodism to the frontiers of England and the empire. As Southey and a host of establishment writers observed, this adventure complicated the geography of center and periphery, reorienting even supposedly secularizing practices in middle-class and gentry culture. Those who wanted nothing to do with Methodism or any other form of enthusiasm found themselves somewhat awkwardly connected to it: as historian Boyd Hilton argues, religious evangelicalism in the postrevolutionary era was an "amorphous set of ideas and attitudes, capable of seeping into minds that were sometimes formally hostile" to its ostensible positions.[75] In 1821, the *Quarterly*'s review of Southey's *Life of Wesley* said much the same thing. While the "two or three hundred thousand" Methodists in the country were "no very appalling amount in a population of sixteen millions," the much wider influence was compelling:

> [I]t is not . . . by the numbers of the professed Methodists alone that we must estimate the moral effect which they have produced. . . . The religious ferment first excited by their preaching has extended far beyond the visible bounds of their society. It has stimulated the clergy to greater seriousness and activity in the discharge of their functions; it has set the laity on thinking for themselves; it has, as an incidental consequence of the rivalry of hostile sects, (roused by the new phenomenon to practice a new means of popularity) forwarded, to a degree never previously contemplated, the education and religious instruction of the lower classes; it has opposed, among these classes a mighty and countervailing principle to the poisonous flood of modern philosophy. It is obvious, even to a careless observer, that religion is more in the minds and mouths of men than formerly; that a greater curiosity is excited by its discussion . . . the major-

---

74. Henry D. Rack, *Reasonable Enthusiast: John Wesley and the Rise of Methodism*, 2nd ed. (Nashville, TN: Abingdon, 1993), 350.

75. Boyd Hilton, *The Age of Atonement: The Influence of Evangelicalism on Social and Economic Thought, 1785–1865* (Oxford and New York: Clarendon, 1991 [1988]), 30.

ity are, on the whole, less ashamed of, and more attentive to the outward appearances of piety than they seem to have been during the preceding century.[76]

The *Quarterly* had profound reservations not only about Methodism, but also about Southey's dignifying it with a sustained two-volume treatment. The small comfort was the irrefutable evidence that these were emphatically religious days, in which what it would call "a great excitation of the public mind" had decisively curbed "the poisonous flood" of "modern philosophy," preserving the clarity of a pure Protestantism across denominational divisions.[77]

The disciplined enterprises of Methodism were the leading edge of a much broader, and not always disciplined, enthusiastic literature descending from the 1640s, as the seventeenth-century prophecies of Christopher Love experienced a dramatic revival in the 1790s, the moment of their supposed culmination.[78] "The awful subject of public enquiry and curiosity," announced Richard Brothers in 1795, was "the wonderful effects of inspiration and prescience in prophecy, waking and sleeping visions, and other forms of communication of the divine will and knowledge."[79] If these "wonderful effects" were loudly trumpeted, the tune didn't please a liberal "Clergyman" who in the same year conceded having "lately heard much respecting Prophets and prophecies"—but lamented the "confident, I had almost said blasphemous manner, many lay claim to inspiration."[80] Nevertheless, a broad spectrum of polite culture, from rational Dissenters to orthodox churchmen, recognized itself as living in a moment of "inspired" writing, though this had little to do with the productions of largely unread Oxbridge poets. Lackington read its more suitable fashion in an "inspired prophet": a "taylor," "elevated above an assembly of old women . . . stript in his shirt, with his wig off, sweating, foaming at the mouth, and bellowing like a baited bull. In the above manner it seems he would often amuse himself and his congregation for near two hours."[81]

---

76. "Southey's Life of Wesley," *Quarterly Review*, 24 (October 1821): 1–55 (3).
77. "Southey's Life of Wesley," 3.
78. Iain McCalman, "New Jerusalems: Prophecy, Dissent, and Radical Culture in England, 1786–1830," in *Enlightenment and Religion: Rational Dissent in Eighteenth-Century Britain*, ed. Knud Haakonssen (Cambridge: Cambridge University Press, 1996), 312–35 (323–24).
79. Richard Brothers, *Wonderful Prophecies, Being a Dissertation on the Existence, Nature, and Extent of the Prophetic Powers in the Human Mind*, 3rd ed. (London: B. Crosby, 1795), iii.
80. *Memoirs of Pretended Prophets. By a Clergyman* (London: J. Johnson, 1795), i, iv.
81. Lackington, *Memoirs*, 173.

The enthusiastic "underworld" so brilliantly excavated by Iain McCalman also poured into the daylight in the Romantic period,[82] and led Coleridge to doubt the framing "so complacently affixed to it by the contemporaries of 'this *enlightened age.*'"[83] The wake of the French and Methodist Revolutions pulled Cambridge intellectuals as well as rural chambermaids into communion with *The Destiny of Nations. A Vision:* "By types, shadows, dreams and visions, I have been led on . . . whereby . . . the future destinies of nations have been revealed to me."[84] This is Southcott, not Coleridge, both sharing the mode of apocalyptic vision. Prophetic imagination, historian James Hopkins argues, constituted an extraordinarily widespread belief that the "existing system of social, economic, and political relationships will be recast in the image and likeness of a vision sufficiently compelling to draw its adherents away from their daily routines and into a life of hyperbole, one in which they and all their endeavors take on an outsized, heroic quality."[85] Hazlitt said as much in 1817 of both poets and prophets, without the heroic gloss: "to speak of them as they deserve, they are not well in the flesh, therefore they take refuge in the spirit; they are not comfortable in the here, and they seek for life to come."[86]

The refuge Hazlitt configured is consistent with what Jerome McGann has marked out as a project of cultural transcendence. *Lake Methodism* argues that this is Romantic culture itself. Escapes into a mental interiority were heard more frequently in Methodist field-preaching than in the library of Rydal Mount. Imaginative transcendence was an elite gesture, but also the hope of the poor Methodist: if it effected displacement and "false consciousness," it was also a source and reflex of considerable unease. No small project of this book is to reverse some of the polarities—secular and sacred, polite and popular—that have taken hold in Romantic studies. This can be done only by recognizing the extent to which "Romantic" culture was an emphatically "religious" culture. It is to this culture, in all its exuberance and orthodoxy, we now turn.

---

82. Iain McCalman, *Radical Underworld: Prophets, Revolutionaries, and Pornographers in London, 1795–1840* (Cambridge: Cambridge University Press, 1988).
83. Samuel Taylor Coleridge, *On the Constitution of Church and State*, ed. John Colmer (Princeton, NJ: Princeton University Press, 1976), 14.
84. Joanna Southcott, *The Strange Effects of Faith: Being a Continuation of Joanna Southcott's* Prophecies, 3rd ed. (London: Galabin and Marchant, 1806), 17. Excerpts from Coleridge's poem were published in Southey's *Joan of Arc* (1796); *The Destiny of Nations* first appeared in full in *Sibylline Leaves* (1817).
85. James Hopkins, *A Woman to Deliver Her People: Joanna Southcott and English Millenarianism in an Era of Revolution* (Austin: University of Texas Press, 1982), xi.
86. Hazlitt, "On the Causes of Methodism," 58.

Chapter 2

"Elocution to the Mute"

Anglican Authority and the Cultural Revolt of Methodism

How might we understand Romanticism without secularization? Coleridge answers, when, in the midst of the chilly restlessness of "Frost at Midnight," he warms himself with a dream "Of my sweet birth-place, and the old church-tower, / Whose bells, the poor man's only music, rang / From morn to evening" (28–30). The intimate nostalgia for these "bells" is an inward turn in an already tortuously introspective poem—but it's also a fleetingly public glimpse of cultural forms that have faded from critical view. As Coleridge's verse quietly underscores, the "music" of the poor men and women of England could be parochial in scope. Novels and poetry, the pleasures of the urban theater, were all unavailable to vast swathes of a country still agrarian, impoverished, and semiliterate. The cosmopolitanisms of the Continent or the treasures of the Orient, however delightful to tourists and connoisseurs, tended to be met as, and with, bewildering violence by the deracinated (and likely press-ganged) legionaries of Wellington and Nelson. In its Biblical stories, festivals, rites of passage and rituals of worship, plebeian culture was still tightly connected to "the old church tower": heavily religious in character, and almost always Anglican in confession. This isn't the Romanticism we anthologize, but it was the culture inhabited by most people in the early nineteenth century. The nation's consensus, such as it was, resided within the Church of England, which possessed "at least the nominal allegiance of 90 percent of the population" in 1800.[1]

To be sure, allegiance wasn't appreciation. The music of most Anglican churches was parlous. Organs were very uncommon. More often a rustic "band" of players supplied the tune. Congregations typically didn't join in the hymns; these were sung by the solitary clerk or a straggling choir, and services barely included any song until the late nineteenth century.[2] The rhetorical performance of the clergyman usually deepened the dismal tone. As "Dion" sighed in the *Examiner* in 1819, even an Establishment somewhat buoyed by the rising tide of Evangelicalism still floated only "miserable specimens" of "Pulpit Oratory."[3] Anyone relying on the Church of England for "music" in the Romantic period was likely to be disappointed. Anyone whose horizons were limited to it lived within a very circumscribed cultural geography.

Coleridge leverages this recollection into a contrast that never quite consoles, pitting blinkered poverty against his own overworked and underproductive mind. The "calm" that "disturbs / And vexes meditation with its strange / And extreme silentness" stirs a deeper moral vacancy, not filled by the wordplay of intellectual games (8–10). "Frost at Midnight" possesses Coleridge with a surfeit of cultural labor, versifying "extreme silentness" into a dissonant parallel of the bells' purity, as the "strange" quiet chimes with the fire's "stranger," which "flutters" as the "sole unquiet thing." Even this "sole unquiet" becomes yet more material for an idle imagination, willing to pun on the unquiet state of the poet's soul and "idling Spirit," which, "By its own moods interprets, everywhere / Echo or mirror seeking of itself, / And makes a toy of Thought" (16–23). This self-mirroring play figures the division between the nostalgic leisure of the gentleman and the plebeian body so occupied by physical labor it lacks all cultural instrumentality. Poor men have only church bells for music, Coleridge implies, because they cannot sing themselves.

These bells herald the subject of this chapter: the conditions, consequences, and collapse of the Anglican constitution, which had encoded strict divisions in thought and feeling as the moral order for the nation.

---

1. Rack, *Reasonable Enthusiast*, 10. See especially James Obelkevitch, *Religion and Rural Society: South Lindsay, 1825–1875* (Oxford: Clarendon, 1976).
2. Anthony Russell, *The Clerical Profession* (London: SPCK, 1984 [1980]), 61, 71–73.
3. "Pulpit Oratory," *Examiner* 603 (July 18, 1819): 461.

Romantic England was organized by religious institutions and differences, themselves organized by figurative laws, conventions of metaphor, and rhetorical dispositions. As we'll see in the next two sections, the Church of England ran the country, but doctrine and discipline were often far removed from its definitions of itself and its antagonists. The formal penalties and privileges of the Anglican hegemony were typically expressed in a nebulous constellation of habits for polite reading, writing, speaking, and worshipping, rather than in explicit confessions of faith. Religion was politics—but the vehicle of religious identity was its tenor.

Even for bishops, style trumped theology. William Warburton, with his own stylistic emphases, warned that "a FANATIC MANNER of preaching, tho' it were the doctrine of an Apostle, may do more harm, to Society at least, than a modest revival of *old* speculative heresies, or, than the invention of *new;* since it tends to bewilder the imagination of some, to inflame the passions of others; and, in that state of things, to spread disorder and disturbance throughout the whole community."[4] Warburton was writing in 1763, but in 1819 "Dion" was still "disposed even to go so far as to maintain, that the precise doctrines [any preacher] entertains are of little consequence, compared with the style and power with which they are enforced."[5]

By this measure, Methodism signified a double threat, against the joint establishments of the Church of England and English culture. I borrow this chapter's title from Eve's final acquiescence, and I mean it as an allegory for Methodism's effects upon the *ancien régime:* the failure of a seemingly inevitable set of social relations, in which radical asymmetries of mind and body had been represented as Providentially determined, and in which revolt is an act of language against the Word, as the Fruit "Gave elocution to the mute, and taught / The Tongue not made for Speech to speak" (*Paradise Lost* 9:748–49). But whether stylized by Satanic "elocution" or Coleridgean "music," these denominational contests over cultural inclinations and standards shaped the situation of Romanticism as fully

---

4. William Warburton, *The Doctrine of Grace: or, the Office and Operations of the Holy Spirit Vindicated from the Insults of Infidelity, and the Abuses of Fanaticism,* 2nd ed. (London: A. Millar and J. and R. Tonson, 1763), 131.

5. *Examiner* 603 (July 18, 1819): 461. In 1823, the *Liberal* reported that "Lady Bluemont declares" the preaching of Edward Irving, especially in its "sound," the "picturesque appearance of the orator," the "grace of action," "the beauty of style," and "the bursts of passion," to "be only inferior to the EXCURSION in imagination," which was probably meant to indict simultaneously the tastes of Bluemont, Irving, and Wordsworth. See "Pulpit Oratory: Dr. Chalmers, and Mr. Irving," *The Liberal* 4 (London: John Hunt, 1823): 299–313 (299–300).

as the successes of Scott, Byron, or Radcliffe. By the end of the eighteenth century, Methodism had made polite complacency over the absence of plebeian culture an urgently studied pose, rather than disinterested description. The dominance, not the existence, of "poor man's music" separate from the Church of England was now at issue. Alexander Knox—Irish clergyman, friend of John Wesley, and correspondent of Southey—took it as "indisputable" not only that "a certain fuel of religious sensation is deeply lodged in man's natural constitution," but that this fuel had the most power in "the least cultivated classes of society," where it abided as "as a natural instinct."[6]

If the instinct felt new, the bond between poor man's music and the Anglican bell was often held as immemorial as that between Church and State. Not everyone was convinced that either constitution belonged to "time out of mind," however. The liberal curmudgeon Joseph Ritson, for example, satirized the antiquarian industry for cleansing folk ballads and songs of plebeian soil, and then reproaching plebeians for having had no culture in the first place. He had little use for Thomas Percy's fantasy of minstrels as "an order of men who united the arts of poetry and music, and sung verses to the harp of their own composing." The true history of English song was instead borne by a "tumultuous rout of FIDLERS, PLAYERS, COBBLERS, [and] DEBAUCHED PERSONS" who acted "as an appendage or appurtenance to the whores and letchers, from whose diversion this respectable order of men . . . were most miserably twanging and scraping in the booths of Chester fair."[7] This was "the real character of a nation," which could be "collected" with "certainty" only from "the manners and diversions of the lower or rather lowest classes of the inhabitants."[8]

---

6. Alexander Knox, "Remarks on the Life and Character of John Wesley," appendix to Robert Southey, *The Life of Wesley and Rise and Progress of Methodism*, 2nd ed., ed. Charles Cuthbert Southey (London: Longman, 1864), 293–360 (334–35). Even some recent work on the history of religion seems to accept this formation of an instinctual theological urge, residing as a chthonic force in the nervous system, rather than as a set of socialized expectations, roles, and institutions. John Kent opens his *Wesley and the Wesleyans* considering "the primary human impulse . . . to seek some kind of extra-human power," as "religion" satisfies essentialized and always already extant spiritual appetites: "the individual's test of a religious system is how far it can supply this 'supernatural' force" (John Kent, *Wesley and the Wesleyans* [Cambridge: Cambridge University Press, 2002], 1–2).

7. Joseph Ritson, *Ancient Songs, from the time of King Henry the Third, to the Revolution* (London: Joseph Johnson, 1790), vi–vii.

8. "There is nothing, perhaps, from which the real character of a nation can be collected with so much certainty as the manners and diversions of the lower or rather lowest classes of the inhabitants. The principal amusement of the common people of every country

Ritson was crankily attuned to the prevailing conceit that economic differences were commensurate with affective and linguistic differences. Francis Jeffrey, though no conservative as the early nineteenth century understood it, was a typical proponent of this view. Commenting on the pseudo-democratic poetics of Southey's *Thalaba* and Wordsworth's "Preface," he deigned to remind readers that the "love, or grief, or indignation of an enlightened and refined character, is not only expressed in a different language, but is in itself a different emotion from the love, or grief, or anger, of a clown, a tradesman, or a market-wench." "The things," Jeffrey emphasized, "are radically and obviously distinct."[9] Jeffrey's very insistence, however, recognized that such distinctions were being countermanded not only by the "new poetry" but also by the new politics from which it drew authority—in short, the reorganizations of print culture, the public sphere, and literary and political representation underway by the turn of the nineteenth century.

Methodism, as much as ballad revivalism or radical pamphleteering, drove this reorganization. The Society's brilliant songs, cheap and diverse anthologies, emotional services rich with audience participation, and techniques for self-study and group socialization altered the symbolic order of the nation, with unprecedented and frequently politically inassimilable senses of self-possession and agency. And this from congregations, as the lay preacher Duncan Wright admitted with affectionate irony in 1781, composed of "objects of universal contempt."[10] Methodist services brought theater and opera to people unfamiliar with either; its large textual catalogue, tailored for different reading levels and purchasing capacities, pushed the frontiers of print. The impact on the social—as well as the individual—consciousness was transformative. As Wesley wrote in 1785:

---

and in every age has been a turn for melody and song. Many of the vulgar songs of France and Spain possess the first degree of poetical merit. . . . The common people of Italy listen with rapture to the sublimest flights of Ariosto, whom they appear to comprehend as well as the ablest critic. . . . The English vulgar have never, perhaps, shewn such a brilliancy of intellect, and therefor [sic] the compositions which they most relish are hardly to be endured by those of any other description. Nothing can be more common than to see a large crowd attending with apparent satisfaction to rhapsodies in which, though written in a jargon, and with a grossness perfectly suitable to such an audience, it is evident that the composer had not understood what he wrote, that the performer does not understand what he sings, and that the auditors do not understand what they hear; and yet, what is most extraordinary, no one of these circumstances appears to render the composition less favourite or delightful." Ritson, *A Select Collection of English Songs*, 3 vols. (London: Joseph Johnson, 1783), 1:lxx–lxxi.

9. Jeffrey, "Southey's *Thalaba*," *Edinburgh Review* 1 (October 1802): 66.
10. WV 2:22.

We had a Love-Feast. I could not but observe the manner wherein several of them spoke, one after the other. Not only the matter, but the language: the accent, the tone of voice, wherewith illiterate persons, men and women, young and old spoke, were such as a scholar needeth not to be ashamed of. "Who teacheth like him?"[11]

Methodists were appreciative students, valuing their emotional reactions to a sermon more than the sermon's theological soundness or rhetorical polish. They often sang their doctrine, in preference to having it preached to them, even by one of the Wesleys. The humblest were eager to testify with their own dramatic crises and conversions; the most inspired were encouraged to abandon their ploughs, tools, and frequently their families and shops, for itinerant lay preaching.

These acculturating developments, more than any doctrinal or political agenda, struck at the core of Anglican authority. The front line, moreover, had never been political ideology. Wesley had been no friend to obvious radicalisms. Especially later in life, he cheerfully accommodated himself to whichever ministry happened to be in at the moment, while taking frequent pains to deny any theological innovation.[12] He declared (somewhat disingenuously) that he taught only "plain, Old Christianity": "I and all who follow my Judgment do vehemently refuse to be distinguished from other men, by any but the Common Principles of Christianity."[13] After his death in 1791, most forms of Methodism still identified with both Church and State, and some Wesleyans were attending Anglican services in the middle of the nineteenth century.[14] There were notable exceptions: the Kilhamites and Primitive Methodists were concentrated in areas of Luddite activity, and most of the Tolpuddle Martyrs were Methodists or sons of Methodists.[15] Yet it wasn't these peripheries but the center of the Methodist movement that produced one of the most dramatic transformations since the Civil Wars. This took shape chiefly against the rules of art, and

---

11. Wesley, *Journal and Diaries* I, ed. W. Reginald Ward and Richard P. Heitzenrater (Nashville: Abingdon, 1988), 57.

12. Rack, *Reasonable Enthusiast*, 374. See also Clark, *English Society*, 284–300.

13. John Wesley, *The Character of a Methodist* (Bristol: Felix Farley, 1742), 15–16.

14. In addition to some forms of worship, Methodists still relied on the Church for its notarizing functions for birth, baptism, marriage, and death, even after the Civil Registration Act of 1836 provided them with alternatives (Knight, *The Nineteenth-Century Church*, 24–36).

15. Semmel, *Methodist Revolution*, 137. For recent accounts of the meanings of Luddism, see Kevin Binfield, ed., *The Writings of the Luddites* (Baltimore: Johns Hopkins University Press, 2004), and Steven Jones, *Against Technology: From the Luddites to Neo-Luddism* (New York: Routledge, 2006), esp. 45–75.

the social distinctions and deferences such rules managed. Even inveterate revolutionaries such as Hazlitt were put off by this insurgency. Methodism, he sneered, "let loose the imagination of the gaping multitude."[16] If Hazlitt was provoked into uncharacteristic sympathy with Burke's contempt for "the swinish multitude" of the Revolution, the Anglican establishment was mortified to discover that its power now extended only as far as its ability to entertain. One of its clergy whined in 1795, as he saw his congregation abandon him for the greener pastures of field preaching, "Is a Christian orator to descend to all the gesticulations of the stage, and to rant like a tragedy king?"[17]

By the last decades of the eighteenth century, "Methodism" bespoke a massive reorganization of the logic, purpose, and demographics of "culture." Wesley himself proposed (modestly) the Apocalypse as the only sufficient scale on which to weigh the impact. Preaching in 1787, he found human nature seeming born again, well in advance of the lesser revolution in France:

> "The times" which we have reason to believe are at hand (if they are not already begun) are what many pious men have termed the time of "the latter-day glory"; meaning the time wherein God would gloriously display his power and love in the fulfillment of his gracious promise that "the knowledge of the Lord shall cover the earth, as the waters cover the sea."[18]

This global promise appalled the left no less than the right. Liberals such as Hazlitt and Hunt, and especially radicals such as Cobbett, saw in Methodism the prospect of the working classes distracted from their own political interests by a new, superstitious conservatism. But a correspondent of Viscount Sidmouth was morally certain that "To be a Methodist is to be a Jacobin in the extreme."[19] Yet one soldier turned preacher recalled in 1781 that Methodists were thought to be heirs to the terrifying discipline of the New Model Army; his officers "feared what our enthusiasm would turn to, and mentioned Cromwell, who could preach and pray one part of the day, and kill and plunder the other."[20] The now-reactionary Poet Lau-

---

16. Hazlitt, "On the Causes of Methodism," 60.
17. George Croft, *Thoughts Concerning the Methodists and the Established Clergy* (London: F. and C. Rivington, 1795), 9.
18. Wesley, *Sermons* II: 34–70, ed. Albert C. Outler (Nashville: Abingdon, 1985), 525.
19. Quoted in Iain McCalman, *Radical Underworld*, 51.
20. WV 2:32.

reate Southey rehearsed a different spiritual warfare, in the well-known story that Wesley was an undercover Catholic agent, out "to make a party among the poor, and when the Spaniards landed . . . join them with 20,000 men."[21] This secretly coiled army of insurrection, averred Sarah Trimmer and Sir Frederic Morton Eden, was in fact a mass of sluggish idiocy, dragging down the State:

> Of late years, there has been a very general Complaint, over every part of the kingdom, of the increase of the parish poor. To what cause are we to ascribe this increase? . . . No cause whatever has a more powerful influence than the increase of Methodists. I have shewn, that this Religion is, in the *first* place, a heavy Tax; and, that in the *second*, it encourages Idleness; and both of these contribute to make men poor, and to keep them in that state.[22]

Jesuit, Jacobin, Jacobite, incendiary and wet blanket: the array of incoherent charges testifies to the alarm, and the emergency. The wildly competing meanings suggest that "Methodism" had complicated the terms for political speech itself, in what Burke mapped as "the most important of revolutions . . . a revolution in sentiments, manners, and moral opinions."[23] Leigh Hunt had hinted in 1808 that "not a day passes, but the Methodists are endeavouring to overthrow the Episcopal Church by a thousand weapons open and secret."[24] John Wesley's older brother, Samuel, was the prophet: the Methodist "societies are sufficient to dissolve all societies but their own."[25]

---

21. Robert Southey, *The Life of Wesley and the Rise and Progress of Methodism, in Two Volumes* (London: Longman, Hurst, Rees, Orme, and Brown, 1820 [New York: William Gilley, 1820]), 2: 21. All quotations, unless otherwise marked, are taken from the 1820 edition.

22. [Sarah Trimmer], *A Review of the Policy, Doctrines and Morals of the Methodists* (London: J. Johnson, 1791), 49–50. Eden approvingly cited this passage in *The State of the Poor: Or, An History of the Labouring Classes in England, From the Conquest to the Present Period, in Three Volumes* (London: J. Davis, 1797), 1:ix–x. Eden seems not to have read Trimmer, but rather an Anglican clergyman's pamphlet that drew from her; see John Howlett, *Examination of Mr. Pitt's Speech* (London: W. Richardson, 1796).

23. Edmund Burke, *Reflections on the Revolution in France, and On the Proceedings in Certain Societies in London Relative to That Event*, ed. Conor Cruise O'Brien (London: Penguin Classics, 1986), 175.

24. Hunt, *An Attempt to Shew . . .* , Essay 1, "On the Ignorance and Vulgarity of the Methodists," 301.

25. Quoted in Anthony Armstrong, *The Church of England, the Methodists and Society, 1700–1850* (London: University of London Press, 1973), 67. Later members of the family would be alienated, as well. In 1791, contemplating the Revolution and the uncertain con-

The Methodists were separating from the emotional regulations that the Church of England established for its communion, as well as the country. Southey, the first non-Methodist to write a biography of Wesley, saw in "The Rise and Progress of Methodism" not only the disestablishment of the Church, dire enough, but also the "moral expatriation" of England from its cultural identity, inextricable from its Church.[26] The security of these identities was no small matter during the Napoleonic wars, which threatened both the Church and its national domain. But the worry had cropped up whenever the Anglican hierarchy suspected cultural agents of foreign and domestic subversion. After the defeat of the Catholic menace in 1745, the Bishop of Exeter alleged its survival in the alternate print cultures and affective scripts of Methodism, that "*Surfeit*" of "*Lives, Characters, Sentiments* and *Actions*," "*Journals, Letters,* and other *Works*" with which the Wesleyan "*Press* has cramm'd the Public."[27] By 1791, two years after the French Revolution, James Lackington opened his parody of a Methodistical "life" by gauging the monstrous "multitude of memoirs under which the press has groaned."[28] Although Jon Klancher reports a complete "absence of a textual countercode of political discourse" before the secularized radicalisms of the 1790s, this report overlooks a vitally present Methodism.[29]

It became very convenient, moreover, to lump Methodism together with Jacobinism, however incommensurate. In 1800, the Rev. Richard Polwhele vouched for a rumor first broached in the *Gentleman's Magazine*, "that Paine's Works, and other books of the like tendency, have been translated into Welsh, and secretly distributed by the leaders" of Wesleyan bands.[30] In the same year Samuel Horsley, then Bishop of Rochester,

---

sequences of Wesley's death, Wesley's grand-nephew fretted over the new "constitution he has established among a people scattered throughout every part of a great, a powerful, and a luxurious nation." John Annesley Colet, *An Impartial Review of the Life and Writings, Public and Private Character, of the Late Rev. Mr. John Wesley* (London: C. Forster, 1791), 17.

26. Robert Southey, "History of the Dissenters," in *Quarterly Review* 10 (October 1813): 90–139 (138).

27. [George Lavington], *Enthusiasm of Methodists and Papists, Compar'd*, "Preface," unpaged.

28. Lackington, *Memoirs*, xv.

29. Klancher, *Making of English Reading Audiences*, 42.

30. Richard Polwhele, *Anecdotes of Methodism, to which is added, A Sermon, on the Conduct that Becomes a Clergyman* (London: Cadell and Davies, 1800), 59. There's some satisfaction in finding that Polwhele, best known today as the calumniator of Mary Wollstonecraft and those he named *The Unsex'd Females* (1798), was loathed by his parishioners. With his *Anecdotes*, he attempted to do to Methodism what he had done to the Rights of Woman. The Methodists proved harder targets, and he quickly found himself besieged

saw Methodists substituting for politically repressed radicals: "these new congregations of non-descripts have been mostly formed, since the Jacobins have been laid under restraint of those two most salutary measures, commonly known by the names of the Sedition and the Treason Bill."[31] Whether the initial objection was ecclesiastic or political, gentlemen of many different convictions and parties could concur, with Southey, that "the confederated and indefatigable priesthood" of the Methodists was a cultural blight. Methodists "barely tolerate literature, and actually hate it," insulating themselves with formal loyalty, while poisoning the soul of the nation with "mildewing superstition, blasting all genius in the bud, and withering every flower of loveliness and innocent enjoyment."[32]

This "blasting" and "withering" uprooted the country's putatively organic politics, since the government of polite taste overlapped, if imperfectly, with polite government. The weak bureaucracy of the state was diffused in its gentry, in occasional turns as Justice of the Peace or as a part-time functionary (such as stamp-collector for Westmoreland), with status rather than technocratic ability the usual qualification. Coleridge, for example, a negative of personal and professional accountability in 1804–5, quickly ingratiated himself into the management of the crucial Mediterranean theater of war with little to recommend him other than his wit at dinner; he was also offered a mission to Russia in order to negotiate an £80,000 grain purchase, and he accepted the role of Acting Public Secretary of Malta, a position of real power and substantial salary, in early 1805.[33] Even this 1790s Jacobin could be entrusted ten years later with the overthrow of France, so long as he was legibly "polite."

The Church of England was the pillar supporting the hegemony of respectability, supplementing the sparse number of formal bureaucrats with an agent in every parish, who fulfilled almost all civil functions. This hegemony, as hegemonies are wont, accommodated substantial diversity in its scientific, economic, and theological positions.[34] The Articles were

---

by a well-organized campaign. Even his shopping trips were haunted by a Methodist laypreacher, who "assailed" Polwhele with a "foaming torrent ... of his tub, or his horseblock eloquence," who called the *Anecdotes* "lies," and who insisted "on my revocation of such palpable falsehoods, and threatening to bring the people around me in the market-place of Helston at some future day, and force me to authenticate my stories, or retract them, there, if I persisted in abusing the fraternity" (Polwhele, *Anecdotes,* 18–22).

31. Samuel Horsley, *The Charge to the Clergy of His Diocese* (London: James Robson, 1800), 19–20.

32. Southey, "On the Evangelical Sects," 507.

33. See Richard Holmes, *Coleridge: Darker Reflections, 1804–1834* (New York: Pantheon Books, 1998), 29–33.

34. But while eminent clergymen such as Paley and Malthus navigated the moral conse-

deliberately vague, and the Church had evolved to encompass doctrinal protest, in order to institutionalize a set of cultural habits that generated social coherence, while authorizing intellectualized disagreement. "Old Dissent," I think, picked battles the Church often thought least important, and was best equipped to manage. Even as they protested some of its doctrines or legal claims, most middle-class Dissenters dutifully conformed to the Church's much more significant expectations of polite reading, writing, and "reasonable Christianity."[35]

Methodism, more than the liberal but well-off strains of Dissent, was a genuine rebellion. Its assault on polite norms, Southey insisted, was all the more lethal because it was so politically and theologically muddled. Even while subscribing to the Articles, the Methodists denied the nation's implicit contract, alienating themselves from "common sympathy":

> It is no light evil for a state to have within its bosom so numerous and active and increasing a party, whose whole system tends to cut them off from all common sympathy with their countrymen, and who are separatists not in religious worship alone, but in all the ordinary observances of life. Not satisfied with exclusive salvation, they must have every thing exclusive, and accommodations for the Methodists are to be found in every place, and of every possible kind. They have not only their own chapels, their own schools, their own mad-houses, and their own Maga-

---

quences of Newtonian mechanics and economic calculus, most men promoted to bishoprics between 1780 and 1820 were substantially more orthodox.

35. There was significant cultural overlap between the Church of England and those forms of Dissent originating in the seventeenth-century ejections: churchmen regularly purchased the works of Nonconforming divines such as Isaac Watts and Richard Baxter, and the reading lists at Dissenting academies included many Church of England theologians. See Isabel Rivers, *Reason, Grace, and Sentiment,* 1:164–204. The case for Toleration was usually made by appeals to the socioeconomic solidarity of Dissenters and churchmen, rather than through any argument for a natural right of conscience. "Most Protestant Dissenters did not claim that they should be eligible for public office because of any right they possessed as men *qua* men, merely that the special privileges won by men of their class, wealth and station should not be denied them purely because of their faith" (Hole, *Pulpits, Politics, and Public Order,* 123). Dan White argues that Dissenters, concentrated among the urbanized and educated "middle sorts," took pride in presenting themselves as serious men of business, pulsing with the lifeblood of English identity: as the "parent and guardian of the nation's own libertarian and commercial spirit" (*Early Romanticism and Religious Dissent,* 28). Southey, confessing in 1834 his "very hearty dislike for dissenters as a body," as it was "hardly possible to believe how dishonestly they write, how impudently they suppress or misrepresent important facts, how rancorously they hate the Church, and with how bitter and uncharitable a spirit they are possessed," still said (if only to perfect the prejudice) that many of his best friends were Dissenters: he had an "abundant liking for individuals among them." *New Letters of Robert Southey,* ed. Kenneth Curry, 2 vols. (New York and London: Columbia University Press, 1965), 2:410–11.

zine, but they have their own Bible, their newspaper, their review, their pocket-book, their cyclopaedia, their Margate-hoys, and their lodging-house at Harrogate, next door to the chapel, and with a bath in the house.[36]

Though his ostensible target was Methodist "exclusivity," the old canard that nonconformists were an *"imperium in imperio,"* Southey read this isolation very differently from cloistered renunciations of the world. Methodism was an alarming *modernity,* pervading every aspect of English cultural life—even its baths. Far from abandoning Englishness, Methodism was rewriting it. Already, Southey conceded, most readers understood "poetry" as the hymns and lyrics of the prolific Charles Wesley: "no poems have ever been so devoutly committed to memory as these, nor quoted so often upon a death-bed."[37] This was a coup against the cultural figures that held the allegiance of all men, Tory and Whig, Unitarian and churchman. The Brothers Wesley had replaced Shakespeare as the emissary of English:

> The works of Voltaire have found their way wherever the French language is read; the disciples of Wesley wherever the English is spoken . . . there may come a time when the name of Wesley will be more generally known, and in remoter regions of the globe, than that of Frederick or of Catharine.[38]

This revolution in national (and imperial) mythmaking was beyond any the Rights of Man might precipitate. English enthusiasm, as much as French atheism, could topple monarchs, by fracturing their conventional buttresses. Methodism was desynonymizing "culture" from polite culture, "society" from polite society, and neither could be assumed any longer to reproduce polite rule—whether headed by "Frederick," "Catharine," or, though unsaid, "Louis" and "George."

"Religion is the Basis of Civil Society"

For the Established Church still governing England, this was catastrophe, not transformation. Stories of the secularization of politics, of post-

---

36. Southey, "On the Evangelical Sects," 510.
37. Southey, *Life of Wesley,* 2:161.
38. Southey, *Life of Wesley,* 1:34–35.

Revolutionary contests between classes and ideologies without denominational identity, make poor sense of the period. The "successive hammer blows" of the repeal of the Test and Corporation Acts (1828), Catholic Relief (1829), and the first Reform Bill (1832) dramatically reshaped the constitution between Church and State.[39] But the fifty years leading up to this transformation do not easily support a progressive narrative of inexorable, secularizing separation from the Church of England. "Reform" was the goal of Catholics and Dissenters; "secularism" and "Toleration" were themselves religious agendas in the early nineteenth century. Moreover, firm churchmen as well as committed reformers received the dismantling of the Anglican constitution as an unexpected and somewhat unprecedented event. The classes and interests supporting the original Settlement and Act of Toleration had very little in common with those agitating for Repeal and Relief.[40] All sides often felt that the late seventeenth-century legal code was the antithesis, rather than precursor, of the arguments a century or more later. Southey thought the 1698 Blasphemy Act clear and generous enough that the "necessity" of the Unitarian Relief Act in 1813 "was not quite obvious,"[41] while Paine violently condemned the sort of "Toleration" enjoined by the Act which bore its name.[42] "Reform was not

---

39. John Walsh and Stephen Taylor, "The Church and Anglicanism in the 'Long' Eighteenth Century," in *The Church of England c.1689–c.1833: From Toleration to Tractarianism*, ed. John Walsh, Colin Haydon, and Stephen Taylor (Cambridge: Cambridge University Press, 1993), 1–64 (61).

40. Mark Canuel argues that the "spirit of toleration . . . could be viewed as a series of legislative enactments extending from the Act of Toleration in 1689" to Repeal and Relief, but such a view may require a historical abstraction occluding the variety of local differences and tensions haunting this spirit (*Religion, Toleration, and British Writing*, 12).

41. The Blasphemy Act had exempted from the benefits of the Toleration Act any Dissenter who denied the Trinity. Southey wrote, "The necessity for the repeal was not quite obvious. . . . We are not aware that any Unitarian was ever deprived of a legacy by the enforcement of this law, or debarred by it from the exercise of any legal right: and certainly that body of dissenters had not been prevented by it, from defending, inculcating and diffusing their peculiar opinions with perfect freedom, whether from the pulpit, or the press. In fact, they had organized themselves as a sect, during the existence of the statute, grown up, and flourished (as far as can be said that they have flourished) under it." Southey, "New Churches," *Quarterly Review* 23 (July 1820): 549–91 (570).

42. "Toleration is not the *opposite* of Intolerance, but is the *counterfeit* of it. Both are despotisms. The one assumes to itself the right of withholding Liberty of Conscience, and the other of granting it. The one is the pope armed with fire and faggot, and the other is the pope selling or granting indulgences. The former is church and State, and the latter is church and traffic. . . . Toleration, therefore, places itself, not between man and man, nor between church and church, but between God and man; between the being who worships, and the BEING who is worshipped; and by the same act of assumed authority by which it tolerates the man to pay his worship, it presumptuously and blasphemously sets itself up to tolerate the Almighty to receive it." Thomas Paine, *The Rights of Man, Part One*, in *The*

seen as inevitable" before Waterloo, argues Jonathan Clark, and it seemed even less likely between 1815 and 1827. Establishmentarians controlled the Parliamentary agenda; their authority was reversed by a sudden rash of deaths and defections, more than by the changing sense of the nation.[43] Burke's dictum, though a motivated (and resented) rhetoric in 1790, ruled the next four decades: "We know, and what is better we feel inwardly, that religion is the basis of civil society."[44]

This wasn't an ecumenical feeling. The vagueness of Burke's "religion" was one of the recognizable ways in which Anglican identity, and its dominance, was encoded. The history of the word "Anglican" until 1800 is a history of absence: it "scarcely occurs" as a noun, since "the Church of England was commonly referred to as 'the church' or 'the establishment'; its members as 'Church of England men' or 'churchmen.'"[45] In its catholicity, the Church declined to qualify itself. Amidst the welter of Dissenting nuance, it remained the (only) Church, sublimely removed from both argument and explanation. While the Anglican establishment is often dismissed as "a moribund institution,"[46] the casual and even indifferent ways in which it theorized itself argued not senescence, but absolute dominion.[47] The Church was normative because it was natural, as well as national. Other denominations—Baptist, Unitarian, Presbyterian, Congregationalist—blazoned their doctrine and discipline, but the Church was beyond theological debate or structural nicety, conceptually and historically synonymous with "England."

The Church was privileged as an organ for expressing and preserving national and racial truths, rather than doctrinal specificities. Disestablishment, then, threatened the existential ordering of Englishness, the hierarchical and exclusionary community Burke projected onto the first-

---

Thomas Paine Reader, ed. Michael Foot and Isaac Kramnick (London: Penguin, 1987), 201–62 (231).

43. Clark, *English Society,* 505–26. See Hole, *Pulpits, Politics, and Public Order,* 240–47, for a rejoinder to Clark's case that the successful case for Emancipation and Repeal "was based solely on expediency, not at all on principle" (243).

44. Burke, *Reflections,* 186.

45. Rack, *Reasonable Enthusiast,* xiii.

46. Goldberg, *Lake Poets,* 32.

47. Walsh and Taylor find Anglicans "quietly confident in the superiority of their own Church over all others": "eighteenth-century English clerics were sufficiently relaxed in their churchmanship to feel little need to defend the integrity of their Church or to define its identity." Moreover, they argue that the period from 1688 to the late 1820s was one of substantial continuity in the structure, doctrine, and political orientation of the Anglican Church, and that this continuity is the material and ideological rationale for conceptualizing "the long eighteenth century" (Walsh and Taylor, "The Church and Anglicanism," 58).

person plural: "We know, and what is better we feel inwardly." "We owe to it," intoned Southey in his *Book of the Church* (1824), echoing both Burke's grammar and its politics, "our moral and intellectual character as a nation; much of our private happiness, much of our public strength."[48] Southey had meant his *Book* as catechism, a replacement for the ancient *Book of Martyrs* as the textbook for theo-patriotism in Andrew Bell's national schools.[49] His abiding moral lesson was that the national Church was also an intimate establishment, bound up in domestic affection rather than legal compulsion. Reform meant not just disinheritance, but parricide and infanticide: "I offer, therefore, to those who regard with love and reverence the religion which they have received from their fathers, a brief but comprehensive record, diligently, faithfully, and conscientiously composed, which they may put into the hands of their children."[50] Southey again borrowed from Burke in his quiet conflation of "religion" with the establishment (as well as in his politicization of domestic sentiment), but for the *Reflections,* the Church was something even grander: the constitution, not simply of the private family or the public "family" of the nation, but of the very possibility of sociopolitical thought and feeling. Burke's constitution was founded in cognition, in the immutable, inaccessible laws of language and logic, rather than in arbitrary (and alterable) legal codes. Attacks on the constitution were thus self-incriminating solecisms in English and Englishness. Men of sound judgment, Burke argued, "do not consider the church establishment as convenient but as essential to their state . . . the foundation of their whole constitution." Such constitutional ties produced, and were derived from, the "natural" workings of a prior mental constitution: "Church and State are ideas inseparable in their minds, and scarcely is the one even mentioned without mentioning the other."[51]

Some clerics were even more direct: "They that secede from the Church may be thought to secede likewise from the State."[52] The Church was certainly the State's most visible and ubiquitous apparatus.[53] If Dis-

---

48. Robert Southey, *The Book of the Church,* 2 vols. (London: John Murray, 1824), 2:511.

49. David Eastwood, "Robert Southey and the Language of Patriotism," *The Journal of British Studies* 31.3 (July 1992): 265–87 (284).

50. Southey, *Book of the Church,* 1:2.

51. Burke, *Reflections,* 197–98.

52. Joseph Eyre, *A Dispassionate Inquiry into the Probable Causes and Consequences of Enthusiasm* (London: J. Long, 1800), 18.

53. W. R. Ward argues that the "legal dependence of the Church upon the state disguised a real dependence of a weak state upon networks of informal influence including those of the Church" (W. R. Ward, "The Religion of the People and the Problem of Control, 1790–1830," in *Studies in Church History,* vol. 8, *Popular Belief and Practice,* ed. G. J.

senters weren't convinced by the representations of churchmen, they remained infuriatingly helpless before Anglican control over their daily lives. Bishops comprised ten percent of the House of Lords, were required to reside in London while Parliament was in session, were active in its deliberations, and voted as a block; for most of the long eighteenth century, divisions were separated by 20 to 30 votes, making the 26 Bishops critical for any government.[54] But more important were the lesser clergy, present in every parish, distinctive by uniform, and comprising an organization matched in human capital only by the army or navy. The Church was staffed by approximately 10,000 men, and the modern nation-state—and its civilian bureaucracy—hadn't yet been fully invented; the advent of the civil service in the middle-to-late nineteenth century posed the first major structural recruitment challenge for the Church. But in the Romantic period, "government" could be a strikingly informal, limited and semi-privatized thing. Though the prosecution of the global war against Revolution, the management of an empire, the annexation of a continent, and the maintenance of discipline at home were obvious strains, between 1790 and 1820, the entire staff of the Treasury peaked at 86, while the Home and Foreign Offices combined employed less than 45 clerks.[55]

In default of a civil bureaucracy, clergy were the functionaries managing all English subjects, regardless of denomination. Parliament, sermonized the rector of Lincoln College in 1792, "justly considers . . . the ministers of the national church . . . the support and bulwark of the state."[56] Anglicans were the only notaries and registrars available: before the 1836 Civil Registration Act, it was nearly impossible to be married (or

---

Cuming and Derek Baker [Cambridge: Cambridge University Press, 1972], 237). Deryck Lovegrove responds that the eighteenth-century consensus was of a constitution of Church and State which preserved, rather than blurred, the distinctions between them, as an arrangement "between two free and equal sovereign bodies" (Lovegrove, *Established Church, Sectarian People: Itinerancy and the Transformation of English Dissent, 1780–1830* [Cambridge: Cambridge University Press, 1988], 8). Jonathan Clark suggests the ties were more intimate: the "authority of any institution or practice" in England "could be traced, usually at no very far remove, to the claim of the Church to embody a specific authorization by Christ, and to be in a sense His continuing body in the world. It was ultimately because the Church was an authoritative hierarchy that the society which was so often held to be identical with it so often claimed to be an authoritative hierarchy also. It was natural that fundamental alienation from society in early-modern England and colonial America should generally have had a religious origin" (*English Society*, 318).

54. Armstrong, *Church of England, the Methodists and Society*, 9–10.
55. Russell, *Clerical Profession*, 19.
56. Edward Tatham, *A Sermon Suitable to the Times* (London: J. F. and C. Rivington, 1792), 9.

to record births, deaths, and burials) outside of the Church of England.[57] In villages especially, the resident Anglican priest was very likely to be the only—and certainly the most familiar—representative of the national political order. Clergymen frequently assumed more powerful positions. Between 1783 and 1794, Anglican priests were the nation's tax collectors, and throughout the Romantic period they seem to have proved the fraction of the gentry most likely to serve as Justices of the Peace.[58] Clergymen controlled the social safety net, tattered as it was, and manipulated it in order to exact submission; in 1794, the lay preacher Joseph Cownley recounted the difficulties he had solidifying Methodist converts in rural communities, as local parsons cut off parish relief for those who went to hear him speak.[59]

The clergy were tied not just to the state, but to its spoils, though this plunder, as Paine and Burke testified in their different ways, was unevenly distributed between the best bishoprics and the worst curacies.[60] But beneficed clergymen were some of the largest beneficiaries of the Acts of Enclosure: between 1757 and 1835, nearly two-thirds of all Acts commuted the parish tithe into land for the rector, usually at a rate of at least one-seventh to one-eighth of the entirety of the parish's land.[61] Romantic England thus saw a substantial redistribution of landed wealth to beneficed Anglicans, producing a remarkably—and newly—entitled group, which owed its ascendancy to the *ancien regime*. Clergymen were among the most committed partisans for the status quo, since the French Revolution prophesied that the confiscation of property would start with theirs. Though they made up only one-third of the Justices in Oxfordshire between 1775 and 1816, Anglican priests were responsible for 80 percent of the convictions

---

57. Knight, *Nineteenth-Century Church and English Society*, 13.
58. Russell, *Clerical Profession*, 142–68.
59. WV 4:134.
60. Burke declared that the English people "can see a Bishop of Durham, or a Bishop of Winchester, in possession of ten thousand pounds a year; and cannot conceive why it is in worse hands than estates to the like amount in the hands of this Earl, or that Squire" (*Reflections*, 203). Paine retorted, "The comparison is out of order, by being put between the bishop and the earl or the 'squire. It ought to be put between the bishop and the curate, and then it will stand thus:—*The People of England can see without pain or grudging, a bishop of Durham, or a bishop of Winchester, in possession of ten thousand pounds a year, and a curate on thirty or forty pounds a year, or less.*—No, Sir, they certainly do not see those things without great pain or grudging" (*Rights of Man*, 230). The poorest curates seem to have been in the Lake District, where some "livings" were significantly below starvation wages, at £10 per year (Armstrong, *Church of England, the Methodists and Society*, 26).
61. Russell, *Clerical Profession*, 31.

issued at the Quarter Sessions; they frequently led armed posses from the front, and weren't shy in reading the Riot Act themselves.[62]

In this post-Revolutionary hardening, liberals within the Church became marked targets. The King himself intervened to forbid William Paley a bishopric, while Richard Watson, a prelate who flirted with heterodox politics—and who provoked Wordsworth with his apostasy, Blake with his sophistry—was frozen until his death as Bishop of Llandaff, the very lowest rung of episcopal preferment and a living worth much less than many well-endowed rectories.[63] The doctrinally tolerant and politically flexible strands of Latitudinarian Anglicanism went into very swift decline. By 1795, the party line was firm: the Bible "embraces every opportunity of enlarging on the duty of subordination, and of shewing how much a respectful and obedient conduct towards the magistrate, honours GOD, while it is a test of Christianity."[64] While this might warm Hannah More, it was too tepid for Bishop Horsley, whose uncompromising publications swiftly translated him up the episcopal ladder between 1788 and 1806. Napoleon was the Beast, France the Whore, Horsley charged, and the End was indeed nigh.[65] The Apocalypse was neither poetical figure, nor marginal enthusiasm, but the concern of the highest circles of Anglican orthodoxy. The events facing the Church had only the Crucifixion as precedent: "No crisis, at any period of time since the moment of our Lord's departure from the earth, has more demanded, than the present, the vigilant attention of the Clergy of all ranks and orders, from the Prelate to the Village-Curate, to the duties of the weighty charge, to which we are called."[66]

---

62. Russell, *Clerical Profession*, 152–9.

63. John Walsh and Steven Taylor, "The Church and Anglicanism," 40–41. On Paley, see G. Cole, "Doctrine, Dissent, and the Decline of Paley's Reputation 1805–1825," *Enlightenment and Dissent* 6 (1987): 19–30.

64. Thomas Thomason [Truebody], *An Essay Tending to Prove that the Holy Scriptures, Rightly Understood, Do Not Give Encouragement to Enthusiasm or Superstition* (Cambridge: Cambridge University Press, 1795), 36. Isabel Rivers cautions that establishment theology, especially in the early eighteenth century, was more diverse: while "social conservatism is undoubtedly an important element in Anglican thought . . . it has been overemphasized by modern historians to the neglect of other elements" (*Reason, Grace and Sentiment*, 1:82).

65. "The democracy of Apostate France seems indeed, in many particulars, to be doing the work of Antichrist before he comes, and preparing his way before him. . . . Insomuch that this odious French Republic, aping the manners, grappling the dominion, speaking to friends and to enemies the high vaunting language of antient Rome, we seem to behold the dreadful Apocalyptic Beast, which, at the time of the desolation of the Pagan whore exhibited in vision to St. John, had been, but was not, but was to be again; we seem, I say, to behold, in the French Republic, this dreadful monster beginning to rise, in its antient form, out of the raging sea of Anarchy and Irreligion" (Horsley, *Charge*, 10–11).

66. Horsley, *Charge*, 3. For a sustained reading of Horsley's thought as "characteristic

But Horsley's notion of "vigilant attention" was unlikely to arrest the Four Horsemen. Chiding that the "Festivals and Fasts of the Church are, I fear, not without some connivance of the Clergy, gone much into oblivion and neglect," he instructed that Whitsuntide should now be observed. One service on Easter morning was no longer satisfactory; Ash Wednesday should be celebrated, as well; churches ought to be unlocked "every day in the Passion week," even if no services were held; the Sacrament should now be given four times a year, which, for most parishes, was three times more than usual.[67] This was milquetoast to sop the blood-dimmed tide—yet the Anglican response to the Revolution was less dramatic in practice than rhetoric. Sunday services, by and large, were still limited to once in the morning, which made attendance in rural parishes difficult; prayer meetings were very unusual until the 1830s; meetings not overseen by the incumbent were typically forbidden.

Moreover, the Church was physically incapable of admitting the masses it attempted to catechize. Its infrastructure hadn't developed after the turn of the eighteenth century; as Southey wrote in 1820, since Queen Anne's reign, "the population of the kingdom has doubled; and that of the circle about London has probably decupled its inhabitants; but no additional churches were built, neither were any means provided for imparting religious instruction to multitudes who were now actually excluded from public worship."[68] The last major allocation of funds for new churches had been in 1711, after which the very few that had been built were speculative investments backed by private consortiums, "financed by sales and rents from pews and burial places, with no room for the poor."[69] As sleepy villages became booming centers of industry, the national Church no longer matched the nation. By 1817, the Church of England in Manchester

---

of the intelligent, conservative, high-church Anglicans of his day," see Hole, *Pulpits, Politics, and Public Order*, 160–73. Hole implies that the alarmism of Horsley's 1800 *Charge* may have been the "onset of senility" (170).

67. Horsley, *Charge*, 27–28. Communion was very rarely administered until the rise of the Oxford movement, and before the 1830s was often performed only on Easter. Though he was never theologically orthodox, Coleridge self-identified as Anglican fairly early in his turn to political conservatism, and was in some ways typical of Anglican practice. While (and perhaps because) he invested the ritual with profound significance, he did not take Communion at any time between his first year of college and 1827. See J. Robert Barth, S.J., "Coleridge and the Church of England," in *The Coleridge Connection: Essays for Thomas McFarland*, ed. Richard Gravil and Molly Lefebure (New York: St Martin's, 1990), 291–307 (301–2).

68. Southey, "New Churches," 563–64.
69. Rack, *Reasonable Enthusiast*, 320.

only had seats for 15 percent of the city,[70] and Southey was certain that Liverpool could admit only 20 percent of its population; in Yorkshire, seating was wanting for 580,000, and in Chester, 1,040,000.[71]

The Discourse of Anglican Authority

The Establishment wasn't wholly passive before this emergency. Parliament gestured toward triage in 1818, granting one million pounds for the construction of new churches, and the project generated surprisingly broad-based support.[72] The Church's prerogatives were defended with ferocious, even eliminationist language,[73] as well as naked violence: one Methodist lay preacher was silenced by a drunk parson hitting him in the face, knocking the legs out from the chair he was standing on, and shaking him by the collar with such force that the cloth ripped, while a band of hired thugs looked on darkly.[74] But the strange distance between frenzy at

---

70. Armstrong, *Church of England, the Methodists and Society*, 91.

71. Southey, "New Churches," 553. Simon Dentith argues that the paucity of seats was a serious problem for Anglican authority, as the carefully mapped geography within each church, with bought pews for the gentry, free pews for the middle sort, and benches for the lower classes, worked "as an institution in which the social hierarchy is precisely reproduced . . . and in which patterns of social command and patronage are reinforced on a weekly basis" (*Society and Cultural Forms in Nineteenth Century England* [New York: St. Martin's, 1998], 31). David Hempton suggests that Methodism didn't erode Anglican power, but profited from these demographic and structural erosions already underway, flourishing where the Church of England had grown weakest (*The Religion of the People: Methodism and Popular Religion c. 1750–1900* [London and New York: Routledge, 1996]).

72. New churches made strange bedfellows. Southey was joined by Keats's friend, Benjamin Robert Haydon, in campaigning for the government grant, and the poet-laureate praised the painter's "forcible appeal" that £10,000 be set aside to commission art for the new churches, which would, according to Southey, "complete the glories of this triumphant age, by producing an age of art in England, equal to any which Greece or Italy can boast" (Southey, "New Churches," 586–88). Benjamin Robert Haydon, *New Churches: Considered with Respect to the Opportunities They Offer for the Encouragement of Painting* (London: J. Carpenter, 1818).

73. Though Southey had ecumenical interests, leading to engagements with (if not endorsements of) a variety of religious experiences, by 1827 he was "persuaded of two things—that nothing is so likely to bring an explosion, and that there can be no tranquility for Ireland till the Romish religion is subdued there, and therefore this is the right course to be pursued. If I were in Orders I would be there" (*New Letters of Robert Southey*, 2:311). Anglican opinion could be much more extreme than even this. Southey himself condemned in 1810 a diatribe arguing that Methodist "vermin . . . must all be caught, cracked, and killed in the manner, and by the instrument which are found most efficacious to their destruction" (*New Letters of Robert Southey*, 1:267).

74. WV 3:74.

impending Apocalypse, and palsied solutions such as Whitsuntide observance, wasn't the Church's failure, but its ideological aspiration. The dominant strain of Anglican thought held the Church's power greatest when least explicit, its function the naturalization, rather than evangelization, of Christianity. The Church had little interest in the attendance of its parishioners, couldn't seat them had they turned up, and reliably bored those who did: but it reserved to itself, and this affective restraint, most venues for formal political and cultural agency.

Anglicanism evaporated disruptive feeling, while confusing antagonistic intellectual positions before their political factionalization. The precedents for powerful, popular religiosity were grim, so the "strict canonical order of our Church," Alexander Knox wrote in 1828, was designed to afford "no proportioned means of awakening an entire people from a moral sleep," insuring they slumbered peaceably.[75] Southey celebrated this enervation as an "infinite blessing": "I am never weary of repeating that faith is an appetite of the mind: our establishment starves it, the Catholics gorge it even to surfeiting and sickness."[76] The Church set a low bar for its dogma,[77] and the nuance of its best theologians was probably irrelevant to the everyday faith of most clergy and almost all communicants.[78] Anglicanism was purposefully messy in the Romantic period, avoiding lucid spiritual thought through its material diffusion, intellectual diffuseness, and rhetorical "reasonability," not at all the same as intellectual "rationality."

Theological nicety, or even self-awareness, had been a hallmark of separation since the first Puritans were called "Precisians." Two hundred years on, the *Quarterly Review* lamented that "needless scruples and ill-judged austerities of manner and deportment have agitated bosoms and darkened countenances which before were guileless, and innocent, and gay as the birds in the thicket."[79] The good churchman was cheerfully relaxed, attached to Christianity by those socialized pressures, familial affections, and uninterrogated overdeterminants Burke heroized as "prejudice," not

---

75. Knox, "Remarks," 331.
76. *New Letters of Robert Southey*, 2:6.
77. Rivers, *Reason, Grace and Sentiment*, 1:32.
78. The disabilities imposed on Dissenters made them acutely aware of their doctrines, and the sacrifices they made for them. Anglicans enjoyed the privilege of an uncritical religiosity; after Reform, the situation didn't change dramatically. Tractarianism was very much an elite phenomenon, even among clergymen, until much later in the nineteenth century (Knight, *Nineteenth-Century Church*, 19).
79. "Southey's *Life of Wesley*," *Quarterly Review*, 4.

any spiritual appeal.[80] The best Anglican was a cultural, rather than faithful, Anglican:

> The majority of the English, as of every other people, follow the religion of the country, because they have been bred up in it, conform to it because they have been told it is true, and never think of questioning its truth, nor of requiring any other reason for their belief. For the purposes of the state this is sufficient; their names are to be found in the parish registers, many of them regularly go to church themselves, and those who do not, send their wives and children there.[81]

For Wordsworth, his "grey-haired dame," Ann Tyson, figured the homey comforts of a benevolently flaccid Anglicanism, so complacent it was genuinely somnolent:

> Her clear though shallow stream of piety,
> That ran on Sabbath days a fresher course.
> With thoughts unfelt till now I saw her read
> Her bible on the Sunday afternoons,
> And loved the book when she had dropped asleep
> And made of it a pillow for her head. (1805 *Prelude* 4:216–21)

This "clear though shallow stream" flowed from a Church identified by regional and racial norms rather than doctrinal commitments, with a long history of jettisoning theological concerns for social cohesion. Anglicanism appears a problematic prefiguration of secularization: before the rise of Tractarianism and widespread Evangelicalism by the 1830s, the Church

---

80. In his defense of the Established Church, Burke wrote, "You see, Sir, that in this enlightened age I am bold enough to confess, that we are generally men of untaught feelings; that instead of casting away all our old prejudices, we cherish them to a very considerable degree, and, to take more shame to ourselves, we cherish them because they are prejudices; and the longer they have lasted, and the more generally they have prevailed, the more we cherish them. We are afraid to put men to live and trade each on his own stock of private reason. . . . Many of our men of speculation, instead of exploding general prejudices, employ their sagacity to discover the latent wisdom which prevails in them. If they find what they seek, and they seldom fail, they think it more wise to continue the prejudice, with the reason involved, than to cast away the coat of prejudice, and to leave nothing but the naked reason. . . . Prejudice is of ready application in the emergency. . . . Prejudice renders a man's virtue his habit; and not a series of unconnected acts. Through just prejudice, his duty becomes a part of his nature." Burke, *Reflections*, 183. See especially Canuel, *Religion, Toleration, and British Writing*, 17–20.
81. Southey, "On the Evangelical Sects," 486–87.

of England restrained disruptive or liberationist intensities within religious identity, modeling a Christianity that naturalized the supernatural mysteries still surviving within orthodox Protestantism.

Very few points of doctrine were so essential that refutation damaged the Church's spiritual or temporal authority. This was, after all, a Christianity carefully insecure on the grounds, mechanisms, and meanings of Salvation. The Thirty-Nine Articles were "often deliberately ambiguous, to leave room for varying interpretations," juggling Calvinism with Arminianism, the grace of election and the work of repentance, fully authorizing neither.[82] The final form of the Articles in 1571 struck a political compromise between fundamentally irreconcilable soteriologies; after the Act of Settlement, many churchmen were pleased that the Church's vague, contradictory teachings derailed doctrinal controversies before they progressed into armed disagreements. Theological rigor suggested moral and cognitive morbidity, fatally discredited by the Civil Wars. The most essential matters were best left unexplored, for the sake of the individual soul as well as the nation. The *Quarterly* praised "the ambiguous and comprehensive wording of some of the articles,"[83] and even the hard-charging Horsley shrank from doctrinal entanglements. Clergy ought "to avoid controversial argument in . . . the dark subject of Predestination and Election," as the Articles were wisely unhelpful: "differences of opinion, upon these subjects, have subsisted among the best Christians from the beginning, and will subsist, I am persuaded to the end." These "differences," Horsley insisted, were ineradicable, arising from "necessity, from the inability of the human mind to reconcile the doctrine of Providence, irresistibly ruling all events, with the responsibility of man as a moral agent." It was far better—and quintessentially establishmentarian—to prioritize the affect of the sermon, and regulate its manner, rather than its details: "I would advise you to use in general, not an argumentative, but a plain didactic style: teach with authority, not as the Scribes," and avoid all mysterious points.[84]

Hazlitt jeered that these mealy-mouthed Anglicans thought with only their pusillanimous bellies: *"men should not quarrel with their bread and butter."* The consensus on the Articles was fuzzy because no churchman had any incentive to think clearly: "Is it likely that a man will intrepidly open his eyes to conviction, when he sees poverty and disgrace staring him

---

82. Barth, "Coleridge and the Church of England," 299.
83. "Southey's *Life of Wesley*," *Quarterly Review*, 8.
84. Horsley, *Charge*, 32.

in the face as the inevitable consequence?"[85] Even subscribers granted that the Articles were a bad-faith document of practical expediency, not Scripture. Southey's doctrinal opportunism, while remarkable, wasn't unusual. The genius of the Articles, he wrote in 1811, was what they didn't say: "The nature of the Fall and the question of the Trinity and the superhuman nature of Christ may safely be left undefined, for every person to understand according to his judgment."[86] But as Southey well knew, "the question of the Trinity and the superhuman nature of Christ" were precisely the matters *not* safe for the individual conscience. Until the repeal of the Blasphemy Act in 1813, both had legally compulsory answers, which Southey eagerly exploited. As soon as a "Barrister," James Sedgwick, mounted a Socinian assault on these "mysteries," Southey did a swift about-face, and pretended that the Church of England was entirely of one mind on the "safely undefined":

> What! The bishops? the dignified clergy? have they then exploded all doctrinal mysteries? have they ceased to hold the doctrines of the Trinity, the corruption of the human will, and redemption by the cross of Christ? Do our clergy solemnly pray to their maker, weekly before God and man, in the words of a liturgy which they know *cannot be believed?* Either this is true, or the Barrister is a libeller, a rank and convicted libeller.[87]

Such gymnastics—confessing in private the insignificance of the Articles, using them in public as a truncheon—fooled no one, even as they extorted temporary acquiescence. But an instrumentalist view of the Church, as a spiritually vacuous institution of political hierarchy and due subordination, wasn't some scandalous Deistic critique. This was the key conceit of the Establishment's defenders: "it saves us from persecution; but its creed will not stand the test of sound criticism."[88] Men who "accepted" the Articles had some freedom to ignore them; those who formally rejected them paid a heavy price for their dissent. Even a scholar such as Southey could be strikingly—and conveniently—ignorant of the terms of his own belief. While considering John Wesley's insistence that *"no good works can be done before justification, none which have not in them the nature of sin,"* he barked, "This doctrine, however, was not preached in all the naked

---

85. "On the Clerical Character" (1818), in *Complete Works of William Hazlitt*, 7:250–52.
86. *New Letters of Robert Southey*, 2:6.
87. Southey, "On the Evangelical Sects," 484.
88. *New Letters of Robert Southey*, 2:6.

absurdity of its consequences." Yet as Coleridge quietly remarked in his marginalia to the *Life of Wesley,* "Did R.S. remember that the words in Italics are faithfully quoted from the Articles of Our Church?"[89]

Few pious frauds were quite as self-aware in their mendacity as Southey's. But this doctrinal deemphasis was an important plank for the Church's program of "reasonable Christianity." As an ideology of social and epistemological orthodoxy, its terms didn't admit much variation: the "Religion, by which alone our salvation is to be obtained, is altogether a reasonable service," opined one cleric in 1792;[90] "Our religion is to be reasonable, consistent, and uniform," agreed a Norrisian medalist in 1795;[91] the "great simplicity and reasonableness" of revelation, prophecy, and miracles were the subjects of the 1824 Warburton lectures.[92] "Reasonable Christianity" wasn't the "rational religion" of progressive Dissent: instead it valued a holistic (and reactionary) "good" over the unaccommodating rigor of the one true faith.[93] Reasonability guaranteed the temperament—and temperance—of an argument more than its conclusions. "Reasonable" men might disagree reasonably, yet still be "consistent, and uniform" in style. This discursive practice had the minor virtue of being unfalsifiable, if not true: no skepticism or heterodoxy challenged a Church rooted in emotional and aesthetic habits, rather than positive doctrinal claims.

---

89. Coleridge, *Marginalia,* ed. George Whalley, 6 vols. (Princeton, NJ: Princeton University Press, 1980–2001), 5:138.

90. Tatham, *A Sermon Suitable to the Times,* 3.

91. Thomason, *An Essay Tending to Prove,* 38.

92. John Davison, *Discourses on Prophecy, in Which Are Considered Its Structure, Use, and Inspiration* (London: John Murray, 1824), 27.

93. Joseph Priestley's "rational religion" was very far indeed from Anglican "reasonability." In 1791, he published the Wesley family's accounts of their haunting by a spirit, Old Jeffrey; against what he took to be the asinine credulity of the founders of Methodism, Priestley offered a neat distillation of the "rational religion" of radical Dissent: "Of what unspeakable value, then, are rational principles of religion; and how happy should that man think himself who has never known any other! and yet the Scriptures teach them in the plainest manner, and uniformly instruct us to judge of ourselves and others, not by uncertain and undescribable *feelings,* but by evident *actions.* As our Saviour says, 'by their fruits ye shall know them;' for where a man's conduct is not only occasionally, but uniformly right, the principle upon which he acts must be good. Indeed the only reason why we value good principles, is on account of their uniform operation in producing good conduct." This is the far edge of eighteenth-century theology, in which the recognizable structures of normative Christian thought have been almost entirely translated into a secularized philosophy. The old tension between faith and works is recast as one between "uncertain and undescribable *feelings*" and "evident *actions,*" the innate grace of "good principles" against the bare-Arminianism of "good conduct." *The Theological and Miscellaneous Works of Joseph Priestley,* ed. John Towhill Rutt, 25 vols. (London: Smallfield, 1817–32), 25:328.

The Church much preferred theologically infelicitous, yet discursively "reasonable" Christianity to strident accuracy. "[T]he proof of religion," argued John Davison in his *Discourses on Prophecy*, "gathers light and strength from the concentrated force of all its moral evidence," the "aggregate" of "concurrent proofs," any one—or even all—of which could be discredited without discrediting the belief built upon them.[94] Davison's lectures on the truth of revelation danced from point to point, conceding weaknesses here and there, secure that skeptics could land only glancing blows. It was a "vicious manner of reasoning to represent any insufficiency of the proof, in its several branches, as so much objection": "if the divided arguments be inconclusive one by one," the result was hardly "a series of exceptions to the truth of religion," but rather "a train of favourable presumptions, growing stronger at every step."[95] Assembled reasonably, an agglomeration of individual arguments, each dissatisfying, was an irrefutably compelling whole. If "rationality" accorded with transcendental principles, Anglican reasonability was an inductive mortar, cementing a brickwork of exceptions, errors, and deficiencies. The theology of the Church mirrored its purpose, fabricating a consensus out of diverse and competing elements, reconciling (or at least occluding) disagreements into a solemn and solid gestalt: "If the single stone or column be sufficient to uphold the edifice, we are not to think that the edifice really presses upon that single support; when it reposes, and with a far greater security, upon the broad united strength of the entire range and system of its fabric."[96]

"Reasonable Christianity" was sociable Christianity: an exhortation to "be reasonable" is a demand for collegiality, an appeal to the sanity of relaxed interpersonal relations, while an injunction to "be rational" is a rebuke made in the name of a hard, often impolitic truth.[97] Churchmen viewed the purity of rational Dissent as an atomizing force of disagreement and solipsistic self-fashioning. Milton might have dedicated himself to "the gracefull symmetry" of "moderat varieties and brotherly dissimilitudes,"[98] but Southey rejected this geometry with a bare antithesis: "There is a spirit of dissent, as well as a spirit of Christianity."[99]

---

94. Davison, *Discourses*, 31.
95. Davison, *Discourses*, 35.
96. Davison, *Discourses*, 43–44.
97. These connotational differences have been extant since the fifteenth century; "reasonable, adj. 6a." *Oxford English Dictionary*, 3rd ed., *OED Online* (Oxford University Press, 2010), February 9, 2011, http://www.oed.com/viewdictionaryentry/Entry/159072.
98. John Milton, *Areopagitica*, in *The Riverside Milton*, ed. Roy Flannagan (Boston and New York: Houghton Mifflin, 1998), 997–1024 (1019).
99. Robert Southey, "History of the Dissenters," *Quarterly Review* 10 (October 1813): 90–139 (130).

"Dissent," Southey elaborated, had neither identity nor history, only Oedipal self-repudiation. The "evil" that "grows out of the principle of dissent" was obvious:

> The minister of an establishment has no temptation from vanity, or the love of singularity, or to any more worldly motive, to labour, as Jeremy Taylor expresses it, in the mine of insignificant distinctions: but among Dissenters the right of private judgment is so injudiciously inculcated that the men who are trained among them learn not unfrequently to despise all judgment except their own. Many of their students seem almost to have considered it a proof of weakness if they should believe as they were taught; as if theology, like chemistry, were a science in which every generation ought to make some discovery beyond its predecessor. Thus the Presbyterian seminaries produced Arians; the Arian school brought forth Socinian pupils, and when the Socinian college was established, they who had sat at Gamaliel's feet came away unbelievers.... The consequence of this has been that the English Presbyterians are rapidly disappearing, and Arianism is so nearly extinguished that we believe at this time a minister cannot be found for the last congregation in which it lingers.[100]

Against this self-righteous balkanization, the Church of England nurtured assent to standards more urgent than logic. Anglican theologians prized iteration and agreement as much as the positions agreed upon—safe theology was redundant theology. Thomas Robinson's massive, four-volume *Scripture Characters* (1792) was a successful foray in Biblical typology, running to a fourth edition by 1800, yet it was symptomatically glad to have small reason for being. No "new information [is] aimed at, as being entirely foreign to the plan," Robinson shrugged. Rather, "those doctrines, which have been generally received in the Christian Church, are taken for granted" here, though such "doctrines" were also left generally undefined. "[A]cknowledged principles" were preferred to "the most ingenious ... arguments": that another clergyman had produced an identical book with identical conclusions a few years earlier—"the same thoughts will naturally offer themselves to the mind"—was hardly preemptive competition, but conclusive proof of Robinson's soundness.[101]

---

100. Southey, "History of the Dissenters," 130. This was a familiar insult; cf. Burke's claim that Richard Price's "zeal is of a curious character. It is not for the propagation of his own opinions, but of any opinions. It is not for the diffusion of truth, but for the spreading of contradiction. Let the noble teachers dissent, it is no matter from whom or from what" (*Reflections*, 95).
101. Thomas Robinson, *Scripture Characters: or, A Practical Improvement of the Prin-*

The most powerful performances of Anglican iterative consensus, however, came from the practical theology preached weekly from thousands of pulpits across the country. Many (perhaps most) of these sermons weren't written by their delivering clergymen. Successful sermons by reputable clerics were published, purchased, and read aloud (often verbatim), a depersonalized economy reinforcing the Church's consensus and extension, the primacy of universal institutionality over fungible individualities. Dissenting ministers took this as one of the more serious differences between nonconforming dedication and establishmentarian apathy; as late as 1820, their preaching manuals still rehearsed Philip Doddridge's eighteenth-century warning: "Never preach a borrowed sermon."[102] While the Church of England didn't celebrate the market for "pre-owned" sermons, neither did it suppress the heavy traffic.[103] The Rev. Dr. John Trusler, whom Blake memorably accused of having "fall'n out of the Spiritual World,"[104] found sufficient demand for a unique enterprise: a line of popular sermons, cleverly engraved into simulated calligraphy, insuring that any congregant surreptitiously glancing at the "notes" for a sermon would be impressed by "handwritten" originality.[105]

Even those clergymen moved to write their own sermons often weren't moved far. Many stopped after one sermon for each Sunday. John Sharp, a well-placed Northumberland cleric and grandson of an Archbishop of York, was typical, using the same fifty-two sermons for 45 years, preaching 2,800 times before his death in 1792, without adding once to his canon.[106] Printed sermons helped excuse staffing deficiencies, as widespread pluralism meant that the parish resident was often a poorly incentivized, and sometimes frankly incompetent, curate; a set of approved texts from which he might read meant that the Church need not trouble itself too much about his zeal or theological acumen. Though some local (usually Evangelical) exceptions attracted national attention by the Regency, Anglican preaching was still a heavily textualized phenomenon until the

---

cipal Histories in the Old and New Testament, 3rd ed., 4 vols. (London, 1793 [1792]), 1:viii–x.

102. *The Preacher's Manual*, 3rd ed. (London: Richard Baynes, 1820), 134.

103. See Françoise Deconinck-Brossard, "Eighteenth-Century Sermons and the Age," in *Crown and Mitre: Religion and Society in Northern Europe since the Reformation*, ed. W. M. Jacob and Nigel Yates (Woodbridge: Boydell, 1993), 105–21 (113–14).

104. Letter to Rev Dr Trusler, 23 August 1799, in *The Complete Poetry and Prose of William Blake, Newly Revised Edition*, ed. David V. Erdman (Berkeley and Los Angeles: University of California Press, 1982), 702.

105. Russell, *Clerical Profession*, 87–88.

106. Deconinck-Brossard, "Eighteenth-Century Sermons," 111.

middle of the nineteenth century. Clergymen took pains to make clear—through flat tones, stolid pacing, and quiet vocal projection—that sermons were scripted artifacts, in which pre-extant truths were read aloud, rather than discovered through improvisatory energy. As Oliver Goldsmith had observed in *The Bee,* the archetypical parson insured that his "audience feels not one word of all he says," so that "he earns among his acquaintance, the character of a man of sense; among his acquaintance only did I say, nay, even with his bishop."[107]

The nineteenth-century *Preacher's Manual* shared Goldsmith's disappointment, grumbling over those who "read all their sermons": it "requires a degree of courtesy to call this preaching; and seems to need no gifts but teeth and tongue—and hardly these as many persons perform it."[108] But a "degree of courtesy" was very much the desired temperature of these lectures. Blandness paved the Anglican *via media,* "the sober golden Mean" of a well-regulated publicity, which brought out in the open, and then quietly canceled, all the private derangements which were "of a dangerous sort and prejudicial to society," in order to produce "mutual Forbearance, general Goodwill, and the Benefit of All."[109] The "peculiar beauty" of established Christianity, argued Joseph Eyre, was the "Moderation and Temperateness which it unquestionably exhibits," the calm of a "mode of Worship" renouncing all "the extravagant distortions of frantic Fanaticism," avoiding those "incoherent effusions" so effective "upon the imagination of credulous adherents."[110] Churchmen were the first to admit that their religion was dull, because it was intentionally so: the ever-recurring round of tired sermons figured a social order as eternal as its rhetoric.[111]

The practical theology of the Church of England swapped spiritual mystery for social mystification. The generalized education at Oxbridge provided no formal training in the composition of sermons; clergy adapted the only form they knew, exporting wholesale the arid textualism of the

---

107. Oliver Goldsmith, *The Bee. Being Essays on the Most Interesting Subjects* (London: J. Wilkie, 1759), 201.
108. *Preacher's Manual,* 71–72.
109. Eyre, *Dispassionate Inquiry,* 2–8.
110. Eyre, *Dispassionate Inquiry,* 20–21.
111. Paul Goring finds that a well-known text for sermonizing in the eighteenth century, Michel Le Faucher's *Traitté de l'action de l'orateur* (1657; translated in English in the eighteenth century as *Essay upon the Action of an Orator*), formally instructed clergyman that well-regulated, "polite" oratory "is a key to social order; it is a pedagogic tool to be wielded paternalistically by those invested with political and religious authority so as to spread and enforce the tenets of Christian belief, sympathy and justice" (*Rhetoric of Sensibility,* 47).

collegiate disputation—often complete with classical allusions—into the pulpit.[112] In 1828, Southey regaled John Gibson Lockhart with a story of Coleridge's father, who "used to astonish and delight the Ottery people" with untranslated passages of Hebrew, Greek, and Latin.[113] But these gentlemen appreciated what the congregation couldn't: Joanna Southcott, after all, was born in John Coleridge's parish and sat in his church, and in 1802 she recounted drifting away from the confusing, sterile lessons of her village parson for the visceral appeal of "Mr. Westley's preachers."[114] Southcott had failed to absorb this most important of all Anglican doctrines, that the ancient languages of Scripture ordained the supremacy of the class of men that decoded them. The alien scholasticism of the sermon, and the larger clerical economy from which it was acquired if not composed, made the university immanent in even wretched curates, confronting congregations with the distant power sanctifying the clergyman, if not the Sacrament.

The rhetoric of Anglicanism made the person of the clergyman inseparable from his structural role, always gesturing toward the immovable Church behind the fallible man, resulting in a Christianity almost Catholic in its commitment to the bureaucracy of the soul. Salvation was better based in hearsay than individual experience, and ought to be mediated through the intercessory representations of the Church: it was "the glory of the Christian Faith . . . that they who are employed in the lower but useful offices of life, should receive religious instruction from others who have greater opportunities to know, and are better qualified to judge," as the "mixed and exalted virtue which is the only means of our Salvation . . . requires not information that is direct, conviction that is immediate, nor the first degrees of knowledge, but . . . can ever grow from a second-hand information and out of a weaker conviction, as its proper soil."[115] The Church cultivated this "mixed and exalted" Christianity as the "proper soil" for the naturalization of its hierarchy. "Salvation" was a technically demanding problem beyond amateurish self-help, requiring the professional services of the cleric. The Anglican ratio between self and God was thus a complicated amalgam of privacy and publicity: if moral thought, feeling, and behavior weren't governed by the secrets of Roman superstition, or guarded by a caste of priests with magical endowments,

---

112. Russell, *Clerical Profession*, 86–87.
113. *New Letters of Robert Southey*, 2:331.
114. Joanna Southcott, *The Strange Effects of Faith* (London: E. Spragg, 1802), 85.
115. Tatham, *A Sermon Suitable to the Times*, 4–5.

they hardly belonged to the priesthood of all believers. The discourses of Christian interiority—the prospects for redemption, the consequences of sin, the qualities of "conviction"—were heavily trained techniques, the privileges of an establishmentarian education rather than a Catholic thaumaturgy. The "glory" of Anglicanism was its "second-hand information," which guaranteed that intimate and individual spiritualities were meaningful only as they were managed, explicated, and transformed by institutionalized authority. Personal intuition was likely to misrecognize the true condition of the soul, which could be safely gauged only by the studious, reasonable, and well-trained clergyman, and the gentry hegemony he represented. Humility before the Lord meant deference to the affective conventions his vicars prescribed: "the apostles . . . exhort the followers of Jesus to ascertain the certainty of their convictions and the ground of their expectations, NOT by any INWARD FEELINGS and EXPERIENCES, but by the weight of *rational* evidence there is for them."[116]

"A Brand Plucked out of the Burning"

As Anglicanism dispersed affective intensities, Methodism threatened a literal cult of sentiment. The spontaneous overflow of powerful feelings, argued Bishop Horsley, was the most serious threat the Establishment faced after the Revolution. Equality of property, universal representation, and philosophical skepticism would never seduce solid Englishmen, who were much more likely to be taken in by a dramatically passionate Christianity:

> Instead of divesting Religion of its mysteries, and reducing it to a mere philosophy in speculation, and to a mere morality in practice; the plan is now to affect a great zeal for orthodoxy; to make great pretensions to an extraordinary measure of the Holy Spirit's influence; to alienate the minds of the people from the Established Clergy, by representing them as sordid worldlings; without any concern about the soul of men; indifferent to the religion which they ought to teach, and to which the laity are attached; and destitute of the Spirit of God.[117]

---

116. Thomas Ludlam, *Four Essays: On the Ordinary and Extraordinary Operations of the Holy Spirit; On the Application of Experience to Religion; and on Enthusiasm and Fanaticism* (London: T. Ludlam, 1797), 44.

117. Horsley, *Charge*, 19.

The Church read Methodist "affect" as pretense, its "great zeal for orthodoxy" as oxymoron, since the "Religion of Jesus, owed nothing to the . . . passions, of the human Heart: but the Religion of J. W. [John Wesley] owes to these almost every thing."[118] Methodistical "Heart Religion" unraveled the soporific arrangement between cleric and congregation at the root of the constitution, and prelates worried that the "wholsom rules" of Church government were "not only broken-through, but notoriously *despised*," as the Wesleyans abandoned parish churches for new "Ministers," with whom "there is no Manner of Relation."[119] The Methodist care of the soul traded professional technique for the "sense" common to all, who "might come to Christ now, without any other qualification than a sense of their own sinfulness and helplessness."[120] The *Examiner* cast this religious sensibility as bodily sensuousness and literary sensationalism, beyond any Cockneyism: the "difference" between "a rational religion" and one "calculated for the uninformed mass of mankind" was that between "those who think without feeling, and those who feel without thinking."[121]

Wesleyans wore the insult with pride. Salvation came from right feeling, without benefit of clergy, theology, or even words: "a man may be saved who cannot express himself properly . . . a man can be saved who has not clear conceptions. . . . Therefore, clear conceptions . . . are not necessary to salvation. Yea, it is not necessary to salvation to use the phrase at all."[122] Here was a cultural program doubling as soteriology. Conventional literacy (and the hierarchy it scripted) was irrelevant to both Methodist salvation and Methodist reading and writing. Wesley blocked the exchange between textual production and consumption: good readers didn't make good writers, and familiarity with the history of ideas disabled, rather than credentialed. As he declared in the "Preface" to *Sermons on Several Occasions* (hereafter *SOSA*), one of the more widely reprinted texts of the eighteenth century:

> Nay, my design is in some sense to forget all that ever I have read in my life. I mean to speak, in general, as if I had never read one author, ancient or modern (always excepting the inspired). I am persuaded that,

---

118. Trimmer, *Review*, 17.

119. [Edmund Gibson], *Observations upon the Conduct and Behavior of a Certain Sect, Usually distinguished by the Name of Methodists*, 2nd ed. (London: E. Owen, 1744), 6.

120. WV 2:101.

121. "Pulpit Oratory," *Examiner* 603 (July 18, 1819): 461.

122. Wesley drafted these principles while "alone in the coach" in 1767; Alexander Knox drew Southey's attention to them in his "Remarks," 342.

on the one hand, this may be a means of enabling me more clearly to express the sentiments of my heart, while I simply follow the chain of my own thoughts, without entangling myself with those of other men; on the other, I shall come with fewer weights upon my mind, with less prejudice and prepossession, either to search for myself or to deliver to others the naked truths of the gospel.[123]

Against the socialized "prejudice and prepossession" that Burke, Southey, and other churchmen identified as the iterative consensus of Anglican reasonability, the Wesleyans celebrated the "naked," inspired insularity of nothing but the heart's affections and the truth of the imagination.[124] But spiritual heat, Southey worried, was socially incendiary: "Fanaticism always comes to this in its progress: first it depreciates learning, then it would destroy it. There have been Christians as they believed themselves, who would have burnt the Alexandrian library upon the same logic as the Caliph Omar."[125]

Wesley might have styled himself "*homo unius libri*," but Methodism's ultimate danger to the archive wasn't arson, but new curation.[126] By himself, Wesley might have restocked the Great Library; the *Quarterly* had begrudging awe for him as "a voluminous author, almost 'de omni scibili.'"[127] In addition to his own sermons, tracts, public *Journals* and private letters, Wesley orchestrated one of the most comprehensive publishing empires of the long eighteenth century, which attempted to bring all knowledge, sacred and secular, under the Methodist imprimatur. The fifty-volume *Christian Library* anthologized the whole of "Practical Divinity" in "the English Tongue,"[128] quietly editing the recalcitrant; Bunyan, for

---

123. Wesley, "Preface" to *Sermons on Several Occasions*, Sermons I: 104-5.
124. Though there were ironies even within Wesley's humility tropes. He had been Fellow of Lincoln College and Lecturer in Greek, and this abjuration of classical learning evidenced its continued possession, allusively flitting from Marcus Antoninus to Pindar. As the *Quarterly* recalled in 1821, Wesley could nimbly shift registers to fit audience and occasion, and "in one of his latest sermons in the neighbourhood of Oxford, observing that many members of the University were among his audience, he introduced into his discourse a dissertation on the second Aorist, with a dexterity and acuteness which evinced that he had neither forgotten nor neglected the studies of sixty years before" ("Southey's *Life of Wesley*," 12).
125. Southey, *Life of Wesley*, 1:93.
126. Wesley, "Preface" to *SOSA, Sermons* I:105.
127. "Southey's *Life of Wesley*," *Quarterly Review*, 47.
128. John Wesley, *A Christian Library: Consisting of Extracts and Abridgments of the Choicest Pieces of Practical Divinity, which have been publish'd in the English Tongue*, 50 vols. (Bristol: E. Farley, 1749-55).

example, appeared without his Calvinism.[129] Along with theology, Wesley marketed histories of England, collections of songs, manuals of folk medicine, and a compendium of "natural philosophy," abridged so "as to not require any large Expence, either of Time or Money."[130] Wesley's savvy eye for "Expence" profited Methodism even more than his personal charisma, pitching products in most price tranches, while advertising, serializing, and reviewing the whole in his *Arminian Magazine*. This vertical integration—decades before similar experiments by Murray, Blackwood, and Longman—earned more than £1,000 p.a., from texts often priced at several pence.[131] And all during what William St. Clair calls the "High Monopoly period" of English publishing, in which the reading available to the poor was otherwise extraordinarily limited in scope and antique in age.[132] Methodism was an oasis in this cultural desert, marking landmarks for inexperienced readers with its collections and periodicals, suggesting more substantial sites for exploration in Wesley's own writing. Most of what was suitable for a Christian could be purchased under the Methodist brand, and for poor men and women uninterested in hoary chapbooks, there were few alternatives. The most enterprising bookseller of the late eighteenth century thought their brand loyalty absolute: "There are thousands in this society who will never read any thing besides the Bible, and books published by Mr. Wesley."[133]

In loving Methodist books, Methodists loved themselves. Wesley trained illiterate men and women to read their subjectivities—those "INWARD FEELINGS AND EXPERIENCES" anathematized by

---

129. Isabel Rivers remarks, "Wesley's editorial practice created certain problems. His decision to delete what he regarded as error and to make all his chosen authors consistent with one another meant that he drastically misrepresented some of them" (*Reason, Grace and Sentiment*, 1:218). Wesley "fused (or confused)" author and editor functions, silently adapting (and not infrequently, plagiarizing wholesale) whatever was at hand (Rack, *Reasonable Enthusiast*, 346).

130. John Wesley, *A Survey of the Wisdom of God in the Creation: Or a Compendium of Natural Philosophy*, 2nd ed., 3 vols. (Bristol: William Pine, 1770), 1:iii.

131. For a survey of the economics of Methodist publishing, see Rack, *Reasonable Enthusiast*, 350. Henry Abelove tabulates that Wesley's income was "as big as, or bigger than, the revenues of *eighteen* of the bishoprics of the Church of England" (*The Evangelist of Desire: John Wesley and the Methodists* [Stanford, CA: Stanford University Press, 1990], 9 n16).

132. St. Clair argues that the "lower boundaries of the reading nation . . . were still reading, or were listening to others read aloud, a body of printed texts which were produced in the pre-modern age. For nearly 200 years a large constituency of the English reading nation was locked into the print of the early years of the reign of King James" (*Reading Nation*, 83).

133. Lackington, *Memoirs*, 69.

the Church—as aesthetic objects superior to any appreciated by more "refined" sensibilities.[134] As he argued in his 1780 essay "Thoughts upon Taste," culture meant cultivation of the moral self, and distinction meant discrimination against everything but the egotistical sublime dwelling within everyone:

> May we not likewise observe, that there is a beauty in virtue, in gratitude, and disinterested benevolence? And have not many, at least, a taste for this? Do they not discern and relish it, wherever they find it? Yea, does it not give them one of the most delicate pleasures whereof the human mind is capable? Is not this taste of infinitely more value, than a taste for any or all the pleasures of the imagination? And is not this pleasure infinitely more delicate, than any that ever resulted, yea, or can result, from the utmost refinements of music, poetry, or painting?[135]

In Wesley's regime of taste, poor men, not the establishmentarian "bells" of "Frost at Midnight," were themselves their "only music." Poverty forbade the beaux arts, but the Methodist self was an inalienable cultural property: the fluxes and refluxes of an unsophisticated field-hand or harried housewife in the throes of salvation ought to be savored with "delicate pleasure," surpassing "the utmost refinements" of leisure.[136]

Wesley's culture of the self was more than figural. Taught to read themselves, Methodists learned to write themselves: "Both Charles and John Wesley wanted everybody to write, and Methodists wrote continually, sometimes compulsively, and in many different genres: diaries, journals, letters, poetry, treatises, sermons, hymns."[137] These were among

---

134. D. Bruce Hindmarsh proposes that Methodism "seemed to name and call into being a new sense of interiority for these converts" (*Evangelical Conversion Narrative*, 139).

135. "Thoughts upon Taste," in *The Works of the Rev. John Wesley*, 14 vols. (London: Wesleyan Conference Office, 1872), 13:465–70 (467).

136. Henry Abelove speculates, "Perhaps the Methodists disapproved of adult play, and especially theater, because they had an ongoing theater of their own, which they liked better than the one that dramatists provided. In their theater they were the stars as well as the audience. Their lines were the lines that were remembered and commented upon afterward" (*Evangelist of Desire*, 105). David Bebbington has documented that while Methodists and Evangelicals "deplored" theater in the nineteenth century, there is strong evidence that they read quite a lot of drama "in the privacy of their own homes" (*Evangelicalism in Modern Britain: A History from the 1730s to the 1980s* [London: Unwin Hyman, 1989], 67).

137. Phyllis Mack, *Heart Religion in the British Enlightenment: Gender and Emotion in Early Methodism* (Cambridge and New York: Cambridge University Press, 2008), 22. See also Vicki Tolar Burton, *Spiritual Literacy in John Wesley's Methodism: Reading, Writing, and Speaking to Believe* (Waco, TX: Baylor University Press, 2008).

Methodism's most popular, and the serialized autobiographies comprising the *Arminian* and *Methodist* magazines modeled the dual promises of salvation and publication awaiting every member of the Society, while smuggling profane pleasures under holy cover. Methodist "Lives" were picaresque, and the Augustinian division between youthful sin and mature Christianity captured the appeal of both. Novels were frowned upon, but one hardly needed *Tom Jones* with stories of sexual, martial, and global adventurism such as Sampson Staniforth's. A revered lay preacher, Staniforth opened his 1783 "Life" debauching a Highland girl; her family, vowing to kill him, pursued him across moors and rivers with drawn swords; an escape to the Continent (and tour as soldier) devolved into a binge, climaxing in Ghent, where he found himself "now engaged with a Negro-man's wife, who was passionately fond of me."[138] The hagiography of the lay preachers could also be Gothic for those who couldn't afford Radcliffe, and more hair-raising. Thomas Hanby curdled the blood in 1780:

> It was in the winter season, and a dark night. All was quiet till I gave out a hymn. Then they approached the house, broke first the window-shutters, and then dashed the windows in. The head of this mob was a forgeman, half an idiot, who had bound himself under an oath he would that night have my liver. He brought the pipe with a large bellows, with which he made a frightful noise, and which was to be the instrument of my death.[139]

If the moral was uncertain, the narrative thrill was palpable. Widespread demand provoked a number of competing (but less successful) periodicals into marketing more "lives," of Methodists as well as others, in the late eighteenth and early nineteenth centuries.[140] George Whitefield and John Wesley were two of the great English sermonizers, and Charles Wesley a mighty lyricist—but the most valued texts of Methodism were often those of the Methodists themselves.

This writing, reading, and discussion solicited the promotion of "Creatures" Sarah Trimmer thought better left to darkness:

> Other Religious Societies have no bait of this kind to hold out to their Members; they can give them no hopes of any kind of preferment. They must rest contented with the humble appointment of Hearers. . . . Every

---

138. *WV* 1:67.
139. *WV* 2:63.
140. Hindmarsh, *Evangelical Conversion Narrative*, 229–33.

member is immediately raised to Consequence, and flattered with Hopes, as soon as he enlists with these people. This Society, above all others, pays the greatest attention to every member, whatever may be their rank, or character in Life.[141]

Subjects consigned to personal incoherence and public disorganization would turn the world upside down in exchanging submissive "Hearing" for self-dramatizing: "Servants" were already "more confident and self-willed, less chearful and tractable."[142] Methodists were the attendant class, not fit for "the greatest attention," and by translating "tractability" into tracts, they upset the economies of feeling, representation, and property. But Trimmer's anxiety was competition as much as revolution. In the "shocking Prostitution" turning housemaids into saints, "these ignorant and unfeeling Creatures" were assuming the privileges of sentiment, the safest grounds on which conservative, middle-class women, themselves circumscribed, might charitably express their authority: "ignorant Lads and Lasses, soon take upon themselves to visit the sick, to administer comfort to the disconsolate. . . . Duties which, require good sense, fine feelings, a discernment of character, and the most delicate attention, to be discharged as they ought."[143]

Southey, too, was concerned that social action and self-knowledge remain bound to "good sense" and "fine feelings." The redistribution of affect was as likely to end in disaster as the redistribution of wealth. Autobiography was class privilege, and Methodists could no more manage themselves than manage an estate:

> Of all morbid habits, that of watching our own sensations is one of the most unfortunate . . . if the act of watching our bodily sensations does itself derange the body, and disturb those vital functions which are only carried on healthily and regularly as long as they are unperceived, it is not less certain that the moral economy of our nature is exposed to a like danger by that system of self-watchfulness which the Methodists require.[144]

The "watchfulness" was morbidly private, but the "derangement" was national. The disruption to the "moral economy" from newly visible subjectivities, valuable only "as long as they are unperceived," distressed the

---

141. Trimmer, *Review*, 8–10.
142. Trimmer, *Review*, 43.
143. Trimmer, *Review*, 9.
144. Southey, "On the Evangelical Sects," 498.

"vital functions" of the body politic. Genetic as well as social codes were transformed, "in proportion as they overspread the country":

> The very character of the English face is altered; for Methodism transforms the countenance as certainly, and almost as speedily as sottishness or opium. Go to their meeting-houses, or turn over the portraits in their magazines, and it will be seen that they have already obtained as distinct a physiognomy as the Jews or the Gipsies—coarse, hard, and dismal visages, as if some spirit of darkness had got into them, and was looking out of them.[145]

This was reading Wesley's favorite trope against its owner. Saved from a house fire by what he thought was Providence, Wesley took as his motto, engraved on portraits, coins, and, finally, a grave: "Is this not a brand plucked out of the burning?"[146] Southey here recast the Methodist "brand" in both molds: the heat of conviction, and the sign for an array of products, which together seared cultural forms onto the flesh. Methodist "physiognomy," as well as the "portraits" and "magazines" hawking it, equally registered the transformations in the "character of the English face." But the exile of Methodism to the pathology of racial difference ("Jews and Gipsies") condemned the illusion of stable national identity, as well. Methodism might be a "dismal visage," but then Englishness was merely one mask among many, and one readily slipped off. The ideological and material forms of polite culture and the confessional state were alarmingly liable to spectral, physical, and economic repossession, as "spirits of darkness got into them," and gazed out from the inside.

This Methodist "brand" was proxy for the much wider transformations—and terrors—of modernity. For Southey, "writing the Life of Wesley" meant writing all "religious history for the last hundred years."[147] In "Methodism," the emergencies of Romanticism collided: the reorganization (and atomization) of print culture and the public sphere by the

---

145. Southey, "On the Evangelical Sects," 503.
146. Suffering from an illness from which he later recovered, he preemptively composed his epitaph: "HERE LIETH THE BODY OF JOHN WESLEY, A BRAND PLUCKED OUT OF THE BURNING: WHO DIED OF A CONSUMPTION IN THE FIFTY-FIRST YEAR OF HIS AGE, NOT LEAVING, AFTER HIS DEBTS ARE PAID, TEN POUNDS BEHIND HIM; PRAYING GOD BE MERCIFUL TO ME AN UNPROFITABLE SERVANT!" (Southey, *Life of Wesley*, 2:253).
147. *The Life and Correspondence of Robert Southey*, ed. Charles Cuthbert Southey, 6 vols. (London: Longman, 1849–50), 4:285.

"market economy of the text,"[148] the revision of the social function of "religion" and the established church, and most urgently, the remaking of religious identity by market desires. The Methodists "Usurp a new, unprecedented *Post,* / And *by Retail* dispense the *Holy Ghost,*" transubstantiating communion into commodity, irrevocably shifting spiritual into economic competition.[149] "Denomination" was no longer a matter of birth, the confessional compulsion of Anglicanism; or a matter of belief, the doctrinal gatherings of Old Dissent; but a matter of being bought, expressed by products and preferences, driven by the unregulated whims of unregulated people. "Nothing can be better calculated for amusing and entertaining," Trimmer complained, than that "catalogue of Anecdotes, Experiences, Visions, Miraculous Interpositions, &c." sold by the Wesleyans: "where is the difference between going to the Theatre and the Tabernacle. . . . It is amusement at the Bottom."[150] But by sinking religion into "amusement," the Methodists exploited a space over which the Church had no purchase.[151] Political dominance didn't translate into market dominance; rather than confronting the Church directly in doctrine or at law, as Dissenters did, the Methodists had seized—and increasingly, monopolized—the domain of cultural authority before other denominations recognized its existence. The Methodists sold Christ well enough to bankrupt the Establishment. "It is folly to suppose the poor do not love reading," Southey noted. But while "the poor" spent their pennies enthusiastically on Methodist songs and sermons, the Society for the Promotion of Christian Knowledge fruitlessly gave its texts away, while the Cheap Repository Tracts rotted "in the high road."[152]

---

148. Klancher, *Making of English Reading Audiences,* 19.

149. Anon., *The Love-Feast: A Poem* (London: J. Bew, 1778), 9.

150. Trimmer, *Review,* 7–8.

151. "Clergy could no longer rely on the combined efforts of the spiritual and secular courts to impose Anglicanism in the parishes, and it was only through pastoral directives, through the efforts of individual clergy, through their powers of persuasion rather than legal coercion, that the Church was likely to make any impression against its rivals." Jeremy Gregory, "The Eighteenth-Century Reformation: The Pastoral Task of Anglican Clergy after 1689," in Walsh, Haydon, and Taylor, *The Church of England c.1689–c.1833,* 67–85 (70).

152. "The Society for the Promotion of Christian Knowledge circulates many excellent books, but they are elementary, or doctrinal, or controversial; highly useful when read; but for the most part such as can only be read as a duty. The Cheap Repository Tracts are often good; but we have picked up papers from this manufactory in the high road, (scattered there by some godly travelers as seed by the way side,) and have found among them baser trash than ever contributed to line the old wall at Privy Garden. It is folly to suppose that the poor do not love reading, if works which are of a nature to interest them be published in such a form as to come within their reach" (Southey, "On the Evangelical Sects," 512).

"The Essence" of Methodism, agreed Sarah Trimmer and Leigh Hunt, was its publicity, which crowded out polite conversation with plebeian voices. "Their Religion" was neither liturgy nor catechism, but discourse, the "religious Gossiping" of "Preaching, their Usual talk, and their Writings."[153] Hunt found "the modern Methodists . . . by no means a 'skulking nation who shun the light, mute in public, and prating in corners'": they "come forward in all places, they thunder out their anathemas in the midst of the sunshine and the bountiful fields."[154] Even after trading "sunshine" and "fields" for chapels and magazines, Methodism's raucous outdoor ceremonies endured as its iconic spectacle. Field preaching was its first and most explicit illegality, a calculated violation of the Conventicle and Five-Mile Acts, which regulated the registration of houses of worship and outlawed open-air religious gatherings. The Bishop of London grumbled, "if this be not an open Defiance of Government, it is hard to say what is."[155] It was also Methodism's first miracle. Though the events shrank as they became more common, initial crowds were the stuff of legend: in the summer of 1742, at the tiny parish of Cambuslang outside of Glasgow, Whitefield attracted a crowd of 30,000, a number "significantly larger than the population of Glasgow itself in the 1740s,"[156] while Wesley claimed to have performed his own Sermon on the Mount, packing 20,000 bodies into a 40 by 100 yard space.[157]

Curiosity was a galvanic force. Churchmen clucked at the vulgar who "ran in droves to hear" the "*Field-preaching,* the *Uncommonness* of which is the very circumstance that *recommends* it,"[158] while the rough language of the lay preachers was keyed to mobbing enthusiasms: "these *charming* vociferations gain the attention, and steal into the hearts of those people of delicacy and discernment, who are wont, on other occasions, to demonstrate the fervor of their hearts in melodious *huzzas,* and W[ilke]s and Liberty for ever!"[159] For those who knew only the parish church, the character of the Methodist service—the frightening accounts of hellfire, the groaning demonstrations of the audience, and the sublimity of the hymns—was unreadable. Wesley himself appeared a "consternation" to settled lives, rooted in the clergyman who sedately preached familiar doctrine, who

---

153. Trimmer, *Review,* 28; 40.
154. Hunt, "On the Ignorance and Vulgarity of the Methodists," 301.
155. [Gibson], *Observations upon the Conduct and Behavior of a Certain Sect,* 4.
156. Hindmarsh, *Evangelical Conversion Narrative,* 193.
157. Rack, *Reasonable Enthusiast,* 346.
158. Lavington, *Enthusiasm of Methodists and Papists, Compar'd,* 12.
159. Anonymous, *Naked Thoughts on Some Peculiarities of the Field-Preaching Clergy. By a Member of the Church of England* (London: J. Priddon, 1776), 6.

remained firmly ensconced in one parish (pluralists rarely shifted from the better living on Sundays), and who embodied the inevitability of the Church of England in the poor man's life. Here is Christopher Hopper's shocked report from 1781:

> [W]e heard a strange report of one Wesley, a Church clergyman, that had been at Newcastle-upon-Tyne, and had preached in Sandgate to many thousands, who heard him with astonishment. This new thing made a huge noise. The populace entertained various conjectures about him; but few, if any, could tell the motive on which he came, or the end he had in view. He made a short blaze, soon disappeared, and left us in a great consternation.[160]

The immediate consequence wasn't conversion, but affective chaos, as the service provoked responses from a congregation unused to performances of feeling. Later seeing Charles Wesley in the fields, Hopper was baffled along with everyone else: "I ran with the multitude to hear this strange preacher. When I saw a man in a clergyman's habit, preaching at a public cross to a large auditory, some gaping, some laughing, and some weeping, I wondered what this could mean."[161]

The wildfire spread, according to the *Quarterly*, from art, not artifice, cabals, or trickery. Methodism introduced rhetoric to those who "had never heard anything like eloquence; and an eloquence like Wesley's, recommended by a dignified manner, an harmonious voice, and a thorough persuasion of the truth and importance of all he asserted, employed on the most awful truths . . . might well thrill the heart and give any direction to their feelings which he thought proper."[162] Whitefield was so irritated by this "thrill" that he gave his own "Directions how to hear SERMONS," ruining the fun he knew he represented for many hearers: "you" ought to "come to hear [sermons], not out of Curiosity, but from a sincere Desire to know and do your Duty. . . . Ears entertained, and not our Hearts reformed, must certainly be highly displeasing to the Most High God."[163]

---

160. WV 1:114.
161. WV 1:114.
162. "Southey's *Life of Wesley*," *Quarterly Review*, 37–38.
163. George Whitefield, *Directions how to hear SERMONS: A Sermon Preached at Christ's Church* in *Spittlefields* (London, 1739), 9. John Rule argues that Methodism challenged the politics of leisure in rural communities. Most approved "games," such as wrestling, bear-baiting, and even drinking bouts were often sites for gentry control, with winners treated by the squire, and competing teams usually assembled from the dependents of different squires. In its pious opposition to such practices, Methodism was eroding not so

But even in these vast crowds, supervised by ordained clerics such as Wesley and Whitefield, Methodist culture always returned to the Methodists. Many congregants had little interest in passive audition. Crowds typically used the preaching as the excuse for their own play. Wesley had dismissed "clear conceptions" and "proper expressions" for spiritual feeling, and an account of his time in Wales from 1781 suggests how overdetermined the emotional responsiveness of his flock had become: though the "people understood no English," nevertheless "their looks, sighs, and gestures showed God was speaking to their hearts."[164] For the faithful, this was proof of Wesley's orphic ability to touch his auditors—for everyone else, proof that Methodists were so restively addicted to self-staging they barely classified as "audience."

"The quiet regularity of domestic devotion must be exchanged for public performances," Southey grimaced in the *Life of Wesley*: "the members are to be *professors of religion*; they must have a part to act, which will at once gratify the sense of self-importance, and afford employment for the uneasy and restless spirit with which they are possessed."[165] Southey's punning critique recognized one more failure of the "moral economy." Sham spiritualisms nauseated as they "afforded employment" to a sweated underclass, whose ignorance led them to misrecognize vulgar playacting as "professional" distinction, and who unwittingly participated in their own

---

much "entertainment" as its hierarchy, with a "bottom-up" organization dissimilar from the moralizing impositions of Evangelicals or Factory Owners, who attacked these "wasteful" exuberances while attempting to preserve the ratios of deference such exuberances reinforced (Rule, "Methodism, Popular Beliefs and Village Culture in Cornwall, 1800–50," in *Popular Culture and Custom in Nineteenth-Century England*, ed. Robert D. Storch [New York: St. Martin's, 1982], 48–70). Both establishment clerics and established entertainers viewed the Methodists as serious threats to their livelihood, and acting troupes, publicans, and ballad singers were well represented in violent mobs. Charles Wesley was almost murdered by a group of "players" in 1740; Whitefield's church was assaulted by mobs in 1755–56 funded by the theaters in its vicinity, and ballad singers were at the front of some particularly brutal gangs (John Walsh, "Methodism and the Mob in the Eighteenth Century," in Cuming and Baker, *Studies in Church History*, vol. 8, *Popular Belief and Practice*, 213–27 [220]). Lackington shrugged that enthusiastic rapture was just a way to fill time: "as I happened to have no other pursuit or hobby horse, there was a kind of vacuity in my mind" that the agonies and ecstasies of conversion filled. Field preaching offered the same opportunities as dances and fairs. Going to a field "at Farmer Gamlin's at Charlton . . . I fell desperately in love with the farmer's handsome dairy-maid," causing him to abound "in spiritual gifts, which induced this honest rustic maid to be very kind to me, and to walk several fields with me . . . while I poured heavenly comfort into her soul, and talked so long of *divine* Love, until I found that my affection for her was not altogether of that *spiritual* nature" (*Memoirs*, 86, 106–7).

164. WV 1:133.
165. Southey, *Life of Wesley*, 2:159.

dispossession: after all, the Methodists didn't own but were rather "possessed" by their dramas.

Feverish emotionalism courted "the Wesleyan Manifestation," a practice abandoning "the *still, small voice*" of reasonably moderated Anglicanism for "storms and tempests . . . tumults and confusion."[166] Methodist enthusiasm, the *Quarterly* reminded its Tory readership, was terrifyingly literal, harboring the capacity for real violence within its revolutions in feeling and representation. Wesley

> had the unhappy art of inoculating his audience with convulsions and frenzy, surpassing the most extraordinary symptoms to which animal magnetism has given rise, and calculated more than any other possible occurrence, short of actual criminality, to alarm and disgust the friends of rational religion, and to bring disgrace on the name of the Christian religion itself. Violent outcries, howling, gnashing of teeth, frightful convulsions, frenzy, blasphemy, epileptic and apoplectic symptoms were excited in turn on different individuals in the Methodist congregations.[167]

In this apoplexy, Southey read the grotesque parody of reputable imaginative energy. Methodism was what happened when ditch-diggers played at being poets, with bodies bred for manual, rather than emotional, labor:

> A powerful doctrine preached with passionate sincerity, with fervid zeal, and with vehement eloquence, produced a powerful effect upon weak minds, ardent feelings, and disordered fancies. There are passions which are as infectious as the plague, and fear itself is not more so than fanaticism. When once these bodily affections were declared to be the work of grace, the process of regeneration, the throes of the new birth, a free license was proclaimed for every kind of extravagance. And when the preacher, instead of exhorting his auditors to commune with their own hearts, and in their chambers, and be still, encouraged them to throw off all restraint, and abandon themselves before the congregation to these mixed sensations of mind and body, the consequences were what might be anticipated. Sometimes he scarcely began to speak, before some of his believers, overwrought with expectation, fell into the crisis, for so it may be called in Methodism, as properly as in Animal Magnetism. Sometimes his voice could scarcely be heard amid the groans and cries of these suf-

---

166. Warburton, *Doctrine of Grace*, 97.
167. "Southey's *Life of Wesley*," *Quarterly Review*, 35.

fering and raving enthusiasts. It was not long before men, women, and children, began to act the demoniac as well as the convert.[168]

Southey's theater of "groans and cries," "disordered fancies," and "bodily affections" performed the catastrophic inversion of the hierarchy of Coleridge's bells, staging a nightmare both of plebeian autonomy within, and, worse, complete dominion over the cultural sphere. For all the horror at the "demoniac" masquerading as "convert," the real object of attention here was the lost attention for "the preacher," as Wesley shrank into irrelevance after his grant of "free license" for expression. The newfound elocution of the Methodists, histrionic and deformed, spoke over the gentleman's "voice scarcely heard," compelling his acquiescence before "he scarcely began to speak."

This "Methodism" localized the generalized anxieties over the fate of a public sphere of reasonable affect, complementary discourse, and due subordination threatened by a populace that will have its will. Enthusiastic "passions" were "as infectious as the plague," as plebeian bodies agitated into communal frenzies, prologue to national paroxysms. But ultimately, the contagion was fatal not to the Methodists infected, but to the consumptive authority of the figure of respectability adjacent to them. In Southey's account, treatment, whether private or public, may no longer be possible—though, as we're about to see, this wouldn't prevent Wordsworth from maintaining his own quarantine, for more than half a century.

---

168. Southey, *Life of Wesley*, 220–21.

Chapter 3

Wordsworth and the Ragged Legion
Poets, Priests, and Preachers

My subject isn't *The Prelude,* so much as its absence: the half-century in which Wordsworth's spiritual autobiography was kept private, if not exactly secret. For Wordsworth's biographers, his self-silencing remains "one of the most puzzling phenomena . . . of literary history," though there's been no shortage of explanations.[1] Perhaps *The Prelude* was a welcome, lifelong distraction from the enduring failure of *The Recluse;* belated publication in 1850 was certainly meant as a commercial bequest in verse to the surviving family, an end run around unsympathetic copyright laws. But if the reasons behind the delay may have been quietly domestic, they quickly took on heroic significance. Both *The Prelude* and its suppression were made "phenomena of literary history" from the very beginning, when Wordsworth rationalized his decision not to publish the poem, conceding to Sir George Beaumont in 1805 that it was "a thing unprecedented in literary history that a man should talk

---

1. Stephen Gill, *William Wordsworth: A Life* (Oxford: Oxford University Press, 1989), 230.

so much about himself."[2] There may well be self-deprecating irony in this ritualistically conventional invocation of things unattempted yet in Prose or Rhime. The similar claim opening Rousseau's *Confessions* is, Eugene Stelzig argues, at once "the most inaccurate," and the most typical, "statement about the genre on record."[3] Droll wit, however, tended to become full-throated apologia. The "high hopes in the poetic future that lay before him, and the spiritual history on which those hopes were founded," writes the editor who brought the 1805 *Prelude* out into the open in 1926, "could not, without arrogance, be proclaimed to the world before he had given some solid earnest of their fulfillment."[4]

Even "without arrogance," this is majesty cloaked as modesty. Paratextual restraint hardly impeded Wordsworth's self-characterization as "a prophet sent by Providence to effect the work of his countrymen's redemption."[5] *The Prelude* often recasts such privilege as sacerdotal devotion: when Wordsworth thought of himself as a poet, he thought of himself as a priest. He and Coleridge were to be the "most assiduous ministers" in "Nature's temple" (1850 *Prelude* 2:463–64); if he "made no vows," nonetheless "vows / Were then made for me . . . that I should be—else sinning greatly— / A dedicated spirit" (1805 *Prelude* 4:341–45). The temple may be Nature's, but its attendant belongs to the supernatural, daring "to tread holy ground, / Speaking no dream but things oracular" (1805 *Prelude* 12:251–52). While the poem records lessons learned and mis-learned under the sometimes competing tutelages of Man and Nature, Wordsworth's education often matters insofar as it testifies to that which is before and beyond education, the poet's aboriginal election as "a chosen son / . . . with holy powers / And faculties" (1805 *Prelude* 3:82–84). David G. Riede argues that this dignity has a mystifying agenda, displacing the social into the sacred, and reifying human hierarchy as immune to correction. In the population of "uncouth vagrants," Riede observes, "Wordsworth's differentiation of himself from other wanderers is asserted . . . with the force of dogma—he was, he repeatedly assures us, a 'chosen son,' a 'favored being,' one 'singled out' for a high purpose."[6]

---

2. *The Letters of William and Dorothy Wordsworth: The Early Years, 1787–1805*, ed. Ernest de Selincourt, rev. Chester L. Shaver (Oxford: Clarendon, 1967), 586.

3. Eugene Stelzig, "Romantic Autobiography in England: Exploring its Range and Variety," in *Romantic Autobiography in England*, ed. Eugene Stelzig (Aldershot and Burlington, VT: Ashgate, 2009), 1.

4. William Wordsworth, *The Prelude (Text of 1805)*, ed. Ernest de Selincourt, rev. Helen Darbishire (London: Oxford University Press, 1969), xvi.

5. Ryan, *Romantic Reformation*, 100.

6. Riede, *Oracles and Hierophants*, 116–17.

Yet this story of election comes with "high, often fearful obligations": the gentleman's burden of living up to gifts so generous that the only adequate measure is grace, dispensed along with the rebuking query, Was it for this?[7]

In this chapter, I reorient the "high argument" of ordination, "assiduous ministers," "holy powers," and "things oracular" away from the pleasures and pathologies of privilege, and toward its unexpected counterweight in the embarrassments and enthusiasms of Methodism. The providential and clerical assertions that fill *The Prelude*, I'll argue, have a social history at odds with the ways the scholarship of Romanticism has come to understand them. At the turn of the nineteenth century, these sorts of declarations were not likely to be "high" (or any) argument in respectable circles. They verged on a countercode to politeness, slogans in a very palpable class struggle, signaling a motivated popular insurgency. If this smacks of the "dogma" David Riede identifies, it was dogma explicitly forbidden not only by the Church of England but also by "reasonable" Dissenters.

As we'll see, the language of self-consecration was the universally recognized cant of those "uncouth vagrants" and itinerant preachers from whom Wordsworth supposedly "differentiated" himself. Absent many of the texts—most notably *The Prelude*—now conflated with it, this "Romantic Imaginary" belonged instead to those irregularly anointed "dedicated spirits" whom the wealthy evangelical Rowland Hill dismissed as laughably "Inspired Ministers": "WESLEY'S ragged legion of preaching barbers, cobblers, tinkers, scavengers, draymen, and chimney-sweepers."[8] Sounding like a convocation of the casts of *Lyrical Ballads* and Blake's *Songs,* here were men speaking to men, after a fashion—a fashion often "without," as an anonymous satire warbled in 1778, "Wit, Shirts, or Shoes."[9]

My story parts ways with the tradition that reads the sacralizing hallmarks of Romantic verse as celebrations of masculine, bourgeois or gentry subjectivity. This critique, I think, puts the cart before the horse, mistaking Wordsworth's private usages for the Spirit of the Age from which they

---

7. Charles J. Rzepka, "Wordsworth Between God and Mammon: The Early 'Spots of Time' and the Sublime as Sacramental Commodity," in *The Fountain Light: Studies in Romanticism and Religion, in Honor of John L. Mahoney,* ed. J. Robert Barth (New York: Fordham University Press, 2002), 73–89 (74).

8. Rowland Hill, *Imposture Detected, and the Dead Vindicated* (London, 1777), 21. No fan of the "Ragged Legion," Leigh Hunt still thought Hill "a Theological Buffoon" ("On the Ignorance and Vulgarity of the Methodists," 301).

9. Anon., *The Love-Feast: A Poem,* 10.

80   Chapter 3

hid. If anything, Wordsworth's keywords scripted another conversation his poetry was willing to figure, but not join. The smoldering enthusiasm of *Home at Grasmere*—closeted until 1888—wasn't likely to assist a reputation that was, for much of his life, uncertain. Its Poet is a man raised out of all avenues of human comprehension, catapulted beyond Miltonic, even Biblical canon, into titanic and frankly blasphemous uniqueness:

> What Being, therefore, since the birth of Man
> Had ever more abundant cause to speak
> Thanks . . .
> The boon is absolute; surpassing grace
> To me hath been vouchsafed; among the bowers
> Of blissful Eden this was neither given
> Nor could be given. (*Home at Grasmere*, MS. B: 117–25)

The problem of grace so surpassing wasn't its absolute arrogance, but the abundant ignorance of the people who were actually making—or more to the point, actually publishing—similar assertions throughout the Romantic period. What Wordsworth might have pitched as high argument retailed far more successfully as high camp among knowing consumers. *La Belle Assemblée*, a self-styled "Court and Fashionable Magazine," regaled its readers with the unintentional absurdities of one of Joanna Southcott's letters, in which she, rather like the poet of *Home at Grasmere*, "*modestly* averred, that she had met with an 'instance such as had never happened to any human being since earth's *foundation* was *placed before.*'"[10] Though the letter dated from 1799, *La Belle Assemblée*'s extensive coverage was from 1814, a year which saw "The 'Prospectus' to *The Recluse*" as well as Southcott's annunciation of her own long-awaited (and long-delayed) work, the Coming of Shiloh, the Prince of Peace. The magazine, like most parts of English culture, was interested only in the latter.

As I'll show in chapter five, Southcott, as much as Milton, was the contemporary for the sort of extravagances Wordsworth typically kept safely to himself and his coterie.[11] But even without the full evidences of either

---

10. *La Belle Assemblée; being Bell's Court and Fashionable Magazine* (London: September 1814), 104.
11. For an account of more respectable—especially Augustinian—resonances in spiritual autobiography and providential self-assertion, see Frank D. McConnell, *The Confessional Imagination: A Reading of Wordsworth's Prelude* (Baltimore and London: Johns Hopkins University Press, 1974), as well as Susan M. Levin, *The Romantic Art of Confession: De Quincey, Musset, Sand, Lamb, Hogg, Frémy, Soulié, Janin* (Columbia, SC: Camden House,

Home at Grasmere or *The Prelude,* Wordsworth's somewhat baffling sympathies with demotic enthusiasms were apparent to his contemporaries. Francis Jeffrey's fight against "the mystical verbiage of the Methodist pulpit" that disfigured Wordsworth's work was no isolated battle, but part of a much wider campaign.[12] In 1818, the otherwise friendly pages of *Blackwood's* accused Wordsworth of versifying a "volume of sermons" on spiritual, emotional, and potentially social revolt, in which "the lower and coarser feelings, stirred up into activity, lose their subordination and rise up."[13] Even Coleridge, thinking of *The Excursion* as well as *Peter Bell,* would complain in 1820 of "the odd occasional introduction of the popular, almost the vulgar, Religion in his later publications."[14]

Coleridge knew better than anyone the company Wordsworth's rhetoric kept, and was kept away from. But what was "odd" and "occasional" for *The Excursion* would have read programmatically in the "high argument" of *The Prelude* in 1805, and for decades after. To sober Christians, "dispositions . . . mine, almost / Through grace of heaven" (1805 *Prelude* 6:188–89) would have sounded—despite the qualifying "almost"—very much like the declarations of war by the "saints" and "elect" on the Church of England. The Church held as its "most important Doctrine, viz. *the cessation of the miraculous operations of the Holy Spirit after the establishment of the Christian faith.*"[15] If Lakers and Methodists thought otherwise, only the latter had the courage to print their convictions. Three years before Wordsworth completed the first draft of *The Prelude,* an Anglican parson complained that Methodism widely "misapplies words and terms" from the Apostolic "condition of the first Christians," "terms applied in the primitive ages, such as saints, elect, chosen generation, &c."[16] The particular egotistical sublime of Wordsworth's "ministry / More palpable," framing "A favor'd Being," was unknown even to Keats, who first intuited it in 1818 (1805 *Prelude* 1:364–72). But as Joseph Butler exclaimed decades earlier, the type was as well-known as it was mortifying:

1998).

12. [Jeffrey], "Wordsworth's *Excursion,*" *Edinburgh Review, or Critical Journal* 47 (November 1814): 1–30 (4).

13. "Essays on the Lake School of Poetry, No. II. On the Habits of Thought Inculcated by Wordsworth," in *Blackwood's Edinburgh Magazine* 4 (December 1818): 257–63 (258).

14. *Collected Letters of Samuel Taylor Coleridge,* ed. E. L. Griggs, 6 vols. (Oxford: Clarendon, 1956–71), 5:95.

15. Warburton, *Doctrine of Grace,* 76.

16. George Croft, *Thoughts Concerning the Methodists and the Established Clergy,* iii.

> Mr. Whitefield says in his Journal, "There are promises still to be fulfilled in me." Sir, the pretending to extraordinary revelations and gifts of the Holy Ghost is a horrid thing, a very horrid thing![17]

Butler was a cultural arbiter more important than any reviewer, Scotch or English. His *Analogy*, along with William Paley's *Natural Theology*, comprised most of the very short list of required readings at both Oxford and Cambridge throughout the nineteenth century.[18] Together, Paley and Butler forbade their readers—which is to say, nearly every gentleman—the lexicon of spiritual power that would form the core of *The Prelude*.

This hegemonic censure, I think, went a long way toward rendering the poem uncomfortable, if not quite unpublishable. Paley's *Caution recommended in the Use and Application of Scripture Language*, running to four editions by 1790, was willing to grant that early Christians, "in opposition to the unbelieving world, . . . were denominated in scriptures by titles of great seeming dignity and import—they were 'elect,' 'called,' 'saints' . . . they were 'a chosen generation, a royal priesthood, a holy nation, a peculiar people.'" But precisely because early Christians used such discourse, it was off-limits for everyone else. These "titles" did not "have a perpetual meaning," and were "in a great measure exhausted and insignificant" by the foundation of the Church. By the end of the eighteenth century, they were radically inappropriate for any use, figural or literal. Now, "the most flattering of these names, 'the elect,' 'called,' 'saints,' have by bold and unlearned men been appropriated to themselves and their own party with a presumption and conceit, injurious to the reputation of our religion amongst 'them that are without,' and extremely disgusting to the sober part of its professors."[19]

The Excursion might never do, but with much of the Anglican hierarchy finding spiritual self-congratulation "extremely disgusting" and "injurious to the reputation," the prospects of *The Prelude* were even dimmer. "High argument" was often a shabby thing in Romantic England, its loudest polemicists usually condemned as fools at best, charlatans at worst. But this wasn't an idle squabble over theological abstractions. It was political

---

17. *The Works of the Rev. John Wesley*, 14 vols. (London: Wesleyan Conference Office, 1872), 13:500.

18. On the formal curriculum for clerical training at both universities, see Knight, *Nineteenth-Century Church*, 110–11. It wasn't onerous, largely amounting to reading four or five specialized books, and attending the very infrequent Norrisian or Regius lectures.

19. William Paley, *Caution recommended in the Use and Application of Scripture Language* (Cambridge: Cambridge University Press, 1777), 3–4.

speech as the early nineteenth century would have recognized it, extreme enough that only the most committed partisans went public with it during the years of revolution and war. The now-familiar variants of "high argument," secularized and metaphorized, were substantially marginal to their moment; only long after the fact did poetical crowd out literal usage. Such conceits placed their propounder squarely within—or, in Wordsworth's case, sometimes on the wrong side of—the brawl over the nature of priestly identity and authority that rocked, and ultimately dissolved, the Anglican constitution. This struggle is as much my story as *The Prelude*. The absence of the poem lets us read "inspiration" as it was understood by hundreds of thousands of men and women who didn't much care about experimental verse, yet whose lives were organized by the division between a professionalized, de-supernaturalized clergy and the "Ragged Legion" of transcendentally sanctioned Spiritual Redressers.

But this divide between profession and inspiration is the story of *The Prelude*, as well. The poem internalizes the social conflicts its textual history avoided, staging in its recollections of Cambridge the debate between Establishmentarian credentials and visionary power. The poem, I think, finds this debate no easier to conclude than did the nation. If, as Jon Mee argues, "*The Prelude* is constantly attempting to show that its prophetic pretensions are properly disciplined," discipline, management, and regulation may not have been the sum of its project.[20] Even after fifty years of revision, *The Prelude* never entirely controlled the enthusiasms of its high argument, to which it often harnessed a clustering of forces: rhetorical sublimity, spiritual potency, social abjection, and political subversion. All of these modes shape Wordsworth's thinking on the work of the poet, and the ironies of cultural production. The Methodistical securities of an elect or chosen status, like many Wordsworthian "securities," play into their own undoing, as the same figures simultaneously sound, across different but equally resonant registers, the undeniable force as well as the tragicomic vulnerability of the poet's self. For Wordsworth, "high argument" was never a confession of faith, or a declaration of solidarity; as Coleridge reminds us in "Frost at Midnight," even "secret ministries" are still "performances." But "high argument" does carry with it a social history every bit as disruptive as the figural and psychological traumas explored in other critical treatments of *The Prelude*. It is a problematic discourse of privilege, within Wordsworth's much deeper instinct for privileging the problematic.

---

20. Mee, *Romanticism, Enthusiasm, and Regulation*, 237.

Natural Piety

Modern readings of *The Prelude* have shown, time and again, its ironies of confirmation: the discourses that develop and stabilize the self also unnerve, and may even humiliate and damage that self, in the "turns and counter-turns, the strife / And various trials of our complex being" (1805 *Prelude* 11:195–96). This is especially true for the poem's highest arguments, which are possessed by enthusiasms that rupture the social and poetic propriety they nominally endorse. The "inspiration" opening *The Prelude* is dangerously Pentecostal, promoting the most recognizable Methodist figures to Miltonic "apt Numbers":

> To the open fields I told
> A prophecy; poetic numbers came
> Spontaneously, and clothed in priestly robe
> My spirit, thus singled out, as it might seem,
> For holy services. (1805 *Prelude* 1:59–63)

This portrait of the poet as field preacher is among the most famous in *The Prelude*. But its force is dissipated by its familiar identification as "possibly Jacobinical pantheism, certainly . . . Unitarian and Dissenting Deism,"[21] and Mark Canuel's sense that "Wordsworth calls upon nature as a place where there are no requirements on belief" may let go of the moment's doctrinal nuance.[22] The subversions here are real enough, but they have little in common with secularizing tolerance, intellectualized spirituality, or nonspecific "Dissent." Preaching (let alone prophesying) in the open fields had been an intensively legislated (and intensively stigmatized) practice since the Restoration, evidence (in real courts of law, not just courts of opinion) of very specific theological and political enthusiasms, rather than emancipation from either. "Holy services" in nature were social forms of some urgency.

In 1744, the Bishop of London censured the Methodists for "the Boldness to preach in *the Fields* and other open Places, and by publick Advertisements to invite the *Rabble* to be their Hearers; notwithstanding an express Declaration in a Statute (22 Car. II. c. 1.) against assembling in a FIELD, by Name."[23] The censure had hardly abated by 1811, when Henry

---

21. Miles, *Romantic Misfits*, 92.
22. Canuel, *Religion, Toleration, and British Writing*, 193.
23. [Edmund Gibson, Lord Bishop of London], *Observations upon the Conduct and Behavior of a Certain Sect, Usually distinguished by the Name of Methodists*, 2nd ed. (London: E. Owen, 1744), 4.

Addington, Viscount Sidmouth, advanced newly draconian legislation against itinerant field preachers.[24] In this, and this only, Leigh Hunt could sympathize with Addington: "If Mr. Whitfield had been an obedient member of the Church, he would not have commenced field-preacher, when the churches were denied him."[25] This was 1808, only three years after Wordsworth completed the first version of *The Prelude*, which he opened with this deliberate array of transgressions: prophesying, field preaching, clerical ordination impelled by the Spirit rather than the Church, and a providential "singling out." Each stance was more subject to official attention and public debate than the boyhood adventures of poaching, egg-thievery, or boat-stealing which introduce other seminal moments of poetic ordering and disordering. The preamble was the real illegality, and the brashly foregrounded seediness of its sanctifications much of their significance. The poem often casts imaginative activity as both disruptive and disrupted, but this is one of its most acute socio-rhetorical crises, as plebeian vulgarity frames poetical authority.

By the middle of the nineteenth century, when *The Prelude* was finally published and read, this dimension was fading, faint, or altogether invisible. Radical transformations in the relationship between church and state, as well as in the ideologies which governed the nature and functions of priests, allowed Victorian piety to see its reflection in its beloved Laureate. Wordsworth, argues Mark Canuel, "had become nothing less than a national icon of social conformity" and decently unexceptionable Christianity.[26] "No poet, perhaps, is so evidently filled with a new and sacred energy when the inspiration is upon him," said Matthew Arnold, celebrating "the peculiar importance . . . of inspiration" to Wordsworth.[27] Even more heterodox disciples such as Pater cherished the notion that the "old fancy which made the poet's art an enthusiasm, a form of divine possession, seems almost literally true of him."[28]

---

24. Sidmouth's proposal, it should be noted, wasn't well received—his own party forced the withdrawal of the bill without a vote. There is, however, quite a bit of evidence that many JPs acted for several years *as though* it had passed, and prosecuted and convicted accordingly. For the shifting political and legal status of Methodist preaching and preachers, see David Hempton, *The Religion of the People: Methodism and Popular Religion c. 1750–1900*, 145–61, and Clark, *English Society*, 501–64.

25. Leigh Hunt, "On the hatred of the Methodists against Moral Preaching," *Examiner* 20 (May 15, 1808): 317–19 (317).

26. Canuel, *Religion, Toleration, and British Writing*, 162. See also Stephen Gill, *Wordsworth and the Victorians* (Oxford: Clarendon, 1998).

27. *The Complete Prose Works of Matthew Arnold*, ed. R. H. Super, 11 vols. (Ann Arbor: University of Michigan Press, 1960–77), 9:36

28. Walter Pater, *Appreciations* (Oxford: Basil Blackwell, 1967), 41.

The Victorian deployment of Wordsworth as the forlorn hope of Culture's opposition to Society took place on a profoundly altered terrain of theological and political discourse, in which the Church of England's established powers had been fatally curtailed. But Georgian England was governed by the Anglican constitution, and this establishment was far less hospitable to claims of "sacred energy" or "divine possession," which had yet to die into metaphor. What was morally benevolent, emotionally tranquilizing, and ideologically conservative in 1879 was precipitating a crisis in national security in 1799, when a Yorkshire parson rehearsed his fears of "inspiration" in a letter to Parliament:

> In these days of Fanaticism, it highly imports the members of the Established Church of this Kingdom to have right notions respecting inspiration; because the better they are grounded in the truth concerning it, the better they will be secured against the seduction of those fanatical Preachers, who want to persuade the world, and who too often succeed in persuading weak minds, that they are more inspired than the Ministers of the National Church.[29]

During the Romantic period, the Church of England was deeply suspicious of the sort of "prophecy" told in fields. Unbridled inspiration, averred another clergyman in 1795, was "a leveling Principle in Religion" and a lethal threat "to King and Constitution," the leading edge in the Methodist program for the destruction of the Church and responsible Christianity—no trivial terms two years after England declared war on the French Republic.[30] The most powerful ideological apparatus in England between 1780 and 1820 relentlessly assaulted—and represented itself as under relentless assault by—the enthusiasms which were savored by Pater and Arnold as politically innocent soporifics. As Thomas Ludlam made clear in his *Four Essays* (1797), the Anglican order was firmly united in treating such discourse as a heretical disease "belong[ing] to the imagination . . . consist[ing] in a conceit of and claim to apostolic or prophetical *powers,* unattended with the possession of apostolical or prophetic *credentials.*"[31]

---

29. Joseph Entwisle, *A Letter to the Author of An Anonymous Treatise on Inspiration, Lately Printed at York* (York: Thomas Wilson and Robert Spence, 1799), 6.
30. Croft, *Thoughts Concerning the Methodists and the Established Clergy,* 49.
31. Ludlam, *Four Essays: On the Ordinary and Extraordinary Operations of the Holy Spirit,* 68–69.

Ministries, Professional and More Palpable

Romantic England was convulsed by the apparent incompatibility of social "*credentials*" and spiritual "*powers*." The "priest" focused conflicts of agenda between polite and plebeian classes, and the opposition between Anglican "vocation" and Methodist "calling" was as significant as that between Jacobin and loyalist. This historical tumult, I think, powers the rhetorical dynamism of the poet-priest in *The Prelude*. Wordsworth is often read as an exemplary theorist of what Paul Keen calls "the most powerful ideological achievement of the long middle-class revolution: the prestige of the professional."[32] But a play on Mark Schoenfield's thesis that "William Wordsworth was the most methodically professional of the major romantics" better captures the poet's hybridity, since this professionalism often assumed an antithetically Methodistical method.[33] If Wordsworth was eager to "give the poet respectable status, while rejecting the institutional bases for authority . . . Church and University in particular," it's important to recognize that the language of the spirit rejected such institutions *precisely because* it also rejected (and was rejected by) "respectable status."[34] In binding the power of his spontaneous "poetic numbers" to an equally spontaneous ordination into "holy services" and "priestly robes," Wordsworth established himself through powerful figures of cultural, political, and religious disestablishment.

There was real hazard to this irony, in an age when the most influential "professionalism" was structured by its hostility to "holy powers." While the secularized roles of lawyers and doctors are heavily featured in many recent critical accounts, the Anglican clergy were not only the largest body among the "high-status occupational groups," they were also "possibly larger than all the other professions put together."[35] Formal academic training by and large meant religious training under the auspices of the Church of England, and the universities still could be characterized with some accuracy as seminaries: throughout the eighteenth century, sixty percent of Oxbridge graduates were ordained as Anglican deacons, a figure which had fallen only to fifty percent by 1840.[36] All clergymen held degrees from either university, as bishops refused ordination

---

32. Keen, *Crisis of Literature*, 78.
33. Mark Schoenfield, *The Professional Wordsworth: Law, Labor & the Poet's Contract* (Athens: University of Georgia Press, 1996), 2.
34. Goldberg, *Lake Poets*, 220.
35. Russell, *Clerical Profession*, 19.
36. Knight, *Nineteenth-Century Church*, 107.

to men otherwise educated until the middle of the nineteenth century. Advanced degrees mainly operated as status signals within the Church hierarchy, since they were automatically awarded upon promotion to the rank of canon or above.[37] Expanding enrollments at both universities in the Romantic era created a crisis for hopeful clergymen not unfamiliar to modern academics, as accelerating supply rapidly began to outstrip inelastic demand. The 1820s saw twice as many applicants for entry-level curacies as did the 1770s, but since the designation of a new parish required an Act of Parliament, the number of available livings remained almost entirely static from 1700 to 1830.[38]

The clerical profession was thus awkwardly situated at the turn of the century. It was institutionally dominant yet increasingly insecure about its own authority and socioeconomic prospects, especially as the "occupational professionalism" of surgeons, attorneys, and civil servants emerged at the expense of the "status professionalism" of the gentleman-cleric, who had often been his parish's main legal, medical, and bureaucratic functionary.[39] In response, clerical training became increasingly regulated (if not more rigorous), with more emphasis placed on examinations of sacred and secular knowledge, and instruction in pastoral ministry and parochial maintenance, especially visiting the sick, alleviating financial distress, and conducting catechisms.[40] Training and technique mattered most to the lowest levels of the hierarchy, and Deryck Lovegrove reports that the majority of vocational publications from 1790 to 1815 came from the parish clergy, "whose position and credibility were most immediately affected" by the transformations in their professional role.[41]

But curates and vicars understood these transformations in terms strikingly different from narratives of a shift in social capital from inherited privileges to technical skills. In its own self-representations, the newfound "occupationalism" of Anglicanism was instead a rejoinder to the topsy-turvy "status" of illiterate men who offered only hierophantic recom-

---

37. Viviane Barrie-Curien, "Clerical Recruitment and Career Patterns in the Church of England during the Eighteenth Century," in Jacob and Yates, *Crown and Mitre: Religion and Society in Northern Europe since the Reformation*, 93–104.

38. Knight, *Nineteenth-Century Church*, 107–8.

39. For an account of the functional transformation of the Anglican clergy in the nineteenth century, and the frictions which attended this transformation, see Brian Heeney, *A Different Kind of Gentleman: Parish Clergy as Professional Men in Early and Mid-Victorian England* (Hamden and Springfield: Archon Books, 1976).

40. See Jeremy Gregory, "The Eighteenth-Century Reformation," 67–85.

41. Lovegrove, *Established Church, Sectarian People*, 58.

mendations.[42] In 1792, Edward Tatham symptomatically warned against anyone who claimed "extraordinary gifts" and "a greater degree of illumination" from the Spirit.[43] "The best qualified to be teachers in one of the most difficult and learned of all professions," Tatham went on, were only those "bred and educated . . . in the study of languages, sciences, and other necessary parts of learning."[44] Inverting the old Horatian logic, a proper man of God was made, not born, and "inspiration" was a social disability. "To commission men notoriously illiterate, under the idea of being divinely inspired," argued another cleric in 1795, "is a notorious offence, not only against God, but against the general order of society."[45]

Southey thought this the admirable skepticism of a Church ready to meet modernity on its own terms; as he "safely affirmed" in 1818, "at no time since the foundation of the English Church, have men been more diligently trained for holy orders than in these, our days; nor has promotion in the church been ever so generally bestowed according to desert."[46] But for the Methodists so reproached, the Anglican affection for sober diligence was a pious fraud. The itinerant John Nelson, having been illegally pressed by a cabal of parsons, was carted in chains to York and imprisoned. When one cleric violently denied the value of "Inspiration" and "the Holy Spirit," the caged Methodist bit back:

> Here he stormed at me, and called me an enthusiast, and said, "To talk of the Spirit is all a delusion." "Hold sir," I replied, "or I shall expose you before the people, which I did not design to do. How could you affirm, before God and the congregation, that you were inwardly moved by the Holy Spirit to take upon you the office of a deacon; and now testify there is no such thing as being moved by the Holy Spirit?" He said, "Did I say so?" "Yes, sir," I answered, "you did, when you received holy orders." He turned pale, spake not ten words more, but went away.[47]

There was, as Nelson pointed out, plenty of residual thaumaturgy underneath the Anglican vocational pretense: clergymen were still required at ordination to profess their "calling" as ultimately one from God rather

---

42. See Russell, *Clerical Profession*, for the transformation of the "priest" into the "clergyman," in which the self-consciously sociological function of the latter replaced the mysterious powers of the former.
43. Tatham, *A Sermon Suitable to the Times*, 12.
44. Tatham, *A Sermon Suitable to the Times*, 8–9.
45. Croft, *Thoughts Concerning the Methodists*, 33.
46. Southey, "New Churches," 580.
47. WV 3:126.

than man. Though bishops and deacons treated this as a polite fiction solemnizing the formal examinations, for the Methodists, it was an ideological fissure in which they made themselves comfortable. Preachers such as Nelson cannily took the Church's dead-letter teachings more seriously than did the Church, which let them dismiss any polite opprobrium as motivated by bigotry rather than by sound doctrine. "Men of all ranks," declared Christopher Hopper in 1781, had "dispensed with two or three awakened clergymen tolerably well: these were regularly ordained, men of learning, gentlemen, and divines; but to see a ploughman, or an honest mechanic, stand up to preach the gospel, it was insufferable."[48]

These ploughmen and mechanics would introduce a host of impressive innovations in labor organization and compensation, including the first pension plan, and the highly efficient itinerants were arguably the earliest group to realize fully the transformative possibilities of the new national turnpike system.[49] But the preachers imagined themselves as the "chosen sons" and "favor'd beings" of a sacred order, not as members of a technocratic occupation. In 1816, the Methodist Conference officially denounced Daniel Isaac, whose *Investigation of Ecclesiastical Claims* had heretically (at least to Methodist orthodoxy) classed as "nonsense" the notion that "priests are a distinct body of men, specifically designated by heaven to their holy employment, and solemnly set apart."[50] Two decades earlier, George Shadford bore witness to the Pentecostal authority of another preacher who annihilated earthly—meaning, Established—power: "I did not suppose he had very learned abilities, or that he had studied either at Oxford or Cambridge; but something struck me, 'This is the Gift of God, this is the Gift of God.'"[51] Even John Wesley, though always careful to appear in the vestments that marked him as an ordained Anglican cleric, laughed away the professionalizing strategies of the Church of England:

> Certainly the practice and the direction of the Apostle Paul was to *prove* a man before he was ordained at all. . . . Proved? How? By setting them to construe a sentence of Greek? And asking them a few commonplace questions? O amazing proof of a minister of Christ![52]

---

48. WV 1:120.
49. On the connection between infrastructural improvements in Britain and the rise of the very possibility of a national itinerancy, see Hindmarsh, *Evangelical Conversion Narrative*, 73.
50. See Hempton, *Religion of the People*, 106–7, for an account of these proceedings.
51. WV 2:175.
52. Wesley, "A Caution Against Bigotry," in *Sermons* IV, ed. Albert C. Outler (Nashville, TN: Abingdon, 1987), 75.

Inflected by the Spirit rather than the classics, the most famous lay preachers carried marks of their otherworldly difference, and even the faithful were wary of their flashing eyes and floating hair. Richard Whatcoat was described shortly after his death as being a second St. Basil, "that so much divine majesty and luster appeared in him it made the wicked tremble to behold."[53]

Anglican churchmen—not without reason—saw in such "luster" the darkness of the Civil Wars, when the universities had been vilified and partly conquered by uncompromising "reformers." Wesley's own contempt for the institution of which he had been a Fellow had worrisome precedents. It was, after all, a Master of Gonville and Caius who in the 1650s had declared Cambridge "the throne of the Beast," and the idea "that universities are the fountain of the ministers of the Gospel" to be "one of the grossest errors that ever reigned under Antichrist's Kingdom."[54] As the Rev. W. Woolley mocked in 1794, the Methodists had adopted the tone of Rant, and its politics would follow soon enough: "[l]et those . . . consult the primitive fathers, or pore their eyes out over the volumes of a Lowth, an Atterbury, a Sherlock, a Tillotson, who cannot trust to their own strength of lungs, violence of gesture, and an unceasing hurly-burly of sounds for an hour or two upon any emergency."[55]

Bookish wisdom paled for most Methodists before dramatic oratory, which was more obviously inspired the less manicured its source. As Peter Jaco testified in 1778, it was only when he went "to hear Stephen Nicols, a plain, honest tinner, [that] the word took strange hold on me, and seemed like fire in my bones."[56] Jaco's encounter with the arresting power of the Word, which—often without warning for the audience, or preparation by the preacher—mysteriously shook bones and limbs along with hearts and minds, was very common. In Shadford's 1790 account of his own first, fumbling attempt at preaching, an unsought Eolism transformed an untutored peasant lad into a vessel for holy wrath: "When I began again to speak for Him His word was like the flaming sword, which turned every way to every heart; for sinners trembled and fell before it, and were both convinced and converted to God."[57] Clergymen habituated

---

53. WV 2:226.
54. Christopher Hill, *Antichrist in Seventeenth-Century England* (London: Oxford University Press, 1971), 140.
55. W. Woolley, *A Cure for Canting; Or, the Grand Impostors . . . Unmasked* (London: Jordan and Ridgeway, 1794), 4.
56. WV 2:9.
57. WV 2:193.

to receive public rhetoric as Ciceronian technique, mastered through serious application, were rather less taken by these spontaneous overflows.[58] Enthusiasts might be impressed by "something like inspiration," scoffed the Rev. Croft, but the "truth is, the common extempory effusions of the Methodists are an insult upon the understanding, and to ascribe them to inspiration, is little short of blasphemy."[59]

But "an insult upon the understanding," insofar as "the understanding" was the mystification of gentry interests into the grammar for thought and speech, was much of the point and most of the pleasure of Methodistical "inspiration." In 1763, Warburton fretted over the "many well attested cases in modern History, . . . where Enthusiasts, in their extasies, have talked fluently in the learned languages, of which they had a very imperfect knowledge in their sober intervals."[60] Even the most staid Anglican doctrine conceded that the Pentecostal Gift of Tongues had been the original intervention of the Holy Spirit; its recurrence would prove God's approbation for the Methodist attack on the Establishment. Warburton's (unsurprising) verdict was that such attestations were inevitably perjured—yet in truth, Methodist preachers rarely had much interest in claiming an ecstatic power in the "learned languages," or the cultural capital they contained. The itinerants often came from semi-literate backgrounds, and could not always boast even of that "solid and religious EDUCATION, which has rendered few books familiar, but the bible, and the liturgy or hymn book." Coleridge argued in the *Biographia* that this was the bare minimum by which "a rustic's language" might be "purified from all provincialism and grossness" into something like "the Language of Real Life."[61] But for the Methodists, this Reality was aspiration, not assumption. Their English was parochial in vocabulary and dialectal in accent, a far cry from the nationally standardized and textually informed speech the universities imparted to even the most worn curate. For the preachers, speaking in Greek, Aramaic, or Ur had little appeal when rhetorical success in what Coleridge called "*ordinary*" English was so improbable as to seem supernatural.[62] The obligations of itinerancy, in which a gardener from Yorkshire would be expected to convert and comfort the families

---

58. For a sensitive reading of the "negotiations" between Methodist oratory and polite literature in the mid-eighteenth century, see Goring, *Rhetoric of Sensibility,* 60–90.

59. George Croft, *Thoughts Concerning the Methodists,* 21.

60. Warburton, *Doctrine of Grace,* 12.

61. Samuel Taylor Coleridge, *Biographia Literaria,* ed. James Engell and W. Jackson Bate (Princeton, NJ: Princeton University Press, 1983), 2:44, 52.

62. Coleridge, *Biographia Literaria,* 2:56.

of Cornish miners, posed sociolectal challenges that could only be solved with divine help. Fifty—or even five—people, earnestly attending to the extemporaneous exhortations of a cobbler or field-hand, often felt like a miracle to everyone involved. As the itinerant Thomas Olivers sighed in 1779:

> Nor shall I ever forget the last sermon I preached in that town [Dundee]: such liberty I never felt before or since. I had such an absolute command of my ideas, language, voice, and gesture that I could say what I would, and also in what manner I pleased![63]

As Olivers's nostalgia underscores, such rhetorical "liberty" was inexplicable in production and incapable of emulation, a fleeting Gift rather than a consciously managed technique of "language, voice, and gesture." "Inspired speech" was wistful memory, not program for future practice.

These irregular gifts were the most public examples of the special providences and palpable ministries we now associate with *The Prelude*. They were also often as pedestrian as they were public. While the soldier John Haime told a harrowing story of God on the battlefield of Fontenoy,[64] John Pawson's 1806 account of a "very narrow escape indeed" from a "very small bit of potato stuck in my throat, as I was eating my supper," was more typical, and typically moralizing. The tuber, Pawson solemnly reflected, was an unexpected lesson, placed and then removed by God in order to impress that "'in the midst of life we are in death.'"[65] If this seems like uncontrolled bathos rather than serious theology, it was still in communion with the Methodist doctrine that the quotidian was rife with transcendental significance. The smallest incident, Wesley taught, could surpass the grandest event on the world-historical stage, since "the eye of God see[s] everything through the whole extent of creation," a gaze that telescoped with "particular notice" onto the "souls" and "bodies" of His favored children, and "all their tempers, desires, and thoughts, all their words and actions."[66] This metaphysic was increasingly isolated from most respectable Christianities, which attempted "reasonable" reconcili-

---

63. *WV* 1:236.
64. According to Haime, God both saved him and chastised the wicked in one economical intervention: "After about seven hours, a cannon-ball killed my horse under me. An officer cried aloud, 'Haime, where is your God now?' I answered, 'Sir, He is here with me; and He will bring me out of this battle.' Presently a cannon-ball took off his head." *WV* 1:34.
65. *WV* 4:54.
66. Wesley, *Sermons* II, 538, 543.

ations with the predictabilities of the Newtonian physics across the long eighteenth century. But it was also a metaphysic long-cherished by many popular Protestantisms, ennobling men and women whose lives were constrained to a narrow round of enervating labor. A potato might figure more largely in God's plan than any potentate, a nourishing bit of natural piety for those on a restricted diet. As Bunyan had taught a century before, though once the Spirit had called out of Palestine from the height of "*Hill Mizar,*" personal revelation could now be sought and found more readily in "*the Close, the Milk-house, the Stable, the Barn.*"[67]

By the end of the eighteenth century, providential exaltation was powerfully associated with social humiliation. The doctrine of "special providence" was abandoned by both the Church and middle-class Dissent; its survival among the poorer readers of Wesley and Bunyan began to imply that peculiar ministrations were found not only in low places, but also perhaps *only* in low places. This, I think, explains Wordsworth's anxiety over the "vulgar hope" behind the spiritual "ministry" that

> Impress'd upon all forms the characters
> Of danger and desire, and thus did make
> The surface of the universal earth
> With triumph, and delight, and hope, and fear
> Work like a sea. (1805 *Prelude* 1:497–501)

Wordsworth may try to evacuate any theology into a secularized appreciation of the "Presences of Nature," but as Southey argued five years later, too much emphasis on the special purposes guiding the natural world suggested only cultural and historical backwardness. The spiritual autobiographies in the *Arminian* and *Methodist* magazines continually claimed "that the itinerant preachers have a special gift for obtaining rain in dry seasons, and that when they prayed against a plague of caterpillars, an army of crows came and cleared the country." This was unnatural superstition, not pantheistic sophistication: such sensibility, Southey warned, could only "bring back into the world the baneful faith in dreams, tokens, apparitions, and witchcraft."[68] But while reasonable Christians scoffed, this sort of magic was still hugely influential—and very real—for most of the country's rural inhabitants. The success of the Methodist preachers often sprang from their ability to read "the characters / Of danger and

---

67. John Bunyan, *Grace Abounding with Other Spiritual Autobiographies*, ed. John Stachniewski and Anita Pacheco (Oxford: Oxford University Press, 1998), 5.
68. Southey, "On the Evangelical Sects," 508.

desire" that many people assumed God and Satan had written around them. The itinerants easily filled positions only recently vacated by wise-women and sorcerers in the early nineteenth century, arriving "as the interpreter, or even agency, of God's will, just as witches or conjurers were agencies through which darker powers operated."[69]

Alexander Knox, Wesley's loyal friend, worked mightily to convince Southey that the children were not the father of the man. Though Wesley had "conceived himself providentially called" to reanimate the church, "as if he had been commissioned by a voice from heaven," Knox assured Southey that "in this material respect John Wesley differed from all vulgar enthusiasts—that he did not imagine any such voice, nor had he the slightest thought of either impulse or intimation from above."[70] But Southey's *Life of Wesley* drew upon Wesley's own *Journal* for countless counterexamples, anecdotes of divine intervention and "vulgar enthusiasm," in which "even frenzy was rebuked before him," as madhouse riots were calmed with a word, rabid dogs with a glance.[71] Accused of both witchcraft and mesmerism, Wesley's explanation was simpler, grander, and rather Wordsworthian. Where the poet "felt / Incumbences more awful, visitings / Of the upholder" (1805 *Prelude* 3:114–16), the preacher knew the "*Spirit is upon me, because he hath anointed me.*"[72] Behind this confident grandeur, however, was the horde of lesser men Wesley had moved to similar declarations. So many men styled themselves "inspired, anointed, and elect" that, between 1800 and 1820, the Justices of the Peace were swamped by petitions for preaching licenses. Here is another demographic for the Romantic imagination:

> One magistrate in the county of Middlesex licensed fourteen hundred preachers in the course of five years. Of six-and-thirty persons who obtained licenses at one sessions, six spelled "ministers of the gospel" in six different ways, and seven signed their mark! One fellow, who applied for a license, being asked if he could read, replied, "Mother reads, and I 'spounds and 'splains."[73]

As the anti-Methodist satire *The Expounder Expounded*—it should have been *The 'Spounder 'Splained*—grumbled earlier, it was impossible

---

69. Rule, "Methodism, Popular Beliefs and Village Culture," 65.
70. Knox, "Remarks," 310.
71. Southey, *Life of Wesley*, 1:198.
72. Southey, *Life of Wesley*, 1:218.
73. Southey, *Life of Wesley*, 2:388.

96   Chapter 3

to maintain the dignity of the sacerdotal profession in the face of these "inspired fellows": they "are well known to be the most senseless and illiteral Part of the human Species."[74]

Illiteral Poetics

"*Senseless*" and "*illiteral*": in what might be a spectacular pun, or a peculiarly Freudian printer's slip, *The Expounder Expounded* dramatized the conjunction between ignorance and metaphoricity active across the long eighteenth century. "Inspiration" was an unreliable vessel for cultural distinction, as itinerant preachers—whether devoted Wesleyans or conniving mountebanks—outnumbered and out-wrote authors of more self-consciously rarefied (if still rhetorically adjacent) poetical enthusiasms. By the time Wordsworth began *The Prelude,* the case had become acute. Worshipping at the altar of spontaneous power and providential selection was a direct affront, not just to the hegemony of the Church of England, but to the ideology of polite professionalism increasingly essential to it. The spiritual autobiographies in the *Arminian* and then *Methodist* magazines had become so widely read—Lackington was sure that they "circulated with the greatest avidity, to the private emolument of the editors, and doubtless to the great edification of all sinners"—that they set terms for the genre.[75] By 1827, the *Quarterly* flatly declared that only "pickpockets," "our weakest mob-orators," and "cabin-boys and drummers" stooped to publish their own lives, replete with "imbecility, quackery, and vice": "few great men—none of the very highest order—have chosen to paint otherwise than indirectly, and through the shadows of imaginary forms, the secret workings of their own minds; nor is it likely that genius will ever be found altogether divested of this proud modesty."[76]

If the "Life" rendered in *The Prelude* was meant to be exemplary, this was following the example of the Methodist "Lives." The pedagogical hallmarks were so reiterated as to be a convention: ministrations of the Holy Spirit transformed reprobate sinner into wayfaring Christian, who then "examine[d] how far Nature"—though the Wesleyans would prefer

---

74. R—ph J—ps—n, *The expounder expounded: or, annotations upon that incomparable piece, intitled, A short account of God's dealings with the Rev. Mr. G——e W—f—d. Wherein Several profound Mysteries, which were greatly subject to Misconception, are set in a clear Light; and the abominable secret Sin, therein mentioned, is particularly illustrated and explained* (London: T. Payne, 1740), 2.

75. Lackington, *Memoirs*, 182.

76. "Autobiography," in *Quarterly Review* 35 (January 1827): 148–65 (149, 164).

"Providence"—"and Education had qualified him for such employment" ("Preface" to *The Excursion, Prose Works* 3:5).[77] To be asked to write an autobiography was the final earthly reward for an itinerant. "For a Methodist a place in the Magazine was something like a niche in the Abbey for a statesman or a poet," John Telford remarked in 1898, when Wordsworth, though interred home at Grasmere, could have claimed a laureate niche.[78] But in fact, this kind of self-confirmatory autobiography was likely to get a gentleman-poet ejected from Westminster. William Cowper provided a sobering example of the damage enthusiastic postures could inflict even on immensely popular poets. When his *Memoirs* were published in a variety of editions between 1814 and 1816, periodicals collectively recoiled from the disgusting spectacle of his addiction to the providential myopia peculiar to Methodist self-fashioning.[79] Pondering the "forced and unnatural connexion" between Cowper's poetical and religious enthusiasms, the *Quarterly* confessed, "We do not like to be carried back to all the particulars. . . . When they are pressed once more upon our notice, they have a tendency . . . to detract somewhat from our respect."[80] *The Monthly Review*'s diagnosis was even harsher: "The secret sufferings of the gifted but most unhappy subject . . . were detailed with a minuteness, which nothing but the unsocial and indelicate taste of *methodism* could for one instance have endured."[81]

---

77. Lackington opens his autobiography parodying this conventional providentialism, while begging the question, "was it for this?": "I shall there not trouble you with a history of predictions which foretold the future greatness of your humble servant, nor with a minute account of the aspects of the planets at the very auspicious and important crisis when I first inhaled the air of this bustling orb; for, extraordinary as it may appear, it has never yet occurred to me that any of the adepts in the astrological science have made a calculation of my nativity." As we learn shortly thereafter, the patrimonial stock of the Lackingtons was not high. His grandfather, "a good honest man," came to "remarkable" end, "though not very fortunate; in the road between Taunton and Wellington, he was found drowned in a ditch, where the water scarcely covered his face: He was, 'tis conjectured, '——Drunk when he died'" (*Memoirs*, 7–9).

78. John Telford, *The Life of John Wesley* (New York: Eaton and Maine, 1898 [London: Hodder and Stoughton, 1886]), 326–27.

79. For an engaging argument that the Methodist *Lives* generated "an acceptable genre of autobiographical writing," adopted by figures outside of the itinerancy, see Helen Thomas, *Romanticism and Slave Narratives: Transatlantic Testimonies* (Cambridge: Cambridge University Press, 2000), 48–81. My reservation is that the reception histories of Thomas's key examples—Joanna Southcott and William Cowper—suggest, on the contrary, the profound *unacceptability* of Methodist models to polite sensibilities.

80. "Cowper's *Poems and Life*," *Quarterly Review* 16.31 (October 1816): 116–29 (123).

81. "*The Rural Walks of Cowper*," *Monthly Review* vol. C (January 1823): 111–12 (111). For this review in a different (and captivating) critical context, see Andrew Elfenbein,

By and large, Wordsworth took the hint. His most public navigations of the intersections between poets and priests carefully evaded the spiritual poses which might damage the respectability of either vocation. By the end of the French Wars, the established poet was doing his part for established priest-craft. One climax of *The Excursion,* the Wordsworthian epic well into the twentieth century, is this hymn to the Anglican Church in general, and to its uncompromisingly trained priests in particular.

> And, as on earth it is the doom of Truth
> To be perpetually attacked by foes
> Open or covert, be that Priesthood still,
> For defence, replenished with a Band
> Of strenuous Champions, in scholastic arts
> Thoroughly disciplined. (1814 *Excursion* 6:53–58)

Though the Church was in danger "perpetually," the adoration of "scholastic arts" and "thorough discipline" here suggests that the most dangerous "foes" were neither ferociously learned Dissenters nor university-educated Solitaries wallowing in continental atheism, but rather those inspired preachers more invested in overturning the professionalizing protocols of the "Priesthood" than in assaulting Christianity itself. Enthusiasm, not secularism, was the enemy best fought by clerical discipline, but this isn't just late-onset conservatism. Since 1802, with the second edition of the "Preface" to *Lyrical Ballads,* many of Wordsworth's public definitions of the "Poet" drew on the occupational ideology of the Anglican priest, to credit the cultural value of the poet in the company of "a lawyer, a physician, a mariner, an astronomer, or a natural philosopher" (*Prose Works* [*PW*] 1:139).

"Taking up the subject, then, upon general grounds, let me ask, what is meant by the word Poet? What is a Poet?" (*PW* 1:138). The question answers itself: the Poet's intellectual precision parses word from thing, forcing the distinction between the arbitrary ("what is *meant* by the *word* Poet?") and the essential ("What *is* a *Poet?*") into difference. The Poet is a coolly skilled practitioner, not an untutored enthusiast: "[h]owever exalted a notion we would wish to cherish of a Poet, it is obvious, that while he describes and imitates passions, his employment is in some degree mechanical" (*PW* 1:138). The "Preface" is of a type with the "gentrified,

---

Romantic Genius: The Prehistory of a Homosexual Role (New York: Columbia University Press, 1999), 82.

late eighteenth-century grammar prefaces," and its prose enacts its own ironic ideal.[82] The argument for plain-speaking unfolds in the syntax of Burkean periodicity, quietly dramatizing the sophistication necessary to arrange "greater simplicity":

> Low and rustic life was generally chosen because in that situation the essential passions of the heart find a better soil in which they can attain their maturity, are less under restraint, and speak a plainer and more emphatic language; because in that situation of life our elementary feelings exist in a state of greater simplicity and consequently may be more accurately contemplated and more forcibly communicated; because the manners of rural life germinate from those elementary feelings; and from the necessary character of rural occupations are more easily comprehended; and are more durable; and lastly, because in that situation the passions of men are incorporated with the beautiful and permanent forms of nature. (*PW* 1:124)

The "real language of men" turns out to have a surprising affinity for semicolons. Following Coleridge's critique in the *Biographia*, John Guillory identifies this "unacknowledged idealization of the bourgeois sociolect" in the "literalization of pastoral speech."[83] I cavil only at "unacknowledged." This is Wordsworth's deliberate poetics: ostensibly in opposition to the artifices of eighteenth-century diction and the false refinements of modern urbanity, but also—and perhaps more deliberately unacknowledged—the low and rustic company of inspiration. So when Wordsworth pits his manly and "accurate taste in poetry" against the emotional excesses of "frantic novels, sickly and stupid German Tragedies" (*PW* 1:128), he sounds for all the world like Lord Bishop Gibson, who valued "due and regular Attendance, paid by good Men in a serious and composed Way," against "those sudden Agonies, Roarings and Screamings, Tremblings, Droppings-Down, Ravings and Madnesses" that typified the Methodist experience.[84]

And Wordsworth was alert to the need to manage this affinity. Not for nothing did *The Excursion* appear in expensive quarto. This was the armature of its ideological safety: at more than two pounds, it was

---

82. Carey McIntosh, *The Evolution of English Prose, 1700–1800: Style, Politeness, and Print Culture* (Cambridge: Cambridge University Press, 1998), 48.
83. Guillory, *Cultural Capital*, 126.
84. [Edmund Gibson], *Observations upon the Conduct and Behavior of a Certain Sect*, 10.

"for its length, perhaps the most expensive work of literature ever published in England," probably priced beyond the reach of its own author.[85] It was just this cover that Jeffrey suspected as a high-class disguise for a covertly Methodist operation. *The Excursion* wouldn't do, not because it was dull, but because (like Cowper's *Memoirs*) it bored in such a denominationally identifiable manner. Enthusiasm led to tedium as easily as agitation: Wesley's own *Journal* had reached one million words, while the diary of Howell Harris sprawled to an improbable 284 volumes.[86] Jeffrey thought Wordsworth's "preposterous minuteness" similarly motivated by "moral and religious enthusiasm," which, "though undoubtedly poetical emotions, are at the same time but dangerous inspirers of poetry; nothing being so apt to run into interminable dullness or mellifluous extravagance, without giving the unfortunate author the slightest intimation of his danger."[87] The threatened *Recluse* and unnamed *Prelude*, advertised by *The Excursion* as the "history of the author's mind," were proof *avant la lettre* that Wordsworth's spiritual narcissism was a private derangement with a public history. Since the 440-page "quarto now before us" contained "an account of one of his youthful rambles in the vales of Cumberland, and occupies precisely the period of three days; so that, by the use of a very powerful *calculus*, some estimate may be formed of the probable extent of the entire biography."[88]

Even more irritating than the length of *The Excursion*, however, was its hero. The Wanderer, the poem's rebranding of the earlier Pedlar into a more glamorously metaphysical itinerancy, has impressed later critics. Philip Connell and Nigel Leask find him "impeccably respectable,"[89] and Jon Mee draws our attention to his "philosophical discipline . . . as a meditative thinker much like Wordsworth himself."[90] Jeffrey, however, read the Wanderer not only as transparently Wordsworth, but, more disagreeably yet, as patently Methodistical, a "moral teacher . . . willfully debased . . . by low occupation," who proselytized the "moral and devotional ravings" all too familiar in the fields of the Wesleyan ministry. The "radical intellectual poet and the itinerant cleric were," observes

---

85. St. Clair, *Reading Nation*, 201.
86. On Harris, see Hindmarsh, *Evangelical Conversion Narrative*, 129.
87. Jeffrey, "Wordsworth's *Excursion*," 7, 4.
88. Jeffrey, "Wordsworth's *Excursion*," 4.
89. Connell and Leask, "What Is the People?" 23.
90. Mee, *Romanticism, Enthusiasm, and Regulation*, 229. For a very different but stimulating account of itinerancy, see Celeste Langan, *Romantic Vagrancy: Wordsworth and the Simulation of Freedom* (Cambridge: Cambridge University Press, 1995).

Brian Goldberg, equally "alienated from establishment authority."[91] Or not equally, exactly: as Sir Frederic Morton Eden reminded his readers in 1797, roving preachers were formally "rogues, vagabonds, and sturdy beggars," of a piece with "Fencers, bearwards, strolling players of interludes or other entertainments, . . . persons who run away and leave their wives and children upon the parish, . . . persons having implements of house-breaking, or offensive weapons."[92] Such was clearly the company in which Jeffrey located the Wanderer.

Like any itinerant moralizer—and by extension, his excursioning poet—he "entertains no doubt that he is the elected organ of divine truth and persuasion." Jeffrey was aghast at the "most wretched and provoking perversity of taste and judgment" which would entrust an entire theo-poetical system to the brittle dignity of a "superannuated Pedlar."[93] Wordsworth felt the heat, and after 1814, he excised a footnote labeling the Wanderer "strongly disposed to enthusiasm poetical and religious."[94] The rough reception for this conjunction of enthusiasms "poetical and religious" may have made publishing *The Prelude* implausible in the poet's lifetime. Had he owned such discourse in his own voice, undisguised by dramatic figuration, Wordsworth would have appeared (or could have been made to appear) entirely conscripted by the Methodist empire of spiritual autobiography that had arisen in the years in which *The Prelude* was written.

Jeffrey's reaction is all the more noteworthy, given Wordsworth's pains to ally with and celebrate the Church of England. *The Excursion* is a deeply establishmentarian poem of catholic reconciliations within Anglicanism, thematized in the gentle compulsion of the parson's garden (rather

---

91. Goldberg, *Lake Poets*, 133.
92. Eden, *State of the Poor*, 1:307–9.
93. Jeffrey, "Wordsworth's *Excursion*," 30, 4.
94. "In Heron's Tour in Scotland is given an intelligent account of the qualities by which this class of men used to be, and still are, in some degree, distinguished, and of the benefits which Society derives from their labours. Among their characteristics, he does not omit to mention that, from being obliged to pass so much of their time in solitary wandering among rural objects, they frequently acquire meditative habits of mind, and are strongly disposed to enthusiasm poetical and religious. I regret that I have not the book at hand to quote the passage, as it is interesting on many accounts." The note has attracted little critical attention, as it was suppressed in favor of its revision until very recently. For the original note, see Wordsworth, *The Excursion, Being a Portion of The Recluse, A Poem* (London: Longman, Hurst, Rees, Orme, and Brown, 1814), 425; absent in *The Poetical Works of William Wordsworth*, ed. Ernest de Selincourt and Helen Darbishire, 5 vols. (Oxford: Clarendon, 1969) 5:411–12; restored in *The Excursion*, ed. Sally Bushell, James A. Butler, and Michael C. Jaye with the assistance of David Garcia (Ithaca, NY, and London: Cornell University Press, 2007), 298.

than the confines of the stone church), a space for conversations that never quite become confrontations.[95] The resolution of enthusiasm, atheism, and establishment over tea advertises its own fancifulness; parsons and preachers might still trade blows as easily as pleasantries, and the itinerant Christopher Hopper insisted that his meetings with clergymen inevitably ended in "dirt, rotten eggs, brickbats, stones, and cudgels."[96] But even with the reticent enthusiasm of the Wanderer, the poem identifies less with any of its characters, and more with an attenuated Anglicanism of reasonable sociability. What the Vicar calls "Narratives [sic] of calm and humble life," and the "sympathy bestowed" in "patient listening," rather than what Jeffrey identified as "the mystical verbiage of the Methodist pulpit,"[97] seem the poem's ideological and affective aspirations (1814 *Excursion* 8:6–9).

Jeffrey prevailed, however, and the satires in the *Edinburgh* probably had a much wider readership than the poem itself. *The Excursion* sold weakly, with some of its 500 quartos remaindered twenty years later.[98] A fashionable narrative took hold: in his swiftly advancing dotage, Wordsworth had confused Methodistical cant for sound poetics. In 1819, *Peter Bell* was further confirmation: its surprising success was an irresistible target for men eager to burnish their *bona fides* at the expense of the ridiculous marriage between lowbrow evangelicalism and High Toryism. Hunt, no less an enemy of the Wesleyans than a champion of political liberty, was appalled by "the bewitching principles of fear, bigotry, and diseased impulses. . . . We are really and most unaffectedly sorry to see an excellent poet like Mr. Wordsworth returning, in vulgar despair, to such half-witted prejudices."[99] The dramatic distance between Wordsworth and his enthusiastic figures was perilously narrow, and in 1823, Hazlitt closed the gap even further. Trading on an insider's "First Acquaintance," he recounted the queer mixture of stuffy self-importance and uncontained farce that resulted from Wordsworth's identification with his anti-hero. The poet couldn't read the earthy ballad as anything less than holy "*chaunt,*" which worked "as a spell upon the hearer, and disarms the judgment." But even

---

95. Mark Canuel argues that *The Excursion* inevitably subordinates heterodoxy to the national church which "absorbs, encloses, and directs it" (*Religion, Toleration, and British Writing*, 163).
96. WV 1:121.
97. Jeffrey, "Wordsworth's *Excursion*," 4.
98. The octavo edition of 1820 performed better, selling out its run of 500 by 1824; see St. Clair, *Reading Nation*, 661–62.
99. [Hunt], *Examiner* 592 (May 2, 1819): 282. For a still useful compendium of the many parodies of *Peter Bell*, see A. E. H. Swann, "*Peter Bell*," *Anglia* 47 (1923): 136–84.

disarmed, Hazlitt's wit kept its edge. He mordantly scored the enthusiastic fit which rewrote the poet's body into contrarian gloss—"the comment made upon it by his face and voice was very different from that of some later critics!"—and finally collapsed fiction into an unexpectedly palpable autobiography: there "was something of a roll, a lounge in his gait, not unlike his own Peter Bell."[100]

Collegiate Methodism

Yet Wordsworth himself privately suggested that the vitality of his poetic vocation sprang from the communications between religious enthusiasm and establishmentarian orthodoxy, most strikingly in the unpublished autobiography. If *The Excursion* and the "Preface" shift the image of the "Poet" on a map of itinerant power, occupational rigor, irregular consecration, and polite decency, "Book Third" of *The Prelude* locates this map within the poet's self, and against the training ground of university education. In the 1805 telling, Wordsworth learns just what Cambridge was designed not to teach, the "higher language" of heart religion:

>   Of genius, power,
> Creation, and divinity itself,
> I have been speaking, for my theme has been
> What passed within me. Not of outward things
> Done visibly for other minds—words, signs,
> Symbols or actions—but of my own heart
> Have I been speaking, and my youthful mind. (1805 *Prelude* 3:171–77)

"Outward things," the practiced civilities of masculine gentility, have charms, as well as limits. But as this style of self is denominationally positioned—a Cambridge man is by necessity a churchman—so too is its critique. The turn from the public rituals of "signs" and "symbols," to the "divinity" of "my own heart," is the turn from Establishment to Dissent that elsewhere describes, at once playfully and quite seriously, the face-off between "loyal students faithful to their books" and "hardy recusants" (1805 *Prelude* 3:62–63). Accomplishment within the university entails the accommodation of its agenda, and when Wordsworth fails to emerge from Cambridge fully conditioned by the professional Anglicanism it institu-

---

100. *Complete Works of William Hazlitt*, 17:117–18.

tionalizes, he gives this emancipatory failure a doctrinal cast: not just a crypto-Catholic "recusancy," or a vague "nonconformity," but the Methodisms of spiritual calling and special powers, which constituted the university's most explicit antagonists.

Going up to Cambridge, Wordsworth recalls that "My spirit was up" likewise, a quiet equivocation that presents the Book's drift between an adolescent's boisterous accession to adulthood, and his embrace of more provocative spiritual inflations, discovered in the cloisters intended to evaporate such enthusiasm (1805 *Prelude* 3:16). Initially, the university encourages social life at the expense of the life of the mind or spirit, status rather than knowledge, and "politeness" is the real object of attention.

> [T]o myself I seemed
> A man of business and expense, and went
> From shop to shop about my own affairs,
> To tutors or to tailors as befel,
> From street to street with loose and careless heart . . .
> Strange transformation for a mountain youth,
> A northern villager. As if by word
> Of magic or some fairy's power, at once
> Behold me rich in monies and attired
> In splendid clothes, with hose of silk, and hair
> Glittering like rimy trees when frost is keen—
> My lordly dressing gown, I pass it by,
> With other signs of manhood which supplied
> The lack of beard. (1805 *Prelude* 3:23–27; 32–40)

In the passage's gentle self-mockery, the "mountain youth" reads the part of a "man of business," learning the "signs of manhood" and manly privilege as a callow parvenu, rather than to the manner born. Tutors and tailors, "as befel," are casually equivalent for a young man learning to be a gentleman—a study that begins by understanding gentility as an economic rhetoric as well as genetic inheritance, the mystification of the hard force of "monies" into the "magic" of "some fairy's power," and the recognition that purchasing power over the empty "signs" of silk, powder, and robe in fact constitutes maturity more completely than any "beard." The university's most valuable reading list covers the pressures, protocols, and exchanges that bond men with men—the "weekly round" of "invitations, suppers, wine, and fruit," all "Liberal and suiting gentleman's array" (1805 *Prelude* 3:40–43).

This generous spread is worldly, but it's Anglican, not secular, in color. The jumbled table is a still-life for the wider "motley spectacle" of Cambridge, and its cornucopia of "Gowns grave or gaudy, doctors, students, streets, / Lamps, gateways, flocks of churches, courts and towers" (1805 *Prelude* 3:29–31). Just as there's no hierarchy among tutors and tailors, churches join lamps and courts as one architecture of power among many, with neither peculiar attraction nor obvious sanctity, having lost their ministerial function: absent congregants, these "churches" stand as their own "flocks" in self-reflexive institutionalism. But this portrait of the Church—social rather than sacred, massively built and personally distant—is securely establishmentarian. Reasonable indifference is also good Anglicanism, which deliberately dampens the holy, and grants sacerdotal distinction only when unaccompanied by supernatural investment. Wordsworth impresses this lesson most deeply when, reeling from Milton's "apartments," the turn from poetical, spiritual and spirituous enthusiasms to "our chapel door" distills the "place itself and fashion of the rites" (1805 *Prelude* 3:297–315).

> Upshouldering in a dislocated lump
> With shallow ostentatious carelessness
> My surplice, gloried in and yet despised,
> I clove in pride through the inferior throng
> Of the plain burghers, who in audience stood
> On the last skirts of their permitted ground,
> Beneath the pealing organ. Empty thoughts,
> I am ashamed of them.... (1805 *Prelude* 3:316–23)

The rumpled "surplice" is a meticulously arranged metaphor for the Anglican priesthood, which "gloried in" material powers and responsibilities, "and yet despised" their derivation from thaumaturgical pretenses. The very "carelessness" of the ostentation reminds everyone involved that this isn't some divine parting of mystified priests from a credulously "inferior throng," but rather an explicitly—and merely—political division between "plain burghers" and privileged students. If it's all "empty thoughts" and "unworthy vanities" (1805 *Prelude* 3:327), spiritual vacuity and social surplus are the essential forms of establishment professionalism. A jauntily "dislocated lump" of clerical linens suits the Church's ideological fashion admirably.

Wordsworth shrinks from "the weakness of that hour" (1805 *Prelude* 3:326), partly out of moralizing antipathy, and partly out of a recognition that this cheerful veniality was always more mirage than promise. A clergyman ensconced in a comfortable living might have the luxury of playing the gentleman, letting the niceties of the Articles slip from attention better spent managing parishioners and parsonage. But it's a university Fellowship, not a rectory, that provokes "melancholy thoughts" over the stifling obligations and transformations necessary for "my future worldly maintenance" (1805 *Prelude* 3:75–78). Though it wasn't uncommon for Fellows eventually to retire to extramural livings, the position itself compounded the pressures of Anglican conformity with few of its relaxations. The ritualized license tacitly encouraged in students and many clerics would be forbidden by the Fellowship for which Wordsworth had "to hope without hope" (1805 *Prelude* 3:77), since it required wholehearted—and substantially more supervised—subscription to the Articles, and an assumption of celibacy as long as the position was held.[101] Wordsworth's "Cambridge" intensifies the aggravations of family expectations, academic strictures, and vocational determination with the prospect of ordination into one of the most spiritually and personally demanding roles within the Church. The price of admission to the teasing banquet of "signs of manhood" offered by the university is the internalization of Anglican vocational ideology at its most intense and uncompromising.

Unlike the "Preface," *The Prelude* rejects this path, while attempting to imagine a calling that might capture some of the heady promise of adult potency that had first excited the poet. In demonstrating his categorical unfitness for Anglican orthodoxy, Wordsworth erupts into its most violent opposite, sounding a series of extraordinary enthusiasms within the institutional heart of the establishment. Abandoning the social and economic foundations of Cambridge with some wit—"I was otherwise endowed" (1805 *Prelude* 3:93)—the poet "dare[s] to speak / A higher language" against the "unworthy vanities" of polite decorum (1805 *Prelude* 3:106–7). Wordsworth himself knew the "strangeness in my mind,"

> A feeling that I was not for that hour
> Nor for that place. But wherefore be cast down,
> Why should I grieve?—I was a chosen son.

---

101. Queen Elizabeth had barred Fellows from marriage in 1570, an ordinance repealed only after Wordsworth's death. Fellowships were often exchanged for parish livings in order to marry. Wesley, for example, resigned his position at Lincoln in 1751 in order to embark on a spectacularly miserable union, not out of any doctrinal difference from the Church.

> For hither had I come with holy powers
> And faculties, whether to work or feel ... (1805 *Prelude* 3:79–84)

This is vocational confidence, but its verbal tense is pure Methodism, repudiating the ideological ground of Cambridge. The University generated a reliable professionalism that might, as the culmination of a deliberate and replicable program of instruction, be dignified with formal sacerdotal powers—all while emphasizing such distinction as socially constructed, rather than naturally inherent. Wordsworth's arrival at Cambridge, *already* arrayed "with holy powers / And faculties" unsupervised by University or Church, resists the link between the two exactly as a Methodist might; puns on alternative "endowments" and "faculties," against the academic "learning, moral truth / Or understanding" of clerical identity, only strengthen the sympathy (1805 *Prelude* 3:91–92).

Sympathy—or at least opportunism. Wordsworth's enthusiastic turn isn't conversion: "Methodism" is a uniquely convenient rhetoric with which to enunciate separation from the demands of Anglican and professional conformity, not an object of attraction in itself. So it's no surprise when the poet is as skeptical of "holy powers," as of the fate from which they liberate. His argument may be hubris, but the grandeur is more Wesleyan than classical, and the anonymous carping of "some" evokes the abstracted ideological conventions that Wordsworth flaunts knowingly, and somewhat guiltily:

> Some called it madness; such indeed it was,
> If childlike fruitfulness in passing joy,
> If steady moods of thoughtfulness matured
> To inspiration, sort with such a name;
> If prophesy be madness; if things viewed
> By poets of old time, and higher up
> By the first men, earth's first inhabitants,
> May in these tutored days no more be seen
> With undisordered sight. But leaving this,
> It was no madness ... (1805 *Prelude* 3:147–56)

The distance between "old time" and "tutored days" is denominational as well as temporal, playing on an Anglicized modernity that's organized by an establishmentarian pedagogy designed to block things once viewed. Poetical community might be one thing—but communion with the "first men" was the sort of fraternizing university tutors took very seriously. For Paley, as we've seen, such connections were "injurious" and "disgusting." For Bishop Warburton, they were imaginary absurdities:

> These men read the History of the dispensations to the first Propagators of our holy Faith: They look with admiration on the privileges and powers conferred on those chosen Instruments: their imagination grows heated: they forget the difference between the *present* and the *past* Oeconomy of things; they seem to feel the impressions they read of; and they assume the airs, and mimic the Authority of Prophets and Apostles.[102]

With rhetorical daring, Wordsworth's own writing admits these reservations—"Some called it madness; such indeed it was"—so that they might be squelched, yet the obliquely concessionary "*if*"-syntax strings together qualifications that do as much harm as good. Within the Methodistical framing that provoked this outburst in the first place, "if prophesy be madness," and whether the spiritual vision of "earth's first inhabitants" still blessed "these tutored days" were hardly open questions for responsible thinkers, but rather the precise issues which divided the Ragged Legion from reasonable Christendom. Wordsworth's implied answers—"madness," *no;* "seen / With undisordered sight," *yes*—for queries left diplomatically rhetorical are diametrically opposed to those that might assuage worries over the moral threat of enthusiasm. The conclusion lamely grants as much, slinking away from an argument that only complicates itself in its execution, "leaving this" game of coy deflection: "It was no madness."

In its largest perspective, the spiritual election to which Wordsworth graduates exalts and embarrasses to equal degrees. If a Methodistical manner helps construct the poet's irregular authority, such manner can't be assumed in good society, whose reaction—"madness," not of the *genus irritabile vatum,* but of the muddy preacher—this passage easily forecasts. Preparing *The Prelude* for publication, Wordsworth revised what he couldn't resolve, attaching doctrinal qualifiers to some enthusiasms, canceling others entirely. The emendations of 1838–39 discard Cambridge's "chosen son," and bracket his enthusiasm with a parenthesis:

> But wherefore be cast down?
> For (not to speak of Reason and her pure

---

102. Warburton, *Doctrine of Grace,* 86.

> Reflective acts to fix the moral law
> Deep in the conscience nor of Christian Hope,
> Bowing her head before her sister Faith
> As one far mightier), hither I had come,
> Bear witness Truth, endowed with holy powers
> And faculties, whether to work or feel. (1850 *Prelude* 3:82–89)

The poetry of the parenthesis, spilling over five of the eight lines of this sentence, has its own effect, syntactically and ideologically overwhelming the "holy powers" that "endow" the poetical self, while retrospectively identifying the socio-doctrinal problem posed by its earlier version. This conflict of poetry and statement is the symptom of an epic negotiation of two politically divergent, but equally "spiritual" discourses. If, as we often hear, the poem of 1850 is more "religious," this is only a matter of being more establishmentarian, and less enthusiastic. But this is a difference between two of the nineteenth century's most substantial religious categories, not between the secular and the sacred, or the pantheistic and the orthodox. Much of the poem's restlessness, both in its initial incarnation, and in its sustained revision, springs from the poet's lifelong struggle with the enthusiasm that made *The Prelude* at once rhetorically arresting and culturally unacceptable. Wordsworth's corrections follow the pattern set by the changes to Book First: the "corresponding mild creative breeze," working the "power" of "storm" and "vernal promises" into "The holy life of music and verse," gets shifted into the high-church "punctual service high, / Matins and vespers, of harmonious verse!" (1805 *Prelude* 1:43–54; 1850 *Prelude* 1:44–45).

Wordsworth relied increasingly on ostentatiously churchy figures to neutralize the theo-political unorthodoxy that might be imputed to his verse. In the 1810s, Parliament was alarmed by census data showing the irregular houses of Dissenting worship superseding the cathedrals of Anglicanism. Yet Wordsworth opened *The Excursion* with a comfortingly immovable image, envisioning his poetry as a structure of scrupulous conformity:

> The preparatory poem is biographical, and conducts the history of the Author's mind to the point when he was emboldened to hope that his faculties were sufficiently mature for entering upon the arduous labour which he had proposed to himself; and the two Works have the same kind of relation to each other, if he may so express himself, as the antechapel has to the body of a gothic church. Continuing this allusion, he

may be permitted to add, that his minor Pieces, which have been long before the Public, when they shall be properly arranged, will be found by the attentive reader to have such a connection with the main Work as may give them claim to be likened to the little cells, oratories, and sepulchral recesses, ordinarily included in those edifices. (*Prose Works* 3:5–6)

Here is an architecture of perfect service to the national church, which stability Wordsworth prays will not be "madly overturned" by "the blinder rage / Of bigot zeal" (1814 *Excursion* 6:33–34). The "spiritual Fabric" of England's only (and fully Anglican) "Church" was "Founded in truth," and proceeds "In beauty of Holiness, with order'd pomp, / Decent and unreproved" (1814 *Excursion* 6:8–12).

Wordsworth's greatest affection, however, was reserved for his parish church, not the National—the humble yet "reverend Pile, / With bold projections and recesses deep" in Grasmere (1814 *Excursion* 8:461–62). Yet this too is fissured with national conflict, recreating within itself all the contests between establishment and enthusiasm that *The Excursion,* and ultimately *The Prelude,* worked over.

The interior of it has been improved lately—made warmer by under-drawing the roof and raising the floor, but the rude and antique majesty of its former appearance has been impaired by the painting of the rafters; and the oak benches, with a simple rail at the back dividing them from each other, have given way to seats that have more the appearance of pews. It is remarkable that, excepting only the pew belonging to Rydal Hall, that to Rydal Mount, the one to the Parsonage, and I believe another, the men and women still continue, as used to be the custom in Wales, to sit separate from each other. Is this practice as old as the Reformation? And when and how did it originate? In the Jewish synagogues and in Lady Huntingdon's Chapels the sexes are divided in the same way. (*PW* 5:443)

Smuggled in among the abandoned customs of the Welsh, the old practices of the Reformation, and the long history of the Jewish synagogues are the very recent, and very contentious chapels of Lady Huntingdon's Connexion, the division of the Methodist movement directed by George Whitefield. Here what would prove to be a familiar, conflicted practice in Wordsworth's verse asserts itself. While *The Excursion* loudly supports the Church of England, his private, long-unpublished recollections dote on this hidden chapel, which verges on the enthusiastic in its organization and practice. Yet even Wordsworth's admiration is ambiguous, as he keeps himself politely removed from the popular energies that otherwise fill the church: it's only the pews unaffiliated with the Wordsworth family, or the handful of other gentry, which are tainted with the possible Methodism of separated genders.

The need to discriminate Establishment from enthusiasm, both in Wordsworth's poetry and in the nation at large, faded as Dissent rose "from contemptible insignificance to the full flower of Victorian Nonconformity," providing England with a new set of religious norms.[103] Jeffrey's campaign against Methodistical excess was gradually abandoned, and Wordsworth's press went from friendly to fetishistic, as *Blackwood's* found in "his most felicitous poetry" a second Scripture, rivaling "the most touching and beautiful passages in the Sacred Page."[104] Despite its revisions, *The Prelude* may have changed less than its England, and it's the poem's richest irony to have been greeted at its Victorian publication in the terms that would have been its Georgian scandal. F. D. Maurice heard in it "the dying utterance of the half century we have just passed through, the expression—the English expression at least—of all that self-building process in which, according to their different schemes and principles, Byron, Goethe, Wordsworth, the Evangelicals (Protestant and Romanist), were all engaged."[105]

---

103. Lovegrove, *Established Church, Sectarian People,* 14.
104. "Essays on the Lake School of Poetry, No. I. Wordsworth's *White Doe of Rylstone,*" *Blackwood's Edinburgh Magazine* 3 (July 1818): 369–81 (371).
105. *The Life of Frederick Denison Maurice,* ed. Frederick Maurice, 2 vols. (New York: Scribner, 1884), 2:59.

Chapter 4

Sage or Sibyl?

A Lay Sermon

The Regency judged the *Lay Sermons* by their covers, or, at least, their titles, and I'd like to read this superficiality as the texture of "Coleridge" for much of the nineteenth century. We've come to know the depths of both *Sermons* well enough—so well, I think, that we've come to mistake what matters most about them. Containing some of Coleridge's most arcane thoughts on continental philosophy, Trinitarian Christianity, conservative politics, and the ultimate identity of all three when each is properly conceived, the *Lay Sermons*, and *The Statesman's Manual* especially, borrow much of their modern reputation from the seminal work on symbol, allegory, and ideology they've provoked.[1] The consolidated reception of the keynote passages is as sophisticated as, and often more systematic than, the *Sermons* themselves, which may be most familiar now through the unrepresentative (and stabilizing) extracts in popu-

---

1. For example, Paul de Man, "The Rhetoric of Temporality," in *Blindness and Insight: Essays in the Rhetoric of Contemporary Criticism*, 2nd ed. (Minneapolis: University of Minnesota Press, 1983), 187–228; Jerome McGann, *The Romantic Ideology*, 1–14; Susan J. Wolfson, *Formal Charges*, 63–99.

lar anthologies. Both *Sermons* can be self-defeatingly crabbed, and neither quite lives up to the devoted praise of their editor as "models of rigorous thinking and penetrating analysis."[2] But in spite—and often because—of their argumentative difficulty, the *Sermons* arrest close attention.

In this, they preserve the drama of their initial appearance. Published in late 1816 and early 1817, before the *Biographia, Sibylline Leaves,* and *The Friend* had been able to stagger into print or reprint, the *Lay Sermons* were Coleridge's debut as the Sage of Highgate. The role had a long run, albeit to mixed reviews. In 1853, the American W. G. T. Shedd confidently hawked the Sage of the *Sermons* as a metaphysical cure-all, a pool of "deep and brooding reflection," whose water had "stimulated and strengthened" the admittedly "lesser number" able to peer into its profundity.[3] Two years earlier, Carlyle—with less genial quackery—recalled Coleridge as the font of "speculations," which had "a charm almost religious and prophetic . . . to the ardent young mind, instinct with pious nobleness, yet driven to the grim deserts of Radicalism for a faith."[4] For the earliest Coleridgeans, these two slim *Sermons* formed the core of their Master's teachings. Shedd wagered the success of his *Complete Works of Coleridge* on the appeal of a lead volume consisting of *The Statesman's Manual* and *Aids to Reflection,* rather than crowd-pleasing "Rimes," and poetry would play a diminished role in this trans-Atlantic rehabilitation. In 1839, Henry Nelson Coleridge brought his uncle and father-in-law to the "ingenuous but less experienced reader," with a My-First-Coleridge edition of the *Lay Sermons* and *On the Constitution of Church and State,* his editorial apparatus translating the "fundamental and more complicated portion of the work."[5]

This alignment of the "fundamental" with the "more complicated" would spin as the axis of Coleridge studies long after the nineteenth century. The gnomic obscurity of the *Lay Sermons* only made "Coleridge" more plausible as "the personification of religious wisdom."[6] This is Tim

---

2. *Lay Sermons,* ed. R. J. White (London: Routledge & Kegan Paul; Princeton, NJ: Princeton University Press, 1972), xxx. Hereafter cited in-text as LS.

3. W. G. T. Shedd, "Introductory Essay upon His Philosophical and Theological Opinions," in *The Complete Works of Samuel Taylor Coleridge,* ed. Professor Shedd, 7 vols. (New York: Harper and Brothers, 1853), 1:9–62 (25, 9).

4. Thomas Carlyle, *The Life of John Sterling,* 2nd ed. (London: Chapman and Hall, 1852 [1851]), 75.

5. Henry Nelson Coleridge, "Preface to the Church and State," in Samuel Taylor Coleridge, *I. On the Constitution of the Church and State, According to the Idea of Each; II. Lay Sermons,* ed. Henry Nelson Coleridge (London: William Pickering, 1839), ix–xxix (xi).

6. Tim Fulford, *Coleridge's Figurative Language* (New York: St. Martin's, 1991), 130.

Fulford's trope—but such personification wasn't entirely figural. Though much of Coleridge is "riddled with a certain ventriloquism of the divine," it's the first *Lay Sermon,* writes Ian Balfour, "that most resolutely," and most earnestly, "adopts a prophetic stance."[7] But this "prophetic stance," while imposing, could shift on its self-sanctified ground. Coleridge, visionary Father of philosophy and philosophic men, could take on the visage of an unlettered yokel turned preacher, or even that of a bloated village wisewoman berating her betters, and this chapter reveals Coleridge's unsteady efforts to harness these socio-sexual tensions as novel sources of cultural energy in the *Lay Sermons.*

"Lay Sermon," I'll argue, names the unlikely transfer between oracular utterance and plebeian presumption that—for a time, anyway—constituted Coleridge's reputation. After the normalizations of two centuries of scholarship, we've lost sight of the calculated offensiveness of the *Sermons,* the provocations to good taste and good sense that shaped their historical meaning, and entirely determined their initial reception. The "Sage" has visibly endured, but in the Regency, his heroics depended—or at least played—on the disastrous enthusiasms of the "Sibyl," Joanna Southcott, and the Methodistical zeal of "lay sermons." The consequence was not just incoherent, but something like a theory of incoherence, as the *Lay Sermons* continually wrecked their own authority in disreputable spiritualisms, while cobbling together an unexpected vitality from this demolition. The *Sermons* were a game of give-and-take between orthodoxy and heterodoxy, Tory and Methodist, Sage and Sibyl—a game they played without ever fully mastering the rules, as their revisions between 1816 and 1839 would concede.

My story runs against one of Coleridge's own. *The Statesman's Manual,* after all, made an emphatic case for "the *distinctness* of our knowledge," and such "*distinctness*" was usually never clearer than in Coleridge's work on "enthusiasm" (*LS* 23). "Enthusiasm" was subjected to one of his most sustained desynonymizations, as the second chapter of the *Biographia,* the "Author's Appendix" concluding *On the Constitution of Church and State,* and several important marginal glosses partitioned benevolent psychosocial elevation from its miserable double, "fanaticism."[8] But Coleridge's distinctions weren't always so neat in the

---

7. Ian Balfour, *The Rhetoric of Romantic Prophecy* (Stanford, CA: Stanford University Press, 2002), 250–51.

8. The marginalia to Walter Birch, *Sermon on the Prevalence of Infidelity and Enthusiasm* [1818], contains a major reflection on that "practice of all scientific men, whether naturalists or metaphysicians, and the dictate of common sense, that one word ought to

Lay Sermons, as the unequivocal Methodism of their titles kept any argument for difference under the sign of stubborn identification. Both *Sermons* were thoroughly conflicted: they preached reactionary politics and sociocultural purity in a form that was the by-word for sedition, heterodoxy induced by ignorance, and an enthusiasm undermining the last decencies of the public sphere. They presented the most acute symptom of the very cultural pathology they diagnosed, screeds against "a popular philosophy and a philosophic populace" that named themselves after one of the most outrageous examples of plebified discourse in the history of English Protestantism (*LS* 38).

This ideological and formal contradiction is the most salient, and the least critically reported, attribute of the *Sermons*. Coleridge himself quickly came to regret it, admitting to John Murray in 1817 that "Laysermon" was a "most unfortunate name."[9] He was even more apologetic with Dr. Brabant a few months earlier, evading generic identity, as well as the definite article: "I attempted to dictate a something that is coming out; what you will think of it, I cannot conjecture."[10] But conjectural indeterminacy was both abject excuse and organizing principle for the *Lay Sermons*. The *Sermons* finally argued for the power to cancel argument: for the genuinely mysterious authority of statements that mean the opposite of what they say, and of authors who are the opposite of who they claim to be. They attempted to figure a writing so flexible it might bend enthusiasm into order, while contemplating the anarchies within the principles of cultural organization. As we'll see, the *Sermons* wore their contradictions on their front pages, with tag-lines—"the Bible the Best Guide," and "Blessed are ye"—that cryptically touched on keywords dear to ultraconservatives as well as prophetic revolutionaries.

These gymnastics don't make the *Lay Sermons* less reactionary, or more radical, than they're usually assumed to be. Their conservative *bona fides* are substantial, and they rarely do more than flirt with subversion. But they are scrambled in argument and effect, and their weird extrem-

---

have but one meaning" (*Marginalia* 1:495). Jon Mee identifies the desynonymization of "enthusiasm" as the analytical register for social control and political differentiation in Coleridge: "[t]o keep its value, inspiration for Coleridge had to be properly regulated. By the end of his life . . . he had come to believe only the institutional authority of the Church could provide the security he sought from the vicissitudes of the 'low-born mind.' . . . The reliance on institutional authority as a restraint on the excess of enthusiasm is the classic Anglican position in the discourse on regulation" (*Romanticism, Enthusiasm, and Regulation*, 135–36).

9. 27 February 1817, *Collected Letters of Samuel Taylor Coleridge*, 4:706.
10. 21 September 1816, *Collected Letters of Samuel Taylor Coleridge*, 4:673.

ism is bound up in weirder enthusiasm. The result is an intellectual recalcitrance that refuses nice summary. Both texts perform a certain style of writing, reading, and ruling, without quite making a case for coherent philosophical principles or reliable conclusions, and the life and afterlife of this style is my real subject. The *Lay Sermons* are political and rhetorical oxymorons, daring the conflation of refinement with vulgarity, recondite wisdom with senseless jargon, plebeian with clerical culture—and they darkly hint that the negative capability of this daring, rather than the practice of nuanced division, is the best evidence of a supple mind and subtle society.

Sage

Coleridge's middle-aged orthodoxy can seem absolute. The "Sage" is evangelical only in that he has a palpable design upon us, and patriarchal benevolence doesn't fully soften his cultural and political authoritarianism. This gregarious aggression still manages most readings of the *Sermons*—Coleridge, in fact, thought of a "Lay Sermon" as the formalization of managed reading. "Appendix A" of *The Statesman's Manual* "presuppose[d] on the part of the reader or hearer, a humble and docile state of mind," repositioning the potential critique of the anonymous "reader" as the intimate submission of the amiable "hearer," moving deracinated text into the immediacy of conversation (*LS* 55). Yet as Coleridge marginalized in Southey's copy of the second *Lay Sermon,* this audience—fit because few—could be a mirage: "From how few dare a Writer hope for the trouble of reading a page aloud, distinctly, and to their own ears and understandings!" (*LS* 139n1). If the communion between the "Writer" and those "few" on the "page aloud" was slow to materialize, the proselytized often chalked it up to the narcissistic echo of the voice and the voiced text, both more interested in deference than participation, in the capitalized dominance of "Writer" over "reader or hearer," Preacher over "ears and understandings." Even the camelion poet had trouble changing his colors fast enough to match the mercurial shifts of a man supposedly without negative capability.[11] Coleridge's "talk," groused Carlyle,

---

11. As Keats wrote to George and Georgiana Keats, "I took a Walk towards highgate and in the lane that winds by the side of Lord Mansfield's park I met Mr Green our Demonstrator at Guy's in conversation with Coleridge—I joined them, after enquiring by a look whether it would be agreeable—I walked with him a[t] his alderman-after dinner pace for near two miles I suppose In those two Miles he broached a thousand things—let me see

was "always, virtually or literally, of the nature of a monologue; suffering no interruption, however reverent. . . . To sit as a passive bucket and be pumped into, whether you consent or not, can in the long-run be exhilarating to no creature; how eloquent soever the flood of utterance that is descending."[12]

Drenched by this flood, Coleridge's disciples came to treat his droughts as particularly fertile, refreshed by those moments when his arguments dammed themselves up altogether. The Sage "embarrassed or irritated" even (and especially) those who have loved him, writes Jerome Christensen.[13] But for those whose affection became a kind of worship, who received the scattering of his writing as a sacramental "blessedness," Coleridge's worst was his best, incarnate in those half-finished, sometimes barely begun "jointless sentences" of hints, regrets, and apprehensions offered up in the middle of *On the Constitution of Church and State* in order to "excite a certain class of readers to desire or to supply the commentary."[14] While the steadfast Gillman confessed "I desire but cannot supply it" (*CCS* 58n1), for the "certain class," the blindness of the Sage brought on the insight of his initiates. Soon after his death, "Coleridge" summoned a club of meaning, a collaborative alternative to the alienated exchange of ideas in commodified print.

When Henry Nelson Coleridge conceded in *On the Constitution of Church and State* and the *Lay Sermons* "a want of detailed illustration and express connexion, which weakens the impression of the entire work on the generality of readers," he meant to train those outside the "generality" to understand this as strength rather than defect.[15] This, he assured a wary audience, was the obscure sublimity of his uncle's mental syntax, which stimulated the recipient to correct, extend, and sometimes entirely intuit arguments that appeared only in sociable interaction. This autho-

---

if I can give you a list—Nightingales, Poetry—on Poetical Sensation—Metaphysics—Different genera and species of Dreams—Nightmare—a dream accompanied with by a sense of touch—single and double touch—A dream related—First and second consciousness—the difference explained between will and Volition—so my [many] metaphysicians from a want of smoking the second consciousness—Monsters—the Kraken—Mermaids—Southey believes in them—Southey's belief too much diluted—A Ghost story—Good morning—I heard his voice as he came towards me—I heard it as he moved away—I had heard it all the interval—if it may be called so." Letter 14 Feb–3 May 1819, in *John Keats: A Longman Cultural Edition*, ed. Susan J. Wolfson (New York: Pearson Longman, 2006), 245.

12. Carlyle, *Life of Sterling*, 72.
13. Jerome Christensen, *Coleridge's Blessed Machine of Language*, 120.
14. *On the Constitution of Church and State*, ed. John Colmer (Princeton, NJ: Princeton University Press, 1976), 58. Hereafter cited in-text as *CCS*.
15. Henry Nelson Coleridge, "Preface to the Church and State," ix.

rial "want" should be the desideratum of the knowing reader, a lack preventing him—and the reader is determinately gendered—from sliding into mere consumer.[16] In the spirit of Coleridgean cooperation, Henry Nelson Coleridge took F. D. Maurice's evaluation of *On the Constitution of Church and State* as his own:

> When I use the word satisfactory, I do not mean that it will satisfy the wishes of any person . . . who expects an author to furnish him with a complete system which he can carry away in his memory, and, after it has received a few improvements from himself, can hawk it about to the public or to a set of admiring disciples. Men of this description would regard Mr. Coleridge's book as disorderly and fragmentary; but those who have some notion of what Butler meant when he said, that the best writer would be he who merely stated his premises, and left his readers to work out the conclusions for themselves;—those who feel that they want just the assistance which Socrates offered to his scholars—assistance, not in providing them with thoughts, but in bringing forth into the light thoughts which they had within them before; these will acknowledge that Mr. Coleridge has only deserted the common high way of exposition, that he might follow more closely the turnings and windings which the mind of an earnest thinker makes when it is groping after the truth to which he wishes to conduct it. To them, therefore, the book is satisfactory by reason of those very qualities which make it alike unpleasant to the formal schoolman and to the man of the world.[17]

---

16. Even with the dedicated editorial and critical efforts of his daughter, those who valued Coleridge's philosophy later in the nineteenth century most often valued it as a technology for raising young men up into a masculinized maturity. But Coleridge, argues Anthony John Harding, tended to represent a crisis of masculine collapse for everyone not won over by his persona as Sage/Father; see Harding, "Gendering the Poet-Philosopher: Victorian 'Manliness' and Coleridgean 'Androgyny,'" in *Coleridge's Afterlives,* ed. James Vigus and Jane Wright (Basingstoke: Palgrave Macmillan, 2008), 65–84. Certainly William Mitchell, one of his most motivated opponents in mid-century America, suggested that Coleridge's only parallel with Socrates was predatory, an addiction to corrupting the Youth with an adolescently queer metaphysics, which should be rejected in the name of a bluff, commonsensical masculinity and unpretentiously orthodox Christianity: "This definition of an idea, making darkness more dark, with all that is said about supersensuous faculties, provokes a complacent laugh as we hear the master and his beardless disciples (for few men of sober age are caught in such a web of mysticism) chafe at our ignorance of his impenetrable system of ethics, and our incapacity to understand it; but really such philosophy, despite our utmost charity, seems to us to be a compound, in Alligation Alternate, of nothingness, mist, and a few grains of truth; and the more we ask for light, the more are we involved in obscurity" [William Mitchell], *Coleridge and the Moral Tendency of his Writings* (New York: Levitt and Trow, 1844), 35.

17. Maurice, *Kingdom of Christ* (1838), in Henry Nelson Coleridge, "Preface to the

For Professor Shedd, this joint activity meant that reading Coleridge was, inevitably, editing him: "the philosophy of Coleridge must be *gathered* from his writings rather than *quoted* from them, and hence the difficulty for the critic which does not exist in the instance of a rounded and finished treatise, to determine the real form and matter of his system."[18]

In its "real form and matter"—in the whole of its essence, then—the Coleridgean "system" was determined by its "critic," without whom it "does not exist." One hundred and fifty years on, Shedd's editorial metaphysic has life in it yet. Elinor Shaffer's reading of Coleridge and the textual practices of the Higher Criticism in *"Kubla Khan" and "The Fall of Jerusalem"* archly takes its title from Coleridge's most famous poems interrupted and never started,[19] while J. Robert Barth regards his *Coleridge and Christian Doctrine* as reconstructive surgery, "an attempt to present in an organized way, as Coleridge himself did not, his matured views on Christian doctrine."[20] But Coleridge was the first to recognize this shared author-function, in a conditional proof of his conditional style of publishing without publicity:

> I am abused, & insolently reproved, as a man, with reference to my supposed private Habits, for *not publishing* . . . but I *could* rebut the charge, & not merely say but prove—that there is not a man in England, whose Thoughts, Images, Words & Erudition have been published in larger quantities than *mine*—tho', I must admit, not *by* or *for* myself.[21]

"*Mine*," but "not *by* or *for* myself": the practice of writing for Socrates, Jesus, and Samuel Taylor Coleridge. This sublime humility has bound the "Sage" to his students for almost two hundred years, tallying the property under consideration—whether notes left in someone else's book, or speculations recomposed by editorial speculation—as both "Coleridge" and "text," a critical communion allegorized in the question heralding the consummation of the *Opus Maximum* in 2002: "Why is it necessary to discuss a work that does not even exist, and to do so at great length?"[22]

Church and State," x–xi.
    18. Shedd, "Introductory Essay," 10.
    19. Elinor Shaffer,*"Kubla Khan'" and "The Fall of Jerusalem": The Mythological School in Biblical Criticism and Secular Literature, 1770–1880* (Cambridge: Cambridge University Press, 1975).
    20. J. Robert Barth, S.J., *Coleridge and Christian Doctrine* (Cambridge, MA: Harvard University Press, 1969), vii.
    21. Letter to Daniel Stuart, 12 September 1814, in *Collected Letters*, 3:532.
    22. *Opus Maximum*, ed. Thomas McFarland, with the assistance of Nicholas Halmi, (Princeton, NJ: Princeton University Press, 2002), xiii.

This alliance between hierophant and clerisy—between unfinished writing, and reading between the lines—was the complex of Coleridge's conservatism. Coleridgeans might call it "scholarship." Coleridge's name for it was "Lay Sermon":

> When I named this Essay a Sermon, I sought to prepare the inquirers after it for the absence of all the usual softenings suggested by worldly prudence, of all compromise between truth and courtesy. But not even as a Sermon would I have addressed the present Discourse to a promiscuous audience; and for this reason I likewise announced it in the title-page, as exclusively *ad clerum;* i.e. (in the old and wide sense of the word) to men of clerkly acquirements, of whatever profession. I would the greater part of our publications could be thus directed, each to its appropriate class of Readers. But this cannot be! For among other odd burs and kecksies, the misgrowth of our luxuriant activity, we have now a READING PUBLIC—as strange a phrase, methinks, as ever forced a splenetic smile on the staid countenance of Meditation; and yet no fiction! (*LS* 35–37)

In the first (and for years, the only) congenial response to the *Lay Sermons,* Henry Crabb Robinson applauded these clean discriminations, since "too many readers presume that they are written for in every book they take in hand, and too many writers aspire to the rare glory of addressing, with effect, readers of every description."[23] Right thinking, Coleridge confided to John Gibson Lockhart, was co-extensive with right breeding, and an address "to the Higher Classes of Society" synonymous with "to the Learned."[24]

The careful epistemology of the *Lay Sermons,* then, was politics by another name, and demographics in masquerade, since the generalizing power of the universalizing Reason was socially particular in composition. In preaching to "men in whom I may hope to find, if not philosophy, yet occasional impulses at least to philosophic thought," Coleridge intoned, "I appeal exclusively to men from whose station and opportunities I may dare anticipate a respectable portion of that '*sound book learnedness,*' into which our old public schools still continue to initiate their pupils" (*LS* 39). As this argument unfolded, in the *Lay Sermons* and later, the philosophical rigor of the initiated pupil became the grammar of social control. The

---

23. [Henry Crabb Robinson], "Coleridge's *Statesman's Manual,*" in *Critical Review* 5.1 (January 1817): 42–48 (42).

24. Coleridge's marginalia from Lockhart's presentation copy (Copy L): "So it was ordered to be printed, and so, I believe, it was advertised" (*Lay Sermons,* 3–4n1).

well-ordered mind ordered a flourishing cultural domain, which ordered the cultivated nation, which ordered its best minds with "a respectable portion of that '*sound book learnedness*'" still lingering at Eton, Harrow, and perhaps Christ's Hospital. Here was the loop of mutual reformation and superintendence, of "equipoise and interdependency," the "*lex equilibri*" that Coleridge would ultimately identify as the real "constitution" of Church, State, and subject (*CCS* 23).

Within this equilibrium, cultural disruptions were urgently political in mode of effect and means of redress. The *Lay Sermons* introduced Coleridge's conviction that unchecked discourse, "the evils of a rank and unweeded Press" (*LS* 151), was cause, not consequence, of "the Existing Distresses and Discontents" announced on the title page of the second *Sermon*. It was "among the miseries of the present age that it recognizes no medium between *Literal* and *Metaphorical*" (*LS* 30). But this meant that the miseries of the present age should be recognized as representational rather than material, since compelling narrative—organizing consciousness as prelude to organizing men—was more dangerous than the hardest fact: "[w]here distress is felt, tales of wrong and oppression are readily believed. . . . Rage and Revenge make the cheek pale and the hand tremble, *worse than even want itself*" (*LS* 163). Even *On the Constitution of Church and State*, witnessing the apocalyptic failure of the Anglican order, still girded itself for combat with a modern Beast. The real Dragon wasn't the old hierarchy of Roman superstition, but the "Reading Public," "the present much-reading, but not very hard-reading age" sapping the nation's fiber, a "Public" Coleridge solemnly placed alongside the Pope within "the Third Possible Church, Neither National nor Universal, or the CHURCH OF ANTICHRIST" (*CCS* 134).

Though this argument would climax in 1829, it began fifteen years earlier with the *Lay Sermons*. They stand, in almost every recent critical account, as the most complete genre of the Romantic Ideology, the idealization of a readership harmoniously attuned to their own self-representations, as reading and representation become the final form of political expression. For Jerome McGann, the *Lay Sermons* propose a "clearly deplorable . . . conceptual-idealist defense of Church, State, and the class interests which those institutions support and defend,"[25] while Lucy Newlyn finds them "a kind of Malthusian nightmare" of a country "overrun by a new race of unreflecting, unspiritual readers."[26] The *Sermons*,

---

25. McGann, *Romantic Ideology*, 5.
26. Lucy Newlyn, *Reading, Writing, and Romanticism*, 55. This population boom, according to Jon Klancher, was checked by only the superintendence of the newly theorized

on David Riede's map, are the pious turn "from poetic anxieties to critical certitudes," the maturation (or senescence) of a prose which "literally glosses . . . over" the "uncertainties and anxieties" that had agitated Coleridge's youthful verse, politics, and faith.[27] But what has become critically normative would have surprised the Regency, where "lay sermons"—and Coleridge's in particular—were understood as just the sort of demotic writing and bad speech threatening the nation.

Sibyl

By the time of the *Lay Sermons,* Coleridge had returned to the faith of his vicar father, and was once again a loyal son of the Church of England. He had precisely dated his abandonment of Unitarianism to one-thirty in the afternoon, 12 February 1805,[28] and his Trinitarianism had only deepened over a period of intense personal crisis in late 1813 and early 1814. J. Robert Barth describes this as a second "kind of conversion,"[29] and Coleridge's soteriology hardened into an increasingly uncompromising Calvinism.[30] But no amount of private conformity could make "the genre

---

clerisy, an institutionalized bulwark of reading and writing "capable of governing the relations between all the emerging audiences of the nineteenth century over whom, individually, no institution could claim control" (*Making of English Reading Audiences,* 151). Robert Keith Lapp has persuasively argued that the *Lay Sermons* attempt to interrupt any "projection into nineteenth-century print culture of the universalizing and democratizing ideals of the coffeehouse culture of the eighteenth-century public sphere"; they instead endorse a "withdrawal into visionary idealism that locates cultural authority in the attractive figure of the poet-prophet" (*Contest for Cultural Authority: Hazlitt, Coleridge, and the Distresses of the Regency* [Detroit, MI: Wayne State University Press, 1999], 12).

27. David G. Riede, *Oracles and Hierophants,* 173.

28. This notebook entry was more sure in its time-stamp than its "Conviction," however, haltingly recording what Coleridge wished to believe, rather than what he did: "No Christ, No God!—This I now feel with all its needful evidence, of the Understanding: would to God, my spirit were made to conform thereto—that No Trinity, no God . . . O that this Conviction may work upon me and in me/and that my mind may be made up as to the character of Jesus, and of historical Christianity, as clearly as it is Christ the Logos and intellectual or spiritual Christianity." *Notebooks of Samuel Taylor Coleridge,* 2:2448.

29. Barth, *Coleridge and Christian Doctrine,* 24n25; see also Barth, "Coleridge and the Church of England," 291–307.

30. In 1813, he bleakly confessed to Thomas Roberts, "our souls are infinite in depth, and therefore our sins are infinite, and redeemable only by an infinitely higher infinity; that of the Love of God in Christ Jesus. I have called my soul infinite, but O infinite in the depth of darkness, an infinite craving, an infinite capacity of pain and weakness, and excellent only as being passively capacious of the light from above . . . O God save me—save me from myself. . . . " (c.19 December 1813, *Collected Letters of Samuel Taylor Coleridge,*

of 'Layman's Sermon' . . . underscore" an "alignment with Tory ideology" and "a pious adherence to the doctrinal authority of the Established Church."[31] From the instantiation of the Clarendon Code in the 1660s, until the amendment of the Act of Uniformity in 1872, the requirements which defined the Church of England in its broadest sense were assent to the Book of Common Prayer, and consent to the episcopal ordination of priests,[32] this latter clause directly forbidding lay preaching within the Anglican communion. In 1824, Southey's *Book of the Church* still celebrated the collapse of nonconforming excess in the 1680s, when the "crazier sects disappeared; and lay preaching, from which so many evils had arisen, was no longer heard of, except among the Quakers."[33] For most of the eighteenth and early nineteenth centuries, churchmen and "reasonable" Dissenters were united in considering "lay sermons" contemptible violations of sound theology and polite society.[34]

Coleridge's *Lay Sermons* exhorted the nation to Fear God, and Honor the King, but their generic history rattled the cage their argument tried to lock shut. The result was politically and tonally akin to the intellectual "muddle" Seamus Perry locates elsewhere in Coleridge's philosophy, that special "kind of comprehensiveness" found only in a "kind of contradictoriness," which took irreconcilable differences, rather than their

---

3:463); by the middle of 1820, he was marginalizing in the *Reliquiae Baxterianae* that the "introduction (& after-predominance) of Latitudinarianism <under the name of> Arminianism," was one of "the grand Evil Epochs of the our present Church," and he anticipated a moment when "*Arminianism,* will be regarded as to express a habit of Belief opposed not to Calvinism or the Works of Calvin, but to the Articles of our own Church, and to the Doctrine in which *all* the first Reformers agreed" (*Marginalia,* 1:358).

31. Lapp, *Contest for Cultural Authority,* 55.
32. Rivers, *Reason, Grace and Sentiment,* 1:32.
33. Southey, *Book of the Church,* 2:475.
34. Anna Barbauld, for instance, was clear that her popularizing *Civic Sermons* made no appeal to the promiscuous audience of Methodist lay preaching. "You are invited, therefore, by those who wish the welfare of their country, and your welfare, to gain just ideas of what concerns it; for, by having false ideas, you may do much harm: but do not mistake me, you are not *all* invited. You who are dissolute, idle, intemperate, savage in your manners, profligate in your principles, without care for yourselves, or for those who depend upon your labour; who prey upon the honest industry of others; who are ignorant, not merely from want of information, but from a debased and besotted understanding—to you I do not speak, you *must* be governed like brutes; for you *are* brutes. You own no law, cannot judge of laws. You *must* be slaves, not thro' the appointment of men, but by the eternal laws of nature." Only those men who, "in whatever rank of life you are," managed to conform to middle-class respectability—"you who have a love of order, a sense of ingenuous shame, a relish for the conveniencies and decencies which civilized life affords"—were admitted to her text and her state. [Anna Barbauld], *Civic Sermons to the People, Number 1* (London: J. Johnson, 1792), 17–19.

dialectical solutions, as the grand labor of "a real, though ruinous, kind of genius."[35] Ruinous, but also self-ruined. If the idea of "Coleridge," especially in its highest mode, depended on the help of others, that handful of men investing their own intelligence and dignity in order to compound both in accounts of the "Sage," the *Lay Sermons* prevented that transaction, identifying instead with a company of preachers, prophets, and madwomen at the very bottom of the "READING PUBLIC," when they were literate at all.

This set of guilty associations made Coleridge appear as one of the most farcical enthusiasts in recent history. Though he would be rescued by the middle of the nineteenth century, what impressed many of his readers in the aftermath of the *Lay Sermons* was that he didn't much want to be rescued. On the contrary, Coleridge was engaged in a sustained effort to advertise Methodistical sympathies even to those who had little reason to suspect them in the first place. For years, he had dreamed: "Socinianism, moonlight; Methodism, a stove. O for some sun to unite heat and light!"[36]

The *Lay Sermons* were not this celestial union of reason and enthusiasm, genteel sense and vigorous sensibility—not in their reception, nor, I think, in their intention. They presented instead deliberate, but incompletely managed, provocations to misreading, burying their most reactionary arguments in enthusiastic code, and flaunting rhetorical extravagances alien to their reactionary agenda, while offering these misdirections as a misrecognized, but absolute, sort of cultural prowess.

Though Coleridge's would be put to more flexible uses, "lay sermons" were rigid parsers for the nation's denominations. Evangelicals within the Church often had mainly disciplinary, rather than doctrinal, differences from Calvinist Methodists outside it, and for many years, Claphamite disdain for lay preaching was the major division between Evangelicalisms that less "awakened" churchmen could detect. Rational Dissent, in demographic decay if not intellectual quiescence from the end of the seventeenth century, armored its ministers with a depth of learning and middle-class respectability that certified they were governed by most of the ideological

---

35. Seamus Perry, *Coleridge and the Uses of Division* (Oxford: Clarendon, 1999), 25; 2.

36. *Notebooks of Samuel Taylor Coleridge*, 1:467. Coleridge voiced a similar (and more clearly political) sentiment in his 1795 *Lectures*, early experiments in a kind of rationalist lay preaching: "He would appear to me to have adopted the best as well as the most benevolent mode of diffusing Truth, who uniting the zeal of the Methodist with the views of the Philosopher, should be *personally* among the Poor, and teach them their *Duties* in order that he may render them susceptible of their *Rights*." *Lectures 1795, On Politics and Religion*, ed. Lewis Patton and Peter Mann (London: Routledge & Kegan Paul, 1971), 43.

pressures that episcopal ordination was meant to signify. Until the end of the eighteenth century, the Methodists were largely unique in sending forth their lay cohort of (in Southey's taxonomy from 1804) "tradesmen of the lowest orders, bakers, barbers and taylors, perhaps servants or labourers" to preach.[37]

Moreover, the insubordination of the Wesleyans only grew more flagrant as the Society grew in strength and its leader in confidence. It was aggravating enough when Wesley deputized hundreds of inadequately educated preachers to move about the country and colonies, but toward the end of his life he began to assume, rather than simply flout, episcopal authority. In 1763, he relied upon an obscure foreigner who spoke no English but claimed to be the exiled Bishop of Crete to ordain his chosen preachers, "upon the principle," which somewhat anticipated by confused parody Coleridge's own sense of *enclesia* and *ecclesia*, "that whoever is episcopally ordained, is a minister of the church universal, and as such has the right to officiate in any part of the globe."[38] By the end of the century, the Methodists were even bolder. In 1784, Wesley ordained Thomas Coke bishop for the "Methodist Church of England in America," on the grounds that these adjectival and prepositional qualifications were security enough against the charge of usurping the powers of the Lords Spiritual; in 1785, he ordained men for service in Scotland, but commanded them to resume the dress and title of lay preachers upon crossing back into England. This delicate balance held for a few years, but by 1789, Wesley had completed his own revolution, cooking up a complicated precedent from the early Church in Alexandria, which made him "as much a Christian bishop as the Archbishop of Canterbury," authorizing him to ordain men in and for England.[39]

The Methodists presented the Establishment with an increasingly pressing conundrum. While the lay preaching by ignorant men clearly eroded one of the two pillars of the Church of England, to which many Wesleyans still professed their support, the Methodist solution—that these men were not lay preachers at all, but just as canonically ordained as any Anglican deacon—traded presumption for schism. The conflict over the

---

37. [Robert Southey], "Myles's History of the Methodists," in *The Annual Review, and History of Literature; for 1803*, ed. Arthur Aikin, vol. 2 (London: Longman and Rees, 1804), 201–13 (210). For experiments in itinerancy and some varieties of lay preaching among other Dissenting denominations during the Romantic period, see Lovegrove, *Established Church, Sectarian People*.

38. Southey, "Myles's History of the Methodists," 206.

39. See Rack, *Reasonable Enthusiast*, 508–23, for a detailed account of the transformations in Methodist ordination.

status and identity of lay preachers drew up along lines which should be familiar by now, and with which Coleridge himself was intimately familiar, as he spent some of 1797 reading preacher's lives in back issues of the *Arminian Magazine*.[40] Whether admiring or acerbic, however, no view of lay preaching found it well-tailored for addressing a "Statesman," or even "the Higher and Middle Classes." They offered the Bread of Life, to be sure, but most lay preachers would have agreed with Thomas Hanson's admission in 1780 that he was "but a brown-bread preacher,"[41] and the great John Nelson gave a sense of the physical platform and social position from which most "lay sermons" were pronounced: on the "washing-tub" he carried with him, turned "mouth downwards, for a standing-place."[42] A Gospel so laundered was ill-fitted for the ostensibly expansive thinking and expensive audience of the *Lay Sermons*. While the Methodists appreciated one preacher in 1790 as an anti-Coleridge, "simple, plain, and clear" in style, a man who "did not perplex his hearers with abstruse reasoning and metaphysical distinctions . . . instead of sending them to a dictionary . . . he pointed them to the Lamb of God,"[43] more familiar voices in Romantic culture were less convinced of even these modest virtues.

According to Leigh Hunt in 1808, the "want of education" among lay preachers was "a satire upon almost every word they utter," conforming to the Methodist conviction that "you must be excessively stupid" in order to "have a perfect comprehension of mysteries": "they utterly reject reason, and then proceed to give you the reason why."[44] *The Preacher's Manual*, an anthology of practical advice for Dissenting ministers popular in the first decades of the nineteenth century, opined in 1820 that while "lay sermons" were not of themselves contrary to Scripture, the Methodists had proved that such sermons were liable to abuse Christianity itself, since the "most ignorant are generally the most conceited; and those who have the least to say, are often the first to speak."[45] The *Examiner* declared lay preachers "bawlers in the highway," and "evangelists who prove their inspiration by abusing the divine gift of language with every possible

---

40. See Brantley, *Wordsworth's "Natural Methodism,"* 38–40, for a sense of the impact this may have had on the *annus mirabilis*.
41. Hanson is quoted in Southey, *Life of Wesley*, 2:60.
42. WV 3:66.
43. WV 2:216.
44. Leigh Hunt, "On the Ignorance and Vulgarity of the Methodists," *Examiner* 19 (May 8, 1808): 301–3 (302).
45. *The Preacher's Manual*, 3rd ed. (London: Richard Baynes, 1820), ii.

barbarism,"[46] syllogizing that as "ignorance produces vulgarity," and "a want of rational conviction produces vehemence," "accordingly our Methodist preachers are vulgar and vehement."[47] When brought out of the highway, and into the pulpit, the results were still rough-hewn. The anonymous *Naked Thoughts* dryly noted that such preachers relied on "a deal of vociferation and rodomontade in their sermons, as if their hearers had but one ear apiece," while using techniques such as "banging the pulpit-cushion" in order to enforce abstruse theology: "when kept in perpetual play under the powerful blows of the preacher," the pillow "strikingly sets forth the insufficiency of all carnal ease, the fluctuation of all terrestrial grandeur . . . these preachers do not always chuse to verbally inform the people what good they do, but wisely let actions speak for them."[48] Even members of the Society could be embarrassed, and Wesley found himself ordering one lay preacher, "scream no more at the peril of your soul. . . . Speak with all your heart, but with a moderate voice."[49]

The Statesman's Manual had announced—in its inside voice, tucked away on the back wrapper—a third *Lay Sermon*, "To the lower and Labouring Classes of Society, Printed in a cheap Form for Distribution," which would take as its text Wesley's favorite verse, "The Poor have the Gospel preached unto them" (*LS* xxxi). This final homily was abandoned in embryo, and R. J. White, the Bollingen editor of the *Sermons*, "must always regret" the lost "spectacle of the middle-aged Coleridge addressing himself in language understood of the people" (*LS* xxxii). But before Coleridge's first two attempts, it's not clear that Romantic culture entertained the possibility of a lay sermon *not* so addressed and "understood." While Coleridge "never dreamt" that the first could be "understood (except in fragments) by the general reader,"[50] and the second sneered that "[i]n the present day we hear much, and from men of various creeds, of the plainness and simplicity of the Christian religion" (*LS* 176), the "general reader" (and believer) was most likely to anticipate such pious "plainness and simplicity" from something styled a "lay sermon." As William Law told John Wesley as the latter was embarking on his preaching career:

---

46. Leigh Hunt, "On the hatred of the Methodists against Moral Preaching, Concluded," *Examiner* 21 (May 22, 1808): 334–35 (334).
47. Hunt, "On the Ignorance and Vulgarity of the Methodists," 302.
48. *Naked Thoughts on Some Peculiarities of the Field-Preaching Clergy*, 2–3.
49. The story is related in Albert Lyles, *Methodism Mocked: The Satiric Reaction to Methodism in the Eighteenth Century* (London: Epworth, 1960), 73.
50. To T. G. Street, 22 March 1817, *Letters of Samuel Taylor Coleridge*, 4:713.

You would have a philosophical religion, but there can be no such thing. Religion is the most plain, simple thing in the world. It is only, *we love him because He first loved us*.[51]

For most of the eighteenth and nineteenth centuries, "lay sermons" were recognized, even by their proudest performers and most attentive listeners, as incapable of accommodating intellectual labor. They were instead the deliberate anathematization of philosophical nuance, rhetorical sophistication, and the tinsel distracting the earnest Christian from the plain truth of salvation.

This was their most positive construction, at any rate. For much of polite culture, however, "lay sermons" denoted the marriage of dogmatic simplicity to obscurantist mystery, both of which appealed to the blank idiocy of lay preachers and their congregations. The "Ignorance and Vulgarity of the Methodists," Hunt fumed, made them dismiss ungodly things like "scholastic learning, which they entitle *worldly wisdom, carnal knowledge,* and *the learning of this world.*"[52] The "unlearned Methodist" preacher, who "wants the regularity and distinctness of a cultivated mind,"[53] came to identify habitual mental darkness as spiritual illumination. "They are," Hazlitt advised his guests at the *Round Table,* "dull and gross in apprehension, and therefore they are glad to substitute faith for reason, and to plunge in the dark, under the supposed sanction of superior wisdom, into every species of mystery and jargon."[54] Such "mystery and jargon" won more converts than it lost, since (in Hunt's arithmetic) "vulgarity and obscurity" inevitably equaled "popularity; and popularity, as Mr. WHITFIELD says, makes one's sermons *every where called for.*"[55] The "popularity" of lay sermons attracted a monster more gruesome than even Coleridge's "READING PUBLIC," a plague cult of "scarecrows," "melancholy tailors, consumptive hair-dressers, squinting cobblers, women with child or in the ague": "a collection of religious invalids . . . the refuse of all that is weak and unsound in body and mind."[56]

If Coleridge was attempting to "clear the faith in supernatural mystery from all taint of weak-minded credulity," as Frederick Burwick argues, no

---

51. Southey, *Life of Wesley,* 1:77.
52. Hunt, "On the Ignorance and Vulgarity of the Methodists," 302.
53. Hunt, "On the Ignorance and Vulgarity of the Methodists," 301.
54. Hazlitt, "On the Causes of Methodism," 58.
55. Hunt, "On the hatred of the Methodists against Moral Preaching, Concluded," 335.
56. Hazlitt, "On the Causes of Methodism," 58–59.

form was worse equipped to handle such a clearance.[57] Tim Fulford's sense that "Lay Sermon" was meant to title "a spiritual language of accepted importance and inherent invulnerability" to "personal fallibilities of style and conduct" seems to me equally unlikely, since the genre localized exactly these "fallibilities."[58] Certainly very few contemporary readers recognized any transvaluation of Methodistical affiliations. On the contrary, the *Lay Sermons*, almost without exception, were received as disturbingly true performances in the genre they named. What would come to be understood as de Manian complexity was originally taken as vulgar mystery, continental metaphysics as homegrown enthusiasm. Even Coleridge's profound conservatism appeared as shocking personal and political disorder. Friendly responses simply didn't exist for several decades. Southey, though begged by him "who was once your Coleridge" to do something for them in the *Quarterly*, left his copies uncut, as did the Wordsworths.[59] Cold indifference was their warmest reception.

The usual foes of lay sermons roused themselves against the *Lay Sermons*, pressing anti-Methodism into service as anti-Coleridgeanism. Hazlitt and Hunt set the tone in two reviews in the *Examiner*, Hazlitt's third following in the *Edinburgh Review*. Each review targeted Coleridge's "senseless jargon,"[60] and an argument so "obscure, that it has been supposed to be written in cipher, and that it is necessary to read it upwards or downwards, or backwards and forwards, as it happens, to make head or tail of it."[61] But this esoterica wasn't Kantean *Kritik*, according to Hazlitt. Rather, it was the flatus of that "state of voluntary self-delusion, into

---

57. Frederick Burwick, "Coleridge and De Quincey on Miracles," in Barth, *Fountain Light*, 193–230 (194).

58. Fulford, *Coleridge's Figurative Language*, 140.

59. Coleridge pleaded with Southey's presentation copy in classical code (perhaps to preserve his fragile dignity against unsympathetic eyes in Southey's household), "*Quod ad hoc opus refert, te rogo ut me, olim tuum Coleridgium, adjuves: potes enim, nec minus vir*" (Copy *RS*; *LS* 243). On the fate, cut and uncut, of the presentation copies, see *LS* 235–40. Though R. J. White finds Southey's "copies of the Lay Sermons were still uncut" upon his death (*LS* xxx), Southey demonstrated some awareness of their argument, which suggests he knew more of them than their covers. He praised (faintly) "some excellent remarks" in the second *Lay Sermon* to Humphrey Senhouse, 22 March 1817: "If Coleridge could but learn how to deliver his opinions in a way to make them read, and to separate that which would be profitable for all, from that which scarcely half a dozen men in England can understand (I certainly am not one of the number), he would be the most useful man of the age, as I verily believe him in acquirements and in powers of mind to be very far the greatest." *Life and Correspondence of Robert Southey*, 4:258.

60. William Hazlitt, "Coleridge's *Lay-Sermon*," *Edinburgh Review* 27.54 (December 1816): 444–59 (451).

61. Hazlitt, "Mr. Coleridge's Lay Sermon," in *Works* 7:114–18 (115n1).

which [Coleridge] has thrown himself," in which "he mistakes hallucinations for truths":[62] a fog of canting mystery which lifted to reveal not the philosopher-seer, but only "a maudlin Methodistical lay-preacher, . . . Mr. Coleridge."[63] Henry Crabb Robinson shrugged that first *Lay Sermon* "will assuredly be but little read, and by its readers be but little enjoyed or understood,"[64] and those few who did dip into them found only a festering swamp of enthusiasm. "'Mystic' rant," wrote the *Monthly Repository*,[65] "absurd rhapsodies," according to the *Monthly Magazine:* "[t]o reason with a person of this cast would be as hopeless an undertaking as to reason with the inmates of Bedlam."[66] This innuendo of generalized insanity coded a denominationally focused slur, as well, since Bedlam "admitted ninety patients between 1772 and 1795 who were suffering from 'religion and Methodism.'"[67] Southey declared in 1803 the "increase of madness, in England, has been proportioned to the increase of methodism."

> This is not lightly hazarded, nor ignorantly affirmed. Positively and knowingly we assert, that the increase of madness, religious madness, the worst form of the worst calamity which flesh is heir to, has been proportioned to, and occasioned by the growth of methodism.[68]

This critique of the *Lay Sermons*—as Methodistically off-kilter in argument, fatuously self-satisfied in tone, and blissfully clueless in authorial persona—became the touchstone for Coleridge's reputation until the 1830s. Morton Paley suggests that the popularity of Coleridge's poetry in the "Annuals" from the 1820s until his death came burnished with the prestige of his heavy-duty thinking elsewhere, and that readers, "whether or not familiar with the Lay Sermons, Philosophical Lectures, or *Aids to Reflection*, would have at least known of them by reputation and could be assumed to regard seriously a poem by Coleridge."[69] But this isn't the

---

62. Hazlitt, "Coleridge's *Lay-Sermon,*" 446.
63. Hazlitt, "The Fudge Family in Paris," in *Works* 7:287–97 (288).
64. [Crabb Robinson], "Coleridge's Statesman's Manual," 43.
65. "Coleridge's *Lay Sermon,*" in *The Monthly Repository of Theology and General Literature* 12 (May 1817): 299–301 (299).
66. "Critical Notices of New Books," *Monthly Magazine and British Reader,* 43 (May 1817), 354.
67. Susan Juster, *Doomsayers: Anglo-American Prophecy in the Age of Revolution* (Philadelphia: University of Pennsylvania Press, 2003), 38.
68. Southey, "Myles's History of the Methodists," 211.
69. Morton D. Paley, "Coleridge and the Annuals," *Huntington Library Quarterly* 57.1 (Winter 1994): 1–24 (5).

whole story. Those who knew Coleridge's prose only by hearsay or periodical review would have had very little reason to be impressed, or to suspect the author even capable of thought more sustained than the lyric before them.

In 1826, the *British Critic* found that as he discoursed on "spiritual religion," Coleridge became, "in proportion," "less and less intelligible."[70] John Wilson, meanwhile, thought the hieroglyphic difficulty of much of the *Biographia* symptomatic of the "miserable pretensions of Mr Coleridge," who affected to believe that "his own wild ravings are holy and inspired," as his prose deliberately darkened "what was dark before into tenfold obscurity." Like any other fraudulent "prophet," Coleridge treated "the most ordinary common-places as to give them the air of mysteries."[71] The eremitical retreat of the Sage that Coleridge presumed for himself was better recognized as the involuntary lock-up of the addled zealot, alleged the *New Monthly Magazine*, which was "as glad to escape from the . . . opinions of Mr. Coleridge, as we would to the light of day from the darkened cell of a religious enthusiast whose visions and prophecies have rendered confinement necessary for himself and society."[72]

As both *Edinburgh* periodicals agreed, the *Lay Sermons*, and the feeble flurry of activity following them, were the pathetic evidence of the final collapse of Coleridge's politics, theology, sanity, and masculinity. The shattered husk of disappointment and delusion that remained found its only echo in the sad fate of the serving-girl who had grown up in Ottery St. Mary alongside the son of its vicar, and who shared with him a presumption to "visions and prophecies." "The vagaries, whimsies, and pregnant throes of Joanna Southcote," Hazlitt thundered in the *Edinburgh Review*, "were sober and rational, compared with Mr Coleridge's qualms and crude conceptions, and promised deliverance in this Lay-Sermon."[73] Wilson wasn't any kinder in *Blackwood's*, marking the precedent for Coleridge's conceit in connecting "his own name in Poetry with Shakspeare, and Spenser, and Milton; in politics with Burke, and Fox, and Pitt; in metaphysics with Locke, and Hartley, and Berkeley, and Kant": "So deplorable a delusion as this has only been equaled by that of Joanna Southcote, who mistook a complaint in the bowels for the divine afflatus;

---

70. "Coleridge's *Aids* and Leighton's *Works*," *British Critic* 3 (October 1826): 239–80 (260).
71. [John Wilson], "Observations on Coleridge's Biographia Literaria," *Blackwood's Edinburgh Magazine* 2.7 (October 1817): 3–18 (2–8).
72. Review of *Biographia Literaria*, *New Monthly Magazine* 43 (August 1817): 50.
73. Hazlitt, "Coleridge's *Lay-Sermon*," 446.

and believed herself about to give birth to the regenerator of the world, when sick unto death of an incurable and loathsome disease."[74]

My story turns to Southcott, and the meaning her writings and "pregnancy" held for the early nineteenth century, in the next chapter. For now, I'd like to dwell on the Coleridgean causes and consequences of this mockery, which laughed his Jeremiad to the polite classes into a potted Joanniad, fit only for those whom Hazlitt called "the refuse of all that is weak and unsound in body and mind." We overlook much of the color "Coleridge" wore for Romantic culture if we discard these judgments as "deliberately unfair," the public expression of (especially) Hazlitt's private animus, and the willful misidentification of an admittedly troubled Sage as the hysterical, menopausally fertile, illiterate woman who had been educated and alienated by his father's sermons, yet with whom Tim Fulford finds "no sympathy" in Coleridge.[75] Hazlitt's barbs were certainly bloodthirsty: "[Coleridge] is the Dog in the Manger of literature, an intellectual Mar-Plot, who will neither let any body else come to a conclusion, nor come to one himself."[76] The sting was only magnified by delivery in an infamously prophylactic "review by anticipation," which appeared in the *Examiner* months before the first *Lay Sermon* had been published, and perhaps even written. But Coleridge's own account, that this was the inevitable issue of family romance, a "rhapsody of predetermined insult"[77] void of substance other than the Oedipal, is partial.[78]

Personal slanders were political critique, and Hazlitt's pre-emptive reviewing disclosed historical, rather than familial, overdetermination. After a century of Methodist preaching, a mere advertisement of title was sufficient proof for an elaborate indictment of enthusiasm. The *Lay Sermons* staged a drama far exceeding the domestic, and though Hazlitt's tripled flayings in the *Examiner* and *Edinburgh Review* stole the show, his was hardly the only role. The consensus which held Coleridge neither

---

74. Wilson, "Observations on Coleridge's *Biographia Literaria*," 5–6.
75. Tim Fulford, "Apocalyptic and Reactionary?: Coleridge as Hermeneutist," *The Modern Language Review* 81.1 (January 1992): 18–31 (19).
76. Hazlitt, "Mr. Coleridge's *Lay Sermon*," 115.
77. *Biographia Literaria*, 2:242.
78. In the long account he gave to Francis Wrangham (5 June 1817), Coleridge martyred himself as Hazlitt's surrogate parent, while alluding to his quondam child's "unmanly vices" and the "infamous Punishment" for sexual assault from which Coleridge and Southey "snatched" him, a gift which festered into Hazlitt's resentment: "his very Father & Mother having despaired of him," Coleridge had "given him all the money, I had in the world, and the very Shoes off my feet to enable him to escape over the mountains"; "He has repeatedly boasted, that he wrote the very contrary of all, he believed—because he was under heavy obligations, and therefore *hated* me" (*Letters of Samuel Taylor Coleridge*, 4:735–36).

"as a major theologian, someone increasingly respected as an *orthodox* thinker,"[79] nor as an advanced proponent of the Higher Criticism, skeptically threatening all the ancient proofs of Christianity, was diverse and tenacious in the 1810s and 1820s, when many of the appreciators of his philosophy could (and often did) fit in Gillman's parlor. In the wake of the *Lay Sermons,* Coleridge owned a reputation as a man socially, intellectually, and temporally *retrograde,* a bizarre fanatic attempting to pass off exploded dogmas and village superstitions as grand writing and serious thought, and explicit identifications with Methodism were still current in the 1840s.[80]

As reviewers pointed out, if this was unjust, the author himself had suggested the critique. Coleridge's strategy for brand management was one part self-promotion, two parts self-immolation: following his skewering as Southcott's heir after her death in 1814, he made the (sublimely poor) decision to style his come-back volume of poetry *Sibylline Leaves.* Early notices, such as that in the *Literary Gazette,* were bemused by such a "strangely christened work," the deliberate reminder of a shared history in Devonshire at a time when it had been "overrun with fanatical preachers" and aspiring prophetesses,[81] in a volume meant to resuscitate rather than annihilate a reputation:

> "Sibylline," says our Dictionary, "of or belonging to a Sibyl or *Prophetess*": the word cannot therefore, we hope, be appropriated by Mr. Coleridge, who is not so humble a poet as to assume, voluntarily, the character of an old woman.[82]

---

79. Jeffrey W. Barbeau, *Coleridge, the Bible, and Religion* (New York: Palgrave Macmillan, 2008), 5.

80. William Mitchell, for example, compared Coleridge's "patchwork system" of "Luther, Jeremy Taylor, Leighton, More, Swedenborg, Jacob Behmen, Spinoza, Kant, Fichte, and Schelling" with that of "Mr W.[esley]," that "certain divine" condemned in the 1770s by his Calvinist opponent (Augustus) "Toplady." Wesley's "very singular mixture of Manichaeism, Pelagianism, Popery, Socinianism, Ranterism, and Atheism" made him, like Coleridge, an indiscriminate pillager of high and low thought, "good and bad" men, and so *"Aliquis in omnibus, nullus in singulis*" (*Coleridge and the Moral Tendency of his Writings,* 16).

81. One biographer of Southcott reminded readers in 1814 of the condition of Ottery St. Mary and its surroundings several decades earlier: "Devonshire was, at that time, overrun with fanatical preachers, a class so well ridiculed in the Spiritual Quixote, the revered writer of which actually lays his scene not far from Joanna's immediate neighbourhood." *La Belle Assemblée,* September 1814, 100.

82. Review of *Sibylline Leaves, Literary Gazette, and Journal of Belles Lettres* 1.27 (July 26, 1817): 49–51 (49).

No one was willing to trek all the way back to Cumae when a West-Country Sibyl was so near at hand. Coleridge unmanned himself in the oracular distinction meant to authorize him, prophetic power doubling into the insanity of a modern peasant. More to the point, few contemporaries were sure whether this was an allusion gone awry, or whether Coleridge had intended Southcott all along. After all, his intricate epistemology climaxed in a wild paean to a wise woman and maddened virgin, which many people knew not as an ancient holiness, but as the bad joke which had consumed the newspapers and embarrassed the nation over the past few years. Knowledge, concluded *The Statesman's Manual*, was where Heraclitus had found it, not in the Sage but the Sibyl:

> Multiscience (or a variety and quantity of acquired knowledge) does not teach intelligence. But the SIBYLL with wild enthusiastic mouth shrilling forth unmirthful, inornate, and unperfumed truths reaches to a thousand years with her voice through the power of God. (LS 26)

Hazlitt, eyeing misbegotten conceptions closer to home than those of the "sad and recluse philosopher," jeered: "It is not easy to conceive any thing better than this."[83]

The abuse of Coleridge, then, was that Coleridge was a self-abuser—not an enthusiast of uncertain sociosexual proclivities, exactly, but an enthusiast for introducing himself as such. Even Hazlitt acknowledged his victim's real capabilities, in an early draft of "My First Acquaintance with Poets" submitted as an anonymous letter "To the Editor of the Examiner," in response to his own reviews of the *Sermons*. The failure of Promethean promise into monstrous accomplishment was the ground for Hazlitt's complaint, and he sued for the "breach of confidence" between "[t]*hat* Sermon" of 1798, eloquently expounding the Good Old Cause of Dissenting liberty, and "*this* Sermon" of 1816, shamelessly toadying for Old Corruption.[84] But Coleridge's crisis of confidence seemed more severe than this familiar apostasy. The self-sabotage of his newfound orthodoxy was immediately provoking: a conservatism clashing with its Methodistical fabric irritated more than the turning of a decades-old coat, and reviewers sympathetic to the Coleridge of *The Courier* were clearly disgusted with the *Lay Sermons*. Reducing the issue to disenchantment or default misses the temporal and ideological peculiarities of Coleridge's betrayal. The *Lay*

---

83. Hazlitt, "Coleridge's *Lay-Sermon*," 456.
84. Hazlitt, "Mr Coleridge's Lay-Sermon, To the Editor of the Examiner," in *Works* 7:128–29.

Sermons certainly contradicted the Unitarian radicalism of the 1790s—but they also contradicted *themselves,* their cronyism and Methodism at cross-purposes. The oscillations between authoritarian politics and enthusiastic cover were at least as dizzying as the turn from "*that*" to "*this* Sermon," and if Coleridge no longer believed in the doctrine of the one, it wasn't at all obvious that he was committed to the other.

The *Lay Sermons* implied not that Coleridge had changed his faith, but that he had lost it entirely—even his faith in the politically expedient. This may have been the self-abnegating insecurity of a man shattered by decades of addiction, tortured erotic and domestic histories, desperate professional and economic failure, suicidal thoughts and a nearly mortal overdose during the dissolution of the Morgan establishment, and depression so acute it was formally managed in his negotiations with publishers.[85] Even so, personal flagellation had a public history. Serious Calvinism often ended in self-loathing, while sanctioning exposure as atonement. George Whitefield's tract on his own compulsive masturbation was a memorable example: "my secret and darling Sin" proved "that I was conceived and born in Sin;—that in me dwelleth no good Thing by Nature;—and that, if GOD had not freely prevented me by his Grace, I must have been for ever banished from his Divine Presence."[86] This was the only

---

85. Listing the points of business to be discussed with Thomas Curtis (April 1817), Coleridge mentioned "Fifthly, Misery, Sickness, Despondence, etc." as reasons for "my resolve never to make even a *conditional* promise for the future." *Letters of Samuel Taylor Coleridge,* 4:727.

86. George Whitefield, *A Short Account of God's Dealings with the Reverend Mr. George Whitfield, A.B., Late of Pembroke-College, Oxford* (Edinburgh: T. Lumisden and J. Robertson, 1741), 5–6. Whitefield's account of his masturbation wasn't short, but it was tragicomically performative. He played up the role of his "hands," and the "groans" and "feelings" of their "Effects": "*Satan*" and some "Evil Communications with my old Schoolfellows soon corrupted my good Manners.—By seeing their evil Practices, the Sense of the Divine Presence I had vouchsafed unto me, insensibly wore off my Mind; and I at length fell into an abominable secret Sin, the dismal Effects of which I have felt, and groaned under ever since. But GOD, whose Gifts and Callings are without Repentance, would let nothing pluck me out of his Hands, tho' I was continually doing Despite to the Spirit of Grace" (*Short Account,* 11–12). One contemporary made Whitefield's self-mortifying irony into pure bawdy: "As the Species of Commerce above-mentioned is generally transacted between a Man and himself, both Agent and Patient being centered in the Individual, I apprehend that Witnesses are seldom needful; nevertheless, as Mr. W——d and his old Crony were seldom asunder, it is not to be supposed that the former had all the Fatigue: *Satan* certainly lent his Friend an *helping Hand* towards the Dispatch of the *Sport* . . . my Reverend Author returned the *Kindness* of his officious Friend, and—the *Devil,* in his Turn: Tho', as Charity exacts from us the most favourable Construction upon Things doubtful, and as the Gratitude of Mr. W——d was never yet called into Question, I shall conclude that the *Benefit* was *reciprocal.*" [R——ph J——ps——n], *Expounder Expounded,* 40–41. More

logic, doctrinal or otherwise, with which *Blackwood's* could make sense of Coleridge's fascination with his own ridiculousness. The *Biographia*, Wilson warned, was miserable for everyone concerned, strengthening "every argument against the composition of such Memoirs" in the exhibition of "many mournful sacrifices of personal dignity, after which it seems impossible that Mr Coleridge can be greatly respected either by the public, or himself."[87]

Coleridge played off any identifications of Sage with Sibyl, philosopher-gentleman with unwashed lay preacher, as unflattering, but not unplanned. They were penance for sins unnamed and perhaps uncommitted, a uniquely contemporary cut of hair-shirt, weaving discourse as the fiber of humiliation, scratching a mortified sanctification out of the sociolect instead of the body. Pausing to review an exhausting, mystically rhapsodic account of the sixth and "inner sense" that consumed "Appendix C" to *The Statesman's Manual,* Coleridge acknowledged that he had no doubt just made charges of enthusiasm inevitable and accurate.

> It has been asked why knowing myself to be the object of personal slander, (slander as unprovoked as it is groundless, unless acts of kindness are provocation) I furnish this material for it, by pleading in palliation of so chimerical a fancy. With that half-playful sadness, which at once sighs and smiles, I answered: why not for that very reason?—Viz. in order that my calumniator might have, if not a material, yet some basis for the poison-gas of his invention to combine with? (*LS* 82)

This melancholy ethic—not turning the other cheek, so much as slapping it oneself in order to justify the assailant's initial violence—preached the sublimity of sublimation, the boundless representational capacity of the "half-playful" self, which, nourished on bitterness, wore a Janus-like visage, "at once sighs and smiles": "There is a grace that would enable us to take up vipers, and the evil thing shall not hurt us: a spiritual alchemy which can transmute poisons into a panacea" (*LS* 35).

In its "grace," this "spiritual alchemy" was a reminder that social degradation might ultimately change into spiritual glorification, though Coleridge's was more modern than medieval in result. Almost no one received it as such, but this strange brew of "poisons into a panacea"—Methodistical extravagance and philosophical method, Southcottian and

---

seriously, see Jon Stachniewski's powerful argument on the role of self-hatred in Calvinist spiritual autobiography, *Persecutory Imagination.*

87. Wilson, "Observations on Coleridge's Biographia Literaria," 5.

Tory sensibilities—was a chemical change in the nature of cultural capital in the Romantic period, and the distillation of something like its modern form. Decades later, Carlyle reported, Coleridge's reputation was still tenuous, his magisterial prophecy sounding like the humbug of a carnival fortuneteller, even to his disciples: "to the rising spirits of the young generation he had this dusky sublime character; and sat there as a kind of *Magus*, girt in mystery and enigma; his Dodona oak-grove (Mr. Gilman's [*sic*] house at Highgate) whispering strange things, uncertain whether oracles or jargon."[88] In its suppressed referent, this syntax was itself "uncertain," as no one—not Carlyle, not those "rising spirits," and not even the "*Magus*" himself—was proof against that doubting "whether," the hinge between pious sense and enthusiastic nonsense. But the clarity of Carlyle's portrait was its perception that this fuzziness was also the magnetic attraction of the Coleridgean persona, which made a virtue out of its vices. Coleridge's genius, argued Professor Shedd, wasn't found in his settled principles, but in what he canceled, complicated, and abandoned to an unsettled energy of "doubts and prejudices": "Like the *Retractions* of Augustine, the retractions of Coleridge, if we may call them such, have a negative worth almost equal to that of the positive statements to which they lead."[89]

Shedd had in mind the dialectics propelling Coleridge's most abstract metaphysics. But the most historically determinate "retraction," which coyly presumed the community between the clerisy of the *Lay Sermons,* and the plebeian audience of lay sermons, has the most "negative worth," as it anticipates the rules of art which would obtain long after the Regency. The sanitary line between polite and popular ordered much of Romantic culture, but Pierre Bourdieu argues that emphatic division would come to be seen as only the most primitive gambit in the game of distinction. Ultimately, only those who declined such a move were seriously playing the game, and a frown at the "vulgar" was a middlebrow sort of furrow, a spasm of incomplete refinement and bourgeois insecurity. The most knowing strategy in the play of post-Kantean taste was instead an artistry of refuse, in which not only a studied interest in the romantically "natural" and the conventionally "unmediated," but the wholesale embrace of the soiled, crude, and calculatedly anti-aesthetic marked the "true" aesthete, in "the audacious imposture of refusing all refusals by recuperating, in parody or sublimation, the very objects refused by the lower-degree

---

88. Carlyle, *Life of Sterling,* 70.
89. Shedd, "Introductory Essay," 14.

aestheticism."⁹⁰ Aesthetics in the shadow of the *Critique of Judgment* qualified "pure taste by the intensity of the impulse denied and the vulgarity refused," yet Bourdieu finds the consummation of this logic in its own contradiction, the ultimate distinction in the denial of distinction: "the most accomplished art has to be recognized in those works which carry the anti-thesis of civilized barbarism, contained impulse, sublimated coarseness, to the highest degree of tension."⁹¹

Hazlitt alone recognized this as the social practice of the *Lay Sermons*. Their titular vulgarity and their stylistic enthusiasms were neither unintended accidents, nor the wounds of the damaged archangel, but a mystified agenda for cultural domination, in which Coleridge demonstrated his Titanism by conquering the arbitrary limits of sense and taste that held smaller men in thrall. *Sibylline Leaves* advertised a perversely Joannian poetics, the *Lay Sermons* a nastily Methodistical theo-politics, because, Hazlitt insisted, Coleridge meant them to. Coleridge might sigh over "personal slander," "as unprovoked as it is groundless," but he was deliberately toying with the forbidden, in order to discover the final shock of the new: "Again, he places the seat of truth in *the heart,* of virtue in *the head;* damns a tragedy as shocking that draws tears from the audience, and pronounces a comedy to be inimitable, if nobody laughs at it; labours to unsettle the plainest things by far-fetched sophistry, and makes up for the want of proof in matters of fact by the mechanical operations of the spirit."⁹² Hazlitt peer-reviewed that these experiments in social chemistry weren't replicable: "There is something, we suspect, in these studies that does not easily amalgamate."⁹³ This failed suspension, Hazlitt theorized, was the real compound of Coleridge's addiction, a dependence on sociohistorical portmanteaus as the materials for his broken genius.

The "cant of Morality, like the cant of Methodism, comes in most naturally to close the scene" of Hazlitt's demolition of the *Biographia*, revealing a stage bare of everything but the unnatural antitheses that might be called Lake Methodism. When writing the etiology of "enthusiasm," whether "lofty," "abstract," or Methodistical, Hazlitt called this the disorder of "preternatural excitements" in body and spirit, a compulsive muta-

---

90. Pierre Bourdieu, *Distinction: A Social Critique of the Judgment of Taste*, trans. Richard Nice (Cambridge, MA: Harvard University Press, 1984), 61.
91. Bourdieu, *Distinction*, 490.
92. Hazlitt, "Mr. Coleridge's Lay Sermon," 116.
93. Hazlitt, "Coleridge's *Literary Life*," *Edinburgh Review* 28 (August 1817): 488–515 (514).

bility that, "if it takes a definite, consistent form, it loses its interest."[94] In the *Biographia,* he called it "the true history of our reformed Antijacobin poets; the life of one of whom is here recorded":

> Always pampering their own appetite for excitement, and wishing to astonish others, their whole aim is to produce a dramatic effect, one way or other—to shock or delight their observers; and they are as perfectly indifferent to the consequences of what they write, as if the world were merely a stage for them to play their fantastic tricks on.—As romantic in their servility as in their independence, and equally importunate candidates for fame or infamy, they require only to be distinguished, and are not scrupulous as to the means of distinction. Jacobins or Antijacobins—outrageous advocates for anarchy and licentiousness, or flaming apostles of persecution—always violent and vulgar in their opinions, they oscillate, with a giddy and sickening motion, from one absurdity to another, and expiate the follies of their youth by the heartless vices of their advancing age. None so ready as they to carry every paradox to its most revolting and nonsensical excess—none so sure to caricature, in their own persons, every feature of an audacious and insane philosophy:—In their days of innovation, indeed, the philosophers crept at their heels like hounds, while they darted on their distant quarry like hawks; stooping always to the lowest game; eagerly snuffing up the most tainted and rankest scents; feeding their vanity with the notion of the strength of their digestion of poisons, and ostentatiously avowing whatever would most effectually startle the prejudices of others.[95]

Hazlitt figured the extremities of cultural capital—whether named by Coleridge's "grace that would enable us to take up vipers," Bourdieu's "audacious imposture of refusing all refusals," or his own sense of the vain "strength" which came from the "digestion of poisons"—as the agents of lethally misrecognized political power. The insatiable "appetite for excitement" wasn't just a fleshly craving, but an ideological instinct for absolutism in all its forms. Coleridge's output of 1816–18, so diffuse, inconclusive, and mislabeled, was in this view all the more tyrannical for its subversion of rhetorical and social regulation. While the *Lay Sermons* reserved the "*Jus divinum*" for "the Scriptures alone" (*LS* 33), they appropriated some of that divine right for themselves, troping an end-

---

94. Hazlitt, "On the Causes of Methodism," 57, 61.
95. Hazlitt, "Coleridge's *Literary Life,*" 514–15.

less empire that contained multitudes—that alone could level the division between Methodist and "cleric," Sage and Sibyl—and that made meaningless any resistance to its dominion, reinventing the enthusiasms of bad thinking, bad writing, and bad faith as the inevitable reinforcements of its own power.

"The Bible the Best Guide"

Hazlitt worried that enthusiastic confusion, not forceful differentiation, was now the weapon of reaction. The *Lay Sermons* were dangerous because they seemed so absurd, trading the crude polemics of the Society for the Promotion of Christian Knowledge for an insidiously subtle hierarchalism. While it's true that Hazlitt was "politically suspicious of the hedonism of the poetic voice," alarm at Coleridge's secret ministerialism wasn't his unique paranoia.[96] In 1844, William Mitchell outed Coleridge's metaphysical complications as the same obfuscating agenda that had rationalized the Congress of Vienna and re-throned the House of Bourbon. Any attempt, Mitchell hissed, "to exhibit the principles of the great theologian in his own phraseology," "scattered" as they are "in mystic paragraphs, through many volumes . . . is no small task, for, like a wary diplomatist, our poetical philosopher and divine is cautious in the disclosure of his sentiments, acting somewhat upon the saying of Talleyrand, that 'the great object of speech is to conceal the thought.'"[97] By the 1810s, Coleridge's "authoritarian cultural politics" had come to lurk, argues Nigel Leask, "in the literal 'mystification' of authority," patterned after the ancient Mystery cults that demystified Roman religion for the imperial elite, secreting "esoteric" doctrine within outward-facing rituals.[98] This mystification, I think, is the best explanation for the conflicted modes of reading and writing the *Lay Sermons* modeled. The enthusiasms the *Sermons* brazened were more than skin deep—but they were also motivated diversions from Coleridge's most reactionary positions, which unfolded with a nudge, wink, and codeword to the wise in place of exposition.

The politics of the *Sermons* were doubly extraordinary: for their extremism, and for their plausible deniability. The first *Sermon* discov-

---

96. Tim Milnes, *Knowledge and Indifference in English Romantic Prose* (Cambridge and New York: Cambridge University Press, 2003), 13.
97. Mitchell, *Coleridge and the Moral Tendency*, 9–10.
98. Nigel Leask, *The Politics of Imagination in Coleridge's Critical Thought* (New York: St. Martin's, 1988), 4; 173.

ered the scriptural mandate for the Constitution of Church and State, in that "direct Relation of the State and its Magistracy to the Supreme Being, taught as a vital and indispensable part of all moral and of all political wisdom." This was a hint at theocratic absolutism, but Coleridge escaped explication with an allusive (and abrupt) dodge to "the latter period of the reign of Solomon, and to the revolutions in the reign of Rehoboam," before drawing himself up short, and abandoning the argument entirely: one step more, and "I should tread on glowing embers" (*LS* 33). Hazlitt, following the thread through Coleridge's labyrinth back to 1 Kings 11.4–43, found at its end the monster of "divine right, with a vengeance," in the "*grand, magnificent, and gracious* answer of the Son of Solomon" to his beleaguered people, which the *Sermon* advertised, but pointedly did *not* quote: "'My father made your yoke heavy, and I will add to your yoke; my father also chastised you with whips, but I will chastise you with scorpions.'"[99] Since half-baked allusion never quite rose to argument, this was having one's authoritarian cake and eating it, too. Coleridge's nod at Biblically scripted tyranny took its cue from the magisterial mystery of Mitchell's Talleyrand, a fleeting gesture of sympathy so decontextualized it might be disavowed, or even explained away as critique, rather than endorsement, of the political efficacy of yokes, whips, and scorpions.

The *Lay Sermons* were steeling "the Higher and Middle Classes of Society" for the brutality required to preserve the liberty of property in the Armageddon signaled by "the existing Distresses and Discontents"— but so quietly that this ideological hardening would remain undetectable to its victims. Yet this was an ostentatious circumspection, confident that the cipher was secure against anyone without the socioeconomically determined key. The murderously practical conclusions of the "*Jus divinum*" might have been buried in that speech of Rehoboam, but the surfaces of the *Sermons* hid blood and iron, as well. The phrases the *Sermons* took as their texts—"*The Bible the Best Guide to Political Skill and Foresight*" for the first, "*Blessed are ye that sow beside all Waters*" for the second—were political dog-whistles, pitched beyond the range of most readers.

Even Hazlitt seems not to have caught completely the tone of the first. He wondered only, if the Bible were indeed the Best Guide, why Coleridge "has not brought forward a single illustration of his doctrine, nor referred to a single example in the Jewish history that bears at all, in the circumstances, or the inference, on our own"?[100] Text *was* argument, however,

---

99. Hazlitt, "Mr. Coleridge's Statesman's Manual," in *Works* 7:123.
100. Hazlitt, "Mr. Coleridge's Statesman's Manual," in *Works* 7:120.

invoking a long tradition of English (rather than Jewish) "illustrations," for those in the know. "*The Bible the Best Guide*" had been shorthand for the doctrines of "passive obedience" and "nonresistance" since James II, summarizing the sort of extreme, High Church Toryism for which Henry Sacheverell was prosecuted in 1710. Even after the decline of Jacobitism, the ultra-orthodox flocked to the phrase. In 1776, William Mason insisted that the "the Bible our guide in government" should teach the American colonies "passive obedience and nonresistance."[101] Sarah Trimmer agreed in 1789 with Mason's catechism that "the bible . . . our best rule in *politics*" made revolution heretical, since "every creature is placed in its station by GOD,"[102] while, in a truth stranger than fiction, Hannah More named her two cats "Passive Obedience" and "Non Resistance."[103]

Coleridge was preaching to the choir a sermon so uncompromising the congregation might have grown restless, had they been able to understand it. Following Hazlitt's early review of the title and text of the first *Sermon*, the second *Sermon* protected itself against similarly unwelcome (mis)understandings. Text and title were now set as traps for the uninitiated, dividing sheep from goats—those intense readers, admitted to inner secrets, from the superficial herd precipitating the nation toward slaughter. As the *Monthly Magazine* observed, without quite seeing, this *Lay Sermon* was oddly indifferent to itself:

> Mr. Coleridge, adopting a scriptural expression, says, "*Blessed are ye that sow beside all waters*"; this is his text—at least his *motto*—no reference to which is made, that we can perceive, throughout his discourse. Now this, we think, is a clear proof that the lay-preacher is not quite an adept in the selection of texts[.][104]

The *Monthly's* irony hit home, and missed the mark entirely. The *Sermon* did indeed drop this line from Isaiah after its first paragraphs, only return-

---

101. William Mason, *The Absolute and Indispensable Duty of Christians, in this Critical Juncture* (London: Pasham, 1776), 16, 9.

102. Sarah Trimmer, *Comment on Dr. Watts's Divine Songs for Children, with Questions; Designed to Illustrate the Doctrine and Precepts to which they Refer; And Induce a proper application of them as instruments in early Piety* (London: J. Buckland, J. F. and C. Rivington, T. Longman, T. Field, and C. Dilly, 1789), 16.

103. J. C. D. Clark, *English Society*, 299. As Susan Wolfson has observed to me, these names were either tribute to improbably well-behaved cats, or practical testaments to More's conviction that no amount of regulation would be sufficient to curb the disobedient spirit, feline or plebeian.

104. "Critical Notices of New Books," *Monthly Magazine and British Reader* 43 (May 1817): 354.

ing to it in the last sentence. But amateurish disorder, Coleridge confided a few pages after the *Monthly* appears to have stopped reading, was just a shell game to take in rubes: exactly the sort of sleight of hand one might expect from "an adept" prestidigitator of mystified truths. For the casually curious—say, for the "READING PUBLIC" that knew the *Sermons* only by periodical review and critical summary—the *"Blessed are ye"* was a bit of trifling exoterica, patronizing the alien with its own exclusion:

> Easy to be remembered from its briefness, likely to be remembered from its beauty, and with not a single word in it which the malignant ingenuity of Faction could pervert to the excitement of any dark or turbulent feeling, I chose it both as a Text and Title of this Discourse, that it might be brought under the eye of many thousands who will know no more of the Discourse itself than what they read in the advertisements in our public papers. (*LS* 140)

But the elect—or, at least, those who read beyond the first few pages—were permitted to glimpse another face. It was, "in point of fact," another "passage of Scripture, the words of another Prophet, that originally occasioned this Address" (*LS* 140). In its fourth paragraph, the second *Sermon* swapped Isaiah for Jeremiah, esoterically adopting a new text unconnected with the title, unannounced in advertisement, unnoticed by hasty reviewers, and substantially more extreme in moral crisis and material cure: "*We looked for Peace, but no good came: for a time of health, and behold, trouble! The harvest is past, the summer is ended: and we are not saved. Is there no balm in Gilead?*" (*LS* 141) The tonal gap between the anodyne Isaiah (*"Blessed are ye"*) and the grim Jeremiah (*"behold, trouble!"*) performed the political gap the *Sermon* contemplated, rousing the better sorts to a sense of their own peril, while soothing the rest back into convenient torpor. This prophetic reversal was the balm Coleridge prescribed in Gilead, 1817: not a display of naked force, but the "gentle and unnoticed . . . controul" the *Biographia* theorized as the shape of the imagination,[105] and that here softly formed the hierarchy of cultural consumption, the division between those who heard the *Sermon*, and those who merely heard of it.

However "gentle," the "controul" in these leading dead-ends and skeletal suggestions were the culminating formation of the "Sage." This is the political logic encoded in that abstract play between the prophetically sug-

---

105. Coleridge, *Biographia Literaria*, 2:16–17.

gestive Writer and the academic reader who completed him, which transforms rhetorical sympathy into a program for class solidarity. But in the enthusiastic gamesmanship of the *Sermons,* the security of such screening was porous, and orthodoxy opened to admit its own inversion. "*The Bible the Best Guide*" was a shibboleth the Tory rump shared with less well-behaved zealots. Its wholesale repudiation of secularized politics was as likely to end in spiritual revolt as the evangelical discipline of the *Cheap Repository Tracts.* Wesley, Southey warned, "had broken through the forms of [the] Church, and was acting in defiance of her authority" out of a critically unsound faith, which dismissed all institutional managers other than the Bible—not just the Best, but the Only Guide: "This irregularity he justified, by a determination to allow no other rule of faith, or practice, than the Scriptures; not, perhaps, reflecting that in this position he joined issue with the wildest religious anarchists."[106] In the reflection of this "irregularity," Coleridge's slogan was the double-image of both purifying "determination" and unlicensed tumult, a dark warning on the tendency of Protestantism's rigorous interiority to devolve into a de-socialized spirituality. The Bible, the prophet Richard Brothers insisted in 1794, unmade the forms of this world, a holy overturning without appeal:

> As the SCRIPTURE is the only great Fountain of Knowledge, or Book of written Truth in the World; as it contains the sacred Records of those Things which GOD has predetermined shall be hereafter—as well as those which have been already; and as it contains the History of our own Creation, with that of every thing besides, It alone, in preference to any Man's opinion, ought to be, without the least doubt, freely believed and confidently depended on.[107]

As we'll see in the next chapter, Brother's "free belief" and "confident dependence" would lead to treason, prophetic regicide, and prison. Bibliolatry was a habit of antinomians and anti-Jacobins alike. Coleridge's ostensibly bland motto was the doctrinal armature for the *ancien regime,* as well as its complete revision in spite of "any Man's opinion."

The original versions of the *Sermons* relished this ambiguity, vesting the *Biographia's* exordium to "the balance or reconciliation of opposite or discordant qualities" in socially specific form.[108] Secure divisions were

---

106. Southey, *Life of Wesley,* 1:235.
107. Richard Brothers, *A Revealed Knowledge, of the Prophecies and Times, Book the First* (London, 1794 [revised and expanded 1794–95]), 2.
108. *Biographia Literaria* 2:16–17.

the epiphenomena of deeper insecurities, and *The Statesman's Manual* gamely played proper and improper appeals to Biblical authority off each other. Coleridge welcomed an enthusiastic faith "in predictions which are permanent prophecies, because they are at the same time eternal truths": such conviction was infinitely preferable to the cold calculations of political economists and mathematical utilitarians, "the guesses of state-gazers, the dark hints and open reviling of our self-inspired state fortune-tellers, 'the wizards, that peep and mutter' and forecast, alarmists by trade, and malcontents for their bread" (*LS* 7–8). This sentiment wasn't beyond the pale—it was the same impeccable suspicion Burke held for the "sophisters, oeconomists, and calculators" dead to the charms of chivalry and Marie Antoinette.[109] But Coleridge unsettled his prophetic politics, approaching the limit of reasonable Christianity set by the Doctrine of the Cessation of Miracles—and then crossing it irrevocably, into a "self-inspired" condition worse than that of any "state-gazer."

To be sure, an assertion that "the Prophet Isaiah revealed the true philosophy of the French revolution more than two thousand years before it became a sad irrevocable truth of history" would provoke only grunts of agreement from High Churchmen after the 1790s (*LS* 34). The doctrinal implications of this claim were safely delimited. This was only an argument that the prophet had disclosed the principle that certain moral tendencies and intellectual errors led to destruction—not a ludicrous declaration that Isaiah had foreseen 1789 as a specific instance of the general cause, since "a sad irrevocable truth of history" was pointedly not a "truth" of Revelation. But after the bait came the switch. Coleridge next suggested that with the words "*Therefore shall evil come upon thee, thou shalt know from whence it riseth,*" the prophet had forecast Napoleon's weather along with his philosophy:

> The Reader will scarcely fail to find in this verse a remembrancer of the sudden setting-in of the frost, a fortnight before the usual time (in a country, too, where the commencement of its two seasons is in general scarcely less regular than that of the wet and dry seasons between the tropics) which caused, and the desolation which accompanied, the flight from Moscow. The Russians, baffled the *physical* forces of the imperial Jacobin, because they were inaccessible to his *imaginary* forces. The faith in St. Nicholas kept off at safe distance the more pernicious superstition of the Destinies of Napoleon the Great. (*LS* 34–35)

---

109. Burke, *Reflections*, 170.

Though hedged as "remembrancer" rather than "prophecy," this was very close to that delusive faith in the meddling of "Special Providence" in the daily lives of men, which many theologians were extraordinarily careful to forbid, even as they defended the ineffably distant mechanisms of the "General Providence."

For respectable students of prophecy inside and outside the Church, the Scriptures revealed philosophical axioms, never current events. Paley's *Principles of Moral and Political Philosophy,* an examination text at the Universities, set the terms: "Whoever expects to find in the Scripture a specific direction for every moral doubt that arises, looks for more than he will meet with."

> Morality is taught in Scripture in this wise. General rules are laid down of piety, justice, benevolence, and purity . . . this is in truth the way in which all practical sciences are taught, as Arithmetic, Grammar, Navigation, and the like—Rules are laid down, and examples subjoined; not that these examples are the cases, much less the cases which will actually occur, but by way only of explaining the principles of the rule, and as so many specimens of the method of applying it.[110]

The local specificity in which Coleridge indulged with his "remembrancer," insinuating a modern "case" within Scriptural "principles," was the most prominent sociodoctrinal attribute of the prophecies of Brothers and Southcott. Ian Balfour finds the "point of such a citation is to suggest ultimately that Coleridge's analysis of contemporary politics and matters of philosophy coincides with God's own," which is true enough.[111] But contextualized within the denominational identities of the early nineteenth century, Coleridge's political "analysis" was nothing of the sort. Churchmen were very guarded in presuming direct evidence for God's approbation, and this "remembrancer" anticipated an outcome gratifying to the Establishment in terms the Establishment couldn't accept. The resulting fantasy of enthusiasm and orthodoxy was an ideological solecism, imagining a cosmos of reactionary Providential intention and intercession, even as claims for such easily identifiable spiritual agency—regardless of political agenda—offended normative Anglicanism.

The *Lay Sermons* were a high-wire act of precariously balanced enthusiasms, and ultimately, they fell back to earth. Immediately after publi-

---

110. William Paley, *Principles of Moral and Political Philosophy,* 12th ed., 3 vols. (London: R. Faulder, 1791), 1:6–7.

111. Balfour, *Rhetoric of Romantic Prophecy,* 263.

cation, Coleridge recanted most of the transferences that have been my subject. The marginalia in Coleridge's presentation copies retreated from the prophetic amalgamations of Sage and Sibyl, qualifying, excusing, and often simply crossing-out problematic passages. As early as December 5, 1816, Coleridge was nervously noting to Brabant (Copy B) that though *The Statesman's Manual* trumpeted "facts" that were "distinguished . . . from all other facts by especial manifestation of divine interference," he didn't mean to suggest that such facts had contemporary relevance, as he had implied with Napoleon's "remembrancer." The Bible was a political guide, but its insight was located in the orthodox principles Paley emphasized, not the "facts" of "manifestation" or "interference": because they were "divine," they were "for this very reason totally unfit to furnish a ground of action under any existing circumstance" (*LS 9a*). Coleridge didn't clarify his most opaque conservatisms—the full text of Rehoboam's outburst would never see the light of day—but his codicils and outright excisions precisely track the enthusiasms of both *Sermons*, disappearing almost every instance of the doctrinal eccentricities that had so exercised his contemporaries.

Sound piety succeeded Methodistical exuberance. Copy A (John Anster's) now calmly supported the Cessation of Miracles, since "We (it may be said) no longer live under a miraculous dispensation similar to that recorded in the Bible" (*LS 9d–e*). Both Copies B and CL (Charles Lamb's) struck out an earlier vision of prophetic Eolism, which had cast all human "agents" as "but surges of the same tide, passive conductors of the one invisible influence, under which the total host of billows, in the whole line of successive impulse, swell and roll shoreward; there finally each in its turn, to strike, roar and be dissipated" (*LS 9b–c*). The second *Sermon* claimed that Jeremiah had "described by anticipation" the condition of England in 1817, "with such historic precision, so plain and so specifically as to render all comment needless, all application superfluous." Coleridge and his nephew seem to have come to consider any "comment" on "such historic precision" in prophecy truly "needless." The argument, and the very long passage surrounding it, was wordlessly deleted in Coleridge's own copy and in that of 1839 (*LS 141a–b*).[112]

Even in their original forms, Coleridge's prophetic experiments had often been self-consciously constrained. His hearing of an explicit warning from Revelations against Henry Hunt, William Cobbett, and other "mob-orators," was mischievously unsure:

---

112. Cf. *On the Constitution of Church and State and Lay Sermons*, ed. Henry Nelson Coleridge, 328.

> But I had dared to imitate the major part of the Commentators, and followed the *fatuous fires* of FANCY, that 'shrewd sprite' ever busiest when in the service of pre-conceived partialities and antipathies, I might have suffered my judgment to be seduced by the wonderful (*apparent*) aptness of the symbols, (many of them at least) and extended the application of the first eleven verses to the whole chapter, the former as treating of the Demagogues exclusively, the latter as including their infatuated followers likewise. For what other images, concorporated according to the rules of Hieroglyphic Syntax, could form more appropriate and significant exponents of a seditious and riotous multitude, with the mob-orators, their *Heads* or Leaders, than the thousands of pack-horses (*jumenta sarcinaria*) with *heads* resembling those of a roaring wild beast, with smoke, fire and brimstone (that is, empty, unintelligible, incendiary, calumnious, and offensively foul language) issuing from the mouths? (LS 146–47)

Coleridge's "Syntax" was as "Hieroglyphic" as the Revelator's. This is a confusing preteritio of assertion and parenthetical reservation, canceling enthusiasm in a wry grimace at its lunacy: "had I dared" (as he did not) "to imitate" the "*fatuous fires* of FANCY," which should not be mistaken for the creative fires of real inspiration, and which only illuminate "preconceived" prejudice rather than truth, he might in such dim light mistake "(*apparent*) aptness" for "wonderful" signs, "(many of them at least)" pointing toward something genuinely universal. This sort of regulation was at least as exuberant as the enthusiasm it "disciplined," and it didn't comport with the model of sagely self-reflection Henry Nelson Coleridge brought to market some decades later. Though the older Coleridge hadn't marked the passage for comment or revision, it vanished from the 1839 text completely. All that survived was an orthodoxy confining Revelation firmly to the dust of history, in a footnote forcibly migrated to modify an entirely different passage, with no record of the lost referent: "My own conception of the Book is, that it narrates in the broad and inclusive form of the ancient Prophets (i.e. in the prophetic power of faith and moral insight irradiated by inspiration) the successive struggles and final triumph of Christianity over the Paganism and Judaism of the then Roman Empire" (LS 147).[113]

The 1839 edition, silently adopting many of these revisions, would supplant the 1816–17 texts for the rest of the century. Shedd imported

---

113. See *On the Constitution of Church and State and Lay Sermons*, ed. Henry Nelson Coleridge, 330.

Henry Nelson Coleridge's version without editorial comment, standardizing for international study a text "as distinct and unmistakable as the Gulf-Stream in the Atlantic."[114] The "Coleridge" I've attempted to recover faded from view, or at least into other, more reputable scandals: better a plagiarism from Schelling than Southcott. Regency indictments, their evidence revised into thin air, might seem themselves unhinged, the phatic noise of the "READING PUBLIC." Critique now rebounded on critic, as both Shedd and Henry Nelson Coleridge brought James Marsh's dictum out of the wilderness of Vermont, into the canon: "I have no fear that any earnest and single-hearted lover of truth as it is in Jesus . . . will find any cause of offence, or any source of alarm."[115] The disappearing act pulled off by the Sage and his clerisy was impressive. But it was amateurish next to the one pulled on the Sibyl.

---

114. Shedd, "Introductory Essay," 11.
115. *The Complete Works of Samuel Taylor Coleridge*, ed. Shedd, 1:71. Shedd reprinted James Marsh's 1829 "Preliminary Essay" to *Aids to Reflection* in his own 1853 edition, as did H. N. Coleridge in the fourth edition of 1836.

Chapter 5

Joanna Southcott's Body, and the Posthumous Life of Romantic Prophecy

We don't read Joanna Southcott much today, a testament to the resounding finality with which Regency England buried her. A Devon upholsterer's servant turned latter-day Sibyl, who at the age of sixty-five mistook a fatal dropsy for a divinely authored pregnancy (and so captivated a nation), Southcott was interred by the *Times* in December 1814 with a sigh of palpable, and typical, relief: "the scandalous delusion which has for several months disgraced the metropolis, and even the character of the times we live in, is now at an end."[1] Twelve days later, the repressed was yet to return, secured as she was with anxiously adamantine chains. As part of its continuing coverage-*cum*-quarantine, the *Times* reported that after "dissection on Saturday se'nnight, the body was put in a plain coffin. . . . When the lid was screwed down, pitch was applied to the edges and rim."[2] Seizing all London's embarrassed attention—to say nothing of inducing a crisis in the "character of the times"—

---

1. *Times,* December 28, 1814, p. 3, col. b.
2. *Times,* January 9, 1815, p. 3, col. c.

was no small feat, yet the emphatic period of the *Times* has remained uncontested. Working on Southcott today can seem like an unwelcome exhumation.

She's largely absent from critical bibliographies, though the recent writing of Susan Juster, Debbie Lee, Helen Thomas, and Kevin Binfield are important exceptions, and apart from Fiona Robertson's *Women's Writing 1778–1838*, she has no representation in any anthology I'm aware of.[3] Even some of the most valuable studies of Romantic-era prophecy have little to say about her. For Anne Mellor, Southcott is the exception who proves the rule that "the female imagination during the Romantic period on the whole [was] *not* inspired by millenarian, apocalyptic thinking," since apocalypse was "antithetical to . . . the 'feminine mode of thought' in the Romantic period."[4] Morton Paley's *Apocalypse and Millennium*

---

3. Susan Juster, *Doomsayers*; Debbie Lee, *Romantic Liars: Obscure Women Who Became Impostors and Challenged an Empire* (New York: Palgrave Macmillan, 2006), 21–78; Helen Thomas, *Romanticism and Slave Narratives*, 50–60; Kevin Binfield, "The French, 'the long-wished-for Revolution,' and the Just War in Joanna Southcott," in *Rebellious Hearts: British Women Writers and the French Revolution*, ed. Kari Lokke and Adriana Craciun (Albany: State University of New York Press, 2001), 135–59. See also *Women's Writing, 1778–1838: An Anthology*, ed. Fiona Robertson (Oxford and New York: Oxford University Press, 2001). Joseph Lew considers the millenarianism of Richard Brothers and Southcott in "God's Sister: History and Ideology in *Valperga*," in *The Other Mary Shelley: Beyond "Frankenstein,"* ed. Audrey A. Fisch, Anne K. Mellor, Esther H. Schor (New York and Oxford: Oxford University Press, 1993), 159–81. Tim Marshall, in *Murdering to Dissect: Grave-Robbing, "Frankenstein," and the Anatomy of Literature* (Manchester and New York: Manchester University Press, 1995), somewhat problematically argues "that the Creature's part in the story, particularly as it affects Justine, can plausibly be read as a reworking of some key elements of the sensational 'Southcottian' controversy" (189).

4. Anne K. Mellor, "Blake, the Apocalypse, and Romantic Women Writers," 139–52 (140). In Mellor's view, a "female apocalypse" is an oxymoron, since apocalypse marks a "conception of time . . . as breakable, rupturable, full of gaps and holes," ultimately derived from masculine physiology, which experiences reproduction "through a process of ejaculation and separation. . . . In other words, the male birth process is one of creation and complete rupture" (141). This is a provocative intervention, but the embodied and somewhat essentialist argument, though explicitly limited to the Romantic period, seems to me an inevitably trans-historical assertion, as well. It's also in unexamined tension with the very long history of women's religious practice in England. Keith Thomas argues that as women were excluded from conventional forms of spiritual and cultural authority, they tended to gravitate toward eccentric versions of both throughout the early modern period; well into the seventeenth century, "recourse to prophecy was the only means by which most women could hope to disseminate their opinions on public events." Keith Thomas, *Religion and the Decline of Magic: Studies in Popular Beliefs in Sixteenth- and Seventeenth-Century England* (London: Weidenfeld & Nicolson, 1971), 138. The abiding interest of women in prophetic writing is powerfully narrated in Phyllis Mack, *Visionary Women: Ecstatic Prophecy in Seventeenth-Century England* (Berkeley: University of California Press, 1992); Orianne Smith, "'Unlearned & Ill-Qualified Pokers into Prophecy': Hester Lynch Piozzi and

invests in precursors, rather than contemporaries, situating canonical male poets "in appropriating, recasting, and radically revising material from the text of John of Patmos," while for Ian Balfour, "her writing is of quite a different character from that of the writers considered" by *The Rhetoric of Romantic Prophecy*, and so Southcott disappears after the second footnote.[5]

These accidental absences and strategic dismissals are understandable. Southcott's writing is hard to like, harder to make sense of. Her most attentive and generous critic concedes, "Southcott did not make it easy for those of us who wish to see in her voluminous writings a critical and discerning intelligence at work."[6] Her prophetic books, a hodgepodge of prose and poetry, were sometimes tame, as when she forecast the weather—which, contemporaries sniggered, was rather like prophesying with the net down, as twenty out of twenty-two harvests failed in Southcott's Devonshire between 1793 and 1814.[7] They were sometimes rather more ambitious, as she consistently cast herself as a mixture of Eve, Mary, and the "Woman Clothed with the Sun," in whom all of history stood complete: here was "a mystery which no man can explain. If it began with the woman at first, it must end with her at last."[8] Regardless of scope, her visions were usually ridiculous, and rarely sublime, prompting one modern critic to quip that "Joanna's characteristic tone is often more petulant than prophetic."[9]

This is an old game. Crafting the most elegant sneer at the unremitting awfulness of Southcott's writing has been a competition among her polite readers for a long time, serving to patrol the boundary between coarse enthusiasms and clerical sensibilities. But this boundary has proven unstable, and genteel critique sometimes identifies with what it condemns.

---

the Female Prophetic Tradition," *Eighteenth-Century Life* 28.2 (2004): 87–112; Ann Taves, *Fits, Trances and Visions: Experiencing Religion and Explaining Experience from Wesley to James* (Princeton, NJ: Princeton University Press, 1999); and Deborah Valenze, *Prophetic Sons and Daughters: Female Preaching and Popular Religion in Industrial England* (Princeton, NJ: Princeton University Press, 1985).

5. Morton D. Paley, *Apocalypse and Millennium in English Romantic Poetry* (Oxford: Clarendon, 1999), 5. Ian Balfour, *Rhetoric of Romantic Prophecy*, 288n2.

6. Juster, *Doomsayers*, 256.

7. On agriculture in Devonshire, see James K. Hopkins, *A Woman to Deliver Her People*, 69.

8. Joanna Southcott, *Prophecies Announcing the Birth of the Prince of Peace* (London: W. Marchant, 1814), 3.

9. Morton D. Paley, "William Blake, The Prince of the Hebrews, and the Woman Clothed with the Sun," in *William Blake: Essays in Honour of Sir Geoffrey Keynes*, ed. Morton D. Paley and Michael Phillips (Oxford: Clarendon, 1973), 260–93 (281).

Robert Southey's putdown of Southcott is surely best-in-show, but it's also nearly undone by the rabid energy she seems to arouse, as it abominates her "rhapsody of texts, vulgar dreams and vulgar interpretations, vulgar types and vulgar applications: the vilest string of words in the vilest doggerel verse, which has no other connection than what the vilest rhymes have suggested."[10] The vigor of Southey's assault comes from something more complicated than mere contempt. For vulgar and vile though they may have been, Southcott's prophecies also humbled the circulation figures of most everyone other than Byron and Scott, moving more than 100,000 copies between 1802 and 1815, according to biographer James K. Hopkins.[11] Her texts were aggressively priced—three shillings at the most, four-pence for brief pamphlets—and like most books, drifted far beyond their original purchasers. Demand was such that overuse may have compromised the resale market, with at least one bookseller complaining that "almost all the copies were worn out at the time by continual thumbing and reading."[12]

As we'll see, Southcott's fame was peculiarly self-consuming. Her cheaply printed texts now tend to survive (when they exist at all) only in microfilm catalogues, and she sold well among a somewhat invisible demographic of people who couldn't afford many books, which may contribute to her total absence from either the narrative, or the vast apparatus, of William St. Clair's *The Reading Nation in the Romantic Period.*[13] But her textual presence in late-Georgian culture was impressive—one of her prophecies went through nine editions of 1,000 copies each, while seventeen others went into multiple editions; forty-eight more sold through only single editions of 1,000 copies.[14] Contemporaries registered her as an overwhelmingly palpable presence, a leaning tower of Babel toppling over on its readers, and Southey joked that he had braved bodily danger, collecting "for you some account of this woman and her system, from a pile of pamphlets half a yard high."[15] Southey's mock-heroics are from 1807, by which time there was already sustained interest in Southcott's prophecies, but after her annunciation of Shiloh, the Prince of Peace, even Bonaparte was forgotten. In the autumn of 1814, an unauthorized biog-

---

10. Robert Southey, *Letters from England*, ed. Jack Simmons (London: Cresset, 1951), 437.
11. Hopkins, *A Woman*, 84.
12. Hopkins, *A Woman*, 85.
13. William St. Clair, *Reading Nation in the Romantic Period.*
14. Hopkins, *A Woman*, 84.
15. Southey, *Letters from England*, 434.

raphy went through eleven editions in a matter of weeks, and the *Sunday Monitor*, taking stock of the public's interest, devoted itself full-time to all things Joanna, as "in every street, alley, court, and house, nothing was heard but the name of Southcott," the fact that "the fate of Europe [was] about to be decided" notwithstanding.[16]

So if Southcott doesn't matter much to our understanding of early nineteenth-century British culture, she mattered very much indeed to that culture, and even beyond it. While lying-in in 1814, she entertained one "Monsieur Assalini, Professor of Midwifery in Paris, and Accoucheur to the Empress of France," along with "General Orloff, Aide-de-camp to the Emperor of Russia," who "treated the old lady with great respect, making a very low obeisance."[17] Southcott certainly worked hard to make herself matter, undertaking (according to William Cobbett) a daring public-relations program meant to capture the tastemakers: "She sent a copy of her book, with her portrait, in which the circumstances attending her impregnation are detailed, to the Prince Regent, to the Archbishops of Canterbury and York, Bishop of Worcester, Duke of Gloucester, Lord Grovesnor, Lord Ellenborough, the Duke of Kent, the Bishop of London, and the Bishop of Salisbury."[18] Anglican bishops would be hounded by Southcottians bearing pamphlets that demanded to be read, and boxes that demanded to be opened, until well after the First World War, but not all members of the peerage had their attention unwillingly conscripted: Byron's letters to John Murray of September 1814 show he was (at least idly) following the conflicting accounts of the "pregnancy" hawked by Southcott's doctors to the London newspapers.

In fact, Southcott's fame had spread throughout the Anglophone world, with coverage in Belfast, Philadelphia, and Boston, where the *Boston Spectator* saw fit to commission a running column (which seems to have meant that it would lift freely from Southey's *Letters from England*), since "Joanna Southcott is now the rage, and makes more noise in England, and commands more columns in their publick journals, than the Congress at Vienna, the negotiation at Ghent, or the war in America."[19] By 1814, Southcott awoke to find herself famously pregnant, and her celebrity escaped the usual forms of authorship into unexpected cultural

---

16. *Sunday Monitor* (London), November 6 and September 11, 1814.
17. *Times*, January 9, 1815, p. 3, col. c.
18. *Cobbett's Political Register*, September 10, 1814, 330.
19. "Joanna Southcott," *Boston Spectator* 1.54 (January 7, 1815): 215–16. See also "Devotional Somnium," *Analectic Magazine* [Philadelphia] 5 (1815): 497–509 (500); "On Credulity," *Belfast Monthly Magazine* 3.12 (July 31, 1809): 20–23 (20).

organs. One of the most serious and sustained accounts of her life and writing was provided by *La Belle Assemblée* (a Regency *Cosmopolitan*), which sandwiched two long, theologically focused essays between advice on fabrics, a "Description of an Autumnal Walking Dress," and an essay on "Slippers," in order "to gratify the curiosity of our fair readers, all of whom must have heard, of late, so many wonderful, and, we are sorry to see, so many *indelicate*, stories about this *heavenly upholsterer*."[20] Very few Romantic-era writers would achieve public attention so intense it could be found in even the most casual locations, and her very celebrity had begun to stymie her readers. Cobbett opened a would-be review in September 1814, shrugging that "the works of this *inspired* maiden have, in fact, been bought up with such avidity, that, admitting I were inclined to look into them, my bookseller says a copy of them is not to be had for love nor money."[21]

My subject is Cobbett's Southcott: the center of so much gossip she vanishes from the record, the object of so much talk she can't be read. I want to get at some of the mechanics behind her astonishing success, and even more astonishing disappearance. My argument isn't that we should be reading Southcott now, but why we aren't. Southcott matters, because her writing—however feeble, flat, and stupid it's usually held to be—contaminates some of the poetically potent and socially estimable systems of the Romantic era. She was one of the most commercially successful instances of "high romantic argument," that cluster of visionary power and prophetic utterance, divine inspiration and ecstatic transcendence. Southcott's England was one in which *The Prelude* and *Home at Grasmere* were unpublished, as were the lofty arguments of the *Defence of Poetry*; Keats was unread, Blake entirely unknown, and Coleridge, as I argued in the last chapter, a farcical wreck, whose attempt to resuscitate his career in 1816 was brutalized by Hazlitt in the *Edinburgh Review* as dangerously Joannian.

It was Southcott, neither polite, nor male, nor much of an authority, who had the copyright on the language of inspiration in Regency England. But for the accidents of textual history, this claim could seem very near a commonplace. *Don Juan*, the best-selling poem of the nineteenth century, opened its jibes at the popular productions of contemporary poetry alleging that *Lyrical Ballads* "is the sort of writing which has superseded and degraded Pope in the eyes of the discerning British Public, and

---

20. *La Belle Assemblée*, September 1814, 99.
21. *Cobbett's Political Register*, September 10, 1814, 327.

[Wordsworth] is the kind of Poet who, in the same manner that Joanna Southcote found many thousand people to take her dropsy for the God Almighty re-impregnated, has found some hundreds of persons to misbelieve his insanities."[22] Here is an almost-allegory for Southcott's almost-fame. Mediating the intersection between Byron and Wordsworth, she also disappears from the records of either—this "Preface" to *Don Juan* was suppressed until 1901, and both the poem she inaugurated, and the romanticism she was made to frame, were received without her. But this wasn't a thoughtlessly casual identification for Byron, whose pet-name for the poet-prophet Percy Shelley was the coyly Joannian "*Shiloh*," and it's worth recovering some of the defamiliarizing force of *Don Juan*'s introduction.[23]

Southcott provides a kind of counter-romanticism, in conversation with familiar rhetorics, yet utterly shorn of their familiar social contexts and ideological commitments. Hers is a tragicomic medley where inspiration is inebriation, and prophetic vision demands optometric correction, as *La Belle Assemblée* rehearsed "her nonsense about the vision at midnight, *like a large bowl* (a punch-bowl no doubt), behind her candle, where there appeared a white hand coming from the bowl, when a voice told her, 'fear not! It is I';—but there is something highly ludicrous in the spirit telling her *to put on her spectacles,* when the jolly dame began to *see double,* the candle appearing parted in two!"[24] This "argument" isn't "high," but "highly ludicrous," and for the early nineteenth century, "prophecy" and "inspiration" weren't the newly revived and gorgeously elevated tropes of an Oxbridge elite, but what a contemporary called "the witless efflorescences of a distracted old woman."[25] Pastiche or no, the spontaneous overflow of the corresponding breeze was hers, and it came as easily as leaves to the tree: it was her "still small voice, as a rustling wind, which dictates the whole of her writings, neither studied, nor submitted to subsequent alteration."[26] These are common conceits, but as Hazlitt's savaging of Coleridge suggests, any echoing correspondence between Southcott and a polite poet might seriously damage the gentleman. Southcott would never be much of a poet, and she abandoned the Wesleyans early in her career. But she was perhaps the Romantic period's most important tributary of

---

22. Lord Byron, *The Complete Poetical Works,* ed. Jerome J. McGann, 7 vols. (Oxford: Clarendon, 1986), 5:81–82.
23. On Percy as "Shiloh," see Paley, *Apocalypse and Millennium,* 195.
24. *La Belle Assemblée,* October 1814, 152.
25. D. Hughson, *The Life of Joanna Southcott* (London: S. A. Oddy, 1814), 4.
26. *Belfast Monthly Magazine,* "On Credulity," 22.

"Lake Methodism," the embodiment of the detour that funneled cultural and social privilege into semi-literate enthusiasm.

Resurrecting Southcott—and in particular, Southcott's inappropriateness—offers an approach different from the scholarship that hears secularized echoes of Revelations or Milton in Romantic-era texts, or that insists that post-Enlightenment "prophecy" be understood as a rhetorical rather than literal system.[27] This reading of the prophetic—materially absent yet abstractly vital, a game of allusive cultural capital attaching poets to a respectable Christian and literary heritage—is compelling, but it's only part of the story. It's also a motivated formation produced by a polite Romantic culture eager to dissociate from the very real (and very contemporary, rather than decently Biblical or metaphorical) prophecies that sold extremely well from 1780 to 1820. Prophecy with a literally predictive agenda—a form with recognizable norms and codified conventions—at once dominated and embarrassed England in the wake of the French Revolution. It certainly attracted more attention than the (at times numbingly) scholastic exercises associated with the Warburton lectures on the prophetic, or the remotely Higher Criticism that "called into question the literal belief in prophecy and its fulfillment."[28] To its casual consumers, of which there were ever more in the Romantic period, "prophecy" was at least as likely to mean Brothers and Southcott as Lowth and Hurd, and even its well-bred students could be alarmingly literal in their enthusiasms.

Take Spencer Perceval. In 1832, this son of the assassinated Prime Minister thundered on the floor of Parliament a Jeremiad against Reform and its plagues (cholera, he deduced). Reports of his shaking body and foaming mouth suggest the survival in even the most distinguished environment of deadly serious doom-saying:

---

27. Ian Balfour writes "there is hardly such a thing as prophecy in the sense of a clearly codified genre with definite contours . . . in European Romanticism generally. . . . It is usually more appropriate to speak of 'the prophetic' than prophecy, if the latter is a genre and the former a mode" (*Rhetoric of Romantic Prophecy*, 1).

28. Elinor Shaffer, "Secular Apocalypse: Prophets and Apocalyptics at the End of the Eighteenth Century," in *Apocalypse Theory and the Ends of the World*, ed. Malcolm Bull (Oxford: Blackwell, 1995), 137–58 (139). Shaffer suggests, "The state of affairs eloquently described by Christopher Hill as obtaining in the English Revolution—'It is difficult to exaggerate the extent and strength of millenarian expectations among ordinary people in the 1640s and early 50s'—had been much altered. England by the middle of the next century was no longer that 'nation of Prophets'" (137). Shaffer's skepticism for easy historical parallels is welcome, but her argument that revolutions in the stratosphere of Biblical textual theory transformed the religious sensibilities of "ordinary people" is problematic. Most Anglican clergy were ignorant of the Higher Criticism until much later in the nineteenth century, and many "ordinary people" during the Romantic period still had deep affection for magical and prophetic practices and explanations.

> Will ye not listen for a few moments to one who speaketh in the name of the Lord? I stand here to warn you of the righteous judgment of God, which is coming on you, and which is now near at hand. . . . Ye have in the midst of you a scourge of pestilence, which has crossed the world to reach ye. Ye brought a bill into the House to retard its approaches, and ye refused in that bill to insert a recognition of your God . . . I told Ministers it was not God they worshipped. The people is the god before whom they bow down in absurd and degraded worship. . . . This mockery of religion God will not away with, he will bring on fasting and humiliation, woe and sorrow, weeping and lamentation, flame and confusion. . . . I tell ye that this land will soon be desolate, a little time and ye shall howl one and all in your streets.[29]

Perceval inspired catcalls rather than pious attention in his peers. But only by mapping this awkward position for prophecy in the early nineteenth century—suspended between fundamentalist conviction, secularized contempt, academic attention, and noncommittal gawking—can we fully situate its most canonical instances. Even as certain types of Romantic-era prophecy were invested with tremendous prestige, others were stigmatized as cultural detritus or certifiable insanity, and the distinctions were easily compromised. The result could be an anxious, apologetic discourse, pervaded with a deep discomfort at its own existence, as Percy Shelley hedged that though "Poets . . . were called in earlier epochs of the world legislators or prophets," it should not be understood "that I assert poets to be prophets in the gross sense of the word."[30]

Prophecy could unite privileged arrogance with dropsical ridiculousness, and as Southcott would remind polite writers (and as they would gleefully remind their competitors), hierophantically masculine potency could easily be identified with an overweight, lunatic old woman. Southcott simultaneously fascinated and repulsed the nation. Yet her fame from 1813 to 1815 was also her undoing, and through the object that attracted the most attention: her body. It's just this body with which recent criticism engages, when it engages with Southcott at all. For Debbie Lee, Southcott's "brilliance" is "a language composed from a grammar of emotions and whose deep structure was the body itself."[31] Susan Juster leverages

---

29. See Boyd Hilton, *Age of Atonement,* 214–15, for an account of this harangue and reactions to it.

30. *Shelley's Prose: or The Trumpet of a Prophecy,* ed. David Lee Clark (New York: New Amsterdam Books, 1988), 279.

31. Lee, *Romantic Liars,* 22.

Southcott as a "place to begin an examination into the shifting place of the body in the history of female mysticism."[32] Helen Thomas draws attention to the ways "Southcott's revisionary female theology implicitly challenged the established religious and patriarchal traditions of late eighteenth-century England and redetermined the female body as an important textual medium."[33] The prophetess created the taste by which she has been judged, playing her most ambitious metaphysical stakes on the outcome of her pregnancy: "if the visitation of the Lord does not produce a son this year, then Jesus Christ was NOT the son of God, born in the manner spoken by the Virgin Mary; but if I have a son this year, then, in like manner, our Saviour was born."[34]

Southcott wasn't alone in viewing her pregnancy as a referendum on Christianity rather than on her. The *Political Register* seized the prospect of Shiloh to satirize the equally absurd consensus He scandalized. All Christian doctrine, Cobbett reminded, was founded on a confusion of physical and spiritual: "the great Author of Nature, in order to redeem his creatures from a portion of the disgrace entailed upon them, in consequence of their first parents eating some fruit from a forbidden tree, he begot, in a supernatural manner, a son upon the body of a young woman, who was betrothed to an old man."[35] But while wryly blasphemous, Cobbett's coverage was in fact almost uniquely temperate. Most of Southcott's contemporaries represented her body as her most outrageous conception. P. Mathias, one of the small army of doctors who regaled an eager nation with accounts of the changes in her breasts, belly, and diet, thought her pregnancy "so disgusting a subject," an idea "so revolting to common sense," that he was compelled to "enter my protest against opinions so blasphemous and profane."[36]

Southcott's pregnancy was less "hysterical" than the response of a besieged medical and literary establishment. The stakes were high, with Reason and Enlightenment in the balance. One biographer lamented that "a period when men are illuminated by philosophy, founded on experience . . . a period for useful knowledge should be perplexed by the wild

---

32. Susan Juster, "Mystical Pregnancy and Holy Bleeding: Visionary Experience in Early Modern Britain and America," *William and Mary Quarterly* 57.2 (April 2000): 249–88 (250).
33. Thomas, *Romanticism and Slave Narratives*, 53.
34. Southcott quoted in *Cobbett's Political Register*, September 10, 1814, 330.
35. "On Religious Persecution," *Cobbett's Political Register*, February 25, 1815, 251.
36. P. Mathias, *The Case of Joanna Southcott, As Far As It Came Under His Professional Observation, Impartially Stated* (London: Printed for the Author, 1815), 4–6.

vagaries of fanciful illusion."[37] But this cultural panic over Southcott's "revolting," "disgusting," and "blasphemous" pregnancy was also a safety valve, which released or displaced the actual tensions she conjured. It wasn't her body, but her *books* that had initially scandalized polite self-representation. As early as 1809, the *Belfast Monthly Magazine* whined that her prophecies, and the inexplicable demand they created, were "occurrences to shake my confidence . . . in the doctrine of the progressive improvement of mankind."[38]

Southcott as author, as poet, as marketing sensation: these were the roles in which she disrupted the norms of Romantic culture. The drama of late 1814 let a breathless nation recast Southcott as a bodily, rather than a cultural producer, a sexual rather than textual phenomenon. Britain knew how to accommodate—which is to say, discipline, pathologize, and disappear—the bodies of disorderly women, particularly by representing their disorders as bodily. The spectacular coverage of Southcott's bizarre "pregnancy" had a paradoxically normativizing force. Even as the coverage became more horrified, Southcott and the country could be returned to models of hysterical monstrosity and female sexuality that comforted in their dismissive familiarity, and allowed *La Belle Assemblée* to remark that "the whole piece is nothing but the production of a silly mad woman, attested by people as silly."[39]

That Southcott's pregnancy was, in fact, *not*—it was her death, rather than the Second Coming growing inside her—only reinforced its corrective function, retrospectively indicting all of her earlier prophecies as similarly fraudulent. After months of intense buildup, even a natural child would have had nearly supernatural consequences, as the *Political Register* suggested:

> [I]t is not of the miraculous conception, of the divine incarnation, which people in general doubt, or which prevents the many from declaring themselves. It is the fact of the pregnancy only which they seem to question . . . if Joanna's pregnancy does not fail, it will be somewhat difficult to prevent the increase of her followers . . . it is not impossible, [that it may] prove a formidable rival, to perhaps totally supercede, all other systems of religion.[40]

---

37. Hughson, *Life of Joanna Southcott*, 3.
38. *Belfast Monthly Magazine*, "On Credulity," 20.
39. *La Belle Assemblée*, September 1814, 102.
40. *Cobbett's Political Register*, September 10, 1814, 332; 327.

But fail her pregnancy did, along with her cultural capital: a narrative quickly coalesced around the prophet's irrelevant anachronism, of an alienation from modernity so profound it proved fatal. A few months after her death, Southcott could be imagined as having been always already posthumous, a weirdly belated fossil of medieval superstition cast up on the hostile shore of Reason. The consensus of History, reviewed by the American *Eclectic Magazine* in 1851, was that her "errors and actions . . . although taking place in the nineteenth century . . . equal in absurdity any that we read of as enacted in what we term 'the dark ages.'"[41] As soon study Margery Kempe as Southcott in order to understand the Regency; both women equally unnecessary to the age's self-representations, and its subsequent histories. Her prophetic books, proving no more fertile than her body, quickly died out of commercial and critical significance.

Posthumous Prophecy

Quickly, but propelled by an anxious urgency. As a practicing and vital prophet, Southcott had exposed a nerve of raw contradiction within orthodox Protestantism. By the late eighteenth century, normative theology in Britain, Anglican and Dissenting, was required to endorse Biblical prophecy, but only in the historical, geographical, and theological removes of the Holy Land. Southcott threatened to shred the thin polite fiction draping the Church of England, as it maintained the self-evident absurdity of contemporary prophecy, while drawing its doctrine from those testamental revelations that distinguished the perpetually holy from the singularly historical, and which kept ancient Judea relevant to modern Europeans. As *Wonderful Prophecies* argued in 1795, "to doubt of the truth and reality of the antient Prophesies, would be to sap the very foundation of religion, and to reject the universally concurring testimony of antient history."[42] The glue that bound faith to its evidences was not for universal application. Southey, for one, was wary of the wild transpositions of enthusiasts such as Brothers, Southcott, and Blake, since "[t]here are not so many points of similitude between Bristol and Jerusalem, as between Monmouth and Macedon."[43] But even otherwise staid churchmen were often heavily invested in some version of prophecy. This was,

---

41. "Curiosities of Eccentric Biography," *Eclectic Magazine* 22.3 (New York: March 1851): 409.
42. Brothers, *Wonderful Prophecies*, 6.
43. Southey, *Life of Wesley*, 1:216.

as Clarke Garrett suggests, a *Respectable Folly:* "millenarianism enjoyed a continued acceptability within educated circles through its association with a long line of distinguished scholars, including Joseph Mede, Henry More, Isaac Newton, and Joseph Priestley."[44] William Warburton, Richard Hurd, and Robert Lowth all made careers out of visionary study, climaxing in Warburton's endowment of lectures promoting prophecy as the bulwark for rational Christianity, devoted by its deed of trust to "prov[ing] the truth of Revealed Religion in general and of the Christian in particular, from the completion of the Prophecies in the Old and new Testament, which relate to the Christian church, especially to the apostacy of Papal Rome."[45]

But Warburton's safety latch was "the *completion* of the Prophecies" in the Testaments. To be socially acceptable, "Prophecies" could make no claim on later history. This was the thesis of Henry Kett's *History the Interpreter of Prophecy, or A View of Scriptural Prophecies and their Accomplishment,* a text that itself demonstrated the impressive network of cultural capital underneath the professional study of prophecy. The work had some popular success, going through two editions in 1799, but its publication by a university press guaranteed its impeccable theology, and Kett (a fellow of Trinity College, Oxford) dedicated *History the Interpreter* to the Bishop of Lincoln, "whose conduct as a man, and whose vigilance as a prelate, demand the grateful acknowledgements of every friend to the Established Church of England; especially at a period when such examples are eminently useful to the cause of Christianity."[46] But as a vehicle of exchange between well-connected clerics, *History the Interpreter* was expected to make the right noises about the historical termination of visionary power. Kett insisted that "since the Revelation by St. John closed the New Testament, 1700 years have elapsed without the appearance of any Prophet in the world . . . the great object of Prophecy being a description of the Messiah, and of his kingdom, the prophetic min-

---

44. Clarke Garrett, *Respectable Folly: Millenarians and the French Revolution in France and England* (Baltimore: Johns Hopkins University Press, 1975), 15. W. H. Oliver has similarly contended that "prophetic theology was . . . a normal exegetical activity, a concern of professional scholars, and a respectable way of saying things about God, man, and their relationship in society and history." *Prophets and Millennialists: The Uses of Biblical Prophecy in England from the 1790s to the 1840s* (Oxford: Oxford University Press, 1978), 13.

45. See Balfour, *Rhetoric of Romantic Prophecy,* 82–105.

46. Henry Kett, *History the Interpreter of Prophecy, or A View of Scriptural Prophecies and their Accomplishment,* 2nd ed., 2 vols. (Oxford: Oxford University Press, 1799), 1: "Dedication."

istry ceased when that object had been sufficiently displayed."[47] Contemporary men might interpret the prophetic Scriptures—though Kett shifted even this agency onto an inevitable and impersonal "History," which forecast only the "Accomplishment" of its subject—but they could never be prophets.

The Church of England would hear formidably erudite treatments of prophecy, but its historicizing projects never lost sight of their social function: the stigmatization of heretically prophetic practice by attending to sacred prophetic texts. The Warburton Lectures faced both ways, recovering the past in order to ignore the present. Genuine prophecy and its genuine "Cessation" were both equally precious blessings. As John Davison's Warburton Lectures (published by John Murray, read by both Coleridge and Southey) argued, prophecy had imitated the Messiah it foretold, sacrificing its historical life for the sake of the Christian cause:

> Prophecy had been the oracle of Judaism, and of Christianity, to uphold the authority of the one, and reveal the promise of the other. And now its latest admonitions, were like those of a faithful departing minister, embracing and summing up his duties. Resigning its charge to the personal *Precursor of Christ*, it expired, with the Gospel upon its tongue.[48]

This was good theology, though not everyone warmed to its melodrama. While Southey thought Davison would be "remembered as one of those men who supported by their ability and their learning the reputation which the Ch. of England has hitherto held above all other Protestant Churches,"[49] Coleridge marginalized "whether from any modern work of a tenth part of the merit of these Discourses, either in matter or in force and felicity of diction and composition, as many uncouth and awkward sentences could be extracted."[50]

The Church of England was emphatic that "prophecy," though the pillar of Christian prehistory, had not only ceased, it had ceased to be necessary. Everything that should have been revealed, had been revealed. As one of the speakers in the 1795 dialogue *The Age of Prophecy!* asserted: "for, by the sacrifice of the Messiah, the end of all prophecy was fulfilled; atonement was made."[51] Moreover, if prophecy had now been put

---

47. Kett, *History the Interpreter*, 1:24–26.
48. John Davison, *Discourses on Prophecy*, 456–57.
49. *New Letters of Robert Southey*, 2:411.
50. Coleridge, *Marginalia*, 2:154–55.
51. Anon., *The Age of Prophecy! Or, Further Testimony of the Mission of Richard*

to rest, it had always led a somewhat posthumous existence, and respectable accounts operated from within an unexpectedly inverted horizon of time. Rather than allowing the mystically palpable model promoted by *Wonderful Prophecies,* where "the direct and immediate influence of the unerring spirit upon the human mind . . . by a forcible impulse, turns its view towards futurity, and imparts to it an intuitive knowledge of succeeding events," scholars insisted on the archeological and retrospective force of prophecy.[52] Prophecy rightly considered, Kett argued, had never been important because of whatever paltry predictive function it had possessed: it was instead valuable as a *reminder* of the Providential organization of the universe, revealed through the rear-facing judgments of history. As humans grew ever more removed from Eden, the Fall, and the promises of Salvation, prophecy prevented this temporal gap from widening into a moral one, and recovered the lessons of the past by telling the future: "The Prophets, who followed Moses in continual succession for above a thousand years, were employed in preserving the remembrance of the gracious promises of future Redemption to fallen man, and the knowledge of a future state of retribution—in keeping up a sense of the constant superintending providence of God upon all the world."[53]

"Futurity" was ontologically subordinate to History, and prophecy had not so much revealed the details of the future, but that the future had always already been written. Only this initial divine inscription of an eternal organic form, rather than its later echoes, was worthy of admiration (and egregious capitalization): "THE HARMONY OF PROPHECY—THE ONE GREAT SCHEME THAT PERVADES ALL ITS PARTS—AND THE CONCURRENCE OF ALL HUMAN EVENTS TO ACCOMPLISH ITS STUPENDOUS PLAN."[54] Prophecy shaped narrative comfort—beginnings, middles, and ends of Aristotelian purity—out of anarchic and arbitrary time. Thus Davison contended that individual predictions were useless, only reaching moral and metaphysical meaning in their "system":

> This, to the serious religionist, is a doctrine of the greatest moment to his rational satisfaction. It gives to him the assurance of knowing that the system, in which his place and being are cast, is in the hands of God, not only as foreknowing that which it is to be, but as administering the plan and executing the ends of his Providential Government, (wise and right that

---

Brothers. By a Convert (London, 1795), 16.
52. Brothers, *Wonderful Prophecies,* 9.
53. Kett, *History the Interpreter,* 1:23–24.
54. Kett, *History the Interpreter,* 1:iii.

government must be) in the midst of all the tumult of the seeming disorders, the vicissitudes, and wayward course of the world.[55]

In this self-styled "rational" treatment, the true utility of prophecy was as a readily grasped thread—provocatively leading, but tattered and thin in isolation—that tugged into revelation the vast skein of God's providence, a sublimely permanent "Government" of markedly increased appeal as the supposedly perpetual kingdoms of earth crashed in Revolution.

The balance of antitheses in this construction of prophecy—the basis of Christianity, yet also superfluous to it; projecting into the future only to read the evidences of the past; black magic in some instances, a valid object of study for the eminently respectable in others—had always been delicate, under long pressure from freethinking Dissent. It finally tipped under the weight of Southcott, and her immediate predecessor Richard Brothers. In the mid-1790s, Brothers, a half-pay lieutenant in the Royal Navy, anointed himself Prince of the Hebrews (and so demanded the British crown, among other spoils), foretelling the death of George III and the total annihilation of London if his requests were not met. Government was alarmed enough to have him arrested for something like treason, but not before Nathaniel Halhed, a scholar of Oriental languages and religions, rose to his defense in the House of Commons, forcing a Parliamentary debate on Brothers's *Revealed Knowledge*.[56] Halhed's conversion stunned his colleagues into a baffled if politic silence, as no one seconded his motion to reconsider the imprisonment of the prophet. But in fact, Brothers represented an amalgamation of the orthodox and enthusiastic, with enough conventionality to appeal to a gentleman, and a certain restraint that offended Southcott (who also resented the competition). Though Brothers's *Revealed Knowledge* would become ferociously specific about impending calamities in its *Book the Second*, he had risen to fame with a visionary temporality not entirely alien to the politely retrospective version of prophecy endorsed by men like Kett and Davison.[57]

Book the First advertised itself as dead-on-arrival, since before any of its prophecies had been published, God had already declared to Broth-

---

55. Davison, *Discourses*, 78–79.
56. For the political and rhetorical entanglements within which Brothers found himself, see John Barrell, *Imagining the King's Death: Figurative Treason, Fantasies of Regicide, 1793–1796* (Oxford: Oxford University Press, 2000), 504–50; and Juster, *Doomsayers*, 151–62.
57. Richard Brothers, *A Revealed Knowledge of the Prophecies and Times. Book the Second* (London: 1794 [revised and expanded throughout 1794 and 1795]).

ers, "ALL, ALL. I pardon London and all the people in it, for your sake: there is no other man on earth that could stand before me to ask for so great a thing."[58] The presumption of this divine tête-à-tête resulted in an awkward circumspection. Brothers found himself pronouncing not *Apocalypse Now*, but *Might Have Been Had Not*, with a wistfully subjunctive admission that while Doom had been rescheduled, it would have been very impressive indeed:

> Had London been destroyed in the year 1791, the place where it stands would have formed a great Bay, or Inlet of the channel: all the Land between Windsor and the Downs would have been sunk, including a distance of eighteen miles each side, but considerably more towards the sea coast; it would be sunk to a depth of seventy fathoms, or four hundred and twenty feet, that no traces of the city might be ever found, or even so much as looked for.[59]

This was a pornography of disaster as compelling as any summer blockbuster, and just as self-consciously fictional: Brothers salvaged his apocalyptic special effects from a prophetic project now languishing in cancellation. Especially in its early versions, the *Revealed Knowledge* allowed itself to be experienced almost as entertainment, producing thrilling scenes of destruction safely neutered as alternative and already circumvented histories.

In this, Brothers was one of the most successful examples of a much larger transformation in prophetic culture. If the Romantic period saw fewer converts to prophetic cults than the 1640s, it had many more idle consumers of prophetic books. Susan Juster argues that while the stakes for prophecy were lower at the end of the eighteenth century—few people were expected to sell their goods and reorient their lives around a charismatic personality—the broadly diffuse influence of prophets may never have been higher, as men and women now casually glanced through pamphlets, or read skeptical and credulous accounts in the press.[60] The serious prophets of the Romantic period were more numerous than its poet-seers.

---

58. Brothers, *A Revealed Knowledge, Book the First*, 44.
59. Brothers, *A Revealed Knowledge, Book the First*, 44–45.
60. Juster's quantification of the scale of this transformation is dramatic: "For every person who joined a millennial sect or heard an inspired prophet in the 1640s and 1650s, hundreds of men and women read a millennial tract, followed the careers of itinerant prophets in the daily newspapers, or attended large open-air assemblies where obscure men and women warned of the dangers to come in the 1780s or 1790s." *Doomsayers*, 7.

Though Brothers and Southcott astonished the nation, they were just the leading edge of an enthusiastic subculture that seemed on the verge of losing its subordinate status: we know of nearly two hundred other British prophets publishing between 1750 and 1820.[61] The French Wars saw the most developed, most insistent market for new prophecy in the modern world, eclipsing even the Civil Wars, and according to an influential pamphlet in 1795, this demand marked an epochal shift: "as the world has seen an age of Reason and an age of Infidelity, so also shall the world see an age of Prophecy."[62]

Like the earlier tumults of the seventeenth century, the Revolutionary crisis seemed to call for visionary accounting. Many people didn't understand the French Revolution, and the ensuing mass mobilization, global war, crop failures, and currency panics in Britain, as political events at all. The available social and economic theories hardly accounted for upheavals so catastrophic they seemed Biblical in scope. Even sober thinkers like Kett granted that prophecy was the only technology up to the task: "it may be presumed, that a summary view of the Prophecies is particularly SUITED TO STRIKE THE MINDS OF THE PRESENT GENERATION, WHO SEEK IN VAIN FOR ANY OTHER ADEQUATE EXPLANATION OF OCCURRENCES SO DEEPLY INTERESTING TO THEMSELVES."[63] The more inexplicable an event seemed, the more attractive any explanation of its divine overdetermination became, and revealed Scripture promised a reliable script for navigating the bewildering. New (yet very old) protocols for prediction and risk-management were called for, Richard Brothers declaimed—now was the time to dispense with the nascent actuarial sciences, and deploy the prophets:

> If this war was like any which has preceded it, a prince might, as usual, sit down at his leisure, and calculate, from his successes, how long to carry it on; or, by his defeats, how soon he must leave it off; but the death of Louis XVI. and the revolution in France, having proceeded from the recorded judgment of God, the two *things which have occasioned it, and which have rendered it so entirely different, that its consequences are already determined.*[64]

---

61. Juster, *Doomsayers*, 64.
62. Anon., *Age of Prophecy!*, 7.
63. Kett, *History the Interpreter*, 1:ii.
64. Brothers, *Revealed Knowledge, Book the Second*, 28.

Prophetic culture, James Hopkins argues, was enormously appealing in its clear answers to complicated problems, offering people who "had virtually no understanding or even awareness of the precipitating factors of the events in France" the brusquely confident response, "It was brought about by God."[65] A mystical reading of the French Revolution was not incompatible with a political one, and informants for the Duke of Portland alleged that Paine's *Rights of Man* was being distributed with Brothers's *Revealed Knowledge* in Hastings.[66] But popular prophecy wasn't necessarily populist politics. Southcott was generally loyalist, her grievances with individual clergymen rather than the institutional Establishment. Even hostile accounts granted that she imagined her followers as a Home Guard, so that "when Napoleon was to effect a landing," he would "be put to death by the *sealed people!*"[67] Even so, as Tim Fulford observes, "Millenarianism was not an addition to radical politics but one of the principal discourses in which that politics was formulated."[68]

In the face of the dramatic rise of contemporary—and so blasphemous, if not Jacobinical—prophecy, it became ever more implausible for an Oxbridge don to meditate on spiritual visions with a straight face. William Pitt's agents planted prophecies in various "newspapers and pamphlets that cast the French Republic in the role of the Beast of Revelation,"[69] but after Waterloo, formal clerical treatments of the "prophetic" became ever more doctrinally detached from their subject. In part, this was due to the increasing importance of new methods of textual scholarship derived from models both domestic and foreign. Robert Lowth's *Lectures on the Sacred Poetry of the Hebrews* (1753) prefigured the Higher Criticism, decoding the Scriptures as performances of various personae rather than emanations of the unitary Divine Voice inspiring them,[70] while Herbert Marsh's translation of Johann David Michaelis's *Introduction to the New Testament* (1793–1801) encouraged theologians to uncouple the assured "genuineness" of the New Testament from its more problematic "inspiration."[71]

---

65. Hopkins, *A Woman*, xvii.
66. Hopkins, *A Woman*, 177. Burke, of course, thought that as Richard Price preached sedition, he "naturally . . . chaunts his prophetic song" (*Reflections*, 94).
67. *La Belle Assemblée*, October 1814, 152.
68. Tim Fulford, "Millenarianism and the Study of Romanticism," in Fulford, *Romanticism and Millenarianism*, 1–22 (3).
69. Garrett, *Respectable Folly*, 167.
70. Robert Lowth, *De sacra poesi Hebræorum* (Oxford: Clarendon, 1753).
71. John [Johann] David Michaelis, *Introduction to the New Testament*, trans. Herbert Marsh, 4 vols. (Cambridge: J. Archdeacon [Printer to the University], 1793–1801). See especially 1:70–97 for this argument.

By the 1820s, sober thinkers were eager to downplay the mystical force even of canonical prophecy. Henry Hart Milman's *The History of the Jews* (1829) coyly demurred whether any of the Testamental prophets in fact had been inspired,[72] while Davison's Warburton Lectures naturalized prophecy as merely a metaphorically exuberant mode of unexceptional theology: "Let the predictions of Prophecy then, for a time, be put out of our thoughts; and let the prophetic books be read for the pure theology which they contain."[73] But these shifts in emphasis are explained only incompletely by an intellectual history that notes the rising influence of the German school, or new strategies meant to secure the Church of England's flank against Unitarians or scientific materialism. Tim Fulford reads the collapse of popular prophetic culture in the 1820s and 30s as a general exhaustion at the failure of Brothers and Southcott, but I think the remarkable celebrity—independent from veracity—of both prophets from 1794 to 1815 shifted the terms of polite millennialism as surely as any continental theory or skeptical polemic.[74]

The years 1780 to 1820 witnessed prophecy's dramatic, and ultimately irreversible, slide down the ladder of demographic respectability, from the Warburton Lectures to "the people," "condemned by the opulent classes as fanatics and imposters, and by historians as cranks and the lunatic fringe."[75] The passage of time falsified Brothers, Southcott, and every lesser prophet. But the vast market demand they aroused was very real, capable of re-determining for its own interests even the most reticent scholarship that took seriously the possibility of prophecy, no matter how historically remote. In the course of debunking Brothers and others, the orthodox *Memoirs of Pretended Prophets* (1795) was most aggravated not by madmen—like the poor, its "Clergyman" author sighed, you will always have these with you—but by an amoral marketplace, which adopted and amplified madness to an unprecedented degree, jettisoning all values other than profit. Editors were now scavenging solid Warburtoni-

---

72. On Milman, see Jeffrey W. Barbeau, *Coleridge, the Bible, and Religion*, 33–35.

73. Davison, *Discourses*, 54. For an account of Anglican efforts in the middle of the nineteenth century to salvage holy "inspiration" from an increasingly implausible "revelation," see J. Robert Barth, S.J., *Coleridge and Christian Doctrine*, 53–84.

74. On the collapse of millenarianism, Fulford writes, "too many prophets had prophesied, too many days of predicted destruction gone without incident. . . . If the French Revolution had once seemed a millennial 'new dawn' and an apocalyptic 'blood-dimmed tide,' it had by now become a familiar, compromised affair." "Millenarianism and the Study of Romanticism," 10.

75. J. F. C. Harrison, *The Second Coming: Popular Millenarianism, 1780–1850* (New Brunswick, NJ: Rutgers University Press, 1979), 5.

ans, along with long-dead prophets from the Civil Wars, for any morsel of prophetic enthusiasm to offer the ravenous disciples of Brothers, and the increased sales mortified rather than gratified:

> We have lately heard much respecting Prophets and prophecies. The reveries of those enthusiastic men, who have formerly disgraced themselves by their pretensions to a prophetic spirit, have been industriously sought for. Even the writings of sober commentators upon the scripture prophecies, have been ransacked, and their modest conjectures have been styled predictions. Many motley collections of extracts, said to contain remarkable predictions, have issued from the press, and have found numerous readers.[76]

This bubble of prophetic speculation precipitated a panic over the determination of moral and social meaning in genuine scholarship: armatures of citation and classical languages might be recklessly discarded by "motley" anthologies, and "modest conjectures" might be unscrupulously excerpted until they would satisfy an antinomian. Fear at this sort of degradation is essential for understanding the deeply equivocal usage of prophecy that emerged even at the margins of Romantic culture; as Morton Paley suggests, Blake's enthusiasm for "prophetic books" in the 1790s may have waxed with the first flush of Brothers's success, and waned sharply following his arrest, which seemed to herald further crackdowns on outspoken enthusiasts.[77]

Nor was Blake isolated in his caution at being misunderstood, or in his case, perhaps being understood too well. Formally studying Biblical prophecy was one thing (and increasingly bad enough), but pretending to be an actual seer was quite another. Only by registering this historical situation for *The Prelude*—in which the two most famous contemporary prophets were an illiterate peasant woman, and a man lucky to be merely incarcerated after being accused of a capital crime against the state—can we recognize the awkwardly abashed way in which it claims the prophetic mantle for Wordsworth, with a humility that may also be a humiliation:

> Dearest friend,
> Forgive me if I say that I, who long
> Had harboured reverentially a thought

---

76. Anon., *Memoirs of Pretended Prophets. By a Clergyman*, i.
77. Paley, "William Blake, The Prince of the Hebrews, and The Woman Clothed with the Sun," 267.

> That poets, even as prophets, each with each
> Connected in a mighty scheme of truth,
> Have each for his peculiar dower a sense
> By which he is enabled to perceive
> Something unseen before—forgive me, friend,
> If I, the meanest of this band, had hope
> That unto me had also been vouchsafed
> An influx, that in some sort I possessed
> A privilege, and that work of mine,
> Proceeding from the depth of untaught things,
> Enduring and creative, might become
> A power like one of Nature's. (1805 *Prelude* 12:298–312)

There's certainly an elevated strain as Wordsworth ascends "reverentially" to the "privilege" of his "peculiar dower," though he would soften the enthusiasm of his "influx" into the simpler safety of an "insight" by 1850. But the polite diffidence before august company—"meanest of this band"—has a syntactical tic, and the entire passage is framed by a recurring entreaty to "Forgive me . . . forgive me." This is as much apology as assertion, one that eagerly reminds Coleridge ("dearest friend . . . friend") of his responsibility to provide a sympathetic reading. The poem ultimately recoils from fully naming Wordsworth—or, critically, any poet—a prophet, instead generating a simile that's also a hedge. Though David Riede reads this passage as "the communion of poets and prophets in a transcendent scheme," there's an equivocation within Wordsworth's equivalence.[78] Poets are "even as" prophets, which highlights rhetorical and even functional similarity while maintaining an essential distinction between the two. This is, the syntax insists, a tropical comparison and not an identification, while "each with each" links as it separates, binding poets to poets, and prophets to prophets, without endangering the clean purity of the categories. This is partly trepidation before Miltonic majesty, but it's also reticence to descend into the miasma of prophetic enthusiasm that was Wordsworth's far more immediate contemporary.

This is a familiar story for Romantic prophecy, which was characterized by an affect of mourning over its own death, anxiously declaring itself bereft of all contemporaries, while preaching a doctrine of "Cessation" that might satisfy any good churchman. Self-consciously polite writers coupled their investment in visionary apocalypse with its emphatic inter-

---

78. Riede, *Oracles and Hierophants*, 106.

ment, constructing a poetics of nostalgia that set the present decay of prophetic power against its historical—and *only* historical—force. Wordsworth's famous sigh "Milton! Thou should'st be living at this hour" may summon the figural power of what David Riede calls "the last prophetic voice in the English tradition," but it also insists on the *lastness* of that voice.[79] If Milton incarnates visionary energy he also ends it, and socially problematic enthusiasms are decently buried in the dust of the seventeenth century. Wordsworth's "prophecy" has no modern life, no material claims on contemporary England—its rhetorical vitality has survived only by embalmment. The lament of the sonnet "London, 1802" not only affiliates Wordsworth with the prestige of a Miltonic lineage, it's also making a very precise argument for spatio-temporal anachronism, inscribed by its title: *London, 1802*. Opposed to "London, 1649," this city, in this year, is a "stagnant fen" of spiritual energies that have "ceased to be," in which prophetic possibilities are hopelessly out of both place and time. If this is glum self-critique, it's also careful self-preservation, reluctantly relinquishing exalted models in order to inoculate against more embarrassing enthusiasms.

Autopsy and the Death of Romantic Prophecy

But London, 1802, also saw Southcott's first runaway success, *The Strange Effects of Faith*, suggesting Wordsworth had greatly exaggerated the reports of prophecy's death. The somber consensus of Southcott's "anachronism" and "alienation" from modernity was of course a motivated formation: she was the most powerful member of a community that reminded Romantic culture that vision, inspiration, and prophecy were hardly dead metaphors. They were increasingly *rude* metaphors, produced and consumed by the marginal and disenfranchised, and the polite pretense of the historical distance of prophecy was meant to salvage these rhetorics from social contamination.

Yet Southcott was especially important, I think, not because she was the ancient shockingly reborn in the present, but because she was so unnervingly modern—not just in the sense that she incarnated prophecy's heyday, but because she, more than any of her competitors, was a creature of the literary marketplace. She sharply deviated from traditional form of female mysticism, which was usually physical and private: the stigmata

---

79. Riede, *Oracles and Hierophants*, 9.

or bodily raptures, occurring in a bedroom or other cloistered space.[80] As Southey complained, if Southcott had had the decency to follow the precedents of charismatic piety, everything might have made sense. She galled insofar as she innovated, and the *Letters from England* regretfully set her against a simpler example of similar heresy:

> In the early part of the thirteenth century there appeared an English virgin in Italy, beautiful and eloquent, who affirmed that the Holy Ghost was incarnate in her for the redemption of women, and she baptized women in the name of the Father, and of the Son, and of herself. Her body was carried to Milan and burnt there. An arch-heretic of the same sex and country is now establishing a sect in England, founded upon a not dissimilar and equally portentous blasphemy. The name of the woman is Joanna Southcott; she neither boasts of the charms of her forerunner, nor needs them. Instead of having an eye which can fascinate, and a tongue which can persuade to error by glossing it with sweet discourse, she is old, vulgar, and illiterate. In all the innumerable volumes which she has sent into the world, there are not connected sentences in sequence, and the language alike violates common sense, and common syntax.[81]

Though this first "English virgin" was spectrally immaterial, having "appeared" in Italy as a deracinated apparition, she was also richly embodied, and Southey compromised her sacrilegious outrage through her corporeality. The virgin's body ultimately marked her as vulnerable and unthreatening, and the chilly casualness that froze her ending—"Her body was carried to Milan and burnt there"—coded discipline as pure inevitability. She posed an entirely unproblematic disobedience, one that was brought under a corrective regime without the sentence's rhetorical, let alone ideological, structures straining in the slightest: she did not contest orthodoxy, but revealed its serene dominance.

Not so Southcott, who broke radically with this earlier model, producing an eruption without a clear regulatory mechanism. As Southey ventriloquized through his Spanish Don, "this phrensy would have been speedily cured in our country; bread and water, a solitary cell, and a little wholesome discipline are specifics in such cases."[82] Here was a cult of personality not susceptible to the bodily controls of "bread and water." Southcott

---

80. See Juster, *Doomsayers*, 96–133, for an account of the enduring importance—from the medieval to the Methodistical—of the flesh in mystical experiences.
81. Southey, *Letters from England*, 433.
82. Southey, *Letters from England*, 441.

had substituted "innumerable volumes" for the captivating charms of "the eye" or the fleshly "tongue," and she "fascinates" not through an eroticized intimacy, but through the economic circulations of the bookseller's shop—her enthusiasms didn't come conveniently cloistered, but were rather packaged, priced, and "sent into the world." Southcott arrested attention with texts, not sex, and her language threatened Southey with a monstrous inversion of the sublime, passing all understanding as it blurred terror and the terrible. At once disgusted and overmatched, he confessed himself unable "to convey any adequate idea of this unparalleled and unimaginable nonsense."[83] Nearly all of Southcott's critics harped over the ineffable nastiness of her words, and Southey's sneer that "the language of Joanna . . . is groveling in the very mud and mire of baseness and vulgarity" was a universal polite opinion.[84] But such assaults could also be surprised by the compulsive attractions of language so catastrophically bad. If her books were disastrous, they also had the morbid appeal of a semantic car crash, from which it was impossible to look away. Her appalling vulgarity could generate solecisms so bizarre they were nearly poetic, bringing one essayist to marvel at her ability to marry "*man,*" "*done,*" and "*go on*" in rhyme, which "would indeed lead us to suppose it was some west country deity who had inspired this apostle."[85]

Southcott was managing to transform rhetorical imbecility into a perverse kind of strength, and no one was quite sure how to correct a set of texts that seemed to generate value out of error. As one of her followers, Elias Carpenter, argued in his *Nocturnal Alarm*, Southcott mattered more the less she meant. The further her texts drifted from any appreciable significance, the more transcendentally important they became:

> She pretends to no knowledge, frequently declaring herself unable to explain what she writes: and, in fact, she often gives proof that she understands not its purport so well as those to whom it is read. Had it been otherwise, we should have had none of those strong evidences of the reality of her work. Her being unable to explain what she writes, and to write so as others can read, are two circumstances which afford me the highest satisfaction.[86]

---

83. Southey, *Letters from England*, 437.
84. Southey, *Letters from England*, 445.
85. *La Belle Assemblée*, September 1814, 103.
86. Elias Carpenter, *Nocturnal Alarm; Being an Essay on Prophecy and Vision* (London: W. Smith, 1803), 68–69.

Southcottians might draw theopneustic "satisfaction" from "her being unable to explain what she writes," but even among the unconverted, the drumbeat of jokes against her incomprehensible "baseness and vulgarity" marked a nervous defense formation. If Southcott violated every grammar, she sold better than many decent authors, and by such a margin that her success called into question the operative force of the very sociolinguistic protocols she transgressed.

Southcott seemed to have an unsettling ability to remake in her image the culture she nominally embarrassed, captivating the establishment meant to restrain her. Southey sat incredulous as the reliable Anglican parsons dispatched to catechize Southcott were *converted by* her, and "listened with reverence, believed all her ravings, and supplied her with means and money to spread them abroad."[87] That she was a functionally illiterate peasant woman, somehow capable of producing a marketing campaign that the House of Murray might envy, only compounded the outrage of her celebrity. William Sharp, an intimate of the Godwin circle who was also Southcott's rapt devotee, engraved a portrait that captured her unique appeal, textually compelling and physically indifferent (see frontispiece).

This is remarkably unlike the portraits of other successful women writers such as Charlotte Smith and Felicia Hemans, who traded on sartorial sophistication and dewy-eyed sex appeal: this is a figure of little personal charisma and an unlikely author, every inch the fusty old serving woman in her Sunday (not very) best. Yet, despite belonging to the below-stairs, Southcott imperiously offers culture; she doesn't consume it. The outsized book of prophecy—the real site of attention for the engraving—nearly spills from its binding as it demands to be read, and even hostile viewers are conscripted into glancing over her open page. Most of all, this is an entirely one-way relationship of political and literary mastery. Her gaze, confidently addressing her spectator rather than the books in her lap, argues no interest in reading, only in being read. As she herself admitted, "I never read any books, at all; but write by the spirit as I am directed. I

---

87. Southey, *Letters from England*, 438. Tim Fulford has diagnosed this is as a chronic symptom of Southey's worries over the polite engagement with enthusiasm, suggesting that Southey also thought Halhed had "'gone native,'" importing an Eastern illness sympathetic to the domestic disorders of Brothers: "Orientalism might infect powerful and educated people with the same kind of irrational belief as that which uneducated people had contracted in ignorant credulity. Fanaticism, Southey feared, was a disease of British India that might leave the educated unfit to govern the uneducated—and the uneducated had already contracted a revolutionary version of it from France." Fulford, "Pagodas and Pregnant Throes: Orientalism, Millenarianism and Robert Southey," in Fulford, *Romanticism and Millenarianism*, 121–37 (127).

should not like to read any books to mix my senses with any works but those of the spirit by whom I write."[88]

Writing sixty-five books in twelve years, Southcott hardly had time to read. She was industrious enough to have become an industry: "dictating books as fast as her scribes can write them down, she publishes them as fast as they are written, and the Joannians buy them as fast as they are published."[89] But here the object of critique shifts from Joanna to the "*Joannians*"—not the private pathology of an isolated enthusiast, but a raucous system of market desire, and it's these Southcottians, even more than Southcott, who irritated. Rather like Byron's remark that the miracle was not that she was pregnant, but that she could find someone to make her so,[90] Southcott mattered not because she wrote, but because so many people wanted, and were able, to buy her prophecies. Her "inspiration" wasn't a rhetorical retreat or a transcendental withdrawal, but a thoroughly socialized system that entranced some, and appalled others. Disciples like Carpenter might celebrate that the prophecies barely had an author-function, belonging entirely "to those to whom it is read," while Southey warned, "when a madman calls himself inspired, from that moment the disorder becomes infectious."[91] But both agreed "Southcott" incarnated something public rather than personal.

For a brief moment, polite literary culture discovered itself floating fragilely atop a popular current that threatened to swamp its cherished self-representations. While the *Times* was "almost ashamed" at its own coverage "of the above-named wretched old woman," it justified itself that, "till her prophecies were made public, few of the better-informed people knew to what a degree of beastly ignorance thousands of their fellow creatures had fallen on religious subjects, by the desertion of their parish churches."[92] It wasn't just that Southcott's vast audience revealed that

---

88. Southcott quoted in Hopkins, *A Woman*, 10.
89. Southey, *Letters from England*, 442.
90. "I long to know what she will produce—her being with child at 65 is indeed a miracle—but her getting any one to beget it—a greater." Byron to John Murray, September 2, 1814, in *Byron's Letters and Journals,* ed. Leslie A. Marchand, 12 vols. (Cambridge, MA: Belknap Press of Harvard University Press, 1973–82), 4:164.
91. Carpenter, *Nocturnal Alarm*, 68. Southey, *Letters from England*, 428.
92. *Times,* January 12, 1815, p. 3, col. c. This "beastly ignorance" of "their fellow creatures" was sometimes driven even closer to home. The *Belfast Monthly Magazine* related the bewildered confusion of socialites calling for breakfast in Bath on the morning of Good Friday, 1808, and receiving only silence in return. The servant classes ("dupes to their superstitions and fears") had decamped *en masse* for the countryside, as a woman pretending to be Southcott had predicted the city would be destroyed for its Austenian sins. "On Credulity," 22.

"the progress of reason" hadn't had much effect on most of the country, and that the rural Devon of the nineteenth century could produce "wise women" as well as the thirteenth; an association between intellectual and class privileges—the demographic non-universality of universal reason—was as much feature as bug of "enlightenment."[93] On the contrary, the Southcottians, by flexing their economic muscle, were poised to seize control of the cultural technologies of Reason—print culture and the public sphere—without being co-opted into ideologies of politeness and rationality supposedly inseparable from them. Southcott's enthusiasms had found national purchase: the Southcottians demonstrated that "vulgar insanity" had a market, and not only of the abject and ephemeral sort catalogued by Iain McCalman's *Radical Underworld,* but one surprisingly well-to-do, with enough mass to redefine cultural norms.

By the autumn of 1814, Southcott's commercial success was forcing Britain to examine itself in a way that we no longer do: to consider the prospect of national tastes and traditions characterized not just by *Waverly, The Excursion,* and *Childe Harold,* but also by *Prophecies Announcing the Birth of the Prince of Peace.* Southcott seems to have been a mirror in which Regency culture discovered itself, and didn't much care for what it saw. Mythologies of the laudably sluggish rationalism of the English race were tarnished by a nation consumed with prophecies of post-menopausal pregnancy, and international prestige was on the line. Southey may have fabricated the Spanish contempt for "these English," whom the narrator of *Letters from England* was "accustomed to consider as an unbelieving people," only to discover they "are in reality miserably prone to superstition," but the press of former and current colonies was eager to trumpet England's absurd fixations.[94] The *Boston Spectator* laundered Southey's critique as its own, crowing that the prophetess conclusively proved that "extreme credulity is more prevalent among the lower classes of people in England, than in any other country that has any pretensions to vie with them in civilization."[95] The *Belfast Monthly Magazine* took some pleasure in hurling accusations of superstition back at the metropole, chortling, "there is more of this dupery in England than

---

93. As John Rule has shown, the folk-culture of Devonshire remained magical long into Victoria's reign, with deeply held beliefs about fairies, "knockers" (underground spirits who helped and hindered miners), witches, and conjurers. Rule suggests that it was precisely this powerful baseline of superstition which accounted for Methodism's striking success in Devon and Cornwall, as "Methodism did not so much replace folk-beliefs as translate them into a religious idiom." Rule, "Methodism, Popular Beliefs and Village Culture," 63.
94. Southey, *Letters from England,* 427.
95. *Boston Spectator,* "Joanna Southcott," 215.

with us: not, I suppose, from their greater credulity or cullibility [sic], but because being a richer nation, they are better able to afford the luxury of being duped."[96] Southcott had made "dupery" into a luxury good, and the nation bought heavily. Along the way, she was yet one more lesson that cultural authority and ostensible orthodoxy were fragile things, given to erratic obsessions and pathological fascinations: "there is no time when popular credulity has not some hobby, The Cock-lane Ghost—Richard Brothers and his prophecies, Perkins' Metallick Tractors—some prodigy or other makes a figure, and seems to engage the attention of a great portion of the nation, either in wondering at the miracle, or in laughing at those who believe it."[97] These hobbies might be risible, but Southcott seemed to evidence that they were not so much disruptive of English culture, as constitutive of it. One either believed or laughed, but the agenda was always already scripted by "popular credulity," and the belated tut-tutting of the self-appointed arbiters of taste was a weak reaction to, rather than a regulation of, the rumblings of enthusiasm.

In the last moments of her life, Southcott hosted anxieties much larger than herself: trepidation at new cultural politics driven by consumers with little interest in what had been hegemonic goods and practices; worries about the absent or insane program of the literary marketplace that she metaphorized, an Eolian machine that mindlessly spewed popular nonsense and stillborn monstrosities, to feed its "herd . . . ready to devour this garbage as the bread of life."[98] Southcott's prophetic certainty ironically figured the unpredictability of Romantic culture, the irresistible conscriptions that could faddishly remake a public sphere increasingly crowded with men and women unmoored from the anchors of serious material or cultural capital. The "Joannians" provoked something like what Lucy Newlyn has called "the anxiety of reception," an ideological rather than psychological unease at the vulnerability of authorial and national meanings, now in the hands of more and more readers, less and less "qualified to understand what they were reading."[99] Southey, one of Southcott's best if most reluctant students, found her the unexpectedly ideal trope for his own unwanted celebrity, which marked him as the victim of the culture he dominated unwillingly. In the midst of the *Wat Tyler* affair, he confided to William Smith, "I have reigned in the newspapers as paramount as Joanna

96. *Belfast Monthly Magazine,* "On Credulity," 20.
97. *Boston Spectator,* "Joanna Southcott," 216.
98. Southey, *Letters from England,* 437.
99. Lucy Newlyn, *Reading, Writing, and Romanticism,* 4.

Southcott during the last month of her tympany."[100] There would be other parallels, though it's hard to say whether they were more or less dignified; in the same letter, Southey suggests that "My celebrity . . . may perhaps have impeded the rising reputation of Toby the sapient pig."

But if Southcott was the personal vehicle for Southey's bitter humor at the absurd helplessness of the individual before the faceless malignity of publicity, for Cobbett, she had become the universal type for the times. Though "every age" had had its "*visionaries, prophets,* and *inspired,*" Southcott made a uniquely modern contribution, since all her "former competitors" were plagued by querulous self-doubt, prophesying "in so *ambiguous* a way, that even their most intimate followers found it difficult to ascertain the meaning of the oracle which they delivered."

> But in Joanna there is no want of *courage*. She seems to have been sufficiently aware that she lived in an *enlightened* age, in a country where *learning* abounds, *amongst scholars,* and with a people accustomed to *investigate* and *criticise*. Nothing of *concealment* marked her progress. From the commencement of, what she considers, her divine inspirations, she has *boldly* announced them; she has *challenged* inquiry; she has held *public conferences;* and she boasts of the *fulfillment* of her predictions—not uttered in *secret,* but in the presence of thousands of her enemies, who now rank themselves among her disciples and warmest supporters.[101]

In Cobbett's italicized community of keywords, parody rubs elbows with seriousness, and Southcott emerges as the unlikely exemplar of—or at least, impossible without—the public sphere of "thousands" of "*scholars*" and "*conferences,*" which "*investigate*" and "*criticise,*" according to the epistemologies of an "*enlightened age.*" These are the agents for Southcott's dissemination, rather than her rebuke, as "enemies" convert to "disciples" under the pressure of her "boldly . . . challenged" invitation to "inquiry." If there's a disorder here, the nation shares it with its prophetess, as contemporary enthusiasm supplants melancholy and "nerves" as what John Wesley's friend George Cheyne had diagnosed as "The English Malady": a madness born of cultural sophistication and imperial power, economic triumph and nice refinement, rather than abjection and alien-

---

100. *Life and Correspondence of Robert Southey,* 4:375. He got some mileage out of his Southcott joke, writing to Humphrey Senhouse in March 1817, "You see I am flourishing in the newspapers as much as Joanna Southcote did before her expected accouchement" (4:257).

101. *Cobbett's Political Register,* September 10, 1814, 326–27.

ation.[102] The rage for Southcott indicted the decadence of a culture so surfeited with leisure and wealth that both were wasted in lavish fruitlessness, and Joanna became the accidental magnet for time, money, and ink so plentiful they had no more urgent—or productive—use. As the *Analectic Magazine* informed curious Philadelphians in 1815, this was a disorder of the English national spirit, which, while at war with both French ambition and American democracy, chose to devote its resources instead to Southcott's "nursery furniture, baby clothes, and gold candle cups and spoons . . . a superb manger fitted up as a child's crib, made of the most costly materials, with draperies, &c., cost 300£. Many dozens of damask and diaper napkins, seriously wrought, designed for solemn occasions; a costly mohair mantle; a purple robe diverse rich frocks bibs, caps &c . . . a large sum of money was subscribed to build a palace for the expected infant."[103]

It's just as she was beginning to mean something far beyond herself that the fatal collapse of her pregnancy could be made to shrink the heady consequences of Southcottianism back into Southcott, and bury them with her. The prophetess's body itself became weirdly composed out of printed matter. After her death, Southcott was autopsied in public, as each of her attending physicians published his own pamphlet on the (increasingly rotten) state of her corpse—all of which were frantically recycled in the London press. The media frenzy allowed her "pregnancy" to be figured as an error of individual, rather than social production, signifying a personal rather than a cultural deformation. "Shiloh"—and all the attention showered upon him—was made symptomatic only of the illness of his "mother," rather than the pathologies of polite taste. Coverage of Southcott's texts had always been exercises in contempt, with one reviewer

---

102. Though Cheyne's interests were ultimately humoral and physiological, he introduced his discussion with a treatment of the cultural pathology that followed from unprecedented affluence: "The Title I have chosen for this Treatise, is a Reproach universally thrown on this Island by Foreigners, and all our Neighbours on the Continent, by whom nervous Distempers, Spleen, Vapours, and Lowness of Spirits, are in Derision, called the ENGLISH MALADY. And I wish there were not so good Grounds for this Reflection. The Moisture of our Air, the Variableness of our Weather, (from our Situation amidst the Ocean) the Rankness and Fertility of our Soil, the Richness and Heaviness of our Food, the Wealth and Abundance of the Inhabitants (from their universal Trade), the Inactivity and sedentary Occupations of the better Sort (among whom this Evil mostly rages) and the Humour of living in great, populous and consequently unhealthy Towns, have brought forth a Class and Set of Distempers, with atrocious and Frightful Symptoms, scarce known to our Ancestors, and never rising to such fatal Heights, nor afflicting such Numbers in any other known Nation." George Cheyne, *The English Malady* (London: G. Strahan, 1733), i–ii.

103. *Analectic Magazine*, "Devotional Somnium," 500.

abandoning his essay with, "Poh!—it smells rank! How long must lewdness and debauchery be thus permitted to insult both religion and common sense!"[104] But her dissection transitioned this valedictory disgust to her body, neatly dropping all notice of her books: that Regency print culture judged the exhumation of a rotting corpse a fitter object for public attention than Southcott's verse-prophecies testifies to the depth of the anxiety they stirred. Time and again, articles emphasized the peculiar, almost unnatural decay of Southcott. The *Times* reported that Joanna's body was coming apart at the seams "in such a high degree of putrefaction, that we could not trust to the limbs to convey it, and it was accordingly moved to the table on a sheet."[105] The *Edinburgh Review* explained, "The dead body was kept warm for four days, according to her own previous directions, in hopes of a revival, and the birth of the promised child; it was not consigned to the dissection, till putrefaction had rendered it extremely offensive."[106] Though Southcott had seemed on the verge of escaping early modern formations of bodily mysticism, here was the return of repressed medievalism. There must have been, the *Times* and the *Edinburgh* implied, a quasi-supernatural judgment in her hasty decomposition, that most ancient test of saints, and her flesh was finally conquered by the ecological and material logics her spiritual pregnancy had claimed to transcend.

So foul had Southcott's body become—layered as it was under the flannel blankets brought by her well-meaning followers, who hoped to keep the infant Shiloh warm—that the autopsy procedure was abandoned midway. The attending physicians spared no gruesomeness. Dr. Mathias offered that "the rest of the viscera were not examined minutely, from the extreme offensiveness of the body,"[107] while Dr. Reece chuckled that "the body was in so highly a putrid state, that it was thought unnecessary to examine the brain, where it was probable all the mischief lay."[108] The medical agreement on her "extreme offensiveness" is exceptional. Paul Youngquist argues that most early nineteenth-century anatomists of the female body were careful to "eschew visceral response," in order "to assert an affective threshold above which disciplined knowledge holds dispassionate sway," as "all that falls below becomes its other," figuring

---

104. *La Belle Assemblée*, October 1814, 152.
105. *Times*, January 9, 1815, p. 3, col. d.
106. "Joanna Southcott," *Edinburgh Review* 24 (February 1815): 453–71 (469).
107. Mathias, *Case of Joanna Southcott*, 16.
108. Reece quoted in Paley, "William Blake, the Prince of the Hebrews, and The Woman Clothed with the Sun," 288.

women as "existentially anonymous, interchangeable husks of flesh."[109] But there was nothing "dispassionate," and certainly nothing "existentially anonymous," about the stylized horror in the medical testimony on Southcott, and the point of this autopsy was, I think, to fixate on the contemptible vileness of her body, rather than on whatever that body might signify.

This was a procedure designed to circumvent knowledge rather than reveal it, excusing the nation from any further reflections on the matter of Joanna Southcott. That Reece thought it "unnecessary" to complete his examination due to the revoltingly "putrid state" of his subject argues that this procedure did not penetrate the body in order to disclose secrets, but to keep them well hidden: it was a form of professional attention that authorized cultural inattention. Southcott's body was made to disclose just enough to disclose no more—having speculatively isolated "all the mischief" in her physiology, no further argument or observation was necessary, and Southcott, and Southcottianism, were silently filed away. Her last creation, like all her prophecies, was fraudulently vacuous, the disgusting result of so much hot air. The final diagnosis of Shiloh, and of Southcott, was that "the flatus of the intestines satisfactorily accounts for the extraordinary size of the deceased."[110]

In a handful of months after her death, Southcott was so successfully reincorporated into disciplinary logics that she became literally unhearable, vanishing from the records that might otherwise have carried her to us today. It would be histrionic to call this a conspiracy of silence, especially as there was nothing secretive about the decision: it was enshrined in the public sentence of the law, for all to see. Southcott's pregnancy had made her into an object of impossible attention, as the ubiquity of the gossip that enveloped her precluded any textual registration—as she became a figure of universal interest, she was, legally, rendered entirely illegible. By 1815, she had been formally recuperated into the grammars of female decorum she had so thoroughly violated, and the case of *Ditchburn v. Goldsmith* allegorizes Southcott's disappearance from Regency culture, and its subsequent histories. "This was," reported the *Annual Register*, "an action between inhabitants of Gravesend, upon a wager laid by the defendant, who was a preacher of the doctrines of the late Joanna Southcott, of £200 to £100 that she would be delivered of a male child on or before the 1st of November last." Yet the preacher was luckier in his

---

109. Paul Youngquist, *Monstrosities: Bodies and British Romanticism* (Minneapolis: University of Minneapolis Press, 2003), 135–38.

110. Mathias, *Case of Joanna Southcott,* 15–16.

defense than in his doctrine. He leaned on a precedent from Lord Mansfield, that any wager "as would 'affect the interest or the feeling of a third person; for instance, that such woman has committed adultery, or that an unmarried woman has had a bastard'" could not be heard by an English court. Lord Chief Justice Gibbs agreed, dismissing the case, refusing to "try the extent of a woman's chastity and delicacy in an action upon a wager," and establishing the impossibility of any future considerations of Joanna Southcott by any court.[111]

This technical act of oblivion figured a more general forgetting. Culture as well as Law exiled into polite silence the chatter and body of an old woman, the last records of her language and form narrating only the anonymity to which both had decayed beyond recovery. As the *Times* reported in its final dispatch, Southcott's fame could never recover from her burial. Her pallbearers masqueraded in silence, "so completely had they succeeded in disguising themselves, that not a feature was visible," while "they abstained from all conversation." These misdirections indicated the darker obscurity of their charge:

> The few people whom curiosity attracted round the grave had not the slightest suspicion that the coffin contained the remains of Joanna Southcott. Such precautions were taken, that it was impossible the secret could prematurely transpire.[112]

The nation interred not just Joanna's enthusiasm, but its own, comfortably secure that neither could be reanimated from beyond the grave. One of the dissecting physicians, triumphing over the wrecked body, confidently jested that "certainly the same power that could raise a putrid body, could raise one that had been opened."[113] But as Mary Shelley would teach a handful of years later, the enthusiasms haunting polite Romantic culture wouldn't stay buried so easily.

---

111. "Ditchburn v. Goldsmith," in *The Annual Register, or, A View of the History, Politics, and Literature for the Year 1815* (London: Baldwin, Cradock, Joy, et alii, 1816), 289–90.
112. *Times,* January 9, 1815, p. 3, col. c.
113. *Times,* January 9, 1815, p. 3, col. d.

Chapter 6

Resurrection, the New Birth, and Vital Christianity

The Methodism to Frankenstein's Madness

Joanna Southcott brings us close to Victor Frankenstein, while seeming to take us very far afield. Intimacy appears in inversion, as Romanticism's most famous pregnancy without a birth, and birth without a pregnancy, each feature their own hysteric bodies, putrescent corpses, and reanimations performed not at all, or only too well: both hideous progeny of what Ellen Moers identified as the "Female Gothic," that discourse of physiological terror at the terror of physiology, rooted in the "glands, muscles, epidermis, and circulatory system" of feminine objects and subjects.[1] Some thirty years ago, *Frankenstein* began to benefit from a critical revolution so entirely persuasive as to become a benevolently *ancien regime*, and it's now difficult (if not fruitless) to attend to the novel without Anne Mellor's invitation to read it as "a book about what happens when a man tries to have a baby without a woman," concerned "with natural as opposed to unnatural modes of production and reproduction."[2]

---

1. Ellen Moers, "Female Gothic," in *The Endurance of Frankenstein: Essays on Mary Shelley's Novel*, ed. George Levine and U. C. Knoepflmacher (Berkeley, Los Angeles, London: University of California Press, 1982 [1979]), 77–87 (77–78).

2. Anne K. Mellor, *Mary Shelley: Her Life, Her Fiction, Her Monsters* (New York:

With only a few deforming transformations, this might be Southcott's story as much as Shelley's. Creation, procreation, and the disappointments of both, a story at once deeply personal and utterly alienated from the woman who authored it: if Southcott's "Shiloh" mirrored the nation rather than its mother, there was never a time, except perhaps in the seminar room, when Shelley's novel was better known than its adaptations.[3]

Yet if one critical tradition might suggest the community between prophetess and prophet's wife, a second, almost as established and compelling, ought to keep them apart. Southcott's eccentric, profound, and profoundly literal religiosity would seem to find scant purchase on Shelley's atheistic materialism, or on the novel which emanates from it. *Frankenstein*'s is, after all, a modern sort of Prometheanism. If there's a mythological registry here, it's decidedly classical and skeptical. The novel's title page banishes Christian dogma into the poem that Percy Shelley thought its fullest indictment, partially voicing Adam's rebellious adolescence, without his subsequent awareness that he is patriarch as well as son, a master by the same logic which subordinates him.[4] The story following this allusive abjuration is "starkly secular," according to Chris Baldick, as it "explores the godless world of specifically modern freedoms and responsibilities."[5] Judith Wilt argues that the only religion left by "Mary Shelley's atheistic trinity" is a theologically savvy parody of a medieval mystery play, in which the "absence of God is celebrated in the presence of metaphor,"[6] what Paul Cantor calls Shelley's "gnostic twist to her creation myth."[7]

Methuen, 1988), 40.

3. See especially St. Clair, *Reading Nation*, 357–73, for the different social lives of *Frankenstein* as book and "Frankenstein" as cultural phenomenon in the nineteenth century. The success of the 1818 novel was modest, and though resurrected in 1831, it again went out of print in a few decades, reappearing only toward the end of the century—all while various dramatic adaptations flourished. Susan Wolfson provides a valuable survey of more modern "Frankentalk," as well as a wittily annotated compendium of film and TV versions, in her edition of *Frankenstein* (Longman, 2007 [2nd ed.]), 402–24; 429–31.

4. As Adam reasons within twenty lines of claiming he never asked to be born:

>   and though God
> Made thee without thy leave, what if thy Son
> Prove disobedient, and reprov'd, retort,
> Wherefore didst thou beget me? I sought it not:
> Wouldst thou admit for his contempt of thee
> That proud excuse? (*Paradise Lost* 10:759–64)

5. Chris Baldick, *In Frankenstein's Shadow: Myth, Monstrosity, and Nineteenth-Century Writing* (Oxford: Clarendon, 1987), 42; 5.

6. Wilt, "*Frankenstein* as Mystery Play," in Levine and Knoepflmacher, *Endurance of Frankenstein*, 31–48 (40; 32).

7. Paul Cantor, *Creature and Creator: Myth-Making and English Romanticism* (Cam-

So the familiar story goes: in the midst of all the uncanny horrors of the novel, the antithesis between Faith and Reason can still be found at its most comfortably extreme. Frankenstein may be mad, but there's a specifically scientific method to his madness: "I paused, examining and analyzing all the minutiae of causation."[8] His Creature, while perhaps woefully anti-natural, has its supernaturalism thoroughly naturalized. Its construction, as Frankenstein makes sure to note, proceeds from a logical series of "discoveries in the improvement of some chemical instruments, which procured me great esteem and admiration at the university" (31–32). "The stages of the discovery were distinct and probable," and there's not a whiff of the mystical: the whole event is explicitly "not . . . like a magic scene" (33). Steven Jones rightly cautions against projecting our contemporary "science" and its discontents onto Victor, who is more alchemist than chemist and "still a long way from the modern technologist,"[9] but Victor's obsessive scholarship, distinct from its quality, situates him socially as well as intellectually. The resurrection that follows seems worlds removed from the miserable absurdities of the Southcottians: Frankenstein's errors are those of a man too well educated, so supremely privileged that his very monsters are the deformities of his class advantages. The Creature, in a perverse way, is the shambling reminder of (but not only of) his creator's dignity, which the very first words of his narrative trumpet: "my family is one of the most distinguished" of Geneva (17).

But Victor's cover of rationalist distinction is thin. If his "workshop of filthy creation" presents an inevitably iconic laboratory of sparking instruments and foaming beakers, this is a readerly intuition determined by centuries of dramatic and cinematic revision. Shelley herself describes his lair in only the vaguest terms, "a solitary chamber, or rather cell, at the top of the house," while leaving the actual mechanics of reanimation entirely undefined (35). The narcissistic entitlement of Frankenstein's self-heroizing is sometimes ludicrous, and often certifiable, as he makes each of the novel's fatally suffering subjectivities "but a type of me" (204). Yet despite his self-absorption, Victor relays a narrative deeply problematic for a member of a ruling elite. Whatever else he is, Frankenstein is an "enthusiast," and not an enthusiast of the better sort. The word is positively endemic in his story, sometimes occurring many times in a single page: it was an "enthusiastic frenzy that blinded me to the horror of my employment," a "mad

---

bridge: Cambridge University Press, 1984), 105.

    8. Mary Shelley, *Frankenstein; or, The Modern Prometheus*, ed. Susan J. Wolfson, 2nd ed. (New York: Longman, 2007), 32. Further citations appear in parentheses.

    9. Steven E. Jones, *Against Technology*, 115.

enthusiasm" that spawns his "enemy," though at times this "enthusiasm was checked by my anxiety" (128, 144, 36). Endemic, and infectious. Frankenstein's disciple Robert Walton breathes the same heady air, feeling his "heart glow with an enthusiasm which elevates me to heaven," where he might hold final communion with Victor; in a fit of "enthusiasm" Walton describes him as "this divine wanderer . . . a celestial spirit, that has a halo around him" (6, 16).

The story of *Lake Methodism* concludes with this "enthusiasm" that bonds these would-be titans of masculine self-aggrandizement. Frankenstein's "enthusiasm," so often received as adventurous hubris, is more deeply and pervasively connected to the besotted lunacies of Southcott and other traditions of religious enthusiasm. Victor—like Southcott, lay preachers, Wordsworth, and Coleridge—declares "I prophesied truly" (52). To take him seriously is also to take him out of the politely deranged laboratory and into the disreputable chapel, from which he emerges with a cultural prehistory more Wesleyan than Newtonian. Scholars who have discovered only the dessicated husk of secularized religion in *Frankenstein* may have been looking for the wrong thing, in the wrong place. While there's very little spiritual orthodoxy (or any other orthodoxy, for that matter) in the novel, it overflows with the most urgently popular—and the most socially problematic—religious forms of the late eighteenth and early nineteenth centuries.

Gospel as much as Galvanism drives Victor's quest to make the dead live again—though, as we'll see, these weren't contradictory formations—and the account which follows his "new birth," filled as it is with self-appointed martyrs, prophets, and devils engaged in cosmic struggle, reads like a pitch-perfect rendition of spiritual warfare. Frankenstein has boldly gone where most enthusiasts tried, and failed, to go. As the American *Eclectic Magazine* recounted in 1851, Southcott herself, before attempting to give birth to God, had been disappointed in giving life to the dead:

> On another occasion, to confirm her disciples, a miracle was announced to be performed on a certain day; and this was to raise a corpse to life. The Devil, however, in the shape of Wortley, an officer of the Union Hall Office, interposed and spoiled the effect, by proposing that the dead man should first be stabbed with a dagger. The corpse not liking such a process got up and ran away, to the great astonishment of the congregation.[10]

---

10. "The Curiosities of Eccentric Biography," *Eclectic Magazine* 23.3 (New York, March 1851): 401–9 (408).

But what had safely devolved into farce by the middle of the century was quite serious several decades earlier, when the rhetorics, and, not uncommonly, the practices of spiritual and physical resurrection, still possessed an electric charge.

Methodism, Southey reminded the nation two years after the first edition of *Frankenstein,* was "Vital Christianity," which "hoped to give a new impulse to the Church of England, to awaken its dormant zeal, infuse life into a body where nothing but life was wanting."[11] These enthusiastic Vitalities were personal as well as national, animating sinners along with churches in what James Lackington, whose firm would publish *Frankenstein* three years after his death, called (along with every other Methodist) "pass[ing] through the *New Birth,*" as vile bodies were changed for glorious bodies, "and (to the great grief of his parents)" one might "become a *new creature.*"[12] If Lackington's Oedipal hint suggests a publishing house uniquely primed to grasp the appeal of new creatures warring with old parents, other Methodist converts described their transformations in language even more strikingly prefigurative of Frankenstein's experiment: "I felt as if Lightning, or a slower ethereal Flame, had been penetrating and rolling through every Atom of my Body."[13] In its atomic power, this "new birth" warns against too easily conflating materialism with atheism in the early nineteenth century; molecular detail could be just one more field for the activation of Providential energy. The sort of narrative which Victor propounds conforms to Methodist as well as scientific conventions. Southey's horrified rehearsal in 1810 of the typifying insanities of Wesleyan autobiography doubles as a remarkably accurate plot summary for Shelley's novel: "They tell us of devils hovering about the death-bed of an unbeliever, and record the ravings of delirium as actual and terrific truths . . . and in one instance, not indeed in direct terms, but in expressions that unambiguously are intended to be so understood, they lay claim to the miracle of having raised the dead!"[14]

These enthusiastic formations—new births and new creatures, death and life-in-death, resurrection and reanimation, and the battle between the elect and the Devil—seem to me essential for understanding some of the peculiar (and peculiarly ironic) force of *Frankenstein,* and later sections of this chapter will explore each in more detail. None of this is to say that the novel is "religious" in any metaphysical sense. Shelley offers

---

11. Southey, *Life of Wesley,* 1:264.
12. Lackington, *Memoirs,* 42.
13. Quoted in Hindmarsh, *Evangelical Conversion Narrative,* 134.
14. Southey, "On the Evangelical Sects," 508.

critique, not confession, one typically oriented around social rather than spiritual effects, the personal and interpersonal disfigurations consequent upon enthusiastic discourse. Yet perhaps even this limited reading of *Frankenstein*'s "religion" seems to miss the mark, frustrated, if not by Shelley's text itself, then by the para-text in Percy Shelley's hand. While Mary's 1831 "Introduction" paints its "pale student of unhallowed arts" (190) as a warlock rather than professor, whose "unhallowed" transgressions are explicitly blasphemous, rather than simply in defiance of the protocols of peer-review, Percy's 1818 "Preface" frames the novel with a doubled skepticism: if the "event on which this fiction is founded has been supposed, by Dr Darwin, and some of the physiological writers of Germany, as of not impossible occurrence," nevertheless "I shall not be supposed as according the remotest degree of serious faith to such an imagination" (3).

These Darwinian and continental attestations build a handbook, not for the science of life and irregular creation, but for the empirical doubt upon which such science might be based, in which experimental "supposition" tracks only to its own falsification ("I shall not be supposed"), prefacing the novelist, if not the novel, as the proponent of a rationalist epistemology which rejects "the remotest degree of serious faith." Yet the uncontrolled pun on "the remotest degree" also suggests that this "Preface" isn't entirely in control of the novel it introduces, a novel that willfully begins in a contrarian embrace of the remotest degrees of frozen temperatures and forbidden latitudes. This gap between Percy Shelley and *Frankenstein* is as much my subject as "enthusiasm," though ultimately they amount to the same thing, as the novel's sociospiritual critique figures the enthusiasms of the poet's own discourse as its object. Percy worked over the original draft meticulously, and somewhat cluelessly: his assertion that the novel's "chief concern" was "the exhibition of the amiableness of domestic affection" (4) is either a piece of very sharp wit, or very dull criticism. But if he had any difficulty reading *Frankenstein*, it reads him, and the cultural privileges invested in him, with sublime irony.[15]

The Shelleys' Enthusiasms

Like Victor Frankenstein, Percy Shelley was an enthusiast, and like Victor, not always one of the better sort. He was, as Stephen Behrendt remarks

---

15. Anne Mellor has painstakingly recreated Percy's editorial attentions and inattentions to *Frankenstein*, in *Mary Shelley*, 58–69 and 219–24.

near the beginning of *Shelley and His Audiences*, "always enthusiastic," an observation which amplifies the poet's insecurities.[16] "Enthusiasm" maps Percy's intersection with what I've tried to identify as "Lake Methodism," the double-crossing of poetical prestige and popular religion, in which even one of the Romantic period's most outspoken skeptics might find himself snared. Not that this Shelley always registered the pressure: in his optimistically unproblematic moods, he figured "enthusiasm" as a blessed relaxation of the social, brought on by tensing imaginative nerves. As he wrote in a letter of 1812 on *Queen Mab*: "You will perceive that I have not attempted to temper my constitutional enthusiasm in that Poem. Indeed a Poem is safe, the iron-souled Attorney general would scarcely dare to attack 'genus irritabile vatum.'"[17]

This "enthusiasm" mediates the poetic and the political: it affiliates Shelley with the vatic tradition (as well as the cultural capital of the classically educated) by force of the Hellenic sense of "a prophetic or poetical rage or fury, which transports the mind."[18] Shelley canonizes himself and his "Poem" within this tradition, as if to work a transport so supremely aestheticized as to be beyond political action, or at least criminal responsibility. In its punning "constitutionality," Shelley's enthusiasm appeals to a metaphorical and metaphysical code conveniently beyond the material chains of the Attorney general's "iron-souled" absolutism.

Even in this bare outline, Percy Shelley's thinking on enthusiasm—as a nexus of rhetorical and class privilege that resolves the historically problematic by virtue of aesthetic transcendence—sketches the unmistakable form of the Romantic Ideology. If, as Bryan Shelley argues, Percy continually twists "biblically informed language against the biblical worldview,"[19] the poet still finds some eremitical attraction in turning inherited spiritualisms against the world with the vigor of a man of faith. Whether secular or sacred, Shelley's enthusiasm cuts against the grain of History. The *Defence* that he worked on just a few years after *Frankenstein* offers an angelology rather than psychology of inspiration, "evanescent visitations of thought and feeling . . . the interpenetration of a diviner nature

---

16. Stephen Behrendt, *Shelley and His Audiences* (Lincoln: University of Nebraska Press, 1989), ix.
17. *The Letters of Percy Bysshe Shelley*, ed. Frederick L. Jones, 2 vols. (Oxford: Clarendon, 1964), 1:324.
18. "Enthusiasm," in Nathan Bailey, *Universal Etymological English Dictionary*, rev. Joseph Nicol Scott (London: T. Osborne and J. Shipton, 1755), pages unnumbered.
19. Bryan Shelley, *Shelley and Scripture: The Interpreting Angel* (Oxford: Clarendon, 1994), vii.

through our own."[20] Such divine visitors invariably crowd out more human contacts, and Shelley's famous trumpet of prophecy can be a muted thing indeed, "unheard" in *Queen Mab* "by all but gifted ear."[21] "Poetry is indeed something divine," and the poet is its prophet—but his auditors, at best, overhear him as "a nightingale, who sits in darkness to cheer its own solitude with sweet sounds" (*Defence* 282).

As we've seen several times already, however, enthusiasm could betray Romantic privilege as well as establish it. The metaphors which Shelley manufactures as vehicles of spiritual insulation and social isolation were easily driven by the vulgarizing forces they were meant to escape. When Shelley "cast himself both privately and publicly in the role of prophet and liberator,"[22] this act was less a daring political vision of the poet than a belated turn at a role in which Southcott was already starring, as poet-prophetess and self-styled "Woman to Deliver Her People." If the overlap was unwelcome, it was hardly limited in scope, and many of Shelley's most refined figures of imaginative potency can seem to have been spawned in the intellectual gutter. Percy's figure of the "poet"—"an instrument over which a series of external and internal impressions are driven like the alterations of an ever-changing wind over an Aeolian lyre"—plays on one of the most reliable Romantic tropes (*Defence* 277). But even as this embodied harp resonates with a sublime Eternity, it could strike more discordant tones. John Langhorne remarked some years earlier that such spiritual mechanics were the most hackneyed conceits of zealous hypocrites, as well: it was impossible to find "an enthusiast that did not declaim against reason—all was to be referred to internal impulses; and man was to become a mere machine, acted upon and impelled by powers not his own."[23] In the grip of either enthusiasm, identity is destabilized and potentially extinguished by the influx of alterior power,[24] and if for Shelley this symptomatized the unsustainably exhilarating communication between "the wise, and great, and good" and that universal force which "dwells

---

20. *A Defence of Poetry*, in *Shelley's Prose*, 275–97 (294). Subsequent references to this edition appear parenthetically.

21. *Queen Mab: A Philosophical Poem with Notes*, I:113, in *The Complete Poetical Works of Percy Bysshe Shelley*, ed. Neville Rogers, 4 vols. (Oxford: Clarendon, 1972), 1:229–337.

22. Behrendt, *Shelley and His Audiences*, 1.

23. John Langhorne, *Letters on Religious Retirement, Melancholy, and Enthusiasm* (London: H. Payne and W. Cropley, 1762), 11.

24. For an exploration of the rhetorical, personal, and political dangers and opportunities of this sort of enthusiastic extinction in the seventeenth century, see Nigel Smith, *Perfection Proclaimed*.

apart in its tranquility / Remote, serene, and inaccessible" (*Mont Blanc* 82; 96–97), Lord Shaftesbury had less charitably advertised the event as "a Puppet-Shew at *Bart'lemy*-Fair," with "the Bodys of the Prophets, in their state of Prophecy, being not in their own power, but (as they say themselves) mere passive Organs, actuated by an exterior Force."[25]

The spectacle of the prophet as Punch, performing to excite the gaping masses, reverses Percy Shelley's poetical project, and its projected reception. *Queen Mab,* refashioned into political importance and popular success only once it was pirated out of Shelley's control, opens with "the wondrous strain" that only "the enthusiast hears at evening" (I:46, 49). As if conscious of the potential pathology of this "strain," Shelley attempted to keep the poem away from the wrong variety of enthusiast: "Let only 250 copies be printed. A small neat Quarto, on fine paper and so as to catch the aristocrats."[26] This is an enthusiasm reconfigured for an audience that would mask the lineage of the discourse. While the Bishop of Exeter had fretted about enthusiasm's tendency to "captivate the Vulgar,"[27] Shelley tries to snare only their landlords, writing, as he remarked about *The Refutation of Deism,* "with a view of excluding the multitude."[28] Even so, Shelley's enthusiasm can't quite shake its Southcottian affinities, and the most forceful assertions in the *Defence* wither into a worried dance of declaration and recantation:

> Poets, according to the circumstances of the age and nation in which they appeared, were called in earlier epochs of the world legislators or prophets; a poet essentially comprises and unites both these characters.... Not that I assert poets to be prophets in the gross sense of the word, or that they can foretell the form as surely as they foreknow the spirit of events: such is the pretence of superstition. (279)

Poets are prophets, but not *that* kind of prophet: Shelley's argument trips over "the gross sense" and the vulgar "pretence" of the prophecies of Southcott and Brothers. This sort of determined, if not entirely persuasive, qualification extended well into the reconstructions of his later rescuers, who were always haunted by the sense of distinctions that never amounted to differences.

---

25. [Anthony Ashley Cooper, 3rd Earl of Shaftesbury], *A Letter Concerning Enthusiasm,* (London: J. Morphew, 1708), 43.

26. *Letters of Percy Bysshe Shelley,* 1:361.

27. Lavington, *Enthusiasm of Methodists and Papists Compar'd,* 3.

28. *The Refutation of Deism,* in *The Complete Works of Percy Bysshe Shelley,* ed. Roger Ingpen and Walter E. Peck, 10 vols. (London: Ernest Benn, 1926–28), 6:25.

In 1839, G. H. Lewes would carry the torch while dutifully attempting to douse its flame, finding in Shelley "the obduracy and strength of a martyr, an angel-martyr, however, not a fanatic."[29] The abstractions contained within Shelley's writings were not always handled so tenderly, but in each case the diagnosis was the same. In 1821, Gold's *London Magazine* found his poetry "the outpourings of a spirit 'steeped to the very full' in humanity and religious enthusiasm," while the *Monthly Chronicle* noted acidly that Shelley's aesthetic was disfigured by its egregious affiliation with "error, enthusiasm, [and] the fanaticism of elevated sentiment."[30] Shelley's cousin, Thomas Medwin, presented the familiar argument of Shelley and the Shelleyans: "Even if Shelley had not set himself up as a reformer, his poetry was never calculated to be popular. His creations were of another world . . . clothed in too mystical a language."[31]

Medwin was looking to rehabilitate Shelley for posthumous reception by softening the poet's idiosyncrasies, but this emphasis on otherworldly mysticism conjures its opposite. It's precisely in Shelley's flights of greatest abstraction, his involvement with rapture, vision, imaginative displacement, and prophetic transfiguration that his poetic could be, perversely, at its most popular, as it recycles the language of enthusiasm. If Shelley and his disciples would craft, in Susan Wolfson's phrase, a "poetics of exclusion,"[32] it was in large part a defense against the disreputable sociability that inhered in his thought.

It's on this instability that Mary Shelley would press, producing a critique of Percy's romanticism that drives to the heart of its clouded negotiation with class resonances and popularity. To be sure, as caretaker of the body of Percy's work, Mary could toe the party line as well as Medwin or Lewes. Her meditations in her 1839 edition of Percy's work, as Susan Wolfson observes, focus on "discriminating two audiences" for her husband, "popular and elite," and "'two classes'" of poetry to accommodate them: one, "'curious and metaphysical poems,'" characterized by their "'huntings after the obscure'" and their "'mystic subtlety,'" and a "'second class'" (in several senses), identified by its representations of "'emotions

---

29. "Percy Bysshe Shelley," *Westminster Review* 35 (1841): 303–44 (307).
30. Gold's *London Magazine* (1821), "On the Philosophy and Poetry of Shelley," in Theodore Redpath, *The Young Romantics and Critical Opinion, 1807–1824* (London: Harrap, 1973), 361. "Shelley's Poems," *Monthly Chronicle* 3 (April 1839): 340.
31. Thomas Medwin, *Medwin's "Conversations of Lord Byron"* [1824], ed. Ernest J. Lovell, Jr. (Princeton, NJ: Princeton University Press, 1966), 250.
32. Susan J. Wolfson, "Editorial Privilege: Mary Shelley and Percy Shelley's Audiences," in Fisch, Mellor, and Schor, *The Other Mary Shelley*, 39–72 (43).

common to us all.'"[33] Yet as Wolfson goes on to argue, Mary found this bifurcation in Percy problematic: "Commenting that he shrugged off her entreaties 'to write . . . in a style that commanded popular favour,' the editor regrets that 'the bent of his mind went the other way,' drawn to 'fantastic creations of his fancy.'"[34] Even as Mary's editorial labor in part reified the quarantine of Percy's enthusiasm as the lamentable symptom of his inability to descend from the sociopoetic stratosphere, she quietly needled just these inflations.

Mary Shelley's rebranding of Percy for Victorian readers, Mary Favret suggests, was also a self-marketing at her husband's expense, signaling that both the "poet and the poetry" were "innately unsympathetic and inaccessible," and that editorial intervention was essential for texts so overwrought, they tended to say nothing at all: "her method successfully alienates the poet and his practice from the reading public, while it reinforces her own literary practice."[35] Even Mary's most unctuous praise for Percy's enthusiastic genius was still subject to the frictions of gender and genre, and hagiography was itself an ironic mode. Her elaborate explanation of his failure to write a companion to *Frankenstein*—"more apt to embody ideas and sentiments in the radiance of brilliant imagery, and in the music of the most melodious verse that adorns our language, than to invent the machinery of a story," the poet "commenced" and soon abandoned "one founded on the experiences of his early life" (188)—was also a backhanded swipe at Percy's self-indulgent mode of creation, which James O'Rourke translates into "Sanchean phrase": "'He's so smart he can't write about anything but himself.'"[36]

The loyal wife was thus an oblique competitor, intimately acquainted with Percy's authorial functions and dysfunctions. As she sighed in the 1831 "Introduction" to *Frankenstein*, "My husband, however, was, from the first, very anxious that I should prove myself worthy of my parentage. . . . He was for ever inciting me to obtain a literary reputation," packing an entire cosmos of domestic and professional drama into that "for ever" (187). *Frankenstein* itself is a subtle entry in Mary's conflicted and life-long treatment of her husband's "very anxious" incitements to enthusiastic ambition, and the force of the commentary Victor Franken-

---

33. Wolfson, "Editorial Privilege," 39–40.
34. Wolfson, "Editorial Privilege," 41.
35. Mary Favret, "Mary Shelley's Sympathy and Irony: The Editor and Her Corpus," in Fisch, Mellor, and Schor, *The Other Mary Shelley*, 17–38 (19; 27).
36. James O'Rourke, "The 1831 Introduction and Revisions to *Frankenstein*: Mary Shelley Dictates Her Legacy," *Studies in Romanticism* 38.3 (1999): 365–85 (371).

stein produces on Percy Shelley derives, in large part, from Victor's mirroring of the pampered scion of Sir Timothy. That one of Percy's earliest, most awkward specimens of poetry was published under the pseudonym "Victor" reinforces the point: Victor Frankenstein is the darkened portrait of Shelley's juvenilities, his privileges, egotism, and self-involved rhetoric magnified as disfigurements. I don't mean to diminish the novel into an artifact of marital and professional tensions, however. I mean to historicize Paul Cantor's sense that "Mary Shelley seems to have turned the creation myth back upon Romanticism, making Romantic creativity itself, in all its problematic character, her subject."[37]

Percy's mystification of the social conditions and appeal of his "enthusiasm" was typical of the displacements which partly constituted a specific form of polite, masculine poetics in the Romantic era. If this discursive privilege addressed an elite Sunetoi in a problematically Southcottian rhetoric, *Frankenstein* collapses this opposition in on itself, forcing the half-hidden tracks of vulgarity to the surface in an idiom of recognizably Shelleyan distinction. Oscillating between the political poles of enthusiasm, Victor Frankenstein seizes the figures of a Romantic aesthetic, and tips them over into the popular cacophony that Percy attempted to silence in his own writings. Frankenstein's "passion arise[s], like a mountain river, from ignoble and almost forgotten sources," but his story never forgets the ignoble, and rather insists on its insuperable vitality (21). This Prometheanism is as attuned to Foxe's *Actes and Monuments* as to Aeschylus: "I trembled with excess of agitation as I said this; there was a frenzy in my manner, and something, I doubt not, of that haughty fierceness, which the martyrs of old are said to possess" (158).

Frankenstein is many things, and as many of its best readings remind us, the ideological patchwork of the novel admits endlessly stimulating critical interpretations, while ultimately rejecting—or at least escaping—them all.[38] Yet it always remains a tale of the obligations of acknowledg-

---

37. Cantor, *Creature and Creator*, 109.
38. For Marshall Brown, "monstrosity" is a figure of ontological complexity, even indeterminacy, which explains why *Frankenstein* (and its Creature) "is so easily but mistakenly allegorized into one or another material or situational problem. It implies all the cases to which critics reduce it, but remains more pervasive than any of them." Brown, "*Frankenstein*: A Child's Tale," *Novel: A Forum on Fiction* 36.2 (Spring 2003): 145–75 (159). For Denise Gigante, the Creature's typifying "ugliness" poses a similar critical and metaphysical conundrum to the reader, and the novel: "he symbolizes nothing but the unsymbolized: the repressed ugliness at the heart of an elaborate symbolic network that is threatened the moment he bursts on the scene, exposing to view his radically uninscribed existence." Gigante, "Facing the Ugly: The Case of *Frankenstein*," *English Literary History* 67.2 (Summer 2000):

ment, confronting cultural and rhetorical authority, which carelessly sends forth emanations and re-inscriptions of its own dominance, with the hideous progeny and precursors of generative enthusiasm. The form of the Creature, at once horrifying and pathetically abject, embodies the return of every sort of psychosocial repression: the spectacular apparition of all that the ruling modernities of the early nineteenth century disappeared in the exercise of power.[39] My sense is that the novel's ironic revelation of the cohabitation of religious and poetical enthusiasm is an important part, but not the whole, of this pursuit of high romanticism—even into its most sacred sites, Chamonix and Cumberland—by what it has tried to abandon and deny: but I don't want to allegorize this oppositional identity in the meeting of Victor Frankenstein and his Creature.

My Creature isn't the immiserated incarnation of enthusiasm haunting its genteel other, but the novel's most relentless, and relentlessly sad, proponent of all the discourses of Enlightenment which ought to elevate a subjectivity capable of harnessing them. Victor himself is sufficient as his own doppelganger, continually performing the discursive schizophrenia which tears him from sanity to madness, sexual mastery to hysteria, and politeness to enthusiastic vulgarity, a personal and political unsteadiness that Walton documents: "Sometimes he commanded his countenance and tones, and related the most horrible incidents with a tranquil voice, suppressing every mark of agitation; then, like a volcano bursting forth, his face would suddenly change to an expression of the wildest rage, as he shrieked out imprecations on his persecutor" (165). Seeing the Creature as a reflection of Victor's own monstrosity is a motivated vision, which Victor's boundless narcissism is eager to frame. The Creature's enduring burden is to be read as symbol rather than subject, representing everything other than himself, encased in a narrative which testifies only to his lack of autonomy. For most of the novel, Frankenstein is the lone enthusiast, plagued by demons and haunted by sin, and if Creature relates to creator, it's to relay the antinomian refusal of the terms of his own constitution, which Victor himself recognizes toward the end: "In a fit of enthusiastic madness I created a rational creature" (173).

565–87 (567).

39. Lee Sterrenburg's account of *Frankenstein* and revolutionary discourse remains seminal; see his "Mary Shelley's Monster: Politics and Psyche in *Frankenstein*," in Levine and Knoepflmacher, *Endurance of Frankenstein*, 143–71. For a fascinating account of education and slave narratives in the novel, see John Bugg, "'Master of their language': Education and Exile in Mary Shelley's *Frankenstein*," *Huntington Library Quarterly* 68.4 (2005): 655–66.

This tension, between creative enthusiasm and created rationalism, is the tragic key to *Frankenstein*, as enlightened positions and strategies are gradually overwhelmed—often over their very powerful protests—by an increasingly fanatical enthusiasm which consumes, co-opts, and re-determines the outlets for Reason and rational subjectivity. The Creature wishes very much he shared a story merely with a scientist, however mad. Instead, Victor's enthusiasm forces him to submit to a narrative of moral warfare and metaphysical violence, which casts the Creature as the "Devil": at once the Adversary, and, in another of its Romantic-era meanings, the lowest agent in textual assembly, trapped in a narrative over which he has no control.

Raising the Dead

"Natural philosophy," Victor insists, "is the genius which has regulated my fate" (21). But this is a peculiarly fatalistic "genius," as the word equivocates between an expansively self-congratulatory view of Frankenstein's scientific aptitude, and the providential ministrations of a spiritual intelligence neither natural nor particularly philosophical. The quality of the epistemological and affective "regulation" of Victor's narrative—whether this is an account governed by the fixed laws of matter and motion, or by forces more darkly arcane—is thus called into question as soon as it's raised, though in fact the issue is settled quickly. Frankenstein's skepticism, such as it is, is ultimately an agent for his credulity. Mary Shelley elaborates this frame of evaluation in the 1831 text, where Victor's initial course selection at the University of Ingolstadt was guided by something even more malevolent than the whims of the Registrar:

> Chance—or rather the evil influence, the Angel of Destruction, which asserted omnipotent sway over me from the moment I turned my reluctant steps from my father's door—led me first to Mr. Krempe, professor of natural philosophy. He was an uncouth man, but deeply imbued with the secrets of his science. (202)

Always a devout believer that physiology is ontology, Victor doubly recoils from this "squat little man" with a "repulsive countenance," and from his equally ill-formed "doctrines" (28). But the attending "Angel" (aided by the sagely handsome Waldman) recalls the young heretic to both magisterium and magister, since the "professor" holds forth the prospect, not of knowledge exactly, but of adeptal mysteries and "secrets," which one does not study, but with which one might be "deeply imbued." To the initiated, "natural" philosophy reveals the supernatural, and Victor learns the zeal of a convert, as his "apathy . . . soon changed . . . into enthusiasm," and a "new light seemed to dawn upon my mind" (22). His experimental ambition to "pioneer a new way, explore unknown powers, and unfold to the world the deepest mysteries of creation" provokes a moral struggle which descends with a Calvinist certainty. These were "words of the fate, enounced to destroy me," "as if my soul were grappling with a palpable enemy" (202). Once acquired, Victor's "palpable" faith in a world motivated by spiritual rather than physical causes moves him from his mountains, transforming his pursuit of the Creature across Tartary into a trek across Tartarus: "I was cursed by some devil, and carried about with me my eternal hell; yet still a spirit of good followed and directed my steps, and, when I most murmured, would suddenly extricate me from seemingly insurmountable difficulties" (160).

It was just this sort of worldview which distinguished a "reasonable" man from his enthusiastic other. Thomas Thomason pronounced in 1795 that the rational Christian, sensitive to the "immutable . . . obligations to virtue," enjoyed an emotional stability and metaphysical consistency unknown to the overheated imaginary of "enthusiasm": "No envious daemon can rob us of our happiness; no propitious guardian avert the punishment of our sins."[40] To be sure, personal ecstasies and cosmic influences weren't wholly antithetical to Frankenstein's position as scientist. In 1815, the *Edinburgh Review* began a discussion of Southcott by suggesting a union between certain forms of religious rapture and scientific delusion:

> Even in cases where the greatest calmness and deliberation might be expected, and among those whose profession it is to investigate truth,—the ambition of forming a sect, or displaying intellectual superiority, . . . and the anxiety to penetrate the mysterious secrets of nature,—have sometimes produced, not modest querists and patient inquirers, but zealous believers in the most fanciful creeds of philosophy.[41]

This language of scientific penetration finds an eerie echo in Frankenstein, who is "embued with a fervent longing to penetrate the secrets of nature" (199). But as John Wesley averred in his *Survey of the Wisdom*

---

40. Thomas Thomason, *An Essay Tending to Prove that the Holy Scriptures, Rightly Understood, Do Not Give Encouragement to Enthusiasm or Superstition*, 21.
41. "Joanna Southcott," *Edinburgh Review* 24 (February 1815): 453–71 (454).

of God in Creation—a work adapted from the writings of a professor at the University of Jena in 1770—this doubling of the experimental and the enthusiastic was as old as the introduction of "the Knowledge of Chemistry into Europe," when men emerged who "were wise above the Age they lived in; and penetrated so far into the secret Recesses of Nature, as scarce to escape the Suspicion of Magic. Such were Roger Bacon and Albertus Magnus."[42]

The enthusiastic scientist, infected with moral and intellectual pathologies so acute they could only be diagnosed as theological defects, was a recognizable type, and Victor Frankenstein a legible instance. Isaac Taylor documented the predictable progress of the disorder in his *Natural History of Enthusiasm* (1829). Deranged zeal produced self-involvement, which culminated in an icy death:

> [T]hey become a freezing centre of solitary and unsocial indulgence; and at length displace every emotion that deserves to be called virtuous. No cloak of selfishness is in fact more impenetrable than that which usually envelops a pampered imagination.[43]

As if anticipating this chilly forecast, Victor warms himself with "enthusiasm" for Cornelius Agrippa, Paracelsus, and Albertus Magnus (22), of whom the latter two were especially beloved by young Percy Shelley. While his subsequent university training is itself problematically superstitious, Frankenstein's generative interests and influences—by another name, his "genius"—were inescapably ancient. His "science," on the cutting edge of the fifteenth century, may not so much represent a grim warning against unchecked technological modernization, as testify to the enduring power of shadowy doctrines in an Enlightenment purporting to banish them.[44]

Yet Victor is also somewhat disingenuous when he suggests, "[i]t may appear very strange, that a disciple of Albertus Magnus should arise in the eighteenth century" (23). His unholy trinity of enthusiastic scripture in fact possessed an energetic position in "modern" Europe, and there were many such disciples, as Richard Graves grumbled in his anti-Methodist novel,

---

42. John Wesley, *Survey of the Wisdom of God in the Creation*, 1:9–10.
43. Isaac Taylor, *Natural History of Enthusiasm* [London, 1829], 4th ed. (New York: J. Leavitt, 1834), 15.
44. See especially Jones, *Against Technology*, 105–36. See also *Frankenstein's Science: Experimentation and Discovery in Romantic Culture, 1780–1830*, ed. Christina Knellwolf and Jane Goodall (Aldershot; Burlington, VT: Ashgate, 2008), which attempts to move the discussion of "science" in the novel beyond "masculinity" and "hubris."

The Spiritual Quixote: "our modern itinerant reformers, by the mere force of imagination, have conjured up the powers of darkness in an enlightened age."[45] All three philosophers were foundational for the folk cultures of alchemy and magic that, as J. F. C. Harrison remarks, "provided a matrix in which millenarian yearnings could be nourished" well into the nineteenth century, while Jakob Boehme, a shoemaker and "the greatest inspiration to mystics in the eighteenth century, [and] the name most frequently mentioned as exemplar," was characterized by "his use of the vocabulary and symbolism of alchemy, astrology, and humoral physiology," centerpieces of Frankenstein's education.[46] Even accounting for flashes of popularizing showmanship like Boyle's air-pump experiment, it's not at all clear that many English people, beyond those literate, urban, middle-class (and often Dissenting) men and women who composed a demographic minority, thought themselves citizens of a world of accelerating scientific materialism. "Older" forms of knowledge were still quite contemporary in many parts of the country, where the "modern" was either unknown or not entirely secure; Keith Thomas has found a Cornish doctor seriously endorsing the virtues of alchemy as a moral and intellectual endeavor in 1784, and in 1804, an Anglican vicar treating a witch's curse on his sick child with a phylactery.[47]

If such practices were curious oddities among professionals and the orthodox toward the end of the eighteenth century, plebeian—and especially Methodist—culture relied upon them very heavily until much later.[48] John Wesley's *Primitive Physic*, first published in 1747, would become one of the best-selling books of the eighteenth and nineteenth centuries, going through twenty-four editions in Wesley's lifetime alone. A manual of folk medicine, it prescribed marigold flowers (eaten "as a salad") for the plague, and cold baths for cancer ("this has cured many").[49] Success wasn't always unqualified, and as Alexander Knox wrote to Robert Southey, "an unfortunate mistake" in one of Wesley's "medical prescriptions . . . was at one time brought against him as involving virtual guilt of homicide."[50] But such unfortunate outcomes did little to dampen the enthusiasm of Wesley and the Wesleyans for an amalgamated array of natural and supernatural

---

45. Richard Graves, *The Spiritual Quixote: or, the summer's ramble of Mr. Geoffrey Wildgoose*, 3 vols. (London: J. Dodsley, 1773), 1:57.
46. J. F. C. Harrison, *Second Coming*, 39, 19, 21.
47. Keith Thomas, *Religion and the Decline of Magic*, 271–76.
48. See James Obelkevitch, *Religion and Rural Society*.
49. John Wesley, *Primitive Physic: or, An Easy and Natural Method of Curing Most Diseases*, 24th ed. (London: Paramore, 1792); for marigold, 82; cancer, 33.
50. Knox, "Remarks," 298.

treatments. Southey alleged that the itinerant preachers and their wives were commonly employed in "making and vending pills, drops, balsams, or medicines" that they would retail to their congregations,[51] while some "perfected" preachers offered more personal cures, proposing to manage eye infections by spitting in them while saying magic words.[52] Wesley himself indulged in his own Frankenscience, championing the rejuvenating powers of electrotherapy in *The Desideratum: Or Electricity Made Plain and Useful* (1790), while owning—and using upon his devoted flock—one of the very first copies of Franklin's "electricity machine" in the world.[53]

Folk magic, faith healing, and the electricity of enthusiasm: this is at least as much Victor's purview as the increasingly formalized life sciences, and Professor Krempe rightly glosses the quality of his early studies, labeling him a young man "who, but a few years ago, believed Cornelius Agrippa as firmly as the gospel" (46). But if Frankenstein outgrows Agrippa at Ingolstadt, "gospel"—especially in its most theologically extreme and socially debased readings—remains his guiding light throughout his exercise in creation. Moreover, "creation," capacious as it is, is perhaps not the most satisfying discourse for representing the "catastrophe" which takes place "on a dreary night of November" (37). While this is an event, as so much strong criticism has taught, supercharged with the anxieties of sexuality, gender, and reproduction, it's not only a "birth myth." These are, after all, the practices and categories which Victor is sedulously determined to avoid and subvert, which in absence and opposition make their critical presence felt. Such denials may imprint in negative a secularized fable of technology displacing physiology, but it seems to me that what Frankenstein does is as important as what he doesn't do. In short, Victor raises the dead. While this event directly (and often, to the unconverted, revoltingly) intersected with representations of sexuality and birth in the long eighteenth century, it's ultimately Resurrection, in all its theological and social complexity, rather than pregnancy or its scientific surrogate, which comes closest to capturing the crisis of the novel.

Above all others, Resurrection was the animating miracle for almost every form of Christianity. In 1791, Joseph Priestley published *An Address*

---

51. Southey, *Life of Wesley*, 2:151. For a powerful account of Methodist practices for the healthy and unhealthy body, as well as the differing theological significances of health and illness for men and women, see Phyllis Mack, *Heart Religion in the British Enlightenment*, 171–96.

52. See Rack, *Reasonable Enthusiast*, 334–42.

53. On the machine, see Mack, *Heart Religion in the British Enlightenment*, 13. See also Abelove, *Evangelist of Desire*, 27–29, for the Methodist interest in electric reanimation.

to the Methodists along with some *Original Letters by the Reverend John Wesley and His Friends,* winning few friends among the Addressed, as both pamphlets assassinated the character of Wesley while impugning the sanity of his Society. Yet despite these frictions, Priestley insisted, Socinians and enthusiasts were still bound by the basic consensus which conditioned the Western world, a faith in Christ's once-and-future conquest of death:

> All Christians, of every denomination, believe that whatever Christ himself was, his mission was divine, and that whatever he taught was from God. They all believe that he wrought unquestionable miracles, that he died, and he rose again from the dead, and that he will come to raise all the dead, and to give unto every man according to his works.[54]

Theological unity only went so far, and in his *Disquisitions Relating to Matter and Spirit* (1777), Priestley carefully demurred whether the indubitable historical fact of resurrection was still a contemporary possibility. While it was certain that "whatever is *decomposed* may certainly be *recomposed,* by the same almighty power that first composed it," it was inconsonant with the divine order for such effects to occur again before the end of history.[55] Only madmen, liars, and the woefully stupid believed in anything like a modern form of the ancient magic.

As Priestley smugly implied to the Methodists mourning the recent death of their beloved Father, they were likely all three: "At this time, I hope there are none of you who believe, as Mr. Wesley originally did, in a miraculous new birth, depending on the sole will of God."[56] This was no innocently speculative "hope": Priestley was knowingly aggravating the nerve at the center of Methodist theology. Even as Wesley (and his heirs) squashed or ejected the lunatic fringe orbiting the Connexion, from which occasional claims to literal powers of resurrection would emerge, mainstream Wesleyanism returned again and again to the "new birth," the metaphorical—yet still dramatically embodied—corollary of the original miracle. As Wesley's *Journal* shows, two passages favored in his foundational sermons anticipate *Frankenstein*'s narrative of creation: "If any man

---

54. Joseph Priestley, *An Address to the Methodists,* in *Theological and Miscellaneous Writings of Joseph Priestley,* ed. John Towhill Rutt, 25 vols. (London: Smallfield, 1817–32), 25:333–34.

55. Joseph Priestley, *Disquisitions Relating to Matter and Spirit* (London: J. Johnson, 1777), 161.

56. Priestley, *An Address to the Methodists,* in *Theological and Miscellaneous Works,* 25:334.

be in Christ, he is a new creature" (2 Corinthians 5:17), and "The hour cometh, and now is, when the dead shall hear the voice of the Son of God, and they that hear shall live again" (John 5:25).[57]

This "new birth" was the operative conceit of Methodism, the spiritual reanimation of the old body, wasted and scarred by sin:

> Unto you I call in the name of him whom you crucify afresh, and in his words to your circumcised predecessors, "Ye serpents, ye generation of vipers, how can you escape the damnation of hell?"
>
> 4. How indeed, except ye be born again! For ye are now dead in trespasses and sins.[58]

The resurrection of "a dead Christian" into "a living man" was the cleansing of the doors of perception, as Wesley suggested in another sermon:

> While a man is in a mere natural state, before he is born of God, he has, in a spiritual sense, eyes and sees not; a thick impenetrable veil lies upon them. He has ears, but hears not; he is utterly deaf to what he is most of all concerned to hear. His other spiritual senses are all locked up. . . . But as soon as he is born of God there is a total change in all these particulars. The "eyes of his understanding are opened" (such is the language of the great Apostle). And he who of old "commanded light to shine out of darkness shining on his heart," he sees "the light of the glory of God," his glorious love, "in the face of Jesus Christ."[59]

"Light," "love," "glory" were the formulae by which new creatures often recognized their new births. As Peter Jaco recalled in 1778, his conversion was "a moment" that "seemed to me as though a new creation had taken place. . . . My soul was filled with light and love."[60] In 1781, Christopher Hopper remembered his own "glorious and undeniable change."[61] Methodist spiritual transfigurations paralleled, in rhetoric if not doctrinal agenda, the experience that dots Percy Shelley's poetry, in which Ianthe

---

57. John Wesley, *The Journal of the Reverend John Wesley*, ed. Nehemiah Curnock, 8 vols. (London: Epworth, 1938), 1:441, 449. "If any man be in Christ, he is a new creature" was the text for Wesley's first sermon upon returning from America.
58. John Wesley, "The Marks of the New Birth" [1746], in *Sermons* I: 1–33 [1746–60], ed. Albert C. Outler (Nashville, TN: Abingdon, 1985), 429.
59. John Wesley, "The New Birth" [1746], in *Sermons* II, 192.
60. *WV* 2:10.
61. *WV* 1:118.

symptomatically "knew her glorious change, / And felt in apprehension uncontrolled, / New raptures opening round" (*Queen Mab* I:192–94).

The Wesleyan "new birth" was often more darkly ambiguous in quality, ineluctably linked to birthing "Pangs." In the words of one convert that Southey recorded, "as my mother bore me with great pain, so did I feel great pain in my soul in being born of God."[62] This transposition of the trauma of birth from mother to son has some resonance for the scrambled reproductive roles in *Frankenstein,* and even when not explicitly sexual, the "new birth" was often viscerally physical, re-enacting in the flesh the spiritual transformations of the sinner, and of Christ. As Wesley observed of a congregation in 1786, "several drop down as dead, and are as stiff as a corpse. But in a while they start up and cry, 'Glory! Glory!' perhaps twenty times together."[63] Such physical effects often intensified into actual disfigurements. Pseudo-resurrection could monsterize before it might save, and "swollen tongues and necks," veins "swelled as if ready to burst" for "some hours," and demoniacal strength that could require "as many as seven men" to restrain were all acceptable, and familiar, proofs.[64] This rebirth, as Ronald Knox remarked in his (somewhat contemptuous) study of seventeenth- and eighteenth-century enthusiasm, was the radical annihilation of nature, the fabrication of the physically and metaphysically alien:

> [T]he assumption of the enthusiast is bolder, and simpler; for him, grace has destroyed nature, and replaced it. The saved man has come out into a new order of being, with a new set of faculties, which are proper to his state.[65]

In the critical event—the reanimation of a monstrously disfigured body—Mary Shelley affiliates the "glorious change" in Percy's visionary aesthetic with the forcible resurrections of enthusiasm.

Frankenstein's search for the mysteries of reanimation rebounds to himself, as the scientist is "animated by an almost supernatural enthusiasm" throughout his labors (32). But it's his refusal to publish his methodology that most clearly casts him beyond the scientific pale. "The

---

62. Southey, *Life of Wesley,* 1:203.
63. Wesley, *Journal and Diaries* I, ed. Ward and Heitzenrater, 67–68.
64. Wesley, *Journal and Diaries* I, ed. Ward and Heitzenrater, 526–28.
65. R. A. Knox, *Enthusiasm: A Chapter in the History of Religion, with Special Reference to the XVII and XVIII Centuries* (New York and Oxford: Oxford University Press, 1950), 3.

Methodists are peculiarly attached to mysteries," groused Leigh Hunt, conclusive evidence of their "Ignorance and Vulgarity,"[66] and Frankenstein chides Walton while denying him the final revelation: "I see by your eagerness, and the wonder and hope which your eyes express, my friend, that you expect to be informed of the secret with which I am acquainted; that cannot be" (33). Percy Shelley had focused some skeptical notes to *Queen Mab* on the manufactured mysteries of life and death, reading chicanery in precisely the behavior Mary Shelley would give to Frankenstein:

> But even supposing that a man should raise a dead body to life before our own eyes, and on this fact rest his claim to being considered the son of God;—the Humane Society restores drowned persons, and because it makes no mystery of the method it employs, its members are not mistaken for the sons of God.[67]

Although Frankenstein's self-aggrandizement stops short of a claim for full divinity, his scene of creation evokes both Shelleyan and Methodist enthusiasm. The implied critique offered in its notes notwithstanding, *Queen Mab* opens with the rapture "How wonderful is death" (I:1)—a sentiment amplified for Frankenstein in a frenzied quest that causes him to "have recourse to death" (32), to "[dabble] among the unhallowed damps of the grave" (35), and to yearn for the "deep, dark, death-like solitude" (65) of the grave as the necessary preludes to the work of resurrection. What for Percy Shelley had been an object of contemplation for the philosopher-poet becomes for Frankenstein a passionate obsession. But if Mary Shelley pathologizes his fascination with death, necrophilia is not Frankenstein's peculiar deviance—it was one of enthusiasm's most remarkable axioms.

Methodism's map of desire was experimentally ambiguous, "apt to confuse," as Jon Mee puts it, "agape and eros, imaging sexual love in gross terms, and barely managing, if at all, to sublimate sexual desire into religious devotion."[68] The famous Methodist "Love-Feasts" were (sadly) falsely advertised, usually characterized by no physical love and less feasting. Nevertheless, the myth of the secret sexualities of the initiated provided salacious opportunities for anti-Methodists to condemn, while voyeuristically savoring, the immorality of the Society. *The Love Feast: A Poem* (1778) regaled its readers with Gothic scenes "of mysterious

---

66. Hunt, *An Attempt,* Essay I: "On the Ignorance and Vulgarity of the Methodists," 302.
67. Shelley's Note 15 to *Queen Mab; Complete Poetical Works,* 1:322.
68. *Romanticism, Enthusiasm, and Regulation,* 52.

Lewdness and Debauchery," staffed only by *"the particular select Societies of Fanatics,"* as the *"main Bodies* are not admitted to these *midnight Mysteries."*[69] The Rev. Polwhele took as "indisputably proved . . . the connection between enthusiasm and lust, or the easy transition from (the methodistic) spiritual love to carnal desire," relating an *Eve* of strangely Keatsian seduction:

> At *St. Agnes,* the society stay up the whole night, when girls of twelve and fourteen years of age, run about the streets; call out, "that they are possess'd.". . . . At a nocturnal meeting at *Mawgan,* a short time since, a girl upon her knees, praying, was seized by some one—*gently* I suppose— and a cry was soon heard "that he was kissing her."[70]

Polwhele's mendacity was rivaled only by his capacity to discover sexual outrage in unlikely situations; he memorably banned "unsex'd females" from the biological sciences, since the "bliss botanic" would make "bosoms heave," and lead them to "pluck forbidden fruit, with mother Eve."[71] More sober commentators such as Southey, while holding it "absurd to believe that any open and scandalous acts of licentiousness are committed at these meetings," nevertheless thought "he must wilfully shut his eyes, who does not perceive what consequences are likely to arise when the assembly breaks up, and the members, in that state of bodily excitement to which they have been wrought, are left to return home in the dead of the night, and in what company they chuse."[72]

Southey's anxieties were heteronormative, but Henry Abelove argues that "sodomy was a Methodist practice."[73] The Society clearly authorized

---

69. Anon., *The Love-Feast: A Poem,* 8.

70. Polwhele, *Anecdotes,* v, 38. Polwhele also accused Methodist itinerants of a sort of proto-Byronism, with one "James *Stephens,* alias *Duffens,* . . . of a notoriously bad character" figuring as Lara *avant la lettre:* "He has gone his rounds for several years, generally accompanied by a young woman in man's cloaths" (39).

71. Richard Polwhele, *The unsex'd females,* lines 29–30.

72. Southey, "On the Evangelical Sects," 496–97. Southey was particularly distressed by the potentially erotic self-examinations practiced in class and band meetings. Women "who have actually any vicious propensities, will soon learn to extract a guilty pleasure from these meetings; they will listen to the avowal of others and recall the thoughts of impurity in themselves with delight; in them the act of confession will be but a repetition of the offence; their inordinate passions will thus be stimulated and strengthened; and the very means devised for keeping them holy accelerate their ruin . . . we do affirm that their practice of confession is likely to make more street-walkers than their preaching reclaims" (499).

73. Abelove, *Evangelist of Desire,* 67.

intense, and intensely bodily, bonding between same-sex converts, and such connections were often more real—if less visible to hostile contemporaries—than the familiar fantasies of "Lewdness and Debauchery." For Sampson Staniforth, the ecstasy of his "new birth" was an awakening into unexpected affective possibilities, which reconfigured and overwhelmed normative relationship roles. A chance acquaintance in the army swiftly became his "dear companion," who "took me by the hand, and led to a place erected about half a mile from the camp"; after the service, "my dear companion took me in his arms," and then "took me to be with him as his comrade, and watched over me as a tender parent over a beloved child."[74] In striking compression, this affection exploits and chafes against the emotional opportunities and limits of the positions of parent, child, comrade, and companionate spouse, while attempting to occupy each role simultaneously; within a few days, this social, sexual, and spiritual confusion had brought Staniforth from joy to despair, and it "was strongly suggested to me that my day of grace was past, that I had sinned the unpardonable sin, and it signified nothing to strive any longer."[75]

Yet these affective enthusiasms were restrained compared with the desire of many Methodists for the suffering, and most especially, the dead, body. Boyd Hilton suggests that the "crucicentrism" (the focus on Christ's agony on the Cross) central to Methodism and Anglican Evangelicalism gave doctrinal sanction for "revelling in pain as though it were a mark of grace."[76] The Wesleyans relished gruesomely detailed accounts of decomposition as *sic transits*, which terrified sinners into the hope of salvation:

> [I]n its grave [the body] turns yellow, then black, then it is covered in white mould—a putrid liquid flows, from which crowds of worms are bred. The worms first devour the flesh, then another. The skeleton becomes dust. Soon it will happen to you.[77]

So warned *A Week's Meditations on the Four Last Things* in 1845, and if many mainstream Victorian churches had begun to use death in order to market the appeal of life-after-death, in the eighteenth and early nineteenth centuries, such morbidities were still firmly, and often horrifically, associated with the Methodists and even more outré enthusiasts. The

---

74. WV 1:70–72.
75. WV 1:74. For a sensitive account of Methodist "women in love," see Mack, *Heart Religion in the British Enlightenment*, 127–70.
76. Hilton, *Age of Atonement*, 10.
77. Quoted in Knight, *Nineteenth-Century Church*, 49.

Wesleyans often evidenced compulsive affection for corpses, a celebration of the resurrection displaced onto (and sometimes entirely eclipsed by) a love for the resurrected object, as a few lines from a hymn by Charles Wesley may indicate:

> Ah, lovely appearance of death!
>   What sight upon Earth is so fair?
> Not all the gay pageants that breathe
>   Can with a dead body compare.
> With solemn delight I survey
>   The corpse when the spirit is fled,
> In love with the beautiful clay,
>   And longing to lie in its stead.[78]

The dissonance between the rhyme-paired *Death* and *breathe,* and the casting of life as lifeless pageant, enacts the peculiar ugliness of the living. But death was not simply aesthetically superior: it was uniquely sacred, the more outlandishly described, the better. Methodists and the related Moravians—"who," according to Hunt, "(to do them justice) seem of all Methodists to have the least guidance of common sense"[79]—stressed that resurrection necessitated a passionate involvement with death, and that the killing wound was also the saving womb; the good Christian was "the worm" who must find "Lodging, Bed and Board in the Lamb's Womb."[80]

The Moravians, self-described "wound-worms," developed a theo-sexual fascination with the mutilated corpse (and specifically with the gash in Christ's side that doubled as a vagina) that makes Frankenstein seem decorous:

> [T]he dearest little opening of the sacred, precious, and thousand times beautiful little side.... It is in this opening the Regenerate rests and breathes. It is there he has his country, his house, his room, his little table. It is there he eats and drinks. It is there in a word he lives.[81]

---

78. Hymn 47, from *A Collection of Hymns for the Use of the People Called Methodists,* ed. Franz Hildebrandt and Oliver A. Beckerlegge, with the assistance of James Dale (Nashville, TN: Abingdon, 1984), 138.

79. Hunt, *An Attempt,* Essay II: "On the hatred of the Methodists against Moral Preaching," *Examiner* 20 (May 15, 1808): 318. Early in his career, John Wesley was heavily influenced by the Moravians, living with them in Georgia, making a pilgrimage to them in Germany, and studying with them in London.

80. Thompson, *Making of the English Working Class,* 371.

81. Quoted in Knox, *Enthusiasm,* 414–46.

Southey was unable to restrain himself in the face of such "freaks of perverted fancy, the abominations of the Phallus and Lingam": "madness never gave birth to combinations of more monstrous and blasphemous obscenity, than they did in their fantastic allegories and spiritualizations."[82] Scholars sympathetic to Methodism have tended to downplay the Society's transgendering of Christ, and its eroticization of death,[83] but they were both important components of the movement's theology, attested to by extraordinarily influential figures rather than isolated extremists. Wesley sang of his "thirst" for the "wounded Lamb of God," and his need to "wash me in thy cleansing blood; / To dwell within thy wounds,"[84] while Whitefield, in a moment of ecstasy regretted by Bishop Lavington, "sweetly sucked on my *Saviour's bosom, sucked* out of the breasts of his *Consolation.*"[85] E. P. Thompson was sometimes ungenerous in his engagement with Methodism, but he was not wrong to hear in its theology the same promise which chillingly thrills Victor Frankenstein, "*I will be with you on your wedding-night*": "No Methodist or evangelical magazine, for the mature or for children, was complete without its death-bed scene in which . . . death was often anticipated in the language of bride or bridegroom impatient for the wedding-night."[86]

The Voice of the Devil

Whether hidden in a garret in a university town, or lurking on the most forsaken outpost of the Gaelic periphery, Frankenstein's psycho-sexual innovations still kept a very wide acquaintance: the reconstitution of life from the wreckage of death, through an erotic syntax which confounded masculine and feminine roles even in the body of God, was not an unspeakably alienated act of technological transgression, but one of the most infamously recognizable pieties of enthusiastic Christianity

---

82. Southey, *Life of Wesley,* 1:188.
83. Mack's *Heart Religion in the British Enlightenment* is a strong exception; as she argues, the emphasis on Christ's blood and womb, which mortified a long line of men from Leigh Hunt to E. P. Thompson, had a very different value for many Methodist women in the eighteenth and nineteenth centuries.
84. *A Collection of Hymns, For the Use of the People Called Methodists,* ed. John Wesley (London: J. Patmore, 1780), 31.
85. Lavington, *The Enthusiasm of Methodists and Papists, Compar'd,* 54. For later versions of the religious gothic, most especially in *Dracula,* see Christopher Herbert, "Vampire Religion," *Representations* 79.1 (Summer 2002): 100–121.
86. Thompson, *Making of the English Working Class,* 374.

in the long eighteenth century. At times, Victor is nervously alert to this theo-social community, as unwelcome as his own offspring. Surveying the scraps of his aborted female creature, he "reflected that I ought not to leave the relics of my work to excite the horror and suspicion of the peasants" (135), as their vulgar superstition might seize such "relics" as grotesque remnants of some misbegotten beatification, rather than cast-off material from biochemical experiments. Yet even as he worries that the benighted "peasants" will misrecognize (and so recognize) the inspirited quality of his "work," Victor himself seems to expect this reception for his firstborn.

His anti-Petrarchan blazon—"His yellow skin scarcely covered the work of muscles and arteries beneath; his hair was of a lustrous black, and flowing; his teeth of a pearly whiteness" (37)—renders a grim parody of the Word made flesh. The resulting Resurrection, of course, is utterly divorced from Redemption. Not joy but "breathless horror and disgust" immediately "filled my heart," says the creator (37). Ardor is extinguished by horror at the "demoniacal corpse": "the change was so rapid, the overthrow so complete" (38). But if the tenor has shifted, the "demoniacal" discourse remains the same. Frankenstein's "science" had always been equivocal, disguising popular intensities in professional acumen—but whatever tenuous claim to cultural distinction might be drawn from the science fiction of creation, it's overwhelmed by the raw enthusiasm of Victor's subsequent relationship with his Creature. To label Frankenstein a sublimely incompetent parent doesn't go far enough: he's beyond the extravagantly Oedipal. The "pangs" of every "New Birth," as the Methodist preachers reminded their flocks time and again, were those of the sinner's struggle with Satan. Every conversion story would ultimately find itself within the genre of the psychomachia, and so, too, does Frankenstein's story. What Victor (to his own mind) has crafted is nothing short of an incarnation of the Devil, set for fatal combat, waged with ferocious enthusiasm, for salvation.

"I began the creation of a human being," Victor confides with some satisfaction, though, much to the chagrin of creator and created alike, he never quite gets around to finishing one (34). This initial admission of the Creature's essential humanity, in authorial intent if not effect, degrades even in the primal scene, as "the lifeless thing" animates into "the creature," only to tumble down the great chain of being in just a few paragraphs, passing "wretch" and "miserable monster" on its way to "demoniacal corpse" (37–38). Once arrived, Victor's conviction of demonic influence sets in with the force of dogma. Not that his faith is entirely without its doubts: Frankenstein asks that this resurrection be read against the hedge-magic he purports to have outgrown in his youth. "The raising of ghosts or devils was a promise liberally accorded by my favorite authors, the fulfilment of which I most eagerly sought; and if my incantations were always unsuccessful, I attributed the failure rather to my own inexperience and mistake, than to a want of skill or fidelity in my instructors," and many critics have accepted Frankenstein's critique of his thaumaturgical roots (23). According to Marshall Brown, "whatever one may say about *Frankenstein,* its monster is, assuredly, no ghost," a being "supernatural only in the older and weaker sense, quantitatively impressive, not qualitatively alien."[87] Chris Baldick insists that the "absence of any demonic tempter" removes "the Faust myth from our list of sources": if "Victor calls his creature a devil and a demon," "he knows better than anyone in the tale that the monster is not literally a paid-up and fork-carrying member of that order."[88]

I'm not convinced, however, that Victor "knows better." Shelley's ironic argument, I think, is that if this isn't a novel of demonic bargains and spiritual malevolence, its eponymous gentleman-scholar certainly thinks it is. Whether begotten or made, the Creature makes a good case for himself as a rational, rights-bearing subject. It's his creator who is determined to superimpose the enthusiastic antagonism between Man and Devil onto a relationship that might have been purely secular and contractarian. As Baldick's own math suggests,[89] Frankenstein's lexicon for the Creature—varieties of "devil," "demon," or "fiend" appear fifty-one times, surpassing the twenty-seven instances of "monster," and dwarfing the sixteen for "creature"—deeply entrenches a hellish sensibility. But if this is a convenient rhetoric for reprobation, it's also a serious metaphysic, and Victor carefully forbids noncelestial categories of difference. When Walton intuits, across a snow-blinded "half a mile," the gap between created and creator as the racialized distance between "an European" and "a savage inhabitant of some undiscovered island" (12), while his lieutenant simply reports "some dogs drawing a sledge, with a man in it," Victor is "aroused" to correct both men's evaluations as insufficiently mystical: "he asked a multitude of questions concerning the route which the daemon, as he called him, had pursued" (14). Frankenstein is doubly eager to record both the Creature's physical "route" over the ice, and its moral trajectory as "daemon," and while Walton momentarily hesitates over this figura-

---

87. Brown, "*Frankenstein:* A Child's Tale," 149–50.
88. Baldick, *In Frankenstein's Shadow,* 41.
89. Baldick, *In Frankenstein's Shadow,* 10n1.

tion, he—like the Creature itself—ultimately acquiesces to its inevitability. The Creature, Victor catechizes, is neither natural nor unnatural, but supernatural in the extreme, motivated by a theological rather than ecological agenda.

Contemplating the consequences of his promised female, "who in all probability was to become a thinking and reasoning animal," Frankenstein grants that she and the male Creature will axiomatically comprise a new "species." Yet at the threshold of sexual reproduction, which would confirm the biological status of the "creature," Victor chokes on brimstone, discovering, in the dangers of the body, the moral threat as old as the Archenemy: "one of the first results of those sympathies for which the daemon thirsted would be children, and a race of devils would be propagated upon the earth, who might make the very existence of the species of man a condition precarious and full of terror" (129). This is an eschatological prophecy, not a forecast of evolutionary competition, envisioning a "race of devils" whose sexuality will be that of the hungering incubus, with a "thirst" which will drain dry "the species of man." As Southey wrote in 1817, "[i]n the school of fanaticism, many a thought . . . has been fathered upon Satan,"[90] a maxim which Victor seems to have taken literally by fathering the Devil, while fearing the Devil's own erotic power. Within a few hours of its animation, Victor classes the Creature as "my enemy" (40), and within a few pages, as cosmic Enemy and Adversary.

Crucially, Frankenstein sees the Devil, not Satan, in his Creature, allowing him none of the ruined excellences of Milton's antihero. The hegemony of "Romantic Satanism" was never as grand as the adjective implies. For many readers in the eighteenth and nineteenth centuries, *Paradise Lost* was the baseline for theological knowledge rather than its critical undoing, a second Scripture from which whatever happened to be the conventional dogma of the moment and denomination might be extracted. John Pawson, the great Methodist preacher, related in 1806 his encounter with a waiter at a rural inn, who, while a "serious young man," was sadly old-fashioned in his reading and religion: "It was evident that the Lord had graciously visited his soul, though he had never heard a gospel sermon in his life, and had solely the Bible, the Common Prayer-Book, and Milton's *Paradise Lost* to read."[91] The intellectualized arguments typical of the Godwin-Shelley circle, which, as David Simpson has suggested, "denarrativized, doctrinally deprogrammed, and depoliti-

---

90. Southey, "On the Life of John Wesley," in *The Correspondent* 1.2 (London: Longman, 1817): 157–76 (162).
91. WV 4:38.

cized" the Puritan epic,[92] were perhaps more influential in posthumous canonization than on the uncritical faith of their contemporaries. Nevertheless, a virtuously alienated Satan, whose furious indignation indicted the fatuous certainties of a God and (especially) Church bloated on moral complacence and political malfeasance, certainly had some currency. A skeptical rhetorician straddling the limits of sacred discourse, this Satan shifted from being to exposing the degenerate underbelly of Christianity, serving as the mouthpiece for a peculiarly blasphemous strain of rationalist philosophy.

But even his admirers confessed that theirs was an unpopular vision. Hazlitt would draw the most pointed distinction between a philosophically aristocratic Satan and the orthodox Devil, whose misery was exposed by his physical monstrosity. Milton's difference from the common convention was clear:

> The deformity of Satan is only in the depravity of his will; he has no bodily deformity to excite our loathing or disgust. The horns and tail are not there, poor emblems of the unbending, unconquered spirit, of the writhing agonies within. Milton was too magnanimous and open an antagonist to support his argument by the by-tricks of a hump and cloven foot. . . . He relied on the justice of his cause, and did not scruple to give the devil his due.[93]

If he is to be a Devil, the Creature desperately hopes that he might be a Satan of this stamp, for whom physical deformities do not mirror moral deficiencies. But his creator isn't as magnanimous as Hazlitt's Milton, and Frankenstein's narrative continually recurs to popular versions of the Devil, where the body signals hellish instinct. Dallying on his way back to Geneva following William's murder, Victor catches a fleeting glimpse of the Creature, which is more than enough for him to construct an elaborate moral machinery:

> A flash of lighting illuminated the object, and discovered its shape plainly to me; its gigantic stature, and the deformity of its aspect, more hideous than belongs to humanity, instantly informed me that it was the wretch, the filthy daemon to whom I had given life. What did he there? Could he be (I shuddered at the conception) the murderer of my brother? No

---

92. David Simpson, "Romanticism, Criticism, and Theory," 5.
93. William Hazlitt, "On Shakspeare and Milton," *Complete Works*, 5:65.

> sooner did that idea cross my imagination, than I became convinced of its truth. . . . Nothing in human shape could have destroyed that fair child. *He* was the murderer! I could not doubt it. The mere presence of the idea was an irresistible proof of the fact. I thought of pursuing the devil. . . . (53)

Victor's conviction of the guilt of this "filthy daemon" is theological rather than forensic, hinging on an ontological proof—"the mere presence of the idea was an irresistible proof of the fact"—unlikely to be admitted even by the compromised judiciary of Geneva. Yet it was just this sort of thinking which characterized enthusiastic encounters with the Devil.

Such encounters, moreover, occurred with a frequency which disturbed the conventionally pious as well as the scattered atheists in early nineteenth-century England. Southey despised the Methodist assurance that the material was magical, and especially John Wesley's "notions of diabolical agency," which "imputed" to Satan "many of the accidents and discomforts of life,—disease, bodily hurts, storms and earthquakes, and nightmare: he believed that epilepsy was often, or always, the effect of possession,—that most madmen were demoniacs."[94] Attacking Wesley's personal credulity was a bit like shooting a Methodist in a barrel following Priestley's unauthorized publication in 1791 of the Wesley family's account of its resident house-ghost, "Old Jeffrey." Though the papers were smuggled to him fourth-hand by a Mr. Badcock, Priestley eagerly publicized them as a useful parable for how even "the best natural understanding, with much acquired knowledge" could be insufficiently "guarded against this species of enthusiasm," which would certainly cause the Wesleyans to renounce Wesley: "This very publication will convince you that you who are now called Methodists, are a very different set of people, and much more rational, than those were first distinguished by that name. . . . You will lament as much as I do the wild extravagance of your predecessors, and will conduct yourselves by very different maxims."[95]

Priestley was operating in bad faith, snidely humiliating the Society while praising them as "a very different set of people" from the man they idolized. But as Southey argued—and as Priestley knew perfectly well—this faith in devilish and ghostly presences was hardly confined to Wesley. The Laureate sardonically observed of *A Short Account of God's Dealings with Mr. John Haime*, "Satan has so much to do in the narrative, that this

---

94. Southey, *Life of Wesley*, 2:137.
95. *Theological and Miscellaneous Works of Joseph Priestley*, 25:331–33.

is certainly a misnomer."[96] "No Devil, No God" had been a lynchpin of many Protestant theologies for centuries, and Percy Shelley himself sneered that "the vulgar are all Manicheans," since a firm belief in the Devil is "all that remains of the popular superstition" of darker ages.[97] William Sharp, the great engraver responsible for the portrait of Southcott presented as this book's frontispiece, was scandalized by a skepticism that denied the Devil as well as God:

> for a man innocently to become the sport of fools, in these days, cannot be any matter of surprise, when the existence of God is denied by some; and the existence of a Devil is treated by numbers as a phantom.[98]

The enthusiastic Devil was no phantom, but a familiar of natural violence. It's telling that Mary Shelley has Frankenstein nearly always meet his "fiend" in thunder, lightning, or in rain, often attempting the sort of physicalized relations which Southey found so contemptible in Haime, who told how "one day, as I was walking alone, and faintly crying for mercy, suddenly such a hot blast of brimstone flashed in my face as almost took away my breath. And presently after, as I was walking, an invisible power struck up my heels, and threw me violently upon my face."[99]

But the Devil was most popular as an intimate antagonist, with none of the towering sublimity of Milton's Satan. He might appear, as he did to Southcott early in her career, at tea-time, greeting her, "Thou infamous bitch!"[100] Methodism's relationship with the Devil was quite as intense as its involvement with Christ, and the two were theologically inseparable: salvation in the one could come only through a war with the other. This was warfare as common (many Methodists, perhaps thousands, experienced these "spiritual slayings" every year) as it was brutal. Minor hysterias—"convulsions, tremblings, jumping, laughing"—were matched by spectacular violence ostensibly against the Devil and his minions, such as that witnessed by Samuel Keimer, a young painter:

> Another time I have seen my sister, who is a lusty woman, fling another prophetess upon the floor, and under agitations, tread upon her breast,

---

96. Southey, *Life of Wesley*, 2:90.
97. Percy Bysshe Shelley, "On the Devil, and Devils," in *Complete Works*, ed. Ingpen and Peck, 7:87.
98. William Sharp, *An Answer to the World* (London: S. Rousseau, 1804), 3.
99. WV 1:41.
100. Joanna Southcott, *A Dispute Between the Woman and the Powers of Darkness* [1802], ed. Jonathan Wordsworth (Poole and New York: Woodstock Books, 1995), 23.

belly, legs, etc, walking several times backwards and forwards over her, and stamping upon her with violence. This was adjudged to be a sign of the fall of the whore of Babylon.[101]

The psychomachia could sometimes be used as psychology: Ann Underwood, Southcott's amanuensis, remarked, "that all derangement proceeds from the working of evil spirits."[102] But its explanatory powers were constrained by a set of performances that usually followed a tight script: "there is a cry, or a roar; usually (not always) the afflicted person drops to the ground . . . Satan is letting his prey go with the utmost reluctance."[103]

Frankenstein's seemingly peculiar hysteria conforms in detail to this enthusiastic semiotic, as he doggedly physicalizes his internal struggles: "I had always experienced relief from mental torment in bodily exercise" (155). The immediate sequel to the creation—a dream that merges the corpses of Elizabeth and Frankenstein's mother in an Oedipal fugue—channels the necrophilia strongly stamped by the doctrines of Methodism, and his encounter at the foot of his bed with "the miserable monster whom I created" is a stock scene for devilish confrontations:

> I then waking, and being alone in the Chamber, fancy'd I heard some *rushing Kind of Noise,* and discern'd something at the *Bed's-Foot* like a *shadow;* which I apprehended to have been a *Spirit.* Hereupon, I was seiz'd with *great Fear* and *Trembling,* rose in Haste, went forth into the *Outer-Chamber* in *great Consternation,* and walk'd up and down as one *amaz'd.*[104]

This is Thomas Trosse's chronicle of his own mental illness, but few Methodists theorized the Devil as an expression of purely psychological, rather than moral, disorder. As John Haime related in a similar account, Satan was in deadly earnest when he came to the bedroom:

> I had no rest day or night. I was afraid to go to bed, lest the devil should fetch me away before morning. I was afraid to shut my eyes, lest I should awake in hell. I was terrified when asleep, sometimes dreaming that many devils were in the room, ready to take me away.[105]

---

101. Keimer is quoted in Harrison, *Second Coming,* 25.
102. Underwood is quoted in Hopkins, *A Woman,* 95.
103. Knox, *Enthusiasm,* 521.
104. Thomas Trosse, with italics dramatizing his hysteria; he is quoted in Alan Ingram, *The Madhouse of Language: Writing and Reading Madness in the Eighteenth Century* (London and New York: Routledge, 1991), 41.
105. *WV* 1:13.

For Southey, these nighttime lunacies proved that Methodists and medics had fatally mixed their metaphors. The "preachers," like "empirics have but one drug" to excite their "religious terrors": "the same powerful medicine which restores the confirmed sinner to health by searching his very bones till the joints open and the teeth are loosened, they administer in all cases, and in those who have weak nerves and warm imaginations, madness is frequently the result . . . [t]hat the increase of religious madness is occasioned by and commensurate with the increase of Methodism, is a fact which may be verified at Bedlam."[106]

Frankenstein, like the most hopeless inmate of this enthusiastic asylum, is compelled to fits as soon as he sees his "devil"—"my teeth chattered, and every limb became convulsed"—and while he is gripped by hysterical convulsions throughout his narrative, these are most often prompted by the Creature or its handiwork (38). It is, as he says, "my abhorrence of this fiend" that produces the routine: "when I thought of him, I gnashed my teeth, my eyes became inflamed" (66). The fury climaxes in a religious mission, a sworn desire to "make a pilgrimage to the highest peak of the Andes, could I, when there, have precipitated him to their base" (66). It's not long before Frankenstein quite literally calls for salvation in the throes of combat with the fiend, faithfully recreating in detail the "Wesleyan manifestation": "'Do not ask me,' cried I, putting my hands before my eyes, for I thought I saw the dreaded spectre glide into the room; 'he can tell.—Oh, save me! Save me!' I imagined that the monster seized me; I struggled furiously, and fell down in a fit" (41).[107]

With each struggle, Frankenstein's fury marks the character of his relationship with the Creature. The traditional form of engagement with the Devil was astonishingly vicious; Wesley granted that "enthusiasm" made its victims "daily more rooted and grounded in contempt of all mankind, in furious anger, in every unkind disposition, in every earthly and devilish temper."[108] Southcott, who in addition to her prophecies wrote the psychomachia *A Dispute Between the Woman and the Powers of Darkness*, wished to conquer the Devil "with his mouth tied," and to "[skin] his face with her nails," and she dreamed "once she bit off his fingers, and thought the blood sweet."[109] Southcott's sanguinary vengeance was an arresting survival into the nineteenth century of the medieval belief that

---

106. Southey, "On the Evangelical Sects," 499–500.
107. See Knox's description of the parallel event in Methodist psychomachia; it is characterized by "people who cried as in the agonies of death, who were struck to the ground and lay there groaning, who were released . . . with a visible struggle then and there from the power of the devil" (*Enthusiasm*, 472).
108. John Wesley, "The Nature of Enthusiasm" [1746], in *Sermons* II, 58.
109. Southey, *Letters from England*, 441.

demonic curses were best treated by scratching the offending warlock,[110] and if most Methodists were now more invested in the blood of Christ than of Satan, their encounters still tended to leave a mark. In the story of one Methodist woman in 1812, the figure of Blakean pathos becomes an excuse for a bathetically lopsided brawl: "I dreamed one night, I had great wrestlings with Satan in the figure of a little black boy—the size of a child of two years old, I got my right hand in his mouth, and after some contest got my foot on his head, awoke."[111] So too, Frankenstein: every time he encounters (or even thinks of) his "scoffing devil," he blazes into raptures of violence. The Creature is no abject yet noble Satan, but a vulgar devil to be dealt with accordingly, and his sublime apostrophes in Chamonix are answered with a crude Manichean logic—"we are enemies; Begone, or let us try our strength in a fight, in which one must fall"—that itself quickly dissolves into a purer form of aggression: "my rage was without bounds; I sprang upon him" (72–73).

That such primitive violence should explode in a geography sanctified by a "high male romanticism" represents a deep and deliberate embarrassment of that tradition. Frankenstein's soliloquy initially channels Percy Shelley, as he's swept away "with a sublime ecstasy that gave wings to the soul," reciting stanzas from "Mutability." But Romantic enthusiasm gives way to its Southcottian other even on these most hallowed slopes, and this rhetorical fluency collapses into incoherent frenzy against the "Devil" (71–72). Again and again, Frankenstein attempts to compel his demon to combat, finding himself "possessed by a maddening rage when I thought of him, and desired and ardently prayed that I might have him within my grasp to wreak a great and signal revenge on his cursed head" (156).

But if Frankenstein craves to bruise this particular serpent's head, it's a script with which his "devil" refuses to participate, at least initially; every time he launches his body towards the Creature, "the devil eluded my grasp" (160). The Creature, though capable of violence, refrains with Frankenstein. His constant injunction is to language—"Listen to my tale . . . But hear me. . . . Listen to me, Frankenstein"—even as the enthusiast is usually engorged by such fury that he is "beyond expression," as "rage choked my utterance" (74, 160). "Instead of threatening," the Creature is "content to reason with [Frankenstein]" (111), begging for a rational dialogue between two civilized subjectivities. His conventionally enlightened "account of the progress of my intellect" (96) struggles

---

110. Thomas, *Religion and the Decline of Magic*, 531.
111. Quoted in Mack, *Heart Religion in the British Enlightenment*, 219.

to sop up the enthusiasm which soaks the surrounding Volumes, carefully desupernaturalizing monstrosity as a social artifact, rather than biological imperative or metaphysical inevitability: "My vices are the children of a forced solitude that I abhor; and my virtues will necessarily arise when I live in communion with an equal" (113).[112] In the Creature's telling, the magical arrives only with plangent irony, in the "supernatural force" with which Felix "tore me from his father" (103) and exiles him from the order of the human. But the supremely literate Satanism which he assumes in reaction—"I, like the arch fiend, bore a hell within me" (104)—still protests socially and theologically against his positioning as the twisted Devil of Methodistical nightmare.

His appeals for audition and compassion are deliberately secular, even materialist in quality, swearing on astronomical bodies rather than the celestial spirits which might reside in them:

> I swear to you, by the earth which I inhabit, and by you that made me, that, with the companion you bestow, I will quit the neighbourhood of man, and dwell, as it may chance, in the most savage places . . . I swear . . . by the sun, and by the blue sky of heaven, [1831: and by the fire of love that burns in my heart,] if you grant my prayer, while they exist you shall never behold me again. (113–14)

"Do your duty towards me, and I will do mine towards you and the rest of mankind," the Creature offers Frankenstein, in a bid of clever *realpolitik* that balances carrots against sticks: "If you will comply with my conditions, I will leave them and you at peace; but if you refuse, I will glut the maw of death" (72). Even in its threatened apocalypse, this is the political calculus of a reasonable agent attempting to bargain with its reasonable opposite: precisely what makes the arrangement so unacceptable to Frankenstein. Victor revolts against the ideological implications of this negotiation—namely that both he and his Creature are social rather than spiritual antagonists, engaged in political transaction rather than ontological aggression—even more than he resents its specific consequence in the female creature. Within a matter of paragraphs, he has recast an incipient

---

112. For some of the Enlightenment contexts of the creature's autobiographical agenda, see Peter Brooks, "'Godlike Science/Unhallowed Arts': Language, Nature, and Monstrosity," in Levine and Knoepflmacher, *Endurance of Frankenstein*, 205–20; Alan Richardson, "From *Emile* to *Frankenstein:* The Education of Monsters," *European Romantic Review* 1.2 (1991): 147–62.

social contract into a pact with the Devil: "The promise I had made to the daemon weighed upon my mind" (115).

It will come to weigh on the Creature, as well, who is increasingly pinned underneath Victor's devilish representations. "'I expected this reception,' said the daemon" (72), but expectation can't manage reception. If the Creature's introduction bows with a wearily heroic fatalism, the subsequent clause enacts his submission to the frame narratives which rewrite him as soon as he finishes speaking, shifting Byronic hauteur into demonic utterance. While the Creature "will keep no terms with my enemies" (73), the terms of his enemies keep him, constructing his discourse as irrevocably as Frankenstein fashioned his body, and his formidable physical prowess can't reverse his radical helplessness before the cultural logics he inherits. He is a "Devil" in all its senses for the Romantic period: the faded remnant of the Miltonic counter-spirit, the vulgar Adversary of vulgar Man, and most especially, the "Printer's Devil," an alienated laborer fabricating someone else's text.[113]

More than the mysterious ritual which raises the dead, the revelation on an Alpine glacier of the Creature's fluency is the novel's most astonishing turn. Yet it leaves little impression on its witness—even Eve, lost in catastrophic naïveté, was able to wonder of her Satan, "How cams't thou speakable of mute" (*Paradise Lost* 9:563), a curiosity that Victor never shares as he berates his uniquely "wretched devil" (72). The Creature's autobiography is moving, especially as it discovers that its story is not its own, and that his true account, already written though poignantly misrecognized and denied, has always been at hand in his own pocket:

> You, doubtless, recollect these papers. Here they are . . . the minutest description of my odious and loathsome person is given, in language which painted your own horrors, and rendered mine ineffaceable. (99)

This birth certificate can't be emended, as Victor's writing on the Creature is "ineffaceable." The Creature is surrounded by cultural forms so absolute in their authority that they press themselves upon him with a naturalized inevitability, as, in a German forest, a "leathern portmanteau" casually sprouts like so many weeds the great works of English,

---

113. The *OED* gives this devil as "the errand-boy in a printing office. Sometimes the youngest apprentice is thus called." "Devil, noun, 5a." *The Oxford English Dictionary*, 3rd edition, *OED Online* (Oxford University Press, 2010), February 9, 2011. http://www.oed.com/viewdictionaryentry/Entry/51468

German, and classical literature, conveniently accessible in French translation (96).

But Goethe, Milton, and Plutarch don't, I think, offer emancipatory models for Creaturely self-fashioning. They instead tease him with subject positions forever off-limits to an abomination trapped in a world where the cultural and the natural are indistinguishable. As Volney and the de Laceys teach (89–91), the Creature is different from difference itself, having no nation, no race, no class, and, without a female with whom to perform his sexual identity, a problematic gender. There's only one script, one set of oppositions, which will admit him and make sense of him, and as the novel progresses, he plays his part with some aplomb:

> "Man, you shall repent of the injuries you inflict."
> "Devil, cease; and do not poison the air with these sounds of malice."
> (131)

Man, Devil: this battle between moral personae is deeply amenable to Victor, but by the end, even the Creature is invested in his role. As Frankenstein pursues his "Scoffing devil," the demon promises a struggle which takes as its type the travails of both Jacob and Job: "Come on, my enemy; we have yet to wrestle for our lives; but many hard and miserable hours you must endure, until that period shall arrive" (162).

The Creature loses himself completely in this drama, and as he confides to Walton, frame narratives frame him criminally and demonically: "I was the slave, not the master of an impulse, which I detested, yet could not disobey" (176). Along with his creator's enthusiastic agenda, the Creature seems to have absorbed his abiding habit for foisting responsibility onto irresistible forces—but if this is a convenient excuse, even the Creature's enemies recognize his genuine submission to discursive structures that aren't his own. The voice of the Devil speaks with none of the rhetorical self-possession of Milton's Tempter, but as a strangled voice of opposition to another's heroics. After the destruction of the female, the Creature croaks to Victor "in a smothered voice" (130), a condition that has only grown more acute when Walton observes that "[h]is voice seemed suffocated" (175). "The completion of my demoniacal design became an insatiable passion," he sighs at the end (176), sadly signaling, in the distance between "demoniacal" and "demonic," that he is the designed, not designer, his adjective identifying with the Demoniac rather than the Devil, the helpless body puppeted by spiritual possession, not the agent of evil itself. Absent an exorcism, the Creature is a figure of devilish abuse as much as devilish abuser—and yet, even in this pathetic complication, the Creature inadvertently advances the novel's enthusiastic argument, as the Devil of enthusiasm is more sinned against than sinning.

Southcott's devil is perpetually vanquished, a moral conquest enacted physically: "but at last she got up in a rage against the Devil, and said her revenge would be sweet to see the Devil chained down, and she should like, with a sharp sword, to cut him to pieces."[114] But also intellectually: Southcott continually wins rhetorical victories over her antagonist, who haplessly exclaims, "Thou eternal bitch! Thou runnest on so fast the Devil cannot overtake thee . . . what room have I to speak if thy tongue runs on so fast?"[115]—a practice that Victor seems to echo when he "recovered only to overwhelm him with words expressive of furious detestation and contempt" (76). The very purpose of this Devil is to be bested, tortured, and tormented by the Christian warfarer. As Southcott's Satan howls, "Thou temptest the Devil and not the Devil thee."[116] His resistance is the foil to the psychomachiac's dominance, and the brutality heaped upon him serves only as an index of the human combatant's moral worth; Hunt was convinced that "pity is not the studied virtue of the Methodist Christians: their tragedy consists of simple terror."[117] The enthusiast is thus doctrinally excused from remorse, and unapologetic oppression cues rejoicing: "I was striving, yea, fighting with all my might under the law, as well as under grace. But then I was sometimes, if not often, conquered; now, I was always conqueror."[118]

In the end, Frankenstein's conquest is as complete as Wesley's, as his Creature parrots a "sad and solemn enthusiasm" by way of valediction (179), while Victor indulges himself in a self-reckoning which issues as a series of exculpatory reimaginings: "I felt as if I had committed some great crime, the consciousness of which haunted me"; then "I was guiltless," and finally, "During these last days I have been occupied in examining my past conduct: nor do I find it blameable" (126, 173). This is the final exploitation of the already much abused Creature: Frankenstein's transition from voluble guilt to serenely detached innocence ironically marries the transcendentalizing displacements of a broadly "romantic ideology"

---

114. Southcott is paraphrased in Southey, *Letters from England,* 444.
115. Southcott, *A Dispute,* 25–29.
116. Southcott, *A Dispute,* 13.
117. Hunt, *An Attempt,* Essay V: "On the Melancholy and Bigotry of the Methodists, Concluded," *Examiner* 29 (July 17, 1808): 461.
118. Wesley, *Journal and Diaries* I, ed. Ward and Heitzenrater, 447.

with enthusiastic self-study, which in Methodist accounting inevitably culminated in the doctrine and delusion of "Assurance." If all New Births, Wesleyan and Frankensteinian, demanded that one begin "as a lost, miserable, self-destroyed, self-condemned, undone, helpless sinner,"[119] as the enthusiast is "'become as it were a monster unto many,' that the zealous of almost every denomination cry out 'Away with such a fellow from the earth,'"[120] the reward was the annihilation of responsibility and shame in the certainty of redemption:

> How long I was in that agony I cannot tell; but as I looked up to heaven I saw the clouds open exceeding bright, and I saw Jesus hanging on the cross. At the same moment these words were applied to my heart, "Thy sins are forgiven thee." My chains fell off; my heart was free. All guilt was gone, and my soul was filled with unutterable peace.[121]

As Hazlitt wrote, self-flagellation reliably gave way to self-congratulation, while confusing the boundaries between elevated and popular discourse:

> The principle of Methodism is nearly allied to hypocrisy, and almost unavoidably slides into it. . . . The first Methodist on record was David. He was the first eminent person we read of, who made a regular compromise between religion and morality, between faith and good works. After any trifling peccadillo in point of conduct, as a murder, adultery, perjury, or the like, he ascended with his harp into some high tower of his palace; and having chaunted, in a solemn strain of poetical inspiration, the praises of piety and virtue, made his peace with heaven and his own conscience.[122]

Like Hazlitt's Milton, his David blurs the lines of class that should parse the strains of enthusiasm: David is emblematic of an unequivocally vulgar religious sensibility, yet his mystification proceeds from the "solemn strains of poetical inspiration," "chaunted" in the tower of class privilege.

Methodist displacement compromises its romantic corollary, and quest romance doubles as Frankenstein's story of a "pilgrimage," during which his pursuit of the fiend "continued with unabated fervor"—a pilgrimage that has spiritually sanctified Frankenstein, whose rhetoric gestures toward theological certainty as his "task enjoined by heaven" comes to its close

---

119. Wesley, "The Marks of the New Birth," *Sermons* I, 419.
120. Wesley, *Journal and Diaries* I, ed. Ward and Heitzenrater, 218.
121. *WV* 1:74–75.
122. Hazlitt, "On the Causes of Methodism," 57.

(165, 162, 161).[123] Ever to the end, his problematic romanticism solicits the critical para-language of enthusiasm, and his concluding gasps, whispered in a cloudy region just beyond a place called, not without motivation, Archangel, serve to solemnize the tradition that has haunted his every step.

---

123. Cf. Boyd Hilton's sense that "only martyrdom, leading to 'assurance'—that is, consciousness of the power of the Holy spirit operating within oneself, independently of sanctification or good works—and so to 'final perseverance,' could suffice to vanquish the Devil," in *Age of Atonement*, 11.

Postscript

This book began, years ago, where it ends now. I was just starting my dissertation, fired by an etymological curiosity: "enthusiasm" didn't mean for Mary Shelley what it did for me. She meant it as many people still did in 1818: not our modern "emotional exuberance," but the older "religious delusion," an "imposture of divine inspiration," a blasphemous zeal marred by social vulgarity and intellectual poverty. This "enthusiasm," while on almost every page of the novel, was out of place in the story I thought I knew, the one about the scientific hubris and technological monstrosities of a university-educated aristocrat. So I tried reading it as a different kind of story. This other story confronted secular modernity with its final delusions: that its very mistakes were secular, that its hegemony was so absolute that even its monsters were the result of reason run amok—and that "enthusiasm" was merely the "ignoble and almost forgotten source" of Enlightenment, rather than its interlocutor, and perhaps even its master.

I've made this "enthusiasm" the story of *Lake Methodism,* and even now, the best sense I have for it is "religious literalism." The demographic, doctrinal, and historical varieties of "enthusiasm" united as a polemic against rhetoric, literalizing the figures shared by polite Christianities. The "politeness" of these other Christianities, in turn, was figural abstraction: declaring that "all original religions are allegorical, or susceptible of allegory," Percy Shelley's skepticism was also the Protestant turn, from the gruesome cannibalism of holy flesh and blood, to the decencies of sacramental symbolism. For many reasonable churchmen and dissenters, miracles needed to be metaphor. As we've seen again and again, the Church of England accepted only distant supernaturalisms: prophecies "accomplished" long ago, mysteries better left underexamined, spiritual "callings" best not taken seriously. "Enthusiasm," by contrast, while suggesting any number of heterodoxies, labeled not so much peculiar beliefs, as peculiar concreteness of belief. It was problematic because it was common, expressing bedrock doctrine viscerally and personally, returning orthodoxy to the strange magics that nominally—if not practically—organized it. "Enthusiasm," I think, outraged less by heresy, more by reminding other Christians of things they already believed, absurd only when explicit. Most people already professed some faith in prophecy, inspiration, and the resurrection of the dead. Joanna Southcott, the Wesleyan preachers, and Victor Frankenstein were distinguished by the completeness with which they thought these figures might be materialized.

The play between religious fact and figure—between preacher and priest, prophet and poet—seems to me much of the drama of Romanticism. It didn't happen off-stage: "enthusiasm," Wesleyan or Southcottian, wasn't an "underworld" or "counter-public," an ideological other to the modernity emerging at the turn of the nineteenth century. It mattered because of its ubiquitous vitality, bringing to prominence anxieties already aroused by the increasing marketability of religion, the popularization of culture, the democratization of political representation. But it mattered most of all because this culture was religious in its self-representations: enthusiastic literalism provoked churchmen, not skeptics, defenders of a particularly modulated form of belief, not critics of belief. My story has been so interested in this "reasonable," Christian consensus—whose security can be misrecognized as secularity—because enthusiasm brought it into unique articulation, sharpening dispositions otherwise deeply implicit, because deeply normative.

For all this sharpening, I confess that the interactions between *Lake* and *Methodism* have sometimes given a fuzzy view. I didn't want to assume, or even suggest, the coherence of either: my *Lake* spills beyond Lakers, my *Methodism* beyond Methodists. I've found fixed positions for either category less important than the velocity between them, the speed with which "high Romantic argument" could shift into a very different style of "enthusiasm." And like my "enthusiasm," my "Lake" and my "Methodism" have been very much styles, imprecise yet recognizable, for which elaborate particularity might schematize away what matters. My guide here has been Henry Abelove, who writes that "Wesley taught the Methodists no particular theology, no particular inflection of the Christian tradition . . . he provided them with an internally contradictory mix of virtually everything Christian, new and old, Protestant and Catholic, Dissenting and Anglican, heretical and orthodox" (*Evangelist of Desire*, 74). This "internally contradictory mix" is the most accurate formula for Methodism ever drafted, making discriminations between Justification and Assurance, Sanctification and Perfection—and, perhaps, between Methodist and Anglican, Methodist and Laker—academic illusions of rigor. Atmospherics have their own substance, and, in Abelove's telling, Wesley's unprecedented effect had little to do with his theology, and much to do with the fashion of his clothes, the cut of his hair, and the electricity of his gaze. This sort of "Methodism" has given me my "Lake," both complexes of fact, innuendo, and misrepresentation, which Hazlitt read as easily in the "consumptive hair-dresser" as in the *Lay Sermons*. The transferences between "Lake" and "Methodist" were figural, not confessional—and yet, as I've tried to suggest, the confessions of Romantic religion were most often recognized by their figures. Figural play, I think, had material significance.

This book has argued that Romanticism can't be written without religion. But I also think that this religion can't be written without romanticists, trained to read metaphor and irony, as others are doctrine or parish records. This work is already well under way, as the literary studies of the last two decades testify. But my ultimate hope is that we teach what we're coming to write. Our anthologies may lag our scholarship; even as "religion" plays a larger role in Romantic studies than ever before, it's still hard to find in the book lists and tables of contents designed for the undergraduate classroom. I was fortunate to be able to teach *Lake Methodism* while writing it, and I was delighted to discover that many students find Romantic belief as engaging as Romantic poetry. Southcott is as easy to sell now as she was then, and Paine's *Age of Reason* retains its urgency for women and men who have come of age amidst a clash of global fundamentalisms. But I've been continually surprised at how readily texts I thought I was inflicting—Paley's *Natural Theology,* for one—became unlikely favorites. The rise of digital archives has gone a long way toward freeing syllabi from the limits of the anthology, but I'd like to see "religion" as pedagogically convenient as Revolution, Abolition, Science, Empire, and the Rights of Woman. This would let us see how well a culture of sermons as well as lyrical ballads, hymns as well as novels—which is to say, a culture more like it was written and read—might be proved upon the pulses of the classroom.

Works Cited

Abelove, Henry. *The Evangelist of Desire: John Wesley and the Methodists*. Stanford, CA: Stanford University Press, 1990.
Abrams, M. H. *Natural Supernaturalism: Tradition and Revolution in Romantic Literature*. New York: Norton, 1971.
The Analectic Magazine [Philadelphia] 5 (1815): 497–509. "Devotional Somnium."
The Annual Register, or, A View of the History, Politics, and Literature for the Year 1815. London: Baldwin, Cradock, Joy, et alia, 1816. 289–90. "Ditchburn v. Goldsmith."
Anonymous. *The Age of Prophecy! Or, Further Testimony of the Mission of Richard Brothers. By a Convert*. London, 1795.
———. *The Love-Feast: A Poem*. London: J. Bew, 1778.
———. *Memoirs of Pretended Prophets. By a Clergyman*. London: J. Johnson, 1795.
———. *Naked Thoughts on Some Peculiarities of the Field-Preaching Clergy. By a Member of the Church of England*. London: J. Priddon, 1776.
Armstrong, Anthony. *The Church of England, the Methodists and Society, 1700–1850*. London: University of London Press, 1973.
Arnold, Matthew. *The Complete Prose Works of Matthew Arnold*. Ed. R. H. Super. 11 vols. Ann Arbor: University of Michigan Press, 1960–77.
Bailey, Nathan. *Universal Etymological English Dictionary*. Rev. Joseph Nicol Scott. London: T. Osborne and J. Shipton, 1755.

Baldick, Chris. *In Frankenstein's Shadow: Myth, Monstrosity, and Nineteenth-Century Writing*. Oxford: Clarendon, 1987.
Balfour, Ian. *The Rhetoric of Romantic Prophecy*. Stanford, CA: Stanford University Press, 2002.
[Barbauld, Anna]. *Civic Sermons to the People, Number 1*. London: J. Johnson, 1792.
Barbeau, Jeffrey W. *Coleridge, the Bible, and Religion*. New York: Palgrave Macmillan, 2008.
Barrell, John. *Imagining the King's Death: Figurative Treason, Fantasies of Regicide, 1793–1796*. Oxford: Oxford University Press, 2000.
Barrie-Curien, Viviane. "Clerical Recruitment and Career Patterns in the Church of England during the Eighteenth Century." In Jacob and Yates, *Crown and Mitre*, 93–104.
Barth, J. Robert. *Coleridge and Christian Doctrine*. Cambridge, MA: Harvard University Press, 1969.
———. "Coleridge and the Church of England." In *The Coleridge Connection: Essays for Thomas McFarland*, eds. Richard Gravil and Molly Lefebure. New York: St. Martin's, 1990. 291–307.
———, ed. *The Fountain Light: Studies in Romanticism and Religion, in Honor of John L. Mahoney*. New York: Fordham University Press, 2002.
Bebbington, David. *Evangelicalism in Modern Britain: A History from the 1730s to the 1980s*. London: Unwin Hyman, 1989.
Behrendt, Stephen. *Shelley and His Audiences*. Lincoln: University of Nebraska Press, 1989.
Belfast Monthly Magazine 3.12 (July 31, 1809): 20–23. "On Credulity."
La Belle Assemblée; being Bell's Court and Fashionable Magazine. London, September 1814, 99–104. "Joanna Southcott."
———. London, October 1814, 151–54. "Joanna Southcott."
Binfield, Kevin. "The French, 'the long-wished-for Revolution,' and the Just War in Joanna Southcott." In *Rebellious Hearts: British Women Writers and the French Revolution*, eds. Kari Lokke and Adriana Craciun. Albany: State University of New York Press, 2001. 135–59.
———, ed. *The Writings of the Luddites*. Baltimore: Johns Hopkins University Press, 2004.
Blackwood's Edinburgh Magazine 2 (October 1817): 3–18. "Observations on Coleridge's *Biographia Literaria*" [John Wilson].
———. 3 (July 1818): 369–81. "Essays on the Lake School of Poetry, No. I. Wordsworth's *White Doe of Rylstone*."
———. 4 (December 1818): 257–63. "Essays on the Lake School of Poetry, No. II. On the Habits of Thought Inculcated by Wordsworth."
———. 5 (July 1819): 462–68. "Chalmers's Sermons."
———. 15 (February 1824): 209–19. "Southey's *Life of Wesley*." [John Gibson Lockhart].
Blake, William. *The Complete Poetry and Prose of William Blake, Newly Revised Edition*. Ed. David V. Erdman. Berkeley and Los Angeles: University of California Press, 1982.
The Boston Spectator 1.54 (January 7, 1815): 215–16. "Joanna Southcott."

Bourdieu, Pierre. *Distinction: A Social Critique of the Judgment of Taste*. Trans. Richard Nice. Cambridge, MA: Harvard University Press, 1984.

Branch, Lori. *Rituals of Spontaneity: Sentiment and Secularism from Free Prayer to Wordsworth*. Waco, TX: Baylor University Press, 2006.

Brantley, Richard E. *Locke, Wesley, and the Method of English Romanticism*. Gainesville: University of Florida Press, 1984.

———. *Wordsworth's "Natural Methodism."* New Haven, CT; London: Yale University Press, 1975.

British Critic 3 (October 1826): 239–80. "Coleridge's *Aids* and Leighton's *Works*."

Brooks, Peter. "'Godlike Science/Unhallowed Arts': Language, Nature, and Monstrosity." In Levine and Knoepflmacher, *The Endurance of Frankenstein*, 205–20.

Brothers, Richard. *A Revealed Knowledge, of the Prophecies and Times. Book the First*. London: 1794 (revised and expanded 1794–95).

———. *A Revealed Knowledge of the Prophecies and Times. Book the Second*. London: 1794 (revised and expanded 1794–95).

———. *Wonderful Prophecies, Being a Dissertation on the Existence, Nature, and Extent of the Prophetic Powers in the Human Mind*. 3rd ed. London: B. Crosby, 1795.

Brown, Marshall. "*Frankenstein*: A Child's Tale." *Novel: A Forum on Fiction* 36.2 (Spring 2003): 145–75.

Bugg, John. "'Master of their language': Education and Exile in Mary Shelley's *Frankenstein*." *Huntington Library Quarterly* 68.4 (2005): 655–66.

Bunyan, John. *Grace Abounding with Other Spiritual Autobiographies*. Ed. John Stachniewski and Anita Pacheco. Oxford: Oxford University Press, 1998.

Burke, Edmund. *Reflections on the Revolution in France, and On the Proceedings in Certain Societies in London Relative to that Event*. Ed. Conor Cruise O'Brien. London: Penguin Classics, 1986.

Burton, Vicki Tolar. *Spiritual Literacy in John Wesley's Methodism: Reading, Writing, and Speaking to Believe*. Waco, TX: Baylor University Press, 2008.

Burwick, Frederick. "Coleridge and De Quincey on Miracles." In Barth, *The Fountain Light*, 193–230.

Byron, George Gordon, Lord. *Byron's Letters and Journals*. Ed. Leslie A. Marchand. 12 vols. Cambridge, MA: Belknap Press of Harvard University Press, 1973–82.

———. *The Complete Poetical Works*. Ed. Jerome J. McGann. 7 vols. Oxford: Clarendon, 1980–93.

Cantor, Paul. *Creature and Creator: Myth-Making and English Romanticism*. Cambridge: Cambridge University Press, 1984.

Canuel, Mark. *Religion, Toleration, and British Writing, 1790–1830*. Cambridge: Cambridge University Press, 2002.

Carlyle, Thomas. *The Life of John Sterling*. 2nd ed. London: Chapman and Hall, 1852 (1851).

Carnall, Geoffrey. *Robert Southey and His Age: The Development of a Conservative Mind*. Oxford: Clarendon, 1960.

Carpenter, Elias. *Nocturnal Alarm; Being an Essay on Prophecy and Vision*. London: W. Smith, 1803.

Cheyne, George. *The English Malady*. London: G. Strahan, 1733.

Christensen, Jerome. *Coleridge's Blessed Machine of Language*. Ithaca, NY; London: Cornell University Press, 1981.
Clark, J. C. D. *English Society 1660–1832: Religion, Ideology and Politics during the Ancien Regime*. 2nd ed. Cambridge: Cambridge University Press, 2000.
Cobbett's Political Register 26 (September 10, 1814): 326–37. "Joanna Southcott."
———. 27 (February 25 [misprinted as 18], 1815): 250–56. "On Religious Persecution."
Cole, G. "Doctrine, Dissent, and the Decline of Paley's Reputation 1805–1825." *Enlightenment and Dissent* 6 (1987): 19–30.
Coleridge, Henry Nelson Coleridge. "Preface to the Church and State." In S. T. Coleridge, *On the Constitution of the Church and State*, ed. H. N. Coleridge, ix–xxix.
Coleridge, Samuel Taylor. *Biographia Literaria*. Ed. James Engell and W. Jackson Bate. Princeton, NJ: Princeton University Press, 1983.
———. *Collected Letters of Samuel Taylor Coleridge*. Ed. E. L. Griggs. 6 vols. Oxford: Clarendon, 1956–71.
———. *The Complete Works of Samuel Taylor Coleridge*. Ed. Professor [W. G. T.] Shedd. 7 vols. New York: Harper and Brothers, 1853.
———. *Lay Sermons*. Ed. R. J. White. London: Routledge & Kegan Paul; Princeton, NJ: Princeton University Press, 1972.
———. *Lectures 1795, On Politics and Religion*. Ed. Lewis Patton and Peter Mann. London: Routledge & Kegan Paul, 1971.
———. *Marginalia*. Ed. George Whalley. 6 vols. Princeton, NJ: Princeton University Press, 1980–2001.
———. *The Notebooks of Samuel Taylor Coleridge*. Ed. Kathleen Coburn. 5 vols. Princeton, NJ: Princeton University Press, 1957–2002.
———. *On the Constitution of Church and State*. Ed. John Colmer. Princeton, NJ: Princeton University Press, 1976.
———. *I. On the Constitution of the Church and State, According to the Idea of Each; II. Lay Sermons*. Ed. Henry Nelson Coleridge. London: William Pickering, 1839.
———. *Opus Maximum*. Ed. Thomas McFarland, with the assistance of Nicholas Halmi. Princeton, NJ: Princeton University Press, 2002.
———. *Poetical Works*. Ed. J. C. C. Mays. 2 vols. Princeton, NJ: Princeton University Press, 2001.
Colet, John Annesley. *An Impartial Review of the Life and Writings, Public and Private Character, of the Late Rev. Mr. John Wesley*. London: C. Forster, 1791.
Colley, Linda. *Britons: Forging the Nation, 1707–1837*. New Haven, CT: Yale University Press, 1992.
Connell, Philip, and Nigel Leask, eds. *Romanticism and Popular Culture in Britain and Ireland*. Cambridge: Cambridge University Press, 2009.
———. "What Is the People?" In Connell and Leask, *Romanticism and Popular Culture*, 3–48.
[Cooper, Anthony Ashley, 3rd Earl of Shaftesbury]. *A Letter Concerning Enthusiasm*. London: J. Morphew, 1708.
Croft, George. *Thoughts Concerning the Methodists and the Established Clergy*. London: F. and C. Rivington, 1795.

Cuming, G. J., and Derek Baker, eds. *Studies in Church History*. Vol. 8, *Popular Belief and Practice*. Cambridge: Cambridge University Press, 1972.

Davison, John. *Discourses on Prophecy, in Which Are Considered Its Structure, Use, and Inspiration*. London: John Murray, 1824.

Deconinck-Brossard, Françoise. "Eighteenth-Century Sermons and the Age." In Jacob and Yates, *Crown and Mitre*, 105–21.

de Man, Paul. *Blindness and Insight: Essays in the Rhetoric of Contemporary Criticism*. 2nd ed. Minneapolis: University of Minnesota Press, 1983.

Dentith, Simon. *Society and Cultural Forms in Nineteenth Century England*. New York: St. Martin's, 1998.

Downes, John. *Methodism Examined and Exposed: or, the Clergy's Duty of Guarding their Flocks against False Teachers*. London: J. Rivington, 1759.

Duff, William. *Essay on Original Genius, and Its Various Modes of Exertion in Philosophy and the Fine Arts*. Ed. John L. Mahoney. Gainesville, FL: Scholars' Facsimiles and Reproductions, 1964 (1767).

Eastwood, David. "Robert Southey and the Language of Patriotism." *The Journal of British Studies* 31.3 (July 1992): 265–87.

The Eclectic Magazine 22.3 (New York: March 1851): 401–9. "Curiosities of Eccentric Biography."

Eden, Frederic Morton. *The State of the Poor: Or, An History of the Labouring Classes in England, From the Conquest to the Present Period, in Three Volumes*. London: J. Davis, 1797.

Edinburgh Review 24 (February 1815): 453–71. "Joanna Southcott."

Elfenbein, Andrew. *Romantic Genius: The Prehistory of a Homosexual Role*. New York: Columbia University Press, 1999.

———. *Romanticism and the Rise of English*. Stanford, CA: Stanford University Press, 2009.

Entwisle, Joseph. *A Letter to the Author of an Anonymous Treatise on Inspiration, Lately Printed at York*. York: Thomas Wilson and Robert Spence, 1799.

Erickson, Lee. *The Economy of Literary Form: English Literature and the Industrialization of Publishing, 1800–1850*. Baltimore: Johns Hopkins University Press, 1996.

Esterhammer, Angela. *Romanticism and Improvisation, 1750–1850*. Cambridge: Cambridge University Press, 2008.

The Examiner 591 (April 25, 1819): 268. "The Catholic Claims." 270: "*Peter Bell, a Lyrical Ballad*."

———. 603 (July 18, 1819): 460–61. *Pulpit Oratory, No. 1*. "The State of the Establishment—The Bill for Erecting New Churches—The Growth of Methodism."

———. 604 (July 25, 1819): 471–74. *Pulpit Oratory, No. 2*. "The Reverend Daniel Wilson."

———. 605 (August 1, 1819): 481–82. "Imputed Ignorance of the Lower Orders." 492–93: *Pulpit Oratory, No. 3*. "The Rev. W. B. Collyer, D.D. F.S.A."

———. 606 (August 8, 1819): 497–98. "Lamented Irreligion of the Reformers." 510–11: "Impudent Mode of Propagating the Gospel."

———. 607 (August 15, 1819): 523–24. *Pulpit Oratory, No. 4*. "The Rev. William Gurney, M.A."

---. 608 (August 22, 1819): 538–39. Sub-*Pulpit Oratory, No. 1.* "Mr. Moses Mims, Parish-Clerk of St. Brides, Fleet-Street."
---. 620 (November 14, 1819): 732. "Price of Worship."
Eyre, Joseph. *A Dispassionate Inquiry into the Probable Causes and Consequences of Enthusiasm.* London: J. Long, 1800.
Favret, Mary. "Mary Shelley's Sympathy and Irony: The Editor and Her Corpus." In Fisch, Mellor, and Schor, *The Other Mary Shelley*, 17–38.
Fisch, Audrey A., Anne K. Mellor, and Esther H. Schor, eds. *The Other Mary Shelley: Beyond Frankenstein.* New York and Oxford: Oxford University Press, 1993.
Fulford, Tim. "Apocalyptic and Reactionary? Coleridge as Hermeneutist." *The Modern Language Review* 81.1 (January 1992): 18–31.
---. *Coleridge's Figurative Language.* New York: St. Martin's, 1991.
---. "Millenarianism and the Study of Romanticism." In Fulford, *Romanticism and Millenarianism*, 1–22.
---. "Pagodas and Pregnant Throes: Orientalism, Millenarianism and Robert Southey." In Fulford, *Romanticism and Millenarianism*, 121–37.
---, ed. *Romanticism and Millenarianism.* New York: Palgrave, 2002.
Fyfe, Aileen. "The Reception of William Paley's *Natural Theology* in the University of Cambridge." *The British Journal for the History of Science* 30.3 (October 1997): 321–35.
Garrett, Clarke. *Respectable Folly: Millenarians and the French Revolution in France and England.* Baltimore: Johns Hopkins University Press, 1975.
[Gibson, Edmund, Lord Bishop of London]. *Observations upon the Conduct and Behavior of a Certain Sect, Usually distinguished by the Name of Methodists.* 2nd ed. London: E. Owen, 1744.
Gigante, Denise. "Facing the Ugly: The Case of *Frankenstein*." *English Literary History* 67.2 (Summer 2000): 565–87.
Gill, Stephen. *William Wordsworth: A Life.* Oxford: Oxford University Press, 1989.
---. *Wordsworth and the Victorians.* Oxford: Clarendon, 1998.
Goldberg, Brian. *The Lake Poets and Professional Identity.* Cambridge: Cambridge University Press, 2007.
Goldsmith, Oliver. *The Bee. Being Essays on the Most Interesting Subjects.* London: J. Wilkie, 1759.
Goring, Paul. *The Rhetoric of Sensibility in Eighteenth-Century Culture.* Cambridge: Cambridge University Press, 2005.
Graves, Richard. *The Spiritual Quixote: or, the summer's ramble of Mr. Geoffrey Wildgoose.* 3 vols. London: J. Dodsley, 1773.
Gregory, Jeremy. "The Eighteenth-Century Reformation: The Pastoral Task of Anglican Clergy after 1689." In Walsh, Haydon, and Taylor, *The Church of England c.1689–c.1833*, 67–85.
Guillory, John. *Cultural Capital: The Problem of Literary Canon Formation.* Chicago and London: University of Chicago Press, 1993.
Habermas, Jürgen. *The Structural Transformation of the Public Sphere: An Inquiry into a Category of Bourgeois Society.* Trans. Thomas Burger with Frederick Lawrence. Cambridge, MA: MIT Press, 1989.

Harding, Anthony John. "Gendering the Poet-Philosopher: Victorian 'Manliness' and Coleridgean 'Androgyny.'" In *Coleridge's Afterlives*, eds. James Vigus and Jane Wright. Basingstoke: Palgrave Macmillan, 2008. 65–84.

Harrison, J. F. C. *The Second Coming: Popular Millenarianism, 1780–1850*. New Brunswick, NJ: Rutgers University Press, 1979.

Hawes, Clement. *Mania and Literary Style: The Rhetoric of Enthusiasm from the Ranters to Christopher Smart*. Cambridge: Cambridge University Press, 1996.

Haydon, Benjamin Robert. *New Churches: Considered with Respect to the Opportunities They Offer for the Encouragement of Painting*. London: J. Carpenter, 1818.

Hazlitt, William. "Coleridge's *Lay-Sermon*." *Edinburgh Review* 27 (December 1816): 444–59.

———. "Coleridge's *Literary Life*." *Edinburgh Review* 28 (August 1817): 488–515.

———. *The Complete Works of William Hazlitt*. Ed. P. P. Howe. 21 vols. London and Toronto: J. M. Dent and Sons, 1930–34.

———. "The Fudge Family in Paris." In *Works* 7:287–97.

———. "Mr. Coleridge's Lay Sermon." In *Works* 7:114–18.

———. "Mr. Coleridge's Statesman's Manual." In *Works* 7:119–28.

———. "Mr Coleridge's Lay-Sermon, To the Editor of the Examiner." In *Works* 7:128–29.

———. "On Shakspeare and Milton." In *Works* 5:44–68.

———. "On the Clerical Character." In *Works* 7:250–52.

———. "On the Causes of Methodism." In *Works* 4:57–61.

Heeney, Brian. *A Different Kind of Gentleman: Parish Clergy as Professional Men in Early and Mid-Victorian England*. Hamden and Springfield: Archon Books, 1976.

Hempton, David. *Methodism: Empire of the Spirit*. New Haven, CT: Yale University Press, 2005.

———. *Methodism and Politics in British Society, 1750–1850*. Stanford, CA: Stanford University Press, 1984.

———. *The Religion of the People: Methodism and Popular Religion c. 1750–1900*. London and New York: Routledge, 1996.

Herbert, Christopher. "Vampire Religion." *Representations* 79.1 (Summer 2002): 100–121.

Hill, Christopher. *Antichrist in Seventeenth-Century England*. London: Oxford University Press, 1971.

———. *Milton and the English Revolution*. New York: Viking, 1978.

———. *The World Turned Upside Down: Radical Ideas during the English Revolution*. London: Penguin, 1991 (1972).

Hill, Rowland. *Imposture Detected, and the Dead Vindicated. Containing some gentle strictures on the false and libelous harangue, lately delivered by Mr. John Wesley, upon his laying down the first Stone of his new Dissenting Meeting-House, near the City-Road*. London: T. Vallance, 1777.

Hilton, Boyd. *The Age of Atonement: The Influence of Evangelicalism on Social and Economic Thought, 1785–1865*. Oxford and New York: Clarendon, 1991 (1988).

Hindmarsh, D. Bruce. *The Evangelical Conversion Narrative: Spiritual Autobiography in Early Modern England*. Oxford: Oxford University Press, 2005.

Hoeveler, Diane Long. *Gothic Riffs: Secularizing the Uncanny in the European Imaginary, 1780–1820.* Columbus: The Ohio State University Press, 2010.
Hole, Robert. *Pulpits, Politics, and Public Order in England, 1760–1832.* Cambridge: Cambridge University Press, 1989.
Holmes, Richard. *Coleridge: Darker Reflections, 1804–1834.* New York: Pantheon Books, 1998.
Hopkins, James. *A Woman to Deliver Her People: Joanna Southcott and English Millenarianism in an Era of Revolution.* Austin: University of Texas Press, 1982.
Horsley, Samuel. *The Charge to the Clergy of His Diocese.* London: James Robson, 1800.
Howlett, John. *Examination of Mr. Pitt's Speech.* London: W. Richardson, 1796.
Hughson, D. *The Life of Joanna Southcott.* London: S. A. Oddy, 1814.
[Hunt, Leigh.] *The Examiner* 19 (May 8, 1808): 301–3. *An Attempt to Shew the Folly and Danger of Methodism. In a Series of Essays. Essay I.* "On the Ignorance and Vulgarity of the Methodists."
———. *Examiner* 20 (May 15, 1808): 317–19. *An Attempt. Essay II.* "On the hatred of the Methodists against Moral Preaching; on their Doctrine of Justification by Faith alone without Morals; their love of Ignorance, and their rejection of Reason in obscure Matters."
———. *Examiner* 21 (May 22, 1808): 334–35. *An Attempt. Essay II, concluded.*
———. *Examiner* 22 (May 29, 1808): 348–49. *An Attempt. Essay III.* "Of Eternal Damnation and Election."
———. *Examiner* 24 (June 13, 1808): 380–82. *An Attempt. Essay IV.* "On Methodistical Inspiration."
———. *Examiner* 28 (July 10, 1808): 444–46. *An Attempt. Essay V.* "On the Melancholy and Bigotry of the Methodists."
———. *Examiner* 29 (July 17, 1808): 459–61. *An Attempt. Essay V, concluded.*
———. *Examiner* 33 (August 14, 1808): 524–25. *An Attempt, Essay VI.* "On the Indecencies and Profane Raptures of the Methodists."
———. *Examiner* 35 (August 28, 1808): 555–57. *An Attempt. Essay VI, concluded.*
———. *Examiner* 592 (May 2, 1819): 273–74. "Catholic Emancipation." 282–83: "Peter Bell, a Lyrical Ballad, by Wm. Wordsworth."
Ingram, Alan. *The Madhouse of Language: Writing and Reading Madness in the Eighteenth Century.* London and New York: Routledge, 1991.
Irlam, Shaun. *Elations: The Poetics of Enthusiasm in Eighteenth-Century Britain.* Stanford, CA: Stanford University Press, 1999.
J—ps—n, R—ph. *The expounder expounded: or, annotations upon that incomparable piece, intitled, A short account of God's dealings with the Rev. Mr. G——e W—f—d. Wherein Several profound Mysteries, which were greatly subject to Misconception, are set in a clear Light; and the abominable secret Sin, therein mentioned, is particularly illustrated and explained.* London: Printed for the Author, sold by T. Payne, 1740.
[Jackson, Thomas, ed.]. *Wesley's Veterans: Lives of Early Methodist Preachers Told by Themselves.* Additions and annotations by Rev. John Telford. 7 vols. London: Robert Culley, 1909–14.

Jacob, W. M., and Nigel Yates, eds. *Crown and Mitre: Religion and Society in Northern Europe since the Reformation.* Woodbridge: Boydell, 1993.
Jager, Colin. *The Book of God: Secularization and Design in the Romantic Era.* Philadelphia: University of Pennsylvania Press, 2007.
———. "Shelley after Atheism." *Studies in Romanticism* 49 (Winter 2010): 611–31.
[Jeffrey, Francis]. *Edinburgh Review* 1 (October 1802): 63–83. "Southey's *Thalaba.*"
———. *Edinburgh Review* 47 (November 1814): 1–30. "Wordsworth's *Excursion.*"
Jones, Steven. *Against Technology: From the Luddites to Neo-Luddism.* New York: Routledge, 2006.
Juster, Susan. *Doomsayers: Anglo-American Prophecy in the Age of Revolution.* Philadelphia: University of Pennsylvania Press, 2003.
———. "Mystical Pregnancy and Holy Bleeding: Visionary Experience in Early Modern Britain and America." *William and Mary Quarterly* 57.2 (April 2000): 249–88.
Keach, William. *Arbitrary Power: Romanticism, Language, and Politics.* Princeton, NJ: Princeton University Press, 2004.
Keats, John. *John Keats: A Longman Cultural Edition.* Ed. Susan J. Wolfson. New York: Pearson Longman, 2006.
Keen, Paul. *The Crisis of Literature in the 1790s: Print Culture and the Public Sphere.* Cambridge: Cambridge University Press, 1999.
Kent, John. *Wesley and the Wesleyans.* Cambridge: Cambridge University Press, 2002.
Kett, Henry. *History the Interpreter of Prophecy, or A View of Scriptural Prophecies and their Accomplishment.* 2nd ed. 2 vols. Oxford: Oxford University Press, 1799.
Klancher, Jon. *The Making of English Reading Audiences, 1790–1832.* Madison: University of Wisconsin Press, 1987.
Knellwolf, Christina, and Jane Goodall, eds. *Frankenstein's Science: Experimentation and Discovery in Romantic Culture, 1780–1830.* Aldershot; Burlington, VT: Ashgate, 2008.
Knight, Frances. *The Nineteenth-Century Church and English Society.* Cambridge: Cambridge University Press, 1995.
Knox, Alexander. "Remarks on the Life and Character of John Wesley." Appendix to Southey, *Life of Wesley* (2nd ed.), 293–360.
Knox, R. A. *Enthusiasm: A Chapter in the History of Religion, with Special Reference to the XVII and XVIII Centuries.* New York; Oxford: Oxford University Press, 1950.
Lackington, James. *Memoirs of the First Forty-Five Years of the Life of James Lackington.* London: Lackington, 1791.
Langan, Celeste. *Romantic Vagrancy: Wordsworth and the Simulation of Freedom.* Cambridge: Cambridge University Press, 1995.
Langhorne, John. *Letters on Religious Retirement, Melancholy, and Enthusiasm.* London: H. Payne and W. Cropley, 1762.
Lapp, Robert Keith. *Contest for Cultural Authority: Hazlitt, Coleridge, and the Distresses of the Regency.* Detroit, MI: Wayne State University Press, 1999.
[Lavington, George]. *The Enthusiasm of Methodists and Papists, Compar'd.* London: J. and P. Knapton, 1749.
Lawson, John. *Lectures Concerning Oratory.* Dublin: G. Faulkner, 1758.

Leask, Nigel. *The Politics of Imagination in Coleridge's Critical Thought*. New York: St. Martin's, 1988.

Lee, Debbie. *Romantic Liars: Obscure Women Who Became Impostors and Challenged an Empire*. New York: Palgrave Macmillan, 2006.

Levin, Susan M. *The Romantic Art of Confession: De Quincey, Musset, Sand, Lamb, Hogg, Frémy, Soulié, Janin*. Columbia, SC: Camden House, 1998.

Levine, George, and U. C. Knoepflmacher, eds. *The Endurance of Frankenstein: Essays on Mary Shelley's Novel*. Berkeley; Los Angeles; London: University of California Press, 1982 (1979).

Lew, Joseph. "God's Sister: History and Ideology in *Valperga*." In Fisch, Mellor, and Schor, *The Other Mary Shelley*, 159–81.

The Liberal 4 (London: John Hunt, 1823): 299–313. "Pulpit Oratory: Dr. Chalmers, and Mr. Irving."

Literary Gazette, and Journal of Belles Lettres 1.27 (July 26, 1817): 49–51. Review of *Sibylline Leaves*.

Lovegrove, Deryck. *Established Church, Sectarian People: Itinerancy and the Transformation of English Dissent, 1780–1830*. Cambridge: Cambridge University Press, 1988.

Lovejoy, David S. *Religious Enthusiasm in the New World: Heresy to Revolution*. Cambridge, MA: Harvard University Press, 1985.

Lowth, Robert. *De sacra poesi Hebræorum*. Oxford: Clarendon, 1753.

Ludlam, Thomas. *Four Essays: On the Ordinary and Extraordinary Operations of the Holy Spirit; On the Application of Experience to Religion; and on Enthusiasm and Fanaticism*. London: Printed by and for T. Ludlam, jun., 1797.

Lyles, Albert. *Methodism Mocked: The Satiric Reaction to Methodism in the Eighteenth Century*. London: Epworth, 1960.

Macdonald, D. L., and Anne McWhir, eds. *Broadview Anthology of Literature of the Revolutionary Period, 1770–1832*. Peterborough, Ont.: Broadview, 2010.

Mack, Phyllis. *Heart Religion in the British Enlightenment: Gender and Emotion in Early Methodism*. Cambridge and New York: Cambridge University Press, 2008.

———. *Visionary Women: Ecstatic Prophecy in Seventeenth-Century England*. Berkeley: University of California Press, 1992.

Marshall, Tim. *Murdering to Dissect: Grave-Robbing, "Frankenstein," and the Anatomy of Literature*. Manchester and New York: Manchester University Press, 1995.

Mason, William. *The Absolute and Indispensable Duty of Christians, in this Critical Juncture*. London: Pasham, 1776.

Mathias, P. *The Case of Joanna Southcott, As Far As It Came Under His Professional Observation, Impartially Stated*. London: Printed for the Author, 1815.

Maurice, Frederick, ed. *The Life of Frederick Denison Maurice*. 2 vols. New York: Scribner, 1884.

McCalman, Iain. "New Jerusalems: Prophecy, Dissent, and Radical Culture in England, 1786–1830." *Enlightenment and Religion: Rational Dissent in Eighteenth-Century Britain*, ed. Knud Haakonssen. Cambridge: Cambridge University Press, 1996. 312–35.

———. *Radical Underworld: Prophets, Revolutionaries, and Pornographers in London, 1795–1840*. Cambridge: Cambridge University Press, 1988.

McConnell, Frank D. *The Confessional Imagination: A Reading of Wordsworth's Prelude*. Baltimore and London: Johns Hopkins University Press, 1974.

McGann, Jerome J. *The Romantic Ideology: A Critical Investigation*. Chicago and London: University of Chicago Press, 1983.

McIntosh, Carey. *The Evolution of English Prose, 1700–1800: Style, Politeness, and Print Culture*. Cambridge: Cambridge University Press, 1998.

Medwin, Thomas. *Medwin's "Conversations of Lord Byron"* [1824]. Ed. Ernest J. Lovell, Jr. Princeton, NJ: Princeton University Press, 1966.

Mee, Jon. *Romanticism, Enthusiasm, and Regulation: Poetics and the Policing of Culture in the Romantic Period*. Oxford: Oxford University Press, 2003.

Mellor, Anne K. "Blake, the Apocalypse, and Romantic Women Writers." In Fulford, *Romanticism and Millenarianism*, 139–52.

———. *Mary Shelley: Her Life, Her Fiction, Her Monsters*. New York: Methuen, 1988.

———. *Mothers of the Nation: Women's Political Writing in England, 1780–1830*. 2nd ed. Bloomington: Indiana University Press, 2002.

Mellor, Anne K., and Richard E. Matlak, eds. *British Literature, 1780–1830*. New York: Harcourt Brace, 1996.

Michaelis, John [Johann] David. *Introduction to the New Testament*. Trans. Herbert Marsh. 4 vols. Cambridge: J. Archdeacon (Printer to the University), 1793–1801.

Miles, Robert. *Romantic Misfits*. New York: Palgrave Macmillan, 2008.

Milnes, Tim. *Knowledge and Indifference in English Romantic Prose*. Cambridge and New York: Cambridge University Press, 2003.

Milton, John. *The Riverside Milton*. Ed. Roy Flannagan. Boston and New York: Houghton Mifflin, 1998.

[Mitchell, William]. *Coleridge and the Moral Tendency of His Writings*. New York: Levitt and Trow, 1844.

Moers, Ellen. "Female Gothic." In Levine and Knoepflmacher, *The Endurance of Frankenstein*, 77–87.

Monthly Chronicle 3 (April 1839): 340–48. "Shelley's Poems."

Monthly Magazine and British Reader 43 (May 1817): 354. "Critical Notices of New Books."

The Monthly Repository of Theology and General Literature 12 (May 1817): 299–301. "Coleridge's *Lay Sermon*."

The Monthly Review Vol. C (January 1823): 111–12. "The Rural Walks of Cowper."

Newlyn, Lucy. *Reading, Writing, and Romanticism: The Anxiety of Reception*. Oxford: Oxford University Press, 2000.

New Monthly Magazine 43 (August 1817): 50. Review of *Biographia Literaria*.

Obelkevitch, James. *Religion and Rural Society: South Lindsay, 1825–1875*. Oxford: Clarendon, 1976.

Oliver, W. H. *Prophets and Millennialists: The Uses of Biblical Prophecy in England from the 1790s to the 1840s*. Oxford: Oxford University Press, 1978.

O'Rourke, James. "The 1831 Introduction and Revisions to *Frankenstein*: Mary Shelley Dictates Her Legacy." *Studies in Romanticism* 38.3 (1999): 365–85.

Paine, Thomas. *The Thomas Paine Reader.* Ed. Michael Foot and Isaac Kramnick. London: Penguin, 1987.
Paley, Morton D. *Apocalypse and Millennium in English Romantic Poetry.* Oxford: Clarendon, 1999.
———. "Coleridge and the Annuals." *Huntington Library Quarterly* 57.1 (Winter 1994): 1–24.
———. "William Blake, The Prince of the Hebrews, and the Woman Clothed with the Sun." In *William Blake: Essays in Honour of Sir Geoffrey Keynes,* eds. Morton D. Paley and Michael Phillips. Oxford: Clarendon, 1973. 260–93.
Paley, William. *Caution recommended in the Use and Application of Scripture Language.* Cambridge: Cambridge University Press, 1777.
———. *Principles of Moral and Political Philosophy.* 12th ed. 3 vols. London: R. Faulder, 1791.
Pater, Walter. *Appreciations.* Oxford: Basil Blackwell, 1967.
Perry, Seamus. *Coleridge and the Uses of Division.* Oxford: Clarendon, 1999.
Pocock, J. G. A. "Enthusiasm: The Antiself of Enlightenment." *Huntington Library Quarterly* 60 (1998): 7–28.
Polwhele, Richard. *Anecdotes of Methodism, to which is added, A Sermon, on the Conduct that Becomes a Clergyman.* London: Cadell and Davics, 1800.
———. *The unsex'd females: A poem addressed to the author of The Pursuits of Literature.* London: Cadell and Davies, 1798.
Potkay, Adam. *Wordsworth's Ethics.* Baltimore: Johns Hopkins University Press, 2012.
Potkay, Adam, and Sandra Burr, eds. *Black Atlantic Writers of the Eighteenth Century: Living the New Exodus in England and the Americas.* New York: St. Martin's, 1995.
The Preacher's Manual. 3rd ed. London: Richard Baynes, 1820.
Prickett, Stephen. "The Ache in the Missing Limb: Coleridge and the Amputation of Meaning." In *Coleridge's Visionary Language,* eds. Tim Fulford and Morton D. Paley. Cambridge: D. S. Brewer, 1993. 123–35.
Priestley, Joseph. *Disquisitions Relating to Matter and Spirit.* London: J. Johnson, 1777.
———. *Theological and Miscellaneous Writings of Joseph Priestley.* Ed. John Towhill Rutt. 25 vols. London: Smallfield, 1817–32.
Quarterly Review 16 (October 1816): 116–29. "Cowper's *Poems and Life.*"
——— 24 (October 1821): 1–55. "Southey's *Life of Wesley.*"
——— 35 (January 1827): 148–65. "Autobiography."
Rack, Henry D. *Reasonable Enthusiast: John Wesley and the Rise of Methodism.* 2nd ed. Nashville, TN: Abingdon, 1993.
Redpath, Theodore. *The Young Romantics and Critical Opinion, 1807–1824.* London: Harrap, 1973.
Richardson, Alan. "From *Emile* to *Frankenstein:* The Education of Monsters." *European Romantic Review* 1.2 (1991): 147–62.
Riede, David G. *Oracles and Hierophants: Constructions of Romantic Authority.* Ithaca, NY; London: Cornell University Press, 1991.
Ritson, Joseph. *Ancient Songs, from the time of King Henry the Third, to the Revolution.* London: Joseph Johnson, 1790.
———. *A Select Collection of English Songs.* 3 vols. London: Joseph Johnson, 1783.

Rivers, Isabel. *Reason, Grace, and Sentiment: A Study of the Language of Religion and Ethics in England, 1660–1780*. 2 vols. Cambridge: Cambridge University Press, 1991–2000.

Robertson, Fiona, ed. *Women's Writing, 1778–1838: An Anthology*. Oxford and New York: Oxford University Press, 2001.

[Robinson, Henry Crabb]. "Coleridge's Statesman's Manual." *Critical Review* 5.1 (January 1817): 42–48.

Robinson, Thomas. *Scripture Characters: or, A Practical Improvement of the Principal Histories in the Old and New Testament*. 3rd ed. 4 vols. London: Printed for the Author, 1793 (1792).

Rule, John. "Methodism, Popular Beliefs and Village Culture in Cornwall, 1800–50." In *Popular Culture and Custom in Nineteenth-Century England*, ed. Robert D. Storch. New York: St Martin's, 1982. 48–70.

Russell, Anthony. *The Clerical Profession*. London: SPCK, 1984 (1980).

Ryan, Robert. *The Romantic Reformation: Religious Politics in English Literature, 1789–1824*. Cambridge: Cambridge University Press, 1997.

Rzepka, Charles J. "Wordsworth Between God and Mammon: The Early 'Spots of Time' and the Sublime as Sacramental Commodity." In Barth, *The Fountain Light*, 73–89.

Schoenfield, Mark. *British Periodicals and Romantic Identity: The "Literary Lower Empire."* New York: Palgrave, 2009.

———. *The Professional Wordsworth: Law, Labor & the Poet's Contract*. Athens: University of Georgia Press, 1996.

Semmel, Bernard. *The Methodist Revolution*. New York: Basic Books, 1973.

Shaffer, Elinor. *"Kubla Khan" and "The Fall of Jerusalem": The Mythological School in Biblical Criticism and Secular Literature, 1770–1880*. Cambridge: Cambridge University Press, 1975.

———. "Secular Apocalypse: Prophets and Apocalyptics at the End of the Eighteenth Century." In *Apocalypse Theory and the Ends of the World*, ed. Malcolm Bull. Oxford: Blackwell, 1995. 137–58.

Sharp, William. *An Answer to the World*. London: S. Rousseau, 1804.

Shedd, W. G. T. "Introductory Essay upon His Philosophical and Theological Opinions." In Coleridge, *Complete Works of Samuel Taylor Coleridge*, 1:9–62.

Shee, Martin Archer. *Elements of Art, A Poem*. London: W. Bulmer, 1809.

Shelley, Brian. *Shelley and Scripture: The Interpreting Angel*. Oxford: Clarendon, 1994.

Shelley, Mary. *Frankenstein; or, The Modern Prometheus*. Ed. Susan J. Wolfson. 2nd ed. New York: Longman, 2007.

Shelley, Percy Bysshe. *The Complete Poetical Works of Percy Bysshe Shelley*. Ed. Neville Rogers. 4 vols. Oxford: Clarendon, 1972.

———. *The Complete Works of Percy Bysshe Shelley*. Ed. Roger Ingpen and Walter E. Peck. 10 vols. London: Ernest Benn, 1926–28.

———. *The Letters of Percy Bysshe Shelley*. Ed. Frederick L. Jones. 2 vols. Oxford: Clarendon, 1964.

———. *Shelley's Prose: or The Trumpet of a Prophecy*. Ed. David Lee Clark. New York: New Amsterdam Books, 1988.

Simpson, David. "Romanticism, Criticism and Theory." In *The Cambridge Companion to British Romanticism*, ed. Stuart Curran. Cambridge: Cambridge University Press, 1993. 1–25.

Smith, Nigel. *Perfection Proclaimed: Language and Literature in English Radical Religion, 1640–1660*. Oxford: Clarendon, 1989.

Smith, Orianne. "'Unlearned & Ill-Qualified Pokers into Prophecy': Hester Lynch Piozzi and the Female Prophetic Tradition." *Eighteenth-Century Life* 28.2 (2004): 87–112.

Southcott, Joanna. *A Dispute Between the Woman and the Powers of Darkness* (1802). Ed. Jonathan Wordsworth. Poole and New York: Woodstock Books, 1995.

———. *Prophecies Announcing the Birth of the Prince of Peace*. London: W. Marchant, 1814.

———. *The Strange Effects of Faith*. London: E. Spragg, 1802.

———. *The Strange Effects of Faith: Being a Continuation of Joanna Southcott's Prophecies*. 3rd ed. London: Galabin and Marchant, 1806.

Southey, Robert. *The Book of the Church*. 2 vols. London: John Murray, 1824.

———. "History of the Dissenters." *Quarterly Review* 10 (October 1813): 90–139.

———. *Letters from England*. Ed. Jack Simmons. London: Cresset, 1951.

———. *The Life and Correspondence of Robert Southey*. Ed. Charles Cuthbert Southey. 6 vols. London: Longman, 1849–50.

———. *The Life of Wesley and the Rise and Progress of Methodism, in Two Volumes*. New York: William Gilley, 1820 (London: Longman, Hurst, Rees, Orme, and Brown, 1820).

———. *The Life of Wesley and Rise and Progress of Methodism*. 2nd ed. Ed. Charles Cuthbert Southey. London: Longman, 1864.

———. "Myles's History of the Methodists." In *The Annual Review, and History of Literature; for 1803*, ed. Arthur Aikin. Vol. 2. London: Longman and Rees, 1804. 201–13.

———. "New Churches." *Quarterly Review* 23 (July 1820): 549–91.

———. *New Letters of Robert Southey*. Ed. Kenneth Curry. 2 vols. New York and London: Columbia University Press, 1965.

———. "On the Evangelical Sects." *Quarterly Review* 4 (November 1810): 480–514.

———. "On the Life of John Wesley." *The Correspondent* 1.2 (London: Longman, 1817): 157–76.

Stachniewski, John. *The Persecutory Imagination: English Puritanism and the Literature of Religious Despair*. Oxford: Clarendon, 1991.

St. Clair, William. *The Reading Nation in the Romantic Period*. Cambridge: Cambridge University Press, 2007 (hdbk., 2004).

Stelzig, Eugene. "Romantic Autobiography in England: Exploring its Range and Variety." In *Romantic Autobiography in England*, ed. Stelzig. Aldershot; Burlington, VT: Ashgate, 2009. 1-12.

Sterrenburg, Lee. "Mary Shelley's Monster: Politics and Psyche in *Frankenstein*." In Levine and Knoepflmacher, *The Endurance of Frankenstein*, 143–71.

Stillinger, Jack, and Deidre Shauna Lynch, eds. *The Norton Anthology of English Literature: The Romantic Period*. 8th ed. New York: W. W. Norton, 2006.

Sunday Monitor [London]. September 11, 1814.

———. November 6, 1814.
Swann, A. E. H. "*Peter Bell.*" *Anglia* 47 (1923): 136–84.
Tatham, Edward. *A Sermon Suitable to the Times*. London: J. F. and C. Rivington, 1792.
Taves, Ann. *Fits, Trances and Visions: Experiencing Religion and Explaining Experience from Wesley to James*. Princeton, NJ: Princeton University Press, 1999.
[Taylor, Isaac]. "Church and State." *Eclectic Review* 6 (July 1831): 1–28.
———. *Fanaticism, By the Author of Natural History of Enthusiasm*. New York: J. Leavitt, 1834 (London, 1833).
———. *Natural History of Enthusiasm*. 4th ed. New York: J. Leavitt, 1834 (London, 1829).
Telford, John. *The Life of John Wesley*. New York: Eaton and Maine, 1898 (London: Hodder and Stoughton, 1886).
Thomas, Helen. *Romanticism and Slave Narratives: Transatlantic Testimonies*. Cambridge: Cambridge University Press, 2000.
Thomas, Keith. *Religion and the Decline of Magic: Studies in Popular Beliefs in Sixteenth- and Seventeenth-Century England*. London: Weidenfeld & Nicolson, 1971.
Thomason, Thomas [Truebody]. *An Essay Tending to Prove that the Holy Scriptures, Rightly Understood, Do Not Give Encouragement to Enthusiasm or Superstition*. Cambridge: Cambridge University Press, 1795.
Thompson, E. P. *The Making of the English Working Class*. New York: Vintage, 1966.
The Times [London]. December 28, 1814, 3. Coverage of Joanna Southcott.
———. January 9, 1815, 3. Coverage of Southcott.
———. January 12, 1815, 3. Coverage of Southcott.
Trimmer, Sarah. *Comment on Dr. Watts's Divine Songs for Children, with Questions; Designed to Illustrate the Doctrine and Precepts to which they Refer; And Induce a proper application of them as instruments in early Piety*. London: J. Buckland, J. F. and C. Rivington, T. Longman, T. Field, and C. Dilly, 1789.
[———]. *A Review of the Policy, Doctrines and Morals of the Methodists*. London: J. Johnson, 1791.
Tucker, Susie I. *Enthusiasm: A Study in Semantic Change*. Cambridge: Cambridge University Press, 1972.
Valenze, Deborah. *Prophetic Sons and Daughters: Female Preaching and Popular Religion in Industrial England*. Princeton, NJ: Princeton University Press, 1985.
Walsh, John. "Methodism and the Mob in the Eighteenth Century." In Cuming and Baker, *Studies in Church History*, 8:213–27.
Walsh, John, Colin Haydon, and Stephen Taylor, eds. *The Church of England c.1689–c.1833: From Toleration to Tractarianism*. Cambridge: Cambridge University Press, 1993.
Walsh, John, and Stephen Taylor. "The Church and Anglicanism in the 'Long' Eighteenth Century." In Walsh, Haydon, and Taylor, *The Church of England c.1689–c.1833*, 1–64.
Warburton, William. *The Doctrine of Grace: or, the Office and Operations of the Holy Spirit Vindicated from the Insults of Infidelity, and the Abuses of Fanaticism*. 2nd ed. London: A. Millar and J. and R. Tonson, 1763.

Ward, W. R. *The Protestant Evangelical Awakening*. Cambridge: Cambridge University Press, 1992.

———. "The Religion of the People and the Problem of Control, 1790–1830." In Cuming and Baker, *Studies in Church History*, 8:237–57.

Wesley, John. *The Character of a Methodist*. Bristol: Felix Farley, 1742.

———. *A Christian Library: Consisting of Extracts and Abridgments of the Choicest Pieces of Practical Divinity, which have been publish'd in the English Tongue*. 50 vols. Bristol: E. Farley, 1749–55.

———. *A Collection of Hymns, For the Use of the People Called Methodists*. London: J. Patmore, 1780.

———. *A Collection of Hymns for the Use of the People Called Methodists*. Ed. Franz Hildebrandt and Oliver A. Beckerlegge, with the assistance of James Dale. Nashville, TN: Abingdon, 1984.

———. *Journal and Diaries* I [1735–38]. Ed. W. Reginald Ward and Richard P. Heitzenrater. Nashville, TN: Abingdon, 1988.

———. *The Journal of the Reverend John Wesley*. Ed. Nehemiah Curnock. 8 vols. London: Epworth, 1938.

———. *Primitive Physic: or, An Easy and Natural Method of Curing Most Diseases*. 24th ed. London: Paramore, 1792.

———. *Sermons* I: 1–33 [1746–60]. Ed. Albert C. Outler. Nashville, TN: Abingdon, 1984.

———. *Sermons* II: 34–70 [1746–60; 1788]. Ed. Albert C. Outler. Nashville, TN: Abingdon, 1985.

———. *Sermons* III: 71–114 [1788–89]. Ed. Albert C. Outler. Nashville, TN: Abingdon, 1986.

———. *Sermons* IV: 115–51 [1789–92; MS. *Sermons*, 1725–41]. Ed. Albert C. Outler. Nashville, TN: Abingdon, 1987.

———. *A Survey of the Wisdom of God in the Creation: Or a Compendium of Natural Philosophy*. 2nd ed. 3 vols. Bristol: William Pine, 1770.

———. *The Works of the Rev. John Wesley. With the last corrections of the author*. 14 vols. London: Wesleyan Conference Office, 1872.

Westminster Review 35 (1841): 303–44. "Percy Bysshe Shelley."

White, Daniel E. *Early Romanticism and Religious Dissent*. Cambridge: Cambridge University Press, 2007.

Whitefield, George. *Directions how to hear SERMONS: A Sermon Preached at Christ's Church in Spittlefields*. London: Printed for C. Whitefield, 1739.

———. *A Short Account of God's Dealings with the Reverend Mr. George Whitfield, A.B., Late of Pembroke-College, Oxford*. Edinburgh: T. Lumisden and J. Robertson, 1741.

Wilt, Judith. "*Frankenstein* as Mystery Play." In Levine and Knoepflmacher, *The Endurance of Frankenstein*, 31–48.

Woolley, W. *A Cure for Canting; Or, the Grand Impostors . . . Unmasked*. London: Jordan and Ridgeway, 1794.

Wordsworth, William. *The Excursion, Being a Portion of The Recluse, A Poem*. London: Longman, Hurst, Rees, Orme, and Brown, 1814.

———. *The Excursion*. Ed. Sally Bushell, James A. Butler, and Michael C. Jaye with the assistance of David García. Ithaca, NY; London: Cornell University Press, 2007.

———. *Home at Grasmere*. Ed. Beth Darlington. Ithaca, NY: Cornell University Press, 1977.

———. *The Poetical Works of William Wordsworth*. Ed. Ernest de Selincourt and Helen Darbishire. 5 vols. Oxford: Clarendon, 1969.

———. *The Prelude (Text of 1805)*. Ed. Ernest de Selincourt. Rev. Helen Darbishire. London: Oxford University Press, 1969.

———. *The Prose Works of William Wordsworth*. Ed. W. J. B. Owen and Jane Worthington Smyser. 3 vols. Oxford: Clarendon, 1974.

———. *The Thirteen-Book Prelude*. Ed. Mark L. Reed. 2 vols. Ithaca, NY; London: Cornell University Press, 1991.

———. *The Fourteen-Book Prelude*. Ed. W. J. B. Owen. Ithaca, NY; London: Cornell University Press, 1985.

Wordsworth, William, and Dorothy Wordsworth. *The Letters of William and Dorothy Wordsworth: The Early Years, 1787–1805*. Ed. Ernest de Selincourt. Rev. Chester L. Shaver. Oxford: Clarendon, 1967.

———. *The Letters of William and Dorothy Wordsworth: The Later Years*. Ed. Ernest de Selincourt. 2nd ed. Rev. Alan G. Hill. 3 vols. Oxford: Clarendon, 1978–79.

Wolfson, Susan J. "Editorial Privilege: Mary Shelley and Percy Shelley's Audiences." In Fisch, Mellor, and Schor, *The Other Mary Shelley*, 39–72.

———. *Formal Charges: the Shaping of Poetry in British Romanticism*. Stanford, CA: Stanford University Press, 1997.

Wolfson, Susan J., Peter J. Manning, and Amelia Klein, eds. *The Longman Edition of British Literature: The Romantics and their Contemporaries*. 5th ed. New York: Pearson Longman, 2012.

Youngquist, Paul. *Monstrosities: Bodies and British Romanticism*. Minneapolis: University of Minneapolis Press, 2003.

Index

Abelove, Henry, 66n131, 67n136, 201n53, 206, 227
Abrams, M. H., 5, 23
anthologies, 2, 227–28
Arnold, Matthew, 10, 85
autobiography, 96–97, 100

Baldick, Chris, 185, 211
Balfour, Ian, 114, 146, 152, 162
Barbauld, Anna, 123n34
Barbeau, Jeffrey, 133, 169n72
Barrell, John, 165n56
Barth, J. Robert, 55, 119, 122, 169n73
Bebbington, David, 67n136
Behrendt, Stephen, 189–91
Binfield, Kevin, 38n15, 151
Blair, Hugh, 28
Blake, William, 60, 79, 155, 170
Bourdieu, Pierre, 137–39

Branch, Lori, 11n20
Brothers, Richard, 31, 144, 161, 164–67, 169–70, 178. *See also* prophecy
Brown, Marshall, 195n38, 211
Bugg, John, 196n39
Bunyan, John, 28, 65–66, 94
Burke, Edmund, 40, 46–47, 49n60, 53–54, 145, 168n66
Burr, Sandra, 7–8n13
Burwick, Frederick, 128–29
Butler, Joseph, 81–82
Byron, George Gordon, Lord, 28–29, 153–56, 176

Cantor, Paul, 185, 195
Canuel, Mark, 45n40, 84–85
Carlyle, Thomas, 113, 116–17, 137
Chalmers, Thomas, 8, 29
Cheyne, George, 179–80

247

Christensen, Jerome, 26, 117
Church of England: condition of churches, 51–52; constitutional role, 42–43, 45–50; doctrine, 53–57; professional theory, 83, 87–92; reasonable Christianity, 57–63, 198; sermons, 60–63; services, 33–35, 51. *See also* Dissent; enthusiasm; inspiration; Methodism; prophecy
Clark, J. C. D., 24–25, 46, 48n53, 85n24
Cobbett, William, 154–55, 159–60, 179
Coleridge, Henry Nelson, 113, 117, 147–49
Coleridge, Samuel Taylor, 4, 18–19, 24n55, 42, 51n67, 62, 78, 81; *Biographia Literaria*, 92, 99, 113, 130, 136, 138–39, 143–44, 155; "Frost at Midnight," 33–34; *Lay Sermons*, 112–17, 120–24, 126–49; *Lectures 1795*, 124n36; *Letters*, 115, 119, 122–23n30, 127, 132n78, 135n85; *Marginalia*, 57, 114–15n8, 120n24, 122–23n30, 163; *Notebooks*, 8, 122n28, 124n36; *On the Constitution of Church and State*, 11n22, 83, 113, 115, 117–18; *Opus Maximum*, 119; *Sibylline Leaves*, 133–34, 138
Colley, Linda, 28
Cownley, Joseph, 49
Cowper, William, 97

Davison, John, 57–58, 163–65, 169
de Man, Paul, 112n1
Dentith, Simon, 52n71
de Selincourt, Ernest, 78
Dissent, 23n53, 24n56, 25, 43, 46, 53n78, 55–56, 57n93, 58–59, 123–25. *See also* Church of England; Methodism

Elfenbein, Andrew, 26n61, 97–98n81
enthusiasm, 7, 9–14, 31–32, 101, 114–15, 123–40, 144–49, 186–97, 198–209, 215–18, 222–24, 225–26. *See also* Church of England; inspiration; Methodism; prophecy

Favret, Mary, 194
Fulford, Tim, 113–14, 129, 132, 168–69, 175n87

Gigante, Denise, 195n38
Gill, Stephen, 77
Godwin, William, 25
Goldsmith, Oliver, 61
Goring, Paul, 21, 61n111
Guillory, John, 13, 99

Habermas, Jürgen, 21–23
Haime, John, 93, 214–15
Hanby, Thomas, 68
Hanson, Thomas, 126
Harding, Anthony John, 118n16
Hawes, Clement, 12n25
Haydon, Benjamin Robert, 52n72
Hazlitt, William, 4, 7, 12–14, 19, 32, 39, 55, 102–3, 128–32, 134–41, 213, 223, 227
Hempton, David, 6n7, 52n71, 85n24
Herbert, Christopher, 209n85
Hill, Rowland, 79
Hindmarsh, D. Bruce, 2, 67n134, 72
Hopkins, James, 32, 152–53, 168
Hopper, Christopher, 73, 90, 102, 203
Horsley, Samuel, 41–42, 50, 55, 63
Hunt, Leigh, 7, 9, 12, 40, 72, 79n8, 85, 102, 126–28, 205, 208, 222

inspiration, 78–86, 90–96, 103–9, 154–56. *See also* Church of England; enthusiasm; Methodism; prophecy
Irlam, Shaun, 10–11, 12n25
Irving, Edward, 35n5

Jaco, Peter, 91, 203
Jager, Colin, 23
Jeffrey, Francis, 4, 14–17, 37, 81, 100
Jones, Steven, 38n15, 186, 199n44
Juster, Susan, 130, 151–52, 158–59, 166–67, 173n80

Keach, William, 13
Keats, John, 116–17n11, 155
Keen, Paul, 22, 87
Kent, John, 36n6
Kett, Henry, 162–64, 167
Klancher, Jon, 13, 23, 41, 121–22n26
Knight, Frances, 27, 82n18
Knox, Alexander, 36, 53, 95, 200
Knox, Ronald, 204, 216, 217n107

Lackington, James, 27–28, 31, 41, 74–75n163, 96, 97n77, 188
Langhorne, John, 191
Lapp, Robert Keith, 121–22n26
Lavington, George, 15, 41, 72, 192, 209
Law, William, 127–28
Leask, Nigel, 140
Lee, Debbie, 151, 158
Lew, Joseph, 151n3
Lewes, George Henry, 193
Locke, John, 24n56
Lockhart, John Gibson, 3, 62, 120
Lovegrove, Deryck, 48n53, 88, 111, 125n37

Mack, Phyllis, 201n51, 201n53, 207n75, 209n83
Marshall, Tim, 151n3
Maurice, Frederick Denison, 111, 118
McCalman, Iain, 31–32
McGann, Jerome, 5, 32, 112n1, 121
Medwin, Thomas, 193
Mee, Jon, 6n9, 9, 14n34, 17, 83, 100, 114–15n8, 205
Mellor, Anne, 22n47, 151, 184

Methodism: definitions, 5–9; erotics and necrophilia, 205–9; interest in "natural philosophy," 199–201; and Moravians, 208–9; muddled politics, 38–41; preaching, 72–76, 79, 84–85, 123–29; print culture, 29–31, 65–71; professional theory, 83, 87, 90–96; resurrection and the "new birth," 188, 201–5, 223; salvation and feeling, 64–65; transforming the Anglican constitution, 37–44, 69–70; "Wesleyan manifestation," 74–76, 204, 215–17. *See also* Church of England; Dissent; enthusiasm; inspiration; prophecy
Miles, Robert, 17, 84
Milnes, Tim, 140
Milton, John, 13–14, 35, 58, 172, 185, 212–13
Mitchell, William, 118n16, 133n80, 140
Moers, Ellen, 184
More, Hannah, 26n63, 142

Nelson, John, 89, 126
Newlyn, Lucy, 121, 178

Olivers, Thomas, 93

Paine, Thomas, 45, 49n60, 227
Paley, Morton, 130, 152, 170
Paley, William, 27n64, 29, 50, 82, 146–47, 227
Pater, Walter, 85
Pawson, John, 6, 93, 212
Perceval, Spencer, 157–58
Perry, Seamus, 123–24
Pocock, J. G. A., 10
Polwhele, Richard, 41, 206
Porteus, Beilby, 25
Potkay, Adam, 7–8n13, 8n16
Prickett, Stephen, 24n55

Priestley, Joseph, 57n93, 201–2, 214
print culture, religious dimensions of, 25–31, 153–57, 160–61, 166–69, 172–80. *See also* secularization
prophecy, 31, 114, 133–34, 144–48, 151–52, 157–58, 161–72, 174–76, 179–80, 192. *See also* enthusiasm; inspiration

Riede, David G., 10, 78, 122, 171–72
Ritson, Joseph, 36–37
Rivers, Isabel, 29, 43n35, 50n64, 66n129
Robinson, Henry Crabb, 120, 130
Robinson, Thomas, 59
Rule, John, 73–74n163, 177n93
Ryan, Robert, 15, 23, 78
Rzepka, Charles, 79

Satan, 212–18, 220–22
Schoenfield, Mark, 23, 87
secularization, 3, 17, 20–32. *See also* print culture
Semmel, Bernard, 8
Shadford, George, 90–91
Shaffer, Elinor, 119, 157n28
Sharp, William, 215
Shedd, W. G. T., 113, 119, 137, 148–49
Shelley, Mary, 20, 193–95, 225; *Frankenstein*, 184–89, 194–99, 201–5, 209–224
Shelley, Percy Bysshe, 20, 156, 189–95, 215, 226; *Defence of Poetry*, 155, 157, 191; "Mont Blanc," 191–92; *Queen Mab*, 190–92, 203–5; *Refutation of Deism*, 192
Simpson, David, 4–5n5, 212–13
Southcott, Joanna, 19, 32, 62, 80, 114, 131–34, 150–62, 172–83, 184–85, 187–88, 215–18, 222, 227. *See also* enthusiasm; inspiration; prophecy
Southey, Robert, 4, 26, 29, 41, 45n41, 47, 51–52, 54, 56, 58–59, 62, 69–70, 71n152, 89, 94, 125, 130, 206, 212, 216; *Book of the Church*, 47, 123; *Letters* and *Life and Correspondence*, 43, 52n73, 53, 56, 70, 129n59, 163, 179; *Letters from England*, 153–54, 173–78; *Life of Wesley*, 3, 30–31, 39–40, 43–44, 53, 55, 57, 65, 70, 73–76, 95, 128, 144, 161, 188, 201, 204, 209, 214–15
Staniforth, Sampson, 68, 207
St. Clair, William, 25, 66, 100, 153, 185n3
Stelzig, Eugene, 78
Sterrenburg, Lee, 196n39

Tatham, Edward, 48, 57, 62, 89
Taylor, Isaac, 11–12, 199
Taylor, Stephen, 45, 46n47
Thomas, Helen, 97n79, 151, 159
Thompson, E. P., 8, 209
Trimmer, Sarah, 40, 64, 68–69, 71–72, 142

Walsh, John, 45, 46n47
Warburton, William, 35, 76, 92, 162
Ward, W. R., 47n53
Watson, Richard, 50
Wesley, Charles, 73, 208. *See also* Methodism
Wesley, John, 29–30, 37–38, 39, 56–57, 64–65, 67, 70, 73–76, 81–82, 90, 93, 95, 100, 125, 127, 133n80, 144, 198–203, 209, 212, 214, 217, 223. *See also* Methodism
Whatcoat, Richard, 91
White, Daniel, 15, 23n53, 43n35
Whitefield, George, 72–73, 81–82, 85, 110, 128, 135n86, 209. *See also* Methodism
Wilt, Judith, 185
Wolfson, Susan, 112n1, 142n103, 185n3, 193–94
Wordsworth, William, 4, 8, 11n22,

14–17, 18, 54; *The Excursion*, 16, 35n5, 98–103, 109–11; *Home at Grasmere*, 80, 155; "London, 1802," 172; *Lyrical Ballads*, 15–16, 79, 155–56; *Peter Bell*, 102–3; "Preface" to *Lyrical Ballads*, 98–99; *The Prelude*, 77–79, 83–85, 87, 94–95, 103–11, 155, 170–71

Wright, Duncan, 37

Youngquist, Paul, 182

LITERATURE, RELIGION, AND POSTSECULAR STUDIES
Lori Branch, Series Editor

Literature, Religion, and Postsecular Studies publishes scholarship on the influence of religion on literature and of literature on religion from the sixteenth century onward. Books in the series include studies of religious rhetoric or allegory; of the secularization of religion, ritual, and religious life; and of the emerging identity of postsecular studies and literary criticism.

Lake Methodism: Polite Literature and Popular Religion in England, 1780–1830
    Jasper Cragwall

Hard Sayings: The Rhetoric of Christian Orthodoxy in Late Modern Fiction
    Thomas F. Haddox

Preaching and the Rise of the American Novel
    Dawn Coleman

Victorian Women Writers, Radical Grandmothers, and the Gendering of God
    Gail Turley Houston

Apocalypse South: Judgment, Cataclysm, and Resistance in the Regional Imaginary
    Anthony Dyer Hoefer